Henry Houston Bonnell

Charlotte Brontë, George Eliot & Jane Austen

Studies in Their Work

Henry Houston Bonnell

Charlotte Brontë, George Eliot & Jane Austen

Studies in Their Work

ISBN/EAN: 9783955630652

Auflage: 1

Erscheinungsjahr: 2013

Erscheinungsort: Bremen, Deutschland

@ Leseklassiker in Access Verlag GmbH, Fahrenheitstr. 1, 28359 Bremen.
Alle Rechte beim Verlag und bei den jeweiligen Lizenzgebern.

Leseklassiker

CHARLOTTE BRONTË
GEORGE ELIOT
JANE AUSTEN

STUDIES IN THEIR WORKS

BY

HENRY H. BONNELL

LONGMANS, GREEN, AND CO.
91 AND 93 FIFTH AVE., NEW YORK
LONDON AND BOMBAY
1902

To

E. C. B.

CONTENTS

I. CHARLOTTE BRONTË.   PAGE
   (a) Her Realism 3
   (b) Her Attitude towards Nature 53
   (c) Her Passion 81

II. GEORGE ELIOT.
   (a) Her Religion and Philosophy 131
   (b) Her Art 199
   (c) Her Sympathy: Further Considered 257

III. JANE AUSTEN.
   (a) Her Place 325
   (b) Her Wonderful Charm . . . 380

CHARLOTTE BRONTË
A STUDY OF PASSION

CHARLOTTE BRONTË
A STUDY OF PASSION

A.—HER REALISM

I

"THERE are three principal influences," says the biographer of Rénan, "which go to shape human character: that of heredity, that of locality, and that of every-day association." And the character may be studied with approximations to truth only after all possible evidence relating to such influences is in hand. If time be the corrector and adjuster, any approach to finality in criticism may be despaired of until the image shall have passed into a more or less fixed atmosphere,—into an atmosphere which has ceased to pulsate with the passions and the prejudices, the friendships and the hatreds of the present hour.

As a pathetic illustration of this essential inability to seize with a full sense of ownership the finished idea of a life whose activities have but just ceased, the memorial paper of Mr. Henry James upon Lowell is worthy of note. "It is his [the critic's] function," says Mr. James, "to speak with assurance when once his impression has become final; and it is in noting this circumstance that I perceive how slenderly prompted I am to deliver myself on such an occasion as a critic. It is not that due conviction is absent; it is only that the function is a cold one. It is not that the final impression is dim; it is only that it is made on a softer part of the spirit than the critical sense. The process is more mystical, the deposited image is insistently personal, the generalizing principle is that of loyalty."

But if the poet had been an offender in the eyes of the critic, and if the critic had lived in a less acutely fair-minded age than the present; if instead of having the latter-day Mr. James as his friendly reviewer, the poet had died far enough back in the century to have fallen under the finger of Gifford, this difficulty of correct judgment would have been all the more urgent. The vast majority of men and women seem to be but the net product of ancestry and environment; and an original man used to be regarded with peculiar suspicion as one whose purpose was not explained by his environment, and whose lack of ancestry had to be accounted for by a kind of spontaneous generation or special creation, which, like all biological departures, is a little disquieting. Indeed, this nervous attitude is even yet a common one.

We are fond of talking about the Republic of Letters, and the capitals have a fine rhetorical look on the printed page. But too many of those immortals who have finally won a free citizenship there would seem to have had their fortunes at first cast among the numbing rigors of an oligarchy, — their radicalism grouped for the while into a forlorn third party, such was that questioning challenge of all new modes of thought and action which was esteemed to be a safeguard of our conservation.

And yet in course of time the true values come to the surface. If there is enough vital excellence in a man's work to buoy up what is not vital in it, that work will be found afloat in after generations. The best books are not the rare books. Every wise writer is, sooner or later, a read writer. However slow the critics may be in differentiating the vitalities from the non-vitalities, the life in them is at last discovered, somehow as tears are discovered in the presence of grief, or a fever in the blood at a tale of wrong.

It is not so very surprising, then, that the reception of 'Jane Eyre' in certain critical quarters was a glaringly mistaken one, and that its appreciation was challenged step by step with refusals to accept its message because of the misunderstandings of its spiritual simplicity. Yet in six months' time the novel was in its third edition.[1] Sales are not the finest test, of course, for 'Queechy,' and 'An Original Belle' are still sold. But it is not only the commonplace which is popular: there is another kind of popularity which is but the acknowledgment that a great chord has been struck true; and this instinctive recognition of a pure, sane genius lasts in an abiding personal interest unattached to the other class of "popular" writers. How many who read, last year, — well, any of the "best-selling books" of that season, can tell even the name of its author? On the other hand, who does not know that Keats lies buried in Rome; and what literary sojourner in the Eternal City does not linger for awhile in that old cemetery near the pyramid of Gaius Cestius? Finally, is there any popular living

---

[1] 'The Life of Charlotte Brontë,' by Mrs. Gaskell, with an Introduction and Notes by Clement K. Shorter. New York and London, Harper & Bros., 1900, p. 363, note. All references to Mrs. Gaskell's work in this study are made from this, the latest and most authoritative edition of her biography.

writer to whose grave, forty years after his death, will flock in one year, as to a shrine, ten thousand pilgrims? That was the number which visited the Brontë Museum at Haworth in 1895.[1]

II

There were popular writers in Miss Brontë's day, too, who are known now only to students of literature. Richardson and Fielding had, each in his own way, marked a path for Realism to follow, but it was not heeded. The love of the marvellous, formerly fostered by the drama, and checked for awhile by Goldsmith, and in a minor way by such books as 'Evelina' and 'Cecilia' (for artificial as her style was, and highly improbable as were some of her incidents, Miss Burney's pictures were in general accord with the principles of realism), found full vent again in the 'Mysteries of Udolpho,' and in the lucubrations of 'Monk' Lewis and 'Anastasius' Hope. While Miss Brontë had, in her formative period, only such knowledge of literature as the parsonage afforded, and while beyond certain standard poets and historians it did not afford much;[2] while her reading was necessarily desultory,

---

[1] 'Charlotte Brontë and Her Circle,' by Clement K. Shorter, London: New York, Dodd, Mead & Co., 1896. p. 23.

[2] We know from 'Shirley' what the Brontë library consisted of in part: "mad Methodist magazines, full of miracles and apparitions, and preternatural warnings, ominous dreams and frenzied fanaticisms;" all of which came from the maternal forbears in Cornwall. It was not until the pleasant relations with her publishers were established that she was put in command of a full supply of literature; and the flood that set in then is an index to the previous drouth. In the earlier days there was no such assistance, and no time for extended reading even if the means had been present.

as the time for it had to be snatched from household drudgery, needlework, and the mistaken art-practising, and the nearest circulating library could be reached only by a stiff four-mile walk over the moors to Keighley (in 1848 we find her complaining that no circulating library is accessible), she had doubtless dipped into the romance writers enough to appreciate their general faults, and to criticise the same in her preface to 'The Professor.'

The story-tellers whose fame was noisiest in Miss Brontë's early days might be divided into two classes, the ultra-romantic and the tiresomely didactic. An encyclopedic list of these would be interesting as showing how like a breeze from a new sphere 'Jane Eyre' and 'Vanity Fair' scattered their unrealities and impossibilities. They are for the most part forgotten, and only by forcibly carrying the attention back to them can we rightly understand what the originality of Charlotte Brontë and Thackeray meant in 1847.

As good specimens as any of the first class are Jane Porter, whose 'Thaddeus of Warsaw' gained such honors (but who reads it now?); the Lee sisters, from one of the 'Canterbury Tales' of whom Byron "borrowed" his 'Werner,' — if, indeed, 'Werner' was written by Byron, and not by the Duchess of Devonshire, as the Hon. Frederick Levison-Gower now claims;[1] Mrs. Radcliffe, of lurid memory; 'Fatal Revenge' Maturin; the gratefully recalled G. P. R. James, with his solitary horseman, his pale moonlight, and his lonely inn; to say nothing of the much-to-answer-for Ainsworth, with *his* Jack Sheppards and Dick Turpins.

[1] *Nineteenth Century*, August, 1899.

In the second division repose, among others, Mrs. Opie; Anna Maria Porter, the child friend of Scott; Hannah More; Maria Edgeworth, and Miss Landon; and that Mrs. Sherwood who in the working heyday of her life produced ninety books.[1] It is significant that the typical didacticists are women. They were forced into it, positively, by an honest natural feminine desire to save fiction, through morality, from utter pruriency, and negatively, by a lack of inspiration to accomplish the reform along the lines of the highest art. It is easy enough for *us* to laugh at Miss Edgeworth's 'Moral Tales;' we ought to think a little, in her justification, of what she was trying to escape from.[2]

Other novelists still famous in Miss Brontë's day who may not be classified so easily were: William Godwin, whose writings she did not know, as she asks to see them in 1849;[3] Henry Mackenzie, whose voice comes down to us a mixed echo of Richardson and Sterne; that sprightly woman, Miss Ferrier; William Carleton and Gerald Griffin, two Irish realists before the days of realism; the excellent Miss Mitford; and the ephem-

---

[1] Mrs. Sherwood is, curiously enough, omitted from such works as the 'Encyclopedia Britannica' and the 'Library of the World's Best Literature.' If such works of reference are intended to chronicle only those of the past who live in the present, her name would certainly be one of the first to be dropped; but the author of 'Roxobel' — still, admired by grandmothers and maiden aunts in primitive homes — surely deserves mention in any book which professes to be not only a recorder of the living dead, but a mausoleum also to the dead dead.

[2] It is just to Miss Edgeworth's memory to say that, but for the didactic interference of her father, the popularity of her works would have remained; and that, notwithstanding this interference, such novels as 'Castle Rackrent,' 'Belinda,' and 'Patronage,' have a fixed place in literary history, and may still be enjoyed by the judicious.

[3] Shorter, p. 195.

eral but fashionable Mrs. Gore.[1] I was about to put Samuel Warren in the list, but Miss Brontë probably read 'Ten Thousand A Year,' as it came from *Blackwood's*, the one strictly literary periodical taken in at the parsonage up to 1832, when *Fraser's* was subscribed to for a short period.

In none of these had Charlotte Brontë any lot or share.[2] Surely the remarkable circumstance of her criticism of Miss Austen is, not that it differs from Sir Walter Scott's (and nearly everybody else's, too), but because of its revelation that she had never seen such a book as 'Pride and Prejudice,' which had then been in print thirty-five years. We are fain to overlook in Charlotte Brontë what in others would seem a slight upon that delightful recorder of tittle-tattle and charming precursor of Trollope. The reader of the biography knows that she was, as a child, uncommonly

---

[1] Among the "curiosities of literature" which I occasionally take down from a dusty top-shelf, I value for the suggestions it invariably awakens a certain sadly faded set of twelvemos, in the doubtful binding of the early '30's, and bearing the imprint of the Messrs. Harper. They are reprints of the most popular of such of the above as had fallen from the press by that time; and the accompanying advertisement of the publishers, long since turned yellow, mentions these productions as "fashionable," in contradistinction to the "standard" work noted on the opposite leaf. Fancy the impossibility of such a distinction between fiction and other literature to-day! Yet for the most part, the distinction was deserved then. Only since then has the novel taken on its more serious side, assuming to itself the characteristics of all the other forms of literature also.

[2] She says, in a letter to Mr. Williams: "The plot of 'Jane Eyre' may be a hackneyed one. Mr. Thackeray remarks that it is familiar to him. But having read comparatively few novels, I never chanced to meet with it, and I thought it original.... *The Weekly Chronicle* seems inclined to identify me with Mrs. Marsh. I never had the pleasure of perusing a line of Mrs. Marsh's in my life." — Shorter, p. 404.

studious, and that her schoolmates were wont to look up to her as a prodigy of learning. It is safe to surmise that of the books she recommends to Ellen Nussey in her letter of July 4, 1834,[1] she had read a goodly number, if not all, herself; and the list is valuable as showing that, however high the omissions, there were still higher inclusions. But that she was not a trained student is evident. Outside of *Blackwood's* she had but little acquaintance with contemporary writers. The favorite heroes of the youthful 'Magazine' were, almost without exception, the famous politicians of the day, — were not literary heroes. The natural periods or turning-points of literary history were not known to her; and she was therefore without any thorough understanding of their reciprocal relations and their influence upon subsequent writing. Her reference to Mr. Atkinson's book as "the first exposition of avowed atheism and materialism" she had ever read,[2] shows she had no acquaintance with the free thought of the preceding century; and if any speculative writing had come in her way (which the environment forbids us to suppose), it is clear from the tone of her letters pertaining to this period that it would have been considered unsafe for a young woman's perusal.

Whether consciously or unconsciously, and without necessarily affecting his originality, nearly every writer is influenced by some predecessor. Bulwer traces to Godwin, Dumas to Scott. The literary father of Dickens is Goldsmith, and his uncles are Smollett and Sterne; while Smollett, for his part, is a disciple of Lesage, and Sterne is the English Rabelais. Much as Thackeray differs from Fielding, if it had not been

[1] Gaskell, p. 134.   [2] Gaskell, p. 517.

Her Realism

for Fielding, he would have differed more. And Fielding's prototype, on his own confession, was Cervantes. But whence came Charlotte Brontë? Stand on the old gray steps of that Haworth parsonage, and cry out the question over the moors billowing up from the horizon to your feet. Echo will answer "Whence?"

There never was author of highest rank so uninfluenced by, because there never was one so unconscious of, literary models. Even the French trash she read to perfect her knowledge of that tongue — a dangerous experiment with less elemental natures — was without any effect upon her modes.[1] Her object

---

[1] So high an authority as Mrs. Humphry Ward thinks differently. ['Jane Eyre.' Haworth edition. New York. Harper & Bros., 1899. Introduction, pp. xxvii–xxx.] There is no more proof, however, that the bale of French books which Charlotte acknowledges receiving in 1840 contained Hugo and De Musset (the possibility of which Mrs. Ward hints at) than that it contained the merely ephemeral writers of the day. Why might it not just as well have held the delectable fiction of the Countess Dash? George Sand may have had some influence upon her style. But the point here contended for is the absolute independence of her *idea*; and Mrs. Ward admits that the differences between the two are fundamental, and that Charlotte Brontë's *stuff* is "English, Protestant, law-respecting, conventional even."

She had only a qualified regard for the French woman. She writes Lewes, in 1848, that she never saw any of her works which she admired throughout, and thinks that 'Consuelo' couples "strange extravagance with wondrous excellence." [Gaskell, p. 361] 'Jane Eyre' and 'Shirley' were published before she had read "some of Balzac's and George Sand's novels," which Lewes "lent her," in 1850, "to take with her into the country," and which she returned with the criticism that George Sand is often a "fantastic, fanatical, unpractical enthusiast," "far from truthful" in "many of her views of life," apt to be "misled . . . by her feelings." "A hopeful point in all her writings," she concludes, "is the scarcity of false French sentiment, I wish I could say its absence; but the weed flourishes here and there, even in the 'Lettres.'" [Ibid., pp. 494, 495.]

was to learn a vocabulary, not to form a style; and she did not come in contact with Balzac until late in life, when Lewes called her attention that way. When we hear of Maupassant apprenticing himself to a literary taskmaster for seven years, as Jacob served Laban, before putting pen to paper, — the Rachel in view, perfection of style; and when we remember that Maupassant is but the perfected flower of a plant which had begun to bloom before Miss Brontë's day, we exclaim: Here, then, is a mystery! if not a soul breathing rather than a mind working, at least a mind drawing its breath of life from the soul, and not from other minds. She was one of the queens of literature, like Mrs. Browning, and yet not a literary woman, like Miss Martineau.

III

Imagination so existed for this Yorkshire girl. Its freedom from literary influence was not only the result of the negations of her surroundings, but was an indication in part of her determination to carve her own way. As we have seen, she knew enough of the romancers to deliberately direct her steps in the opposite direction; and that was realism. Realism to her meant simply — as it must mean to all of us when we get back to fundamental conceptions — truth to nature. By that test she can say, "Read Scott alone; all novels after his are worthless."[1] She wrote that before Thackeray had startled the world with a new form of realism; but even after that happy day she would still have defended Scott on the ground that

[1] Gaskell, p. 135.

his romantic situations did not interfere with his sane portrayals of character. Though she tells us that, in sketching Miss Ainley, she is not depicting a figment of the imagination ["we seek the originals of such portraits in real life only"], she also makes Caroline Helstone say, in the same volume, in answer to Shirley's question who prompted her assertion that certain natures, like Cowper's and Rousseau's, were never loved: "The voice we hear in solitude told me all I know on these subjects." Jane Eyre remarks that the three marvellous water-colors which she has shown to Rochester she saw "with the spiritual eye."

The trouble with the latter-day realism is that the outside voices are so loud it cannot hear the voices of solitude; and the spiritual eye has become dim through its constant employment in unspiritual investigations. The story of the life of Miss Brontë admits us to a wonderful picture of simplicity and innocence, — the simplicity rising to spiritual proportions as the morning light of intellectual aspiration blazes through it, and the innocence, like that softer light of evening, taking on deeper colors as the knowledge comes. Realism was to her a vital conception; but we see it exalted by this independence, this ideality, this simplicity and innocence. It stood, first and foremost, for truthfulness, and her life not being full of varied experiences, this truthfulness would not allow her to deal imaginatively with situations beyond them. But what sets it apart from other forms of reality is its sublimation, the actualities studied filtering through her sweet maidenly heart before taking their final shape. How could the critics suppose for a moment that 'Jane Eyre' was the work of a man?

In the filtration it underwent the change. When the bitterness of physical isolation, the sweetness of purity of spirit, the faculty of great receptiveness, and the habit of dogged obstinacy, born of devout conscientiousness, meet in one person, there is likely to result a certain hardness, touched and fired by a purifying egoism. No competent critic would ever apply Chatfield's witty definition of egoism to Miss Brontë, — "suffering the private I to be too much in the public eye;" and yet no critic, competent or otherwise, could fail to note the intensity of the predominant inborn self-emphasis in everything she has written. Such subjectivity is simply the product of conditions fostered by extreme loneliness of life, quickened by intense loftiness of thought. It was not the forced atmosphere of voluntary seclusion which she breathed, but the clean breeze of native loneliness. Hence the natural wildness of the flavor, and the purity of the bouquet. "It is moorish," says Charlotte, of 'Wuthering Heights,' "and wild and knotty as a root of heath. Nor was it natural that it should be otherwise, — the author being herself a native and nursling of the moors." And this is true only in less degree of the sister who wrote it. Picture once more the scene: three motherless girls, with restless, searching brains hungered for lack of food; with a father whose idyllic selfishness left no room in his thoughts for a proper comprehension of their difficulties, and a brother whose presence was a torment; cut off from the busy world, and with a total ignorance of its passwords and divining rods; wearing out body and soul with fruitless plans to remove the load of poverty; feeling conscious power in their veins, and seeing the beckoning hand of fate, but discerning not whither it led, and groping in tracts far more desolate than any surrounding moors; the silence all about broken only by the tumult of rushing thought.

The result is idealized realism, the ideality not antagonizing the realism, but clarifying it. The objective *milieu* was her physical isolation; the subjecttive force was her purity of spirit which penetrated it; the result was the glorious landscape of an apocalypse. It is unconscious, artless. Indeed, her lonely independence is constantly manifesting itself in artlessness of one form or another. That her work has art notwithstanding is because genius inevitably is thus attended: the kindly god provides fairy spades to dig withal. Untutored genius involves unlabored art; and when the tongue is touched by fire, the form of the issuing words is of kindling beauty.

We have in Charlotte and Emily Brontë the most shining of all examples of pure genius. In George Eliot the genius is alloyed by learning. Gold of the purest texture may not be put to as many uses in the arts as the alloyed metals, but it is harder to supply the purity than the alloy. Because of her narrower horizon, Charlotte Brontë had a more compelling genius than her successor, whose acquaintance with the world's philosophies so overlay her thought that the piled up learning was constantly threatening a blockade of the tap-root of genius, whence flow the living juices which color the whole. The development of spiritual strength depends upon intensity, rather than comprehensiveness, of thought; and intense thinking, narrowed by surroundings, and driven in on itself, must result, if the conditions are otherwise favorable, in intense spirituality. Innocence of life of the world energizes and drives down to its deepest springs the search into the life of self. The utter absence of world-knowledge becomes the utter presence of self-penetration. For we must remember that the root idea of genius does not only not involve extraordinary culture, but, on the contrary, conveys a meaning which such culture may succeed in obliterating. So, if Charlotte Brontë could not have drawn Tito Melema, George Eliot could not have drawn Edward Rochester. If the former could not have portrayed with like skill such a subtle analysis of character as is presented in Lydgate, — an analysis which gets its power from a wide knowledge of motives and men, — still more certainly could George Eliot not have made the voice of Rochester ring through the night, "Jane! Jane! Jane!" to be heard miles and miles away by Jane — the wind blowing where it listeth, and no one telling whence it cometh or whither it goeth. And yet it is truth itself; and Miss Brontë once said, "in a low voice, drawing in her breath," "But it is a true thing; it really happened."

I am very far from meaning to compare the genius of George Eliot unfavorably with that of one who so wholly differed from her. But I do mean that there is danger of a loss of the purest spirituality in the broadening out of the intellectual sympathies, and, conversely, that the intense light of a pure spirituality throws a shadow over those sympathies. It is one of many indications that Charlotte Brontë did not write novels with a purpose; for with all their nobility, the specialized interest of George Eliot's later works bears the same relation to Miss Brontë's simple utterance as a hymn which is at the same time a prayer does to a hymn of praise. George Eliot's genius shone through talent, Charlotte Brontë's in spite of talent. Each kind has its peculiar dangers, makes its specific mistakes. Only, the errors of genius led astray by talent are more far-reaching than the accidental lapses of genius pure and simple. The character of Lydgate is perfectly drawn; the most searching analysis fails to find the slightest flaw in the workmanship. There are many incidental errors, on the other hand, in the building up of Rochester. But the book which contains Lydgate is a failure, so far as it fails to establish a doctrine which had taken such an insistent hold upon its author as to warp her mind from its proper contemplation. The nervous intelligence of genius prevented such a failure in 'Jane Eyre.' In that one respect, 'Middlemarch' *is* a mistake. 'Jane Eyre' merely contains mistake.

She was aware of her dangers. She acknowledges some affinity between 'Jane Eyre' and 'David Copperfield,' but exclaims: " Only, what an advantage has Dickens in his varied knowledge of men and things!"[1] See what her conception of realism here stood for. " Details, situations which I do not understand and cannot personally inspect, I would not for the world meddle with, lest I should make a more ridiculous mess of the matter than Mrs. Trollope did in her 'Factory Boy.' Besides," she continues, " not one feeling on any subject, public or private, will I ever affect that I do not really experience. Yet though I must limit my sympathies; though my observation cannot penetrate where the very deepest political and social truths are to be learnt; though many doors of knowledge which are open for you are forever shut for

[1] Shorter, p. 397.

me; though I must guess and calculate and grope my way in the dark, and come to uncertain conclusions unaided and alone where such writers as Dickens and Thackeray, having access to the shrine and image of Truth, have only to go into the temple, lift the veil a moment, and come out and say what they have seen, — yet with every disadvantage, I mean still, in my own contracted way, to do my best."[1]

This lack of experience which she regrets is the cause of whatever failures we have to reckon against her; for no matter how deliberate a realism, and how absolute a conscientiousness, it cannot but transpire that a sparse acquaintance with men and women will lead the wayfarer into occasional culs-de-sac through a failure to appreciate the altered values in the wholeness of a character which the side-lights of motive and circumstance thrust into it. It was the passion of this woman to study the character in its wholeness; but the absence of the world-knowledge at times exaggerated, in her pure vision, faults which such a knowledge would condone, and minimized virtues which it would extol. She saw the world, of necessity, too much through the eyes of self. And yet the failures are unimportant; for, we say again, elementary genius is too intelligent to make fundamental mistakes, while intellectuality forces such mistakes upon the intelligence.[2]

---

[1] Shorter, p. 409.

[2] Could we indulge in impossible speculations as to what Currer and Ellis Bell would have brought forth had their father's lot been cast in a busy city parish, we might easily imagine very different results. Take three examples from Mrs. Gaskell as indicating Charlotte's sturdy ignorance of the world, and incidentally emphasizing the reflection of the quaint beauty of her isolation upon her thoughts and actions. Is there, for example, in all the tearful history of liter-

IV

Not to affect what she did not really experience did not mean that she must physically experience everything she wrote about, but only that she must

ary aspirations, a more touching instance of unacquaintance with ways and means than the record of the travels of the manuscript of the 'Professor' in search of a publisher? Having experimented with house after house, it occurred to this brave struggler, *as a last resource*, to send the, to her precious, but by this time hated, package to Messrs. Smith & Elder, a firm which the sophisticated candidate for fame would have selected among the first of his choice. And the bundle arrives at Cornhill in its original wrapping, with all the other directions and cancelled stamps upon it: so each publisher to whom it had been submitted must have known perforce of all the other publishers who had declined it! Like her Jane and her Lucy, there it stood in all its disadvantages; she would not strip it of a single one. Let it be accepted on its inside merits or not at all.

The second scene is one which stands out in Rembrandt-like colors which leave a deep impress for all time upon the heart. When Mr. Brontë took his daughters to Brussels, their night in London was passed at the famed Chapter Coffee House of Paternoster Row; and thither, "for very ignorance where else to go," drifted the two shrinking girls when they went up to town to break the news of their identity to their publishers. Never before, I conceive, in the history of those walls, which had heard the wordy talk of Johnson and echoed the laughter of Fielding, had such guests been harbored there; and the one female servant of the place — whom I like to fancy a good woman — must have taken a motherly interest in the wanderers, whom Mr. Smith found "clinging together on the most remote window-seat," below which came up to them — not the "mighty roar of London," but an occasional "footfall on the pavement ... of that unfrequented street."

Finally, Miss Brontë's constitutional timidity was so intense that the meeting of strangers was a positive torment. Whenever it was possible, she refused the kind offers of her publishers of introductions to the literary lions of the day, even declining Dickens, whose fame was then growing daily. Yet this painfully diffident woman nerves her almost uncontrollable bashfulness to the point of addressing a Frenchman in an English railway carriage, — eager to snatch every opportunity to improve herself in his language!

feel mentally the absolute truth of it. Whatever faults there are lie in the exaggeration her intense fidelity placed upon this conception. Her anxiety not to falsify, her determination to paint people as she sees them, warts and all, results in a rather slim number of agreeable people. Always excepting Shirley — for Shirley, be it always remembered, is Emily — the only characters in her novels free from sorrowful humors of some sort are the Misses Rivers, Mrs. Fairfax, and Miss Temple, — all in her first great fiction; which, with the addition of little Henry Sympson from 'Shirley,' and Miss de Bassompierre from 'Villette' complete the list. I do not include Caroline Helstone in the category, although she is a lovable girl, because she is in part an idealized portrait of Charlotte Brontë herself, — she coyly placing herself in a romantic atmosphere for once (as if she could not bear to part from Emily after having placed her there first), and attempting to hide from discovery in such an unusual course by speaking in the third person.

The rigor of her portrayals, we cannot but feel, is occasionally overdone. Her portrait of Madame Beck, for example, is too severe, although we know the provocations. It is difficult to believe that "not the agony in Gethsemane, not the death on Calvary, could have wrung from her eyes one tear." Lucy had, at least, considerable freedom there, and was apparently allowed to go out evenings, even to the theatre, with Dr. John, when she so desired. She just mentions some of Madame Beck's good points, showing, in spite of her antipathy, and except for its Jesuitry, that the school was a rationally managed one, and that if the pupils were not happy, it was not wholly Madame Beck's fault. Because Miss Brontë believed all men and women to be imperfect, her characters reflect this belief, — sometimes to an unpleasant degree of truthfulness. Even Robert Moore, fine fellow as he is, is made to sacrifice to Baal by turning his back on Caroline, and seeking matrimonial alliance with a pecuniary end in view. And on the night of Robert's confession of his meanness, the sturdy Yorke himself tells a "dark truth," namely, that if *his* old sweetheart had loved him as he once fancied he loved her; if he "had been secure of her affection, certain of her constancy, been irritated by no doubts, stung by no humiliations . . . the odds were (he let his hand fall heavy on the saddle) that he should have left her!" No marvel that after this, "they rode side by side in silence." Miss Brontë does not express any scorn of men, as apart from women, here, but holds the glass to human nature. For she who drew Edward Crimsworth and Brocklehurst also painted Jane Eyre's aunt and Madame Beck, — to say nothing of Mrs. Yorke, into whose mouth she puts the spitfire of the *Quarterly's* very words, thus showing herself capable of bright revenge.

But, though we feel the austerity of her treatment, though we see that the arrow aimed at exactness may fall below the heart of the centre because not directed above it, though the truth which she finds is at times a little too harsh for common vision, still — such is her general truthfulness — her impersonations do not cease to interest because 'disagreeable;' nay, none of her strongest characters are among the exceptions.

And the severity is always keen against herself. Her portraits of the Professor, Jane Eyre, and Lucy

Snowe intend to urge the next to impossible likelihood of their originals to win that affection for which they were perishing because of the natural obstacles their dispositions offered to popular esteem. Who does not remember how their author is constantly checking and subduing their dreams of happiness? Such dreams are madness, she says again and again; and she makes her heroines plain and unprepossessing and prim and outwardly cold, in order to make the chances of happiness fantastic. She was aiming, as we know from the preface to the 'Professor,' against the fallacious romanticism of the day, — the "passionate preference for the wild, wonderful, and thrilling." "I said to myself that my hero should work his way through life as I had seen real living men work theirs; that he should not get a shilling he had not earned; that no sudden turn should lift him in a moment to wealth and high station; that whatever small competency he might gain should be won by the sweat of his brow; . . . that he should not even marry a beautiful girl or a lady of rank. As Adam's son he should share Adam's doom, and drain throughout life a mixed and moderate cup of enjoyment."

And so she places Jane and Lucy in adverse circumstances such as she was personally acquainted with, that they may look the hardest facts of life full in the face. When Lucy — in whom there is even more of Charlotte Brontë than in Jane — is, in her incomparable way, endeavoring to propitiate the future by realizing the present, she soliloquizes:

Is there nothing more for me in life — no true home — nothing to be dearer to me than myself, and by its paramount preciousness to draw from me better things than I care to cultivate for myself only? Nothing at whose feet I can willingly lay down the whole burden of human egotism, and gloriously take up the nobler charge of laboring and living for others? I suppose, Lucy Snowe, the rule of your life is not to be so rounded; for you the crescent phase must suffice. Very good! I see a huge mass of my fellow-creatures in no better circumstances. I see that a great many men, and more women, hold their span of life in conditions of denial and privation. I find no reason why I should be of the few favored. I believe in some blending of hope and sunshine sweetening the worse lots. I believe that this life is not all; neither the beginning nor the end. I believe while I tremble; I trust while I weep. . . . It is right to look our life accounts bravely in the face now and then, and settle them earnestly. And he is a poor self-swindler who lies to himself while he reckons the items, and sets down under the head "happiness" that which is misery. Call anguish anguish, and despair despair; write both down in strong characters with a resolute pen; you will the better pay your debt to Doom. Falsify; insert "privilege" where you should have written "pain," and see if your mighty creditor will allow the fraud to pass, or accept the coin with which you would cheat him. Offer to the strongest, if the darkest, angel of God's host water when he has asked blood — will he take it? Not a whole pale sea for one red drop.

That she carries it too far in her supreme effort is evidenced by the ending of 'Villette.' Her father, generally wrong, was right in insisting upon a happy conclusion there. The matter of endings is always to be determined by the logical drift of the plot. If without an insult to rational intelligence Jack may have Jill, we poor mortals who love a lover want it brought about; but if it can be done only by a gymnastic performance, we would prefer a little heartache and great spiritual satisfaction to a reconciled father, a made-up quarrel, and a happy marriage, — all accompanied by strong mental depression. But surely, Paul Emmanuel's ship might have come back, and the "pain-pressed pilgrim" ended her days in certain joy, without any shock to the trained perceptions. I suspect she had been led, somewhat against her conscience, to make 'Jane Eyre' and 'Shirley' close happily; and in her final work, into which the whole strong essence of her suffering was infused, she was determined not to be swayed from her fell tragic purpose. She, who is usually so logical, is forced by this Spartan fixedness not to be led into paths of dalliance to an illogical, and therefore inartistic, conclusion.

Her feelings were kept under the surveillance of distrust, owing to her nervous shrinking from outward display. So, while there is a consequent inward expansion, the published result is often a lack of warmth in the portrayal of character. It was as if she dreaded to praise too eagerly through fear of a rejection of the gift from such an insignificant giver: the fancied repulse overcame the actual impulse. For example: —

I liked her. It is not a declaration I have often made concerning my acquaintance in the course of this book. The reader will bear with it for once. Intimate intercourse, close inspection, disclosed in Paulina only what was delicate, intelligent, and sincere, therefore my regard for her lay deep. An admiration more superficial might have been more demonstrative. Mine, however, was quiet.

Because of this her minor characters are forgotten, except by her close students, and only her great creations, like Rochester and Emmanuel, are remembered, because with them only does the passion burn through the timidity.

One feels a primness, a restriction; but it is not owing, as has been supposed, to an old-maidenish prudery, but to a young-maidenish modesty, — the modesty of a maid of her time, which is different from that of the present day; and which was exaggerated even for her time by the seclusion of her surroundings. But — such are the happy recompenses of genius — nearly every negation in such an order of mind stands for the corresponding acquisition. The primness results in a fine logical exactness, and fulfils one of the minor definitions of genius, — "infinite painstaking."

It is her logic, in general, that makes her delineations so sharp, — her logic leagued with her stout conscientiousness. Nearly every other author would have softened the picture of the death-bed of Mrs. Reed. Not she. It is a splendid, if terrible, picture of death-bed remorse, without any death-bed repentance, — the pain of a guilty conscience without the change of the spiritual attitude towards her sin which is signified in the more effective word, and without which the remorse is futile and cowardly. The author pities her, and makes Jane forgive her. Miss Brontë's attitude is eminently Christian; but her clear-eyed genius penetrates the mists of sentimentality raised by those who conjure up final events in accordance with pious hopes as against assured certainties, and perceives that "it was too late for her to make now the effort to change her habitual frame of mind: living, she had ever hated me — dying, she must hate me still." Inexorable, you say. Yes, but bravely true; and though to be contemplated with tears, yet full of a stronger morality than that of the eleventh-hour repentance of average fiction. As she sowed, she reaped. It is stern, just, perfect. But it required courage to set it forth; and it is perhaps the finest evidence in Miss Brontë's work of her logical mind and conscientious spirit, — two characteristics, I believe, more pre-eminently twined in her than in any other author. To such a marriage must we trace her "severity," — a legitimate child of honest parents.

V

One might ask, if she did not affect what she did not really experience, how she came to make those social blunders in 'Jane Eyre' which gave the reviewers such a turn. Miss Brontë doubtless thought she had found the experience in the homes in which she had led the life of a dependant; and Miss Ingram was doubtless intended to reflect some supercilious miss who had crossed the path of the little governess, wincing at the contrast between careless freedom and careworn slavery,— between proud looks and a high stomach and their utter physical and psychical opposites. It is quite possible she exaggerated the contrast, her natural retiring shyness magnifying what seemed to her the reverse of shy into something bolder than it really was. It is simply one of the faults of intensity unchecked by experience, — one of the marks of a lack of technical training. It does not interfere with her general veracity. Even in such details as pertained to the fashionable life she was ignorant of, the falsity is only *in* the details. The *character* of Miss Ingram is clearly enough seen through all the faults of manner in telling it.

Veracity was more than a study with Miss Brontë; it was a passion. The emphasis laid upon it at times had its outcome in an exaggeration which defeated the very purpose of its aim, making the situation unlikely where it was only meant to be intense. It is hard to believe, for example, that the silence following the interruption of the marriage ceremony of Jane Eyre and Rochester lasted for ten minutes. A ten-minutes silence at such a time is a sizable slice. Of the same sort is her description of Graham conferring with Lucy about his impending interview with Mr. Home. His fate hung on the outcome of that interview; and yet so anxious is the author to keep before the reader the idea of the gay, debonair Graham, — the picture set forth at the beginning of the story ["a handsome, faithless-looking youth . . . his smile frequent, and destitute neither of fascination nor of subtlety"], — that, although she makes his hand tremble and a "vital suspense alternately hold and hurry his breath," she can calmly assure us that in all this trouble "his smile never faded." It is also a tax upon our credulity to accept the cool statement that the knowledge possessed by Helstone and Moore that they stood a good chance of being shot from behind a wall, that drizzling night they went on their dangerous errand to Stillbro' Moor, made them "elate." I am convinced that Richard Cœur de Lion himself would hardly be elated with the idea of being shot in the dark. But her notion was to lay emphasis on the fact of their "steely nerves and steady-beating hearts." It is merely another example of over-emphasis, almost her only fault in character drawing, and a natural fault of writers who feel their convictions intensely, and whose faithful realism is harassed by ideality.

Not to multiply instances, let us say, in conclusion, that delirious persons do not talk just like Caroline Helstone in her wanderings. What causes some of Miss Brontë's conversations to seem unreal is her making her characters say *to*, what other novelists would make them say *of*, each other. This is also the fruit of the unusual conditions of her life. She thought, as it were, out loud, as is the habit of persons much accustomed to solitariness.

There is a lack of skill, too, in the management of the plot, and for the same reasons. For, given simplicity, innocence, love of truth, as the basic character, and intensity as the temperament, and such mechanical complexities as the arrangement and joining together of all the parts (which requires a technical gift quite different from that of the pure conceiving of character) will only bewilder and confuse. It is extremely improbable that the presence of the maniacal wife in Thornfield could have been concealed from Mrs. Fairfax and the servants, and that their suspicions should not have been conveyed to Jane. There is no need for the elaborate portraiture of the king and queen of Belgium in 'Villette.' They have nothing to do with the story, and are of no interest in themselves: with such matter crowded into it, the book ceases to be a story, and becomes a journal. And all that intense picturing of Miss Marchmont's sufferings, at the beginning of the same book, might have been omitted.

It was a too careful notice of such seeming carelessness that moved the criticisms of those reviewers who made such a stir in their day, but who are now forgotten, while the object of their attack lives on. They were honest enough, though mistaken and not far-seeing. They could not penetrate the veil of the mystery; nor could they know what we know of the personal life and aspirations of one who was to them simply a new novelist to earn some daily bread over; whose name and whose sex was a riddle, and who used a language not before heard, and therefore open to conservative opposition. The famous *Quarterly Review* article [1] would have been *in*famous only on

---

[1] The subsequent history of this article is one of the most curious instances in literary records of mistaken application. Its supposed author was Lockhart, and Miss Brontë's defenders have made it hot for his memory. For over forty years he was held up to public beating, — Mr. Swinburne ['A Note on Charlotte Brontë.' London: Chatto & Windus, 1877] and Mr. Birrell ['Charlotte Brontë.' London: Walter Scott, 1877] laying on particularly heavy strokes as they passed by. Yet they were not certain of the authorship; and, of course, it did not cross their minds that the writer might have been a woman. "Who wrote the article," says Mr. Birrell, "is not publicly known" [p. 108]. And yet thirty-eight years before that, Charlotte and her publishers knew that Miss Rigby (afterwards Lady Eastlake) was the author [Shorter, p. 347]; and the Memoirs of Sara Coleridge containing a letter to Quillinan referring to Miss Rigby in this connection were published several years before Mr. Swinburne and Mr. Birrell wrote their monographs. The article was certainly in Lockhart's style, and in keeping with the traditions of the *Quarterly*. Charlotte said, before she was informed of the authorship, that the writer was "no gentleman" [Shorter, p. 190]. What Miss Rigby felt when she read Swinburne, Birrell, and others may be surmised, for I believe she must have repented of her wounding judgments. And it is still open to suspicion that Lockhart tinctured the article with his venom.

There were other reviews that hurt also, one of which was our own *North American* of October, 1848, which may be here alluded to as an instance of cocksureness now, happily, not so prominent as in the past. The heading of the notice ran thus:

"1. Jane Eyre, an Autobiography. Edited by Currer Bell. Boston: Wilkins, Carter & Co., 1848. 12mo.

the supposition that the writer was personally acquainted with the novelist. As it stood, it was merely brutal through ignorance and spiritual dullsightedness. Miss Brontë's description of the house party at Thornfield is a failure, of course. She had no real leaning towards that kind of writing, and not enough experience to do it well; nor had she the gift of many lesser writers to absorb into their descriptions the essential masterly qualities of the descriptions of others. The main point overlooked by her critics was, and is, to see through this crudeness to the vitalities beyond. The critics took roughness for coarseness. She drew coarse characters, but they were not coarsely drawn. We see the picture, and we say

---

2. Wuthering Heights. By the author of Jane Eyre. New York: Harper & Bros., 1848. 2 vols., 12mo.

3. The Tenant of Wildfell Hall, by Acton Bell, author of Wuthering Heights. New York: Harper & Bros., 1848. 2 vols., 12mo."

That is, Acton Bell, or Anne Brontë, wrote all three! The writer says, however, that 'Jane Eyre,' bears the mark of more than one mind and one sex. The descriptions of dress, "the minutiæ of the sick chamber," and the "various superficial refinements of feeling in regard to the external relations of the sex" are feminine; but the "clear, distinct, decisive style of its representation of character, manners, and scenery . . . continually suggests a male mind." It is taken for granted that Acton is a man, and is the portrayer of that portion of 'Jane Eyre' which has to do with Rochester. "We are gallant enough to detect the hand of a gentleman in the composition." It is more difficult for us to discover the hand of a gentleman in the review, or to deduce from its tone what constituted the reviewer's right to pass judgment upon what gentlemen do. And certain kinds of gallantry are the worst kinds of insult.

Quarterly reviewers have had their little day. That evil trinity, Gifford, Lockhart, and Croker, are overthrown Olympians, and the insistent fairness of our age prohibits any succession to the office. They were only fit to crush Della Cruscans and the like; and their pronouncements were not based upon what a later generation demands in the way of judgment. Think of the critical ability of a man who could deliberately put Charlotte Brontë, as a poet, before Emily!

it is coarse; but that is because the coarse object is delineated with truth. One looking for coarseness must go elsewhere.[1]

[1] Lewes' article in the *Edinburgh Review*, Jan., 1850, while striving to do her justice, was quite unpardonable in its flippancy, and was far worse, considering the fuller knowledge he possessed of the real facts of her life, than the *Quarterly's;* and her letter to him was a deserved rebuke. [Gaskell, p. 449.] Lewes was an acute, not a profound man. The only critic of her work during her life who really understood her, and the first to understand Emily (too late, alas! for her earthly satisfaction), was Sydney Dobell, in the *Palladium* (bound volume of 1850). His correspondence with Miss Brontë should be read by every student of her life. See 'Life and Letters of Sydney Dobell,' London, Smith, Elder, & Co., 1878. The *Palladium* article is reprinted in the first volume.

It is interesting to note, in this connection, that if the identity of the Brontë sisters was not known to certain persons in London before the question "Who is Currer Bell?" passed from lip to lip over England, it argues for much lack of penetration. Charlotte began her correspondence with the firm of Aylott & Jones concerning the production of the Poems by the Bells as early as January, 1846. She wrote from Haworth, and under her own name, as sponsor for Currer Bell. It is very remarkable that this firm contributed nothing to the elucidation of the problem which sprang up upon the publication of 'Jane Eyre,' for they knew at least that Currer Bell was the friend of Charlotte Brontë, and that Charlotte Brontë's home was Haworth. The identity of the initials must also have seemed suspicious. If they knew and kept silence, it is one of the most notable silences on record. Messrs. Smith and Elder must also have had their unpublished suspicions, for the same reason.

One of the most significant indications of the entire change of view we have undergone in our social attitude towards women may be found in Southey's well-known letter to Miss Brontë. It is quite possible that some old-fashioned gentlemen may still applaud the advice, but the point is that if Southey had to deal with the subject now, he would write differently: it is not now the view of literary men. What gave our author special offence in the criticisms of her work was the folly and crime of blaming her for writing, as a woman, what would have been condoned in a man. She was one of the first to stand for the sexlessness of art. She asked for praise or condemnation for the work's sake, not because she, a woman, did it; and her struggle had a good deal to do with the final literary emancipation of womanhood. "Literature cannot be the business of a woman's life,

VI

Her artlessness is shown on many sides. For example, it is everywhere evident in her failing to screen the locality of her story. All the places mentioned in the books are places known on the maps. Whinbury is Oxenhope. Nunnely is Oakworth. Morton is Hathersage. "Field Head" is Oakwell Hall near Birstall, and all the other 'Shirley' scenery is equally patent. The Haworth edition of the novels is sprinkled with photographs of the originals of the localities she describes under other names. She has not only been to the Brussels she writes of (unlike Mrs. Radcliffe, whose vivid *mise en scène* is wholly fanciful), but one may visit the city, with copies of 'Villette' and the 'Professor,' in hand and discover the places therein made famous, — the Rue d'Isabelle, the Protestant cemetery, the church where the confession was made, the park to which Lucy stole at midnight on the feast of the Martyrs. And because the original of

---

and it ought not to be," wrote Southey, on the ground that the seeking in imagination for excitement would be rendered unnecessary by the vicissitudes and anxieties of that other life which, as a woman, she must accept. Of course, he could not foresee the after-fame of this timid seeker for help; and he would even in his own day have acknowledged, I think, that in cases of real genius, there is no voluntary, arbitrary "seeking" in imagination, but that the imagination exists involuntarily, a hungry call on nature, demanding vent. Had Charlotte Brontë been less of a genius, this letter of Southey might have done her harm. It is a pity that he did not live, as Wordsworth did, to know the matured woman to whom, as a girl, he gave his asked-for advice. And it should be remembered that it was a specimen of Charlotte's verse that he saw: his answer was appropriate enough for that special exhibition. But it is his generalizing that we of a later day have corrected.

Brocklehurst was immediately detected, Brocklebridge church was seen to be no other than Tunstall's, over which that pious gentleman presided. Finally, as all the world knows, Lowood is no fiction, but another name for the all too real Cowan's Bridge.

Edward Crimsworth curses his brother as a "greasehorn," — a term which is explained to be "purely ——shire;" as if the dash would not spell York to all who knew the district. On the other hand, it is only by roundabout methods that one may discover that St. Oggs is Gainsborough. Indeed, George Eliot departs from geographical veracity by giving the Floss (*i. e.*, the Trent) a tributary, as if to throw a too eager searcher after originals off the track.[1]

It is the same with the characters: they are simply the occupiers of the places, all personally or traditionally known to the author. The name of Eyre was not invented. Dr. John stood for Mr. George Smith, and his mother was the prototype of Mrs. Bretton. Cyril Hall's original was Canon Heald. The curates immediately recognized themselves, much to Miss Brontë's dismay, and made a joke of the matter, — which showed them to be as bad as they were painted. Mr. Nicholls was let off easily in the passing reference to Mr. Macarthy. As Morton is recognized as Hathersage, it is fair to assume that St. John Rivers is the fictional name of Henry Nussey, who

---

[1] Those wishing to identify scenery in George Eliot should consult, among other papers, Mr. George Morley's article in the *Gentleman's Magazine* for December, 1890 (reprinted with illustrations in the 1897 volume of the *Art Journal*); 'George Eliot's Country,' in the *Century* for July, 1885; also articles in *Munsey's*, Aug., 1897, and the *Bookman*, vol. ii., p. 376.

was vicar there, especially as the characters fit. We have seen that her discoverer has acknowledged that Miss Ainley was drawn from life. The other old maid in the story was also known, and afterwards married. Mr. Cartwright's works at Liversedge were attacked, as were Robert Moore's at Hollow's-mill. Everybody knows who Paul Emmanuel was in real life. It is evident that the Vashti she describes in 'Villette' was the Rachel she saw in London. There was "absolute resemblance" in Hortense Moore to Mlle. Haussé; and the originals of the other teachers in 'Villette' are mentioned in the letters from Brussels. A Miss Miller sat for the portrait labelled Ginevra Fanshawe. Miss Nussey says[1] Charlotte had met the original of Helstone, although she blended his characteristics with those of her father. Mr. Brocklehurst, if you will pardon me for mentioning it again, is the Rev. Carus Wilson. Miss Nussey herself is commemorated in Caroline Helstone. Miss Wooler's memory is preserved in the picture of Miss Temple, and Miss Scratcherd was equally well known in the flesh. Helen Burns was Maria Brontë. The demoniacal wife in 'Jane Eyre' was not an invention, nor, as we have seen, was that voice in the night. Mme. Beck and her previous study in the 'Professor' were recognized at once. Compare the reference to the time wasted in art-practising —

I have in my day wasted a certain quantity of Bristol board and drawing paper, crayons and cakes of color, but when I examine the contents of my portfolio now, it seems as if during the years it had been lying closed some fairy had changed what I once thought sterling coin into dry

[1] *Scribner's*, May, 1871.

leaves, and I feel much inclined to consign the whole collection of drawings to the fire; I see they have no value.

with what Lucy Snowe says of the same thing:

> I sat bending over my desk drawing — that is, copying — an elaborate line engraving, tediously working up my copy to the finish of the original, for that was my practical notion of art; and strange to say, I took extreme pleasure in the labor, and could even produce curiously finical Chinese fac-similes of steel or mezzotint plates — things about as valuable as so many achievements in worsted-work, but I thought pretty well of them in those days.

Because Lucy Snowe is Charlotte Brontë, as is Jane Eyre, and as is the Professor. "Mrs. Pryor was well known to many, who loved the original dearly." The very animals of the novels were the pets of the parsonage. This faithfulness of reproduction extends in one case to the name of the character, her most typical Yorkshireman being Mr. Yorke himself; for, says Mrs. Gaskell of the original, "No other country but Yorkshire could have produced such a man."[1] Mary Taylor recognized the Yorke group away off in New Zealand where she read the novel, and acknowledged its truthfulness. There is, indeed, a veritable triumph for Miss Brontë's art in Miss Taylor's statement that she and the others were made to talk very much as they would have talked if they had talked at all.[2] That shows both the faithfulness of her realism and her logical power in building an imaginative structure upon a well-ascertained base. The realism was not mere phonography. The conversations were created to suit the known characters. Imagination had full sway; but, recklessly unmodifiable to every recog-

[1] Gaskell, p. 158.   [2] Shorter, p. 251.

nized norm as the talk of the Yorke children seems, it is welcomed by the most intelligent of them as finely true.[1]

No such list as this can be made of any other writer, and it is of the highest interest as illustrating the veracity of Miss Brontë's method. She describes what she knows. She had not had much acquaintance with sea scenery, so there is hardly any mention of the sea in her books. In making Hortense Moore foreign in dress, she makes the foreignness Belgian.

VII

Her range of vision being narrow, and her truthfulness not permitting her to extend it beyond the limits of experience, we find not only known characters, but a similarity of type and situation. There are not many men of many minds in her novels. Hunsden's peculiarities are an early study of Yorke's. Dr. John talks to Lucy somewhat as Rochester talks to Jane. There is a recurrence of the master-and-pupil situation of the 'Professor' in 'Shirley' and 'Villette.' Paul Emmanuel is a moral Rochester, in a Roman Catholic environment. Jane Eyre and Lucy Snowe are twin sisters, — which, knowing as we do their one original, is a dazzling evidence of their beautiful truth. Even in the incidental situations of the stories is this similarity to be found. Louis Moore's trifling with Shirley's desk is a counterpart of Paul Emmanuel's with Lucy's. Indeed, this fondness for meddling with other persons' affairs is quite an alarming symptom in her heroes.

[1] Regarding Emily's work, one walking from Keighley to Haworth may see the name Earnshaw on a sign before an inn.

Her Realism

And that the artistic imagination did not run away with the verisimilitude which she made a matter of course, is sufficiently proved by the outcome of the Lowood controversy. To revert to George Eliot once more,—the comparison is inevitable,—if the latter writer had had to speak of a past experience at a school which, but for some care, would have been immediately recognized as Cowan's Bridge, she would have so cloaked the identity that such a recognition would have been impossible, or would have cleverly intimated that the story was of the long ago and that the abuses had for a century or so been eradicated. Charlotte Brontë erred in these fine distinctions, because of an absorption in her theme which allowed no time for other than setting it forth downright. She maintained that every word of the Lowood matter was in accordance with fact, and Mrs. Gaskell substantiated it from personal investigation.[1] It is not surprising that there was a hubbub about it. But Charlotte did not expect its original would be discovered. She was not a reformer, like Dickens. 'Jane Eyre' was not a novel with a purpose. Lowood was not intended as a companion picture to Dotheboys Hall. Dickens thundered against evils which he believed to be present. There were no evils at Cowan's Bridge when Charlotte Brontë wrote, for the school had been removed to Casterton, and its objectionable features were a thing of the past.[2] Indeed, she tells us as much in the story. Its bitterness had so pierced her memory, however, that her on-rushing thought did not take the prudent steps

---

[1] Gaskell, pp. 65 *seq.*
[2] See her letter to Miss Wooler, Shorter, p. 262.

which a more deliberative judgment would have dictated.[1]

And I take it that this delineation of known persons and places is a very different thing from the "local color" of the more modern novelists. With them it is the celebration of the district, the town, the street. Miss Brontë had no such artistic photography in mind. Her scenery was not intended to be recognized; she fancied she had concealed it behind fictitious names. She had an inherent terror of publicity, and wished the identity between Currer Bell and Charlotte Brontë to remain unknown. The things she had experienced came to her as the natural things to be described; and in the bright innocence of her heart, and the quaint self-deception of her seclusion, she wove her magic web around the people

---

[1] Local tradition, according to Mr. Candy [*Gentleman's Magazine*, vol. 267, p. 415: Some Reminiscences of the author of 'Jane Eyre'] supports Charlotte's statement that "some died at the school and were buried quietly and quickly," notwithstanding Mrs. Gaskell's statement to the contrary. "In Leck churchyard, a short distance from Cowan's Bridge, are two gravestones, the inscriptions on which record the deaths of pupils at the school (one of the names is Becker) at the time of the epidemic described in the novel. If the date of the year — which is somewhat illegible from age — is correctly deciphered, the pathetic record in 'Jane Eyre' is literally true." This writer also vouches, from personal investigation, for the general unsanitary situation of the place, and the unsuitability of the building for the purpose to which it was put. In this connection, it should be insisted that she is, distinctly, *not* a "governess novelist." Anne might fairly be called that, but not Charlotte. She did not have the idea before her of righting any particular wrongs; the absolute freedom of her genius saved her from that. Her direct progression towards truth, taking the steady road of Realism, compelled her to write of the heart-depressing and brain-wearying trials of the one dependent life which she knew with a personal knowledge which inflamed her soul. She was not moved by the philanthropic impulse of Dickens; only thus could her mind flame out its painful message.

she knew, and made them move in the only paths which occurred to her, — the paths her own feet had trod.

As a matter of fact, we learn but little of the customs and manners of the localities of which she writes. The subjective crowds the objective. We hear a little, it is true, of the peripatetic "missionary basket" of parochial fame; there is some mention of the Whitsuntide festivities of the neighborhood; and it may be discovered that in those days Mrs. Sweeney dispensed the soothing syrup which Mrs. Winslow has since made her own. But were Miss Brontë attempting "local color," surely we should find some description of the funeral arvils which the Nonconformist Yorkshire conscience reconciled itself to as a substitute for the Popish wake, and which had a tendency, it would seem from Mrs. Gaskell's description, to change griefs of the heart to pains in the head. She is silent, too, concerning that other Yorkshire custom referred to by her biographer, which would have furnished Mr. Bunner, let us say, with delicious morsels, had he been born in Thornton, — that wedding anthem sung in chapel, upon the first appearance of a newly married couple, by a band of choristers who, with the earnings of the occasion, invariably spent the following night carousing in honor of Hymen, to the great scandal of the neighborhood. Another author — Hardy or Blackmore, for example — would have made much more out of the Gytrash than Miss Brontë does in 'Jane Eyre.' Her first consideration was the portrayal of the radical elements of character, not the painting of scenery; and all the vivid beauty of her descriptive powers, and all the rare marvel of her rich poetic prose when engaged in the depiction of woods and moors and weather, she would have held as secondary and accidental.

In truth, she who in her own field is the most purely imaginative of all writers except Emily, is not an imaginative writer at all either in the portrayal of incidents or in the fashioning of character with other than her native clay. Yorkshire and Belgium are her only hall-marks. Her apocalyptic visions have other sources, — which is, perhaps, why they are apocalyptic. Her stories are thin, and have little outward excitement, the maniacal adventures in 'Jane Eyre' being the only really stirring exception. She could not romance for the mere pleasure of it. Only once did she break loose, when her affection lured her into the dream of Emily happily in love. But it may be that she was a better judge of her limitations than others, for 'Shirley' ranks below her two greatest works.

Hence the curates. Unlike George Eliot, she could not draw a really fine clergyman, never having met one. Mr. Hall's picture is kindly painted, but the talk of him is too didactically pious for our unregenerate taste. The purely priestly in Rivers is excellently, if sternly, emphasized, but the asceticism drowns the humanity. The others seem to us mere caricatures. Caricatures they are not; they are of the type that came under her vision.

VIII

I would not say that Miss Brontë had the old-maid's attitude towards children, for that would put an unjust classification in view, my observation being that among the best friends of children must be

Her Realism

reckoned their maiden aunts. Actual motherhood is not necessary to awaken the mother-love lying dormant in virgin breasts. But she was enveloped with the peculiar shyness which is as a repelling atmosphere to the approach of child-confidence. In regard to the little ones, we do not find in Currer Bell any of those sweet springs of understanding which are fed from the rills of a joyous instinctive uncritical affection. Not that she does not observe; she observes keenly, but too aloofly. She is too individual: her truthfulness to the special portrait stands in the way of a general truthfulness.

Knowing as we do some of the characteristics of Maria Brontë, we should hesitate to say that Helen Burns, her fictional representative, is an impossible child. On the contrary, this portrait is not a proof that Charlotte did not understand children, but is a proof that she did understand Helen Burns. But she is so individual that she is not typical, and we do not recognize any of childhood's qualities in the character. It is not that her talk is big; but when a precocious infant uses large words, what gives charm and humor to the situation is the incongruousness of the childish mind grappling with thoughts as yet imperfectly conceived, — the developing fancy trying to take root in an undeveloped intellect. His words share the fate of his building-blocks; they are apt to come tumbling about his head before they reach the upper stories. There is the undivorcible child-atmosphere even in the clever talk of unusual children; and what makes the conversation of an extraordinarily developed child quaint is the language *in* the atmosphere. But there is no such atmosphere about Helen Burns. She talks like an eighteenth-century essayist. Her mind is not even a palimpsest, through the later writing of which you may discern the earlier. It is a grown-up mind of sixty years, without a trace of childhood.[1] Currer Bell's children are portraits, but portraits only of extremely rare species, as if a natural historian should confine his observation to the grotesque in nature.

The subject suggests an interesting topic. Knowing a little of the originals of some of her extraordinary characters — Helen Burns, among others — is not this result of her labors an argument against a too keenly followed realism? Surely, the passion to set down all the accidents of each particular person is a mistaken attitude towards truth. For while there is no substance without accidents, actual specific observation should be toned into a conformity with general laws before it is set forth to view, unless it be of that kind which is of itself the cause of new law. Hence Romance, which supplies accidents as well as realism, and which supplies them when the resources of realism fail.

Miss Brontë's strongest characteristics are her truthfulness and her intensity. She is, indeed, intense in her truthfulness, which, when combined with a too insistent realism, irritates the attention. If the child Helen Burns, if the child Polly, if the Yorke children, are the outcomes of this truthfulness to particular details, are we not justified in asking for a little less concentration on the specific, and a little more evolution from the general?

This fault of particularization differs, however, from the fault which at first sight seems akin to it, — the fault

[1] Remembering what the father said about Maria, what might have been ours if she and that other had lived!

of the school which has arisen since her day, and which also aims at reality. Realism, pressed ruthlessly to all its minor logical outcomes, passes to its wintry death; and indeed, in our latter-day work, art has been so exclusively employed in developing all the nice shades of— not character so much as every muscle which controls every motive which prompts every desire which works the piston of every will, that the vital juices run thin and dry as they sluggishly return to the heart of the structure. When several paragraphs are devoted, in the finest play of the subtlest of current English-writing realists, to an analysis, of as intricate a delicacy as the workmanship of a Damascus blade, of the dainty set of ideas started in the brain of a Boston lady by the discovery of the brightly polished condition of her door-knob, we feel that in the passing of that other James, there is somehow gone a glory from the earth. Miss Brontë would have had as little sympathy with such an outcome as she had with the romanticists; for any system which involves in its last analysis the absence of large imaginations it would be impossible to connect with the name of one in whom realism was baptized in imagination, and whose style was fired by passion. She was too true to herself to be other than herself in her writings. The mechanical mysteries of her art had no charm for Currer Bell. In very truth, she would have denied fellowship with any craft which would narrow art into the grooves of a cunningly learned trade.

A more extended acquaintance with these mysteries would have saved her from the obvious lapses of her straightforward method; but as the peculiar charm and unique power of this writer are wrapped up in her faults, — as the lapses we speak of are the necessary accidents of that method, — it would be worse than folly to speak of them except gratefully. They could not be safely followed by imitators; it would be impossible to form a school upon them, because that would imply a dependence upon faults which, separated from the independence of Charlotte Brontë, would glare balefully. The art which conceals the art of the narrator in the impersonal third person, for example, is the only safe art for the majority; and to Currer Bell's personal note, a reflection of which is seen in the form of all her stories (for even in 'Shirley,' Caroline Helstone, while intended as a portrait of Miss Nussey, is instinctively felt to be in a much larger way a picture of Charlotte Brontë also), are due most of her shortcomings. Yet what would have become of Jane Eyre and Lucy Snowe if their stories had been told by a manifest outsider? The passion of a personal spiritual experience could only be wrought into them by this particular writer making them stand for her particular self. The first person comes naturally with such a complete emptying of the absolute into the fictional self. Maybe if Miss Brontë's brilliant powers could have been more steadily controlled by the acquired skill of managing details, her realism would have been guided into the narrow streams over which the later school floats so passively. But we are profoundly thankful it was not so, for we should then have had to look elsewhere for the pre-eminent prose-poet of feeling.

There is in 'Villette' as little plot as in any production of the modern realists; but the mark of divergence between the two lies in the importance which incidents occupy in the latter, with whom Dryden's dictum is law: "No person, no incident . . . but must be of use to carry on the main design." Miss Brontë was so captivated by the study of character that what may be called the circumstances of her story are frequently quite accidental and apart from the principal motive. Her accidents do not control; and excellent as her logic is, in life logic does not always control, and accidents often do, which are generally illogical. In our progression towards the end of the age, we have reached the days of composite photography in art. The present realist bases his work upon types. Miss Brontë took the individual individually; we now take the mass representatively. Who would call Edward Rochester a typical man? or Jane Eyre a representative woman? On the other hand, in Silas Lapham do we not recognize, not one man but fifty of our acquaintance? This is the glory of Charlotte Brontë, this is her fame. The romanticists who preceded her made their heroes impossible by making them do impossible things, from the standpoint of supposable experience. The histories of Rochester and Paul Emmanuel are the reverse of impossible; Emmanuel's is even humdrum in its commonplaceness. Yet the characters themselves are two of the most extraordinary in fiction. Rochester is preposterous, not because he is called upon to do things contrary to nature, but because he acts strictly in accordance with his nature. And if the natural man within us grows weary of the extravagances of these gentlemen, the artistic man is bound to acknowledge that there is reason in their madness, and that their words and deeds are in the finest accord with the laws of their being. "Was ever woman in this humor wooed?" will be asked of Jane Eyre only by those whose experience is bounded by the four walls of a conventional home.

IX

Purified realism is a rare enough thing to be thankful for. That is the sun, and the defects we have noticed are mere specks on its surface. The sunspots do not hinder the sunshine.

We are told in 'Shirley' that all her characters will be found imperfect; yet she is also determined not "to handle degraded or utterly infamous ones. Child-torturers, slave masters and drivers, I consign to the hands of jailers; the novelist may be excused from sullying his page with the record of their deeds." Even as we find but few agreeable persons in her books, so also do we find no debasing realisms. There are a few jackasses, clerical and lay, one sanctimonious hypocrite, a spoiled beauty or two, some hard continental characters, a family of tyrannical children, and Mrs. Reed,—strictly speaking, no villains. She is a pure realist in one sense, although she placed her characters in situations which a pure realist of another sense would delight in making that sense all too evident.

She has been blamed for those situations, and 'Jane Eyre' is still considered by some honest persons a dangerous book. But without temptation what is virtue? The glory of Charlotte Brontë is her spotless purity, her making virtue to shine through the temptation and by means of it. She is really a severe moralist. She condemns the 'Life of Mirabeau' because it could not be put in the hands of the young without danger of impressing the grandeur of vice on a colossal scale, "whereas in vice there is

Her Realism 47

no grandeur, . . . only a foul, sordid, and degraded thing."[1] This seems like a commonplace, yet she wrote bitterly, for Miss Brontë's critics ventured to charge her with such portrayals. If the weak only were considered in the writing of books, no books worth the writing would ever be written. To the pure all things are pure is a hard doctrine, for so few are pure. Her realism never shied at ugliness, but it flew unharmed past sin; nor did she commit crimes against art in the name of art. She holds Burns above Bulwer. Truth is better than art is her creed, just as a man is better than his clothes. But she refuses to dwell on such aspects of the truth as are instinctively known, and which could only do harm in the telling, — the finer the art, the worse the harm, — and which would thus militate against the ideal truth.

We live in an age when advice from high quarters — if the dove-like innocence of such advice were not made unlikely by the hardly acquired wisdom of the editorial serpent — not to read a certain book because of alleged immoralities would be hailed with delight by the wicked publisher, before the bulging eyes of whose fancy would dance, in the best tricks of type, the magic words, " twentieth edition ! " How such a warning could have been passed upon the possible readers of 'Jane Eyre' has been deemed one of the problems of literature. The reason, perhaps, lay in the mixed conventionality and pruriency of the age, — this novel being the first to shock the first, in the falsely safe folds of which it was wont to seek the second. It was an age too dull to recognize bright innocence, all the brighter because innocently near darkness; and too materialistic to

[1] Shorter. p. 385.

undertake the analysis of a situation which is obviously (to those who know Miss Brontë) free from all intention of evil, because the situation is objectively one for evil to select. In the intention lies the harm, and the critics could not see it. Let us cherish the pious hope that somebody kicked the gaping puppy who compared his book with hers, in that each was "naughty."

It was the author of 'Jane Eyre' who said:

A lover masculine so disappointed can speak and urge explanation; a lover feminine can say nothing; if she did the result would be shame and anguish, inward remorse for self-treachery. Nature would brand such demonstration as a rebellion against her instincts, and would vindictively repay it afterward by the thunderbolt of self-contempt smiting suddenly in secret. Take the matter as you find it: ask no questions, utter no remonstrances.

and

On my reason had been inscribed the conviction that unlawful pleasure, trenching on another's rights, is delusive and envenomed pleasure; its hollowness disappoints at the time; its poison cruelly tortures afterwards; its effects deprave forever.

and

I hate boldness, — that boldness which is of the brassy brow and insensate nerves; but I love the courage of the strong heart, the fervor of the generous blood.

And this is the key-note of all her work, which she sounds in a more professional way in the preface to the second edition of 'Jane Eyre':

Conventionality is not morality. Self-righteousness is not religion. To attack the first is not to assail the last.

To pluck the mask from the face of the Pharisee is not to lift an impious hand to the Crown of Thorns.

This is why she admires Thackeray so profoundly; and yet she takes even him to task for his Fielding lecture, and cries out in her splendid innocence, "I trust God will take from me whatever power of invention or expression I may have before he lets me become blind to the sense of what is fitting or unfitting to be said!"[1]

There are strong points of similiarity between her male heroes: there is in all of them the eagle quality, the note of dominance. That was her ideal of a man: she could not look up to any other kind. She found this also in Thackeray, and, I venture to suggest, there is a hint of him in Paul Emmanuel. Shirley acknowledges the estimable qualities of Sir Philip Nunnely, but she cannot accept him because he is not her *master* (the italicized word is Miss Brontë's). "I could not trust myself with his happiness; I would not undertake the keeping of it for thousands; I will accept no hand which cannot hold me in check." "Improving a husband!" exclaims Shirley, scornfully. "No. I shall insist upon my husband improving me, or else we part."

Charlotte Brontë had no fear of the word "obey" in the marriage service, and would have had no sympathy with the women who jest about it; for she would have known that such women have not had their noblest natures touched, or suffer from an in-

---

[1] What a subject for an Imaginary Conversation would be her two-hour talk with the great, lovable, faulty giant, in which she gravely reproved him for his shortcomings, and to which he as gravely listened; defending himself, however, "like a great Turk and heathen; that is to say, the excuses were often worse than the crime itself!"

capacity of full affection. Obedience is involved in love. She took the Scriptural view that man is stronger than woman in judgment, and that obedience is therefore due him. There is no fear in that love, for it is of the perfect kind which casteth it out,— the love of complete confidence. Such is her ideal man, and she tries to build her heroes along those lines. Rochester is a trifle too grand, gloomy, and peculiar for the taste of the average woman of this present day, although I understand he created great havoc among the sentimental ladies of the late '40's. Louis Moore is our old friend the Professor over again (and the Professor is a dreadful prig, with his *besicles*, "guiding by smile and gesture," and, as if that was not enough, also "smiling inwardly" and "bestowing" "proud and contented kisses"). In our unsanctified moments, we have even called him a solemn donkey. His talk with Shirley about his "friendless young orphan girl" is as outrageous as Rochester's ramblings with Jane. Yet that is a love scene of great strength, notwithstanding; and Shirley yields to the man who can master her Tartar better than she can herself.

The genius of this girl was equal to her drawbacks; and through the immaturity — one might almost say because of the immaturity — we see it conquering. Immaturity, so far from being wholly a fault, is, negatively, in given cases, an indication of genius. That is, the genius is so demonstrable that the immaturity cannot hide it; the immaturity is seen at once as the thin gossamer through which the sunlight shines. The temporal qualities of immaturity are, by their very poverty, contrasted with the lasting powers of genius, just as the sun shining through a window may show hitherto unsuspected defects in the glass. Miss Brontë knew too well, from the home experience, the lapses of men from her high standard, which, I repeat, is the Scriptural standard. The quotation recently made from her works concerning unlawful pleasure had its direct source in Bramwell's life, as may hardly be doubted when the full context is seen:

> I had once had the opportunity of contemplating, near at hand, an example of the results produced by a course of interesting and romantic domestic treachery. No golden halo of fiction was about this example. I saw it bare and real, and it was very loathsome. I saw a mind degraded by the practice of mean subterfuge, by the habit of perfidious deception, and a body depraved by the infectious influence of the vice-polluted soul. I had suffered much from the forced and prolonged view of this spectacle.

Read also the first paragraph of Chapter XIX. of this same book, the 'Professor,' to see how this example had weighed upon her soul.

Now, just as faith is strong only in the midst of faithlessness, so does she not deny her ideal because of her acquaintance with the actual. The actual was only too real to her, but the ideal was more real. Jane Eyre is not blinded to the moral transgressions and spiritual sins of Rochester. Both morally and spiritually she is stronger than he. Where conscience existed — and it existed everywhere in Charlotte Brontë's vision — not even love had sway, — the point that her critics missed; and it was not until conscience had reconciled the love to its absolute demands that the sway was accepted. But then it *was* accepted. Rochester is a brute, you say. Yet the brute in him was conquered before Jane marries him. It is Una and the lion. There is a mighty strength in her heroes, especially Rochester, which shines back of and out of their weaknesses — the original strength of man as he stood in his Creator's plan. Her women, through love for the strength, subdue the weakness by accepting the strength —

> He for God only; she for God in him.

This is the woman's point of view, and not even the new woman can find fault with it as portrayed in Charlotte Brontë; for she makes the men to whom her heroines give such love acknowledge, once it is gained, not their superiority, but the equality of giver and receiver. "This is my equal," says Rochester of Jane. Shirley is Moore's "leopardess," — hardly an animal to be fondled. No reader of Charlotte Brontë can ever forget the magnificent repudiation of Milton's Eve, in 'Shirley,' yet the quotation from Milton stands, nevertheless. For she bows to the godlike in the man, and the man acknowledges the divinity in her. None but those who are entitled to queenhood may marry kings.

We have seen her attempts at minute delineations are, unlike Miss Austen's, occasionally burdensome, because uncorrected by the application of general principles. It is only when her thought is freed from the petty harassments of her realism that she becomes the great writer that we know, — the greatest writer of passion in the English tongue. Then she rises into her pure native empyrean above these levels, and takes her rank along the high places of the immortals.

B. — HER ATTITUDE TOWARDS NATURE

I

It may be stated without much fear of contradiction that the majority of her readers will always pre-eminently cherish Miss Brontë as a painter of scenery. Atmosphere possessed her. She was enveloped in the storm, the sunset was a personal glory, moonshine was the footstool of deity. She had both the "golden dreams" of Turner and the golden realities of Constable. She could picture the seraphim in ethereal splendor, and she could paint wind.

Let us not take low views of this marvellous gift. It is not merely as scenery that we should view it. There is no mechanical contrivance cunningly intended to give the picture title and rank as a character study through the medium of the surrounding weather conditions; the scenery is imbedded in her imagination, and is not arbitrarily selected for the purposes of interpretation. It is like the music which is more than a running commentary upon the text, — nay, at times like the music which itself forms the text; and the text is ever the passion of the human heart.

One might relate the fluctuations in the history of Jane Eyre by a series of canvases picturing the atmospheric descriptions accompanying them; or might transform into the sister art these descriptions in a symphonic manner which would tease the ear with the rapt enthusiasm which the eye feels at the pictures of the words. For, as in that highest form of musical composition, so in this scenic power of our author, the rhythms are contrasted and the keys are related.

Follow this history for a space, and feel the effect. The book opens in a depressed atmosphere, corresponding to that surrounding the little heroine's life. In the very first paragraph there is a "cold winter wind," bringing with it "sombre clouds." "Raw and chill was the winter morning" she left Gateshead. The afternoon of that long day's drive "came on wet and somewhat misty;" and, arrived at Lowood, "rain, wind, and darkness filled the air," like the spiritual demons which were about to encompass her in that abode. In the night she wakes to "hear the wind rave in furious gusts and the rain fall in torrents;" and when she was compelled to rise, in the grim dawn, "it was bitter cold." She goes out into the garden: "all was wintry blight and brown decay."

In the evening, during the play-hour, she "lifted a blind and looked out. It snowed fast, a drift was already forming against the lower panes; putting my ear close to the window, I could distinguish from the gleeful tumult within the disconsolate moan of the wind outside." And mark that this is not intended merely to emphasize the wintry desolation of her young life, but to drive deep into the spirit her sympathy with the storm, and the storm's sympathy with her, — the two loveless outcasts when others were indoors and loved. "Reckless and feverish, I wished the wind to howl more wildly, the gloom to deepen to darkness, and the confusion to rise to clamor."

There is always throughout the history the same correspondence between outside nature and inside life. But one does not think of this " pathetic fallacy" in following Jane Eyre's experience, with such beautiful unconsciousness does she enclose nature in the framework of her thought. It was to be expected, then, that the Sunday afternoon walk back from Mr. Brocklehurst's ministrations (remembering the physiological condition of the pupils after a day of starvation spent in a paralyzingly cold church) would be set forth in the usual weather strain. "At the close of the afternoon service we returned by an exposed and hilly road, where the bitter wind, blowing over a range of snowy summits to the north, almost flayed the skins from our faces."

The raging wind carries on its wings the raging spirit. And as the first note of peace is touched when Helen Burns calms little Jane with her quaint and patient piety, so then for the first time we see an unclouded night in the sky. "Resting my head on Helen's shoulder, I put my arms round her waist; she drew me to her, and we reposed in silence. . . . Some heavy clouds, swept from the sky by a rising wind, had left the moon bare; and her light, streaming in through a window near, shone full."

After the gloom and decay of Lowood, she sees before her a reawakened life at Thornfield-Hall, as she views the grounds from the battlements: "the horizon bounded by a *propitious* sky, azure, marbled with pearly white." The tameness of the governess-lot soon tells on her, however, and on the evening of her return from that walk to Hay made memorable by her first meeting with Rochester at the scene of his accident, the excitement of that episode thrills all the more vehemently because of the returning stagnation. She had caught a glimpse of the outside world, and there is a momentary rebellion against slipping on again " the viewless fetters of an uniformed and too still existence."

I lingered at the gates; I lingered on the lawn; I paced backward and forwards on the pavement: the shutters of the glass door were closed; I could not see into the interior; and both my eyes and spirit seemed drawn from the gloomy house — from the gray hollow filled with rayless cells, as it appeared to me — to that sky expanded before me, — a blue sea absolved from taint of cloud; the moon ascending it in solemn march; her orb seemed to look up as she left the hill tops, from behind which she had come, far and farther below her, and aspired to the zenith, midnight-dark in its fathomless depth and measureless distance: and for those trembling stars that followed her course, they made my heart tremble, my veins glow when I viewed them. Little things recall us to earth: the clock struck in the hall; that sufficed; I turned from moon and stars, opened a side-door, and went in.

The house was her life, filled with " rayless cells; " and in that spotless night was symbolized that ideal life beyond the range of her piteously feeble grasp.

The day on which she formally makes Rochester's acquaintance is fittingly " wild and stormy." At the second meeting, the winter rain beats against the panes; and he unloads his Parisian memories upon her in " a freezing and sunless air." The night the maniac wife paid her terrifying visit to the second story was "drearily dark; " and later on, as the tragedy advances, and just before she confronts that grisly terror again, from peaceful sleep Jane opens her eyes on the full moon, "silver white and crystal-clear. It was beautiful but too solemn." Her fate was approaching her,—"beautiful" because she carried duty in her closed hand, but "too solemn" because that duty was so grievous to be borne. It is as descriptive as the music of 'Parsival.' The sympathy of and with nature is, as it were, sacramentally complete.

Hope was shining high for Jane. Rochester was, in anticipation, hers.

A splendid Midsummer shone over England: skies so pure, suns so radiant as were then seen in long succession, seldom favor, even singly, our wave-girt land. It was as if a band of Italian days had come from the South, like a flock of glorious passenger birds, and lighted on the cliffs of Albion. The hay was all got in; the fields round Thornfield were green and shorn; the roads white and baked; the trees were in their dark prime: hedge and wood, full-leaved and deeply tinted, contrasted well with the sunny hue of the cleared meadows between.

Then the catastrophe draws very near.

A waft of wind came sweeping down the laurel-walk, and trembled through the boughs of the chestnut: it wandered away — away — to an indefinite distance — it died. The nightingale's song was then the only voice of the hour: in listening to it I again wept.

You hear the far-away echo-like sobbing of a Fate that would be kind, but must be harsh; and it blends with the voice of the nightingale which makes her weep. And at the moment of his proposal, and while he is madly justifying to himself that crime, the night changes.

But what had befallen the night? The moon was not yet set and we were all in shadow: I could scarcely see my master's face, near as I was. And what ailed the chestnut tree? it writhed and groaned; while wind roared in the laurel-walk, and came sweeping over us . . . a livid vivid spark leapt out of a cloud at which I was looking, and there was a crack, a crash, and a close rattling peal; and I thought only of hiding my dazzled eyes against Mr. Rochester's shoulder. . . . Before I left my bed in the morning, little Adèle came running in to tell me that the great horsechestnut at the bottom of the orchard had been struck by lightning . . . and half of it split away.

There was the Lord speaking out of Sinai,—the Lord who had been defied. The nearest approach to it in music that I can think of is the awakening of the trombones in the last act of 'Don Giovanni.'

The third appearance of the foul nightly visitant immediately precedes the wedding ceremony.

"But, Sir, as it grew dark, the wind rose: it blew yesterday evening not as it blows now — wild and high — but with a sullen moaning sound, far more eerie. I wished you were at home. I came into this room, and the sight of the empty chair and fireless hearth chilled me. For some reason, after I went to bed, I could not sleep — a sense of anxious excitement distressed me. The gale still rising seemed to my ear to muffle a mournful undersound: whether in the house or abroad I could not at first tell, but it recurred, doubtful yet doleful, at every lull: at last I made out it must be some dog howling at a distance. . . . On sleeping I continued in dreams the idea of a dark and stormy night. I continued also the wish to be with you, and experienced a strange, regretful consciousness of some barrier dividing us. During all my first sleep I was following the windings of an unknown road; total obscurity

environed me; rain pelted me; I was burdened with the
charge of a little child; a very small creature too young and
feeble to walk, and which shivered in my cold arms, and
wailed piteously in my ear. I thought, Sir, that you were
on the road a long way before me; and I strained every
nerve to overtake you, and made effort on effort to utter your
name and entreat you to stop — but my movements were
fettered; and my voice still died away inarticulate; while
you, I felt, withdrew farther and farther every moment. . . .
I dreamt another dream, Sir; that Thornfield-Hall was a
dreary ruin, the retreat of bats and owls. I thought that
of all the stately front nothing remained but a shell-like wall,
very high and very fragile-looking. I wandered on a moonlight night through the grass-grown enclosure within: here
I stumbled over a marble hearth, and there over a fallen
fragment of cornice. Wrapped up in a shawl, I still
carried the unknown little child; I might not lay it down
anywhere, however tired were my arms. . . . I heard the
gallop of a horse at a distance . . . I was sure it was you;
and you were departing for many years, and for a distant
country. I climbed the thin wall with frantic, perilous haste,
eager to catch one glimpse of you from the top: the stones
rolled from under my feet, the ivy branches I grasped gave
way, the child clung round my neck in terror, and almost
strangled me: at last I gained the summit. I saw you like
a speck on a white track, lessening every moment. The
blast blew so strong I could not stand. I sat down on the
narrow edge; I hushed the scared infant in my lap: you
turned an angle of the road; I bent forward to take a last
look; the wall crumbled; I was shaken; the child rolled
from my knee; I lost my balance, fell, and woke."

"Now, Jane, that is all."

"All the preface, Sir; the tale is yet to come. On
waking, a gleam dazzled my eyes: I thought — oh, it is
daylight! But I was mistaken: it was only candlelight.
Sophie, I supposed, had come in. There was a light on

the dressing table, and the door of the closet where, before going to bed, I had hung my wedding dress and veil, stood open: I heard a rustling there. I asked, 'Sophie, what are you doing?' No one answered, but a form emerged from the closet: it took the light, held it aloft and surveyed the garments pendent from the portmanteau. 'Sophie! Sophie!' I again cried; and still it was silent. I had risen up in bed, I bent forward: first surprise, then bewilderment came over me; and then my blood crept cold through my veins. Mr. Rochester, this was not Sophie, it was not Leah, it was not Mrs. Fairfax: it was not — no, I was sure of it, and am still — it was not even that strange woman, Grace Poole."

While awaiting Rochester's return, and feverish to tell him this story —

I sought the orchard, driven to its shelter by the wind, which all day had blown strong and full from the south; without, however, bringing a speck of rain. Instead of subsiding as night drew on, it seemed to augment its rush and deepen its roar: the trees blew steadfastly one way, never writhing round, and scarcely tossing back their boughs once in an hour; so continuous was the strain bending their branchy heads northward — the clouds drifted from pole to pole, fast following, mass on mass: no glimpse of blue sky had been visible that July day.

It was not without a certain wild pleasure I ran before the wind delivering my trouble of mind to the measureless air-torrent thundering through space. Descending the laurel-walk, I faced the wreck of the chestnut tree; it stood up black and riven: the trunk, split down the centre, gasped ghastly. The cloven halves were not broken from each other, for the firm base and strong roots kept them unsundered below; though community of vitality was destroyed — the sap could flow no more: their great boughs on each side were dead, and next winter's tempests would be sure to fell one or both to earth: as yet, however, they might be said to form one tree — a ruin, but an entire ruin.

"You did right to hold fast to each other," I said: as if the monster splinters were living things, and could hear me. "I think, scathed as you look, and charred and scorched, there must be a little sense of life in you yet; rising out of that adhesion at the faithful honest roots: you will never have green leaves more — never more see birds making nests and singing idyls in your boughs; the time of pleasure and love is over with you; but you are not desolate: each of you has a comrade to sympathize with him in his decay." As I looked up at them, the moon appeared momentarily in that part of the sky which filled their fissure; her disk was blood-red and half overcast; she seemed to throw on me one bewildered, dreary glance, and buried herself again instantly in the deep drift of cloud. The wind fell for a second, round Thornfield; but far away over wood and water, poured a wild melancholy wail.

"The sap could flow no more!" But love, deeper than death, stronger than strength, righter than right, not even God's lightning can destroy.

Rochester stills her fears by explaining that it was Grace Poole she saw, and bids her think of the morrow. "Look here" (he lifted up the curtain) — "it is a lovely night."

It was. Half heaven was pure and stainless: the clouds, now trooping before the wind, which had shifted to the west, were filing off eastward in long, silvered columns. The moon shone peacefully.

That mirage passes, and the secret is at last divulged.

A Christmas frost had come at midsummer; a white December storm had whirled over June; ice glazed the ripe apples, drifts crushed the blowing roses; on hay-field and corn-field lay a frozen shroud; lanes which last night blushed full of flowers to-day were pathless with untrodden snow; and the woods, which twelve hours since waved leafy and fragrant as groves between the tropics, now spread waste, wild, and white as pine forests in wintry Norway. My hopes were all dead-struck with a subtle doom, such as in one night fell on all the firstborn in the land of Egypt. I looked on my cherished wishes, yesterday so blooming and glowing; they lay stark, still, livid corpses that could never revive.

Thus is the ardent expectancy of bridehood turned for Jane Eyre into the bitter-cold desolation of disappointment; and how subtle the elemental feeling by which wintry nature is transmuted, through withering descending scales, into the conditions of her life! It is not a mere likeness between the blight of winter and the death of hope: what chills her to the marrow is that her faith and confidence in her lover are destroyed,—that "the attitude of stainless truth was gone from his idea," the rich full flower of his manhood had perished fruitless. "Signs," she says, "for aught we know, may be but the sympathies of Nature with man."

II

The true nature-lover is the true nature-sympathizer. There is complete reciprocity between what Nature gives to him and what he to her. There is not necessarily a complete comprehension, but there is that highest form of faith, — a complete acceptance even of the incomprehensible. Such faith partakes too largely of reverence to allow fear to enter its despoiling wedge; for this attitude towards nature understands spiritually what it cannot comprehend by reason, and the product is awe. The "most natural" natures have it; and wherever there is any spiritual possession of a man, there may it be found, though the mind be also possessed of shifting quirks. Charlotte Brontë had no love for the Jesuits, but she is candid enough to include the "good father" who had her in spiritual tow with herself in her freedom from fright at the awful storm which overtook them in the house of Mme. Walravens. He had some grandeur in him; he had a simple faith in an elementary God back of his theological complexities, and that simplicity saved him from vulgar fear. In that presence, the socially timid Miss Brontë had none, either. For Lucy says: "I, too, was awe-struck. Being, however, under no pressure of slavish terror, my thoughts and observations were free." Of course. That is a part of her spiritual glory, and which she shares with others of lesser fame, but of similar attitudes.

Only, she goes farther into nature than others: she goes farther into it, without consciously pursuing it. She is not striving for effect by a ceremoniously evident attachment; and she would, without doubt, if living now, disclaim alliance with the class of present writers which takes objective delight in the delineating of scenery. I have said that atmosphere possessed her, and I have tried to demonstrate how it entered into her work. It was of the fibres of her brain, which, of necessity, wrapped the brain's concept with its texture. Her use of nature is more than natural; it is inevitable.

In dealing with Charlotte Brontë, we are dealing with spirit as opposed to flesh. She does not divorce the two in the old scholastic way; there is no theological enmity between them; she suffered, on the contrary, from their close alliance. But she was touched, almost exclusively, on the spiritual side. Pure imagination ruled her. More than any other author, I believe, she exemplifies the idea of the metaphysicians in their term " productive imagination," — " that faculty by which the parts of the intuitions of space and time are combined into continua." It is untutored, untamed, pure. The three sketches which Jane Eyre produces from her portfolio at Rochester's request are, I submit, the three finest examples in any one book of this spiritual power.

The first represented clouds low and livid, rolling over a swollen sea: all the distance was in eclipse; so, too, was the foreground; or rather, the nearest billows, for there was no land. One gleam of light lifted into relief a half-submerged mast, on which sat a cormorant, dark and large, with wings flecked with foam; its beak held a gold bracelet, set with gems, that I had touched with as brilliant tints as my palette could yield, and as glittering distinctness as my pencil could impart. Sinking below the bird and mast, a drowned corpse glanced through the green water; a fair arm was the only limb clearly visible, whence the bracelet had been washed and torn.

The second picture contained for foreground only the dim peak of a hill, with grass and some leaves slanting as if by a breeze. Beyond and above spread an expanse of sky, dark blue as at twilight: rising into the sky was a woman's shape to the bust, portrayed in tints as dusk and soft as I could combine. The dim forehead was crowned with a star: the lineaments below were seen as through the suffusion of vapour; the eyes shone dark and wild; the hair streamed shadowy, like a beamless cloud torn by storm or by electric travail. On the neck lay a pale reflection like moonlight; the same faint lustre touched the train of thin clouds from which rose and bowed the vision of the Evening Star.

The third showed the pinnacle of an iceberg piercing a polar winter sky: a muster of northern lights reared their dim lances, close serried, along the horizon. Throwing these into distance, rose, in the foreground, a head, — a colossal head, inclined towards the iceberg, and resting against it. Two thin hands, joined under the forehead, and supporting it, drew up before the lower features a sable veil; a brow quite bloodless, white as bone, and an eye hollow and fixed, blank of meaning but for the glassiness of despair, alone were visible. Above the temples, amidst wreathed turban folds of black drapery, vague in its character and consistency as cloud, gleamed a ring of white flame, gemmed with sparkles of a more lurid tinge. This pale crescent was "the likeness of a Kingly Crown;" what it diademed was "the shape which shape had none."

On that magnificent night of the fête, when Mme. Beck endeavored, through the operation of a sedative, to hold her English teacher in subjection, the drug merely excited her.

Instead of stupor came excitement. I became alive to new thought — to reverie peculiar in coloring. A gathering call ran among the faculties, their bugles sang, their trumpets rang an untimely summons. Imagination was roused from her rest, and she came forth impetuous and venturous. With scorn she looked on Matter, her mate. "Rise!" she said. "Sluggard! this night I will have my will; nor shalt thou prevail."

"Look forth and view the night!" was her cry, and when I lifted the heavy blind from the casement close at hand — with her own royal gesture, she showed me a moon supreme, in an element deep and splendid.

To my gasping senses she made the glimmering gloom, the narrow limits, the oppressive heat of the dormitory, intolerable. She lured me to leave this den and follow her forth into dew, coolness, and glory.

She recalls having seen a gap in the paling of the park fence. She determines that she will try thus to steal into this deserted park, where she will be absolutely alone at such an hour. "The whole park would be mine, the moonlight, midnight park!" She does not find it deserted, as we know; but after all the fever and the glamour of the fête had passed, as Lucy seeks again the "dim lower quarter," she finds the moon of her search.

Dim I should not say, for the beauty of moonlight, forgotten in the park, here once more flowed in upon perception. High she rode, and calm and stainlessly she shone. The music and the mirth of the fête, the fire and bright hues of those lamps had outdone and outshone her for an hour, but now, again, her glory and her silence triumphed. The rival lamps were dying: she held her course like a white fate. Drum, trumpet, bugle, had uttered their clangor and were forgotten: with pencil-ray she wrote on heaven and earth records for archives everlasting. She and those stars seemed to me at once the types and witnesses of truth all regnant. The night-sky lit her reign: like its slow-wheeling progress, advanced her victory, — that onward movement which has been, and is, and will be from eternity to eternity.

Paul Emmanuel, lingering in the garden, looks "at the moon, at the gray cathedral over the remoter spires and house roofs fading into a blue sea of night-mist. He tasted the sweet breath of dusk, and noted the folded bloom of the garden." Who else has so delicately expressed that exquisite sense of perfumed eventide, — that unnamable sacred-human presence of the haunting vesper spirit?

Her finest similes are based on nature. Saint Pierre's power over her unruly pupils held "them in check as a breezeless frost-air might still a brawling stream." The fair visitors at Thornfield-Hall descend the staircase "almost as noiselessly as a bright mist rolls down a hill." These fine ladies "all had a sweeping amplitude of array that seemed to magnify their persons as a mist magnifies the moon." It is not every day that one may read in one book two such similes based on the effects of mist. When the Orders in Council were repealed, "Liverpool started and snorted like a river-horse roused amongst his reeds by thunder."

So, too, the adjectives which come at her nod have the fine fitness which nature demands, — the fitness which makes one cry out, "None other would have done at all!" The rain falls "heavy, *prone*, and broad." The beck sends a "*raving*" sound through the air. She has twice put into living words the swelling emotions all travellers open to its influence must feel who stand below the great dome of St. Paul's in the solemn night time:

It, too, is dear to my soul; for there, as I lay in quiet and darkness, I first heard the great bell of St. Paul's telling London it was midnight; and well do I recall the deep deliberate tones, so full charged with colossal phlegm and force.

I had just extinguished my candle and lain down, when a deep, low, mighty tone swung through the night. At first I knew it not; but it was uttered twelve times, and at the twelfth colossal hum and trembling knell, I said, "I lie in the shadow of St. Paul's." . . . Above my head, above the house-tops, co-elevate almost with the clouds, I saw a solemn orbed mass, dark-blue and dim — THE DOME. While I looked my inner self moved; my spirit shook its always fettered wings half loose; I had a sudden feeling as if I, who had never yet truly lived, were at last about to taste life; in that morning my soul grew as fast as Jonah's gourd.

This grave bass glides into softest treble when she writes, with equal insight, of "sweet, soft, *exalted*" sounds. Oh, carillons of Bruges!

III

In discussing Charlotte, one must speak of Emily also, — that untamed virgin of the moors, to whom they were as the call of the sea to the mariner, and as strong drink to the drunkard. Younger in years and in grace, she was yet the elder sister in her attitude towards nature, as paganism is older than Christianity. With her, nature was the thing worshipped, not the *milieu* through which worship was done. It is expressed in Catherine's dream:

"If I were in heaven, Nelly, I should be extremely miserable."

"Because you are not fit to go there," I answered. "All sinners would be miserable in heaven."

"But it is not for that. I dreamt once that I was there; . . . heaven did not seem to be my home; and I broke my heart with weeping to come back to earth; and the angels were so angry that they flung me out into the middle of the heath on the top of Wuthering Heights, where I woke sobbing for joy."

Her Attitude towards Nature

I shall have to show, in the next section, how she was like Charlotte, and yet greater than Charlotte, in her conception of love; but let me here point out, in passing, her place, along with her less terrible sister, among the great nature portrayers.

Emily Brontë has been called the Sphinx of literature. We have only 'Wuthering Heights' to tell us, in a mystery, what she was, — that and a handful of poems, Charlotte's loving testimony, and this from 'Shirley':

A still, deep, inborn delight glows in her young veins; unmingled, untroubled, not to be reached or ravished by human agency, because by no human agency bestowed: the pure gift of God to his creature, the free dower of Nature to her child. This joy gives her experience of a genii-life. Buoyant, by green steps, by glad hills, all verdure and light, she reaches a station scarcely lower than that whence angels looked down on the dreamer of Beth-el, and her eye seeks, and her soul possesses, the vision of life as she wishes it. No, not as she wishes it: she has not time to wish: the swift glory spreads out, sweeping and kindling, and multiplies its splendors faster than Thought can effect his combinations, faster than Aspiration can utter her longings. . . .

If Shirley were not an indolent, a reckless, an ignorant being, she would take a pen at such moments; or at least while the recollection of such moments was yet fresh on her spirit: she would seize, she would fix the apparition, tell the vision revealed. Had she a little more of the organ of acquisitiveness in her head, a little more of the love of property in her nature, she would take a good-sized sheet of paper and write plainly out, in her own queer but clear and legible hand, the story that has been narrated, the song that has been sung to her, and thus possess what she was enabled to create. But indolent she is, reckless she is, and most ignorant, for she does not know her dreams are rare, her feelings peculiar: she does not know, has never known, and will die without knowing, the full value of that spring whose bright fresh bubbling in her heart keeps it green.

And as Moore soliloquizes of Shirley, so Charlotte of Emily:

... her deep dark eyes: difficult to describe what I read there! Pantheress! — beautiful forest-born! — wily, tameless, peerless nature! She gnaws her chain: I see the white teeth working at the steel! She has dreams of her wild woods, and pinings after virgin freedom... Some hours ago she passed me, coming down the oak-staircase to the hall: she did not know I was standing in the twilight, near the staircase window, looking at the frost-bright constellations. How closely she glided against the banisters! How shyly shone her large eyes upon me! How evanescent, fugitive, fitful, she looked, — slim and swift as a Northern Streamer!... In her white evening dress; with her long hair flowing full and wavy; with her noiseless step, her pale cheek, her eye full of night and lightning, she looked, I thought, spirit-like, — a thing made of an element, — the child of a breeze and a flame, — the daughter of ray and raindrop, — a thing never to be overtaken, arrested, fixed.

The vigor of her feeling may be pretty accurately described in the younger Catherine's breezy idea of "heaven's happiness," as opposed to Linton's:

He said the pleasantest manner of spending a hot July day was lying from morning till evening on a bank of heath in the middle of the moors, with the bees humming dreamily about among the bloom, and the larks singing high up overhead, and the blue sky and bright sun shining steadily and cloudlessly. That was his most perfect idea of heaven's happiness: mine was rocking in a rustling green tree, with a west wind blowing, and bright white clouds flitting rapidly above; and not only larks, but throstles, and blackbirds, and linnets, and cuckoos pouring out music on every side, and the moors seen at a distance, broken into cool dusky dells; but close by great swells of long grass undulating in waves to the breeze; and woods and sounding water, and the whole world awake and wild with joy. He wanted all to lie in an ecstacy of peace; I wanted all to sparkle and dance in a glorious jubilee. I said his heaven would be only half alive; and he said mine would be drunk; I said I should fall asleep in his; and he said he could not breathe in mine. . . .

We have seen how picturesquely Charlotte impresses the word "beamless" into use. So Emily: "all that remained of day was a *beamless* amber light along the west." The gaunt thorns around Wuthering Heights "stretch their limbs one way, as if craving alms of the sun." There is a picture which dwells in the memory for all time. And she shares with Charlotte her power to select the one word, of all the words she might have selected, which hits consciousness as a blow hits the face, nailing the thought into the attention by an almost physical force. In the description of Vashti, Charlotte contrasts the heavy, sensual 'Cleopatra' she has previously been criticising with the vivid living force of the wonderful actress: "Place now the Cleopatra or any other *slug* before her as an obstacle, and see her cut through the pulpy mass, as the scimitar of Saladin clave the down cushion." Thus, Emily speaks of the "*smiting* beauty" of a face. Her eye had pierced the dark veil which hangs before the penetralia of that nether world which the Furies call their home, and in one burning sentence she gives us a whirling glance thereat: "the clouded windows of hell flashed a moment towards me."

Like Emily, Charlotte is never afraid of Nature, and does not realize her terrors.

Strong and horizontal thundered the current of the wind from northwest to southeast; it brought rain like spray, and sometimes a sharp hail like shot. . . . I bent my head to meet it, but it beat me back. My heart did not fail me at all in this conflict. I only wished that I had wings, and could ascend the gale, spread and repose my pinions on its strength, career in its course, sweep where it swept.

One night a thunder storm broke; a sort of hurricane shook us in our beds: the Catholics rose in panic and prayed to their saints. As for me, the tempest took hold of me with tyranny: I was roughly roused and obliged to live. I got up and dressed myself, and creeping outside the casement close to my bed, sat on its ledge, with my feet on the roof of a lower adjoining building. It was wet, it was wild, it was pitch-dark. Within the dormitory, they gathered round the night-lamp in consternation, praying loud. I could not go in: too resistless was the delight of staying with the wild hour, black and full of thunder, pealing out such an ode as language never delivered to man — too terribly glorious the spectacle of clouds, split and pierced by white blinding bolts.

Who can ever forget Shirley's sublime apostrophe which was doubtless a reflection of Emily's unspoken thought?

"Nature is now at her evening prayers: she is kneeling before those red hills. I see her prostrate on the great steps of her altar, praying for a fair night for mariners at sea, for travellers in deserts, for lambs on moors, and unfledged birds in woods. Caroline, I see her! and I will tell you what she is like: she is like what Eve was when she and Adam stood alone on earth."

"And that is not Milton's Eve, Shirley."

"Milton's Eve! Milton's Eve! I repeat. No, by the pure Mother of God, she is not! . . . He saw heaven: he looked down on hell. He saw Satan, and Sin his daughter, and Death their horrible offspring. Angels serried before him their battalions: the long lines of adamantine shields flashed back on his blind eye-balls the unutterable splendor of heaven. Devils gathered their legions in his sight: their dim, discrowned, and tarnished armies passed rank and file before him. Milton tried to see the first woman; but, Cary, he saw her not."

"You are bold to say so, Shirley."

"Not more bold than faithful. It was his cook that he saw; or it was Mrs. Gill, as I have seen her, making custards in the heat of summer, in the cool dairy, with rose trees and nasturtiums about the latticed window, preparing a cold collation for the Rectors. . . . I would beg to remind him that the first men of the earth were Titans, and that Eve was their mother: from her sprang Saturn, Hyperion, Oceanus; she bore Prometheus — "

"Pagan that you are! what does that signify?"

"I say there were giants on the earth in those days: giants that strove to scale heaven. The first woman's breast that heaved with life on this world yielded the daring which could contend with Omnipotence: the strength which could bear a thousand years of bondage, — the vitality which could feed that vulture death through uncounted ages, — the unexhausted life and uncorrupted excellence, sisters to immortality, which, after millenniums of crimes, struggles, and woes, could conceive and bring forth a Messiah. The first woman was heaven-born: vast was the heart whence gushed the well-spring of the blood of nations; and grand the undegenerate head where rested the consort-crown of creation.

"I saw — I now see — a woman-Titan: her robe of blue air spreads to the outskirts of the heath, where yonder flock is grazing; a veil white as an avalanche sweeps from her head to her feet, and arabesques of lightning flame on its borders. Under her breast I see her zone, purple like that horizon: through its blush shines the star of evening. Her steady eyes I cannot picture; they are clear — they are deep as lakes — they are lifted and full of worship — they tremble with the softness of love and the lustre of prayer. Her forehead has the expanse of a cloud, and is paler than the early moon, risen long before dark gathers: she reclines her bosom on the ridge of Stilbro' Moor; her mighty hands are joined beneath it. So kneeling, face to face, she speaks with God. That Eve is Jehovah's daughter, as Adam was his son."

"She is very vague and visionary! Come, Shirley, we ought to go into church."

"Caroline, I will not: I will stay out here with my mother, Eve, in these days called Nature. I love her — undying, mighty being! Heaven may have faded from her brow when she fell in paradise; but all that is glorious on earth shines there still. She is taking me to her bosom, and showing me her heart. Hush, Caroline! you will see her and feel as I do, if we are both silent."

"It is well that the true poet," says Miss Brontë, "can measure the whole stature of those who look down on him, and correctly ascertain the weight and value of the pursuits they disdain him for not having followed. It is happy that he can have his own bliss, his own society with his great friend and goddess, Nature, quite independent of those who find little pleasure in him, and in whom he finds no pleasure at all."

Nature is her "great friend" also, but more of a divine priestess than a "goddess," as she was with Emily. Unlike Emily, she looks through nature, up to nature's God; and if in the rush of her emotion, she at times confuses the glory and its reflection, it is as if one might, in rapt moments, fail to distinguish the image from the imaged. Nature was to her, not so much a sacred book to be unsealed only with mystic rites, as it was a solemn running commentary upon a passionately conceived, dimly understood, and bravely borne existence. *Life* was the mystery, Nature the priest, she the pale but ready victim. Hence the eloquence of her descriptions. The priest-like Nature stands between her and life, and pleads for her to Life. Nature is not the mystery — that lies beyond; but Nature expounds and exemplifies. That is why we do not think of rhetoric when we think of all this passionate writing. It is rhetoric; but, as when in the glow of a noble liturgy, we are not conscious of it.

There is, in the place of world-knowledge, what is so much better, earth-knowledge. Happy the union! For old Nature soothes the dumb ague of despair into something resembling calm.

Yonder sky was sealed: the solemn stars shone alien and remote; . . . she felt as if Something far round drew nigher. She heard as if Silence spoke. There was no language, no word, only a tone. Again, a fine, full, lofty tone, a deep soft sound, like a storm whispering, made twilight undulate.

That Presence, invisible but mighty, gathered her in like a lamb to the fold; that voice, soft but all-pervading, vibrated through her heart like music. Her eye received no image; and yet a sense visited her vision and her brain as of the serenity of stainless air, the power of sovereign seas, the majesty of marching stars, the energy of colliding elements, the rooted endurance of hills wide-based, and above all, as of the lustre of heroic beauty rushing victorious on the night, vanquishing its shadows like a diviner sun.

Twilight was falling, and I deemed its influence pitiful; from the lattice I saw coming night clouds trailing low like banners drooping.

and that matchless passage,

The moon reigns glorious, glad of the gale, — as glad as if she gave herself to his fierce caress with love,

which causes Mr. Swinburne to exclaim, "The words have in them the very breath and magic, and riotous radiance, the utter rapture and passion and splendor of the high sonorous night." "It is," he declares, "the first and last absolute and sufficient and triumphant word ever to be said on the subject." Surely, surely, if ever the stigmata of inspiration were stamped with ineffaceable imprint on any work, in hers may the miraculous marks be found.

IV

There is no painter of scenery, no painter of atmosphere, like her.

Dawn was just beginning to steal on night, to penetrate with a pale ray its brown obscurity, and give a demi-translucence to its opaque shadows; . . . no color tinged the east, no flush warmed it. To see what a heavy lid day slowly lifted, what a wan glance she flung along the hills, you would have thought the sun's fire quenched in last night's floods; . . . a raw wind stirred the mass of night-cloud, and showed, as it slowly rose — leaving a colorless, silver-gleaming ring all round the horizon — not blue sky, but a stratum of paler vapor beyond.

But it is remarkable that this descriptive power is yoked with her studies of character; her finest passages inevitably lead up to some effect upon the mind. The scenery is a parable, a miracle; a human life is the thing signified, the thing wrought upon. As William Crimsworth walks home from Frances Henri's abode, his affections stirred, and his ambitions aroused to meet them, he feels "the West behind him;" and before him rose "the arch of an evening rainbow." Brain, not only eye, absorbed the scene, for that night in a dream it was reproduced.

I stood, methought, upon a terrace; I leaned over a parapeted wall; there was space below me, depth I could not fathom, but hearing an endless dash of waves, I believed it to be the sea; sea spread to the horizon; sea of changeful green and intense blue. All was soft in the distance; all vapor-veiled. A spark of gold glistened on the line between water and air, floated up, approached, enlarged, changed; the object hung midway between heaven and earth, under the arch of the rainbow; the soft but dusk clouds diffused behind. It hovered as on wings; pearly, fleecy, gleaming air streamed like raiment round it; light, tinted with carnation, colored what seemed face and limbs; a large star shone with still lustre on an angel's forehead; an upraised arm and hand, glancing like a ray, pointed to the bow overhead, and a voice in my heart whispered, — *Hope smiles on Effort.*

I have referred to the passage where Yorke confesses the meanness of his attitude towards Mary Cave. As he is about to utter the words, —

"The moon is up," was his first not quite relevant remark, pointing with his whip across the moor. "There she is, riding into the haze, staring at us wi' a strange red glower. She is no more silver than old Helstone's brow is ivory. What does she mean by leaning her cheek on Rushedge i' that way, and looking at us wi' a scowl and a menace?"

Why does the moon scowl at Yorke? Why is not her light silvery for him? Because of his guilty conscience. She sets her pure light against his turgid wilfulness, and its purity is tinged with the defiling color of his sin. Had he been spotless, she would have had no menace in her glow. He is arrested like Saul of Tarsus. She stands a divine advocate for the innocence he has lost.

We thus see that nature does not exist for her by and for itself, but as mysteriously wrapped about human destiny, and as in sympathy with human character. Human character she undoubtedly considered her first and foremost study, and all her glowing scenic descriptions bear a close approximation to such a study. She was, indeed, a keen analyzer of character; and although at times, through her ignorance of the world, too prim and too severe, the mistakes she makes are on the safe side of overconscientiousness. Take her study of this same Yorke. Let us put his contradictions into parallels:

Sometimes spoke broad Yorkshire.	Sometimes pure English.
Blunt and rough.	Polite and affable.
Without ideality.	Yet a fine ear for music.

Indocile, scornful, sarcastic.	Unusual taste, a connoisseur of art, a travelled man, a scholar, and a gentleman.
Grossly intolerant against lords and parsons.	Excellent general doctrines of mutual toleration.
His religious belief without awe, imagination, tenderness.	Not irreligious.
Family pride.	Professor of "equality."
Haughty as Beelzebub to those above him.	Very kind to all beneath him.
Impatient of imbecility.	Honorable, capable, and respected.

THE KEY.

He was a *Yorkshire* gentleman. He had no veneration, "a great want, . . . which throws a man wrong on every point where veneration is required." He was without the organ of comparison, "a deficiency which strips a man of sympathy." "He had little of the organs of benevolence and ideality, which took the glory and softness from his nature." Every contradiction in this highly original character (are not all original characters contradictory?) is thus explained, and the picture is as clear-cut as the Vienna onyx.

As for me, whenever a purple sunset streaks the West, whenever the moon rises "in an element deep and splendid," whenever the soul swells with killing pains on silent moon-filled nights, I think of Charlotte Brontë. I think of the pang of all the world, the unutterable cries, the low moans, the stifled sobs, which well up into the pitying skies, and shine there on the stricken earth. Whenever I lie awake in the night watches listening to the wind ["Peace, peace, Banshee, keening at every window!"], I think of a pure uplifted face at a parsonage lattice in a Yorkshire wilderness: God and the awful stars above, the graves of buried loves beneath, and all about the ineffable haunting witchery of the loud-whispering moors.

C. — HER PASSION

I

It is a significant commentary upon numan nature that the word *passion* should have come to have a meaning directly opposite to its original import, because the secondary definitions indicate the lapses of that nature from the ideal equipoise of character. The word means, in its simplicity, passivity, as opposed to activity, — hence, susceptibility, receptivity; which implies, when the active force at work is painful, *suffering*. As the greatest suffering known in history, resulting from the most acute susceptibility, made the most intense by the completest passivity, the agony of Christ preceding His death upon the cross is, with an immediately recognized perfect appropriateness, termed for all time THE PASSION. The secondary meanings attached to the word as now generally used relate, as do most secondary meanings, to a state of mind proceeding from such susceptibility as the original meaning sets forth, viz., vehement emotion, evidenced by violent displays of feeling. That is to say, from a perfect passivity, as in the ideal historical case, the word flies to the opposite meaning of extreme activity, because the imperfections of human nature are so rarely under the control of the rational faculties when their springs are disturbed.

All true passion, then, is simple suffering, due to extreme susceptibility, and is opposed by a whole circumference to the idea of action. As such passion approximates to the ideal passion, it is perforce noble; differing from that in the degree of its nobility by the difference between the nobly human, and yet because human, imperfect, and the inevitably divine.

I claim for Charlotte Brontë a place in this pantheon. She suffered and was still, except for her books not meant to be discovered as hers, and through which we feel her shaken soul. It was not *a* pleading *for* passion, as the critics vainly imagined, but *the* pleading *of* passion. "My God, my God, why hast Thou forsaken me?" Let those who impugn Charlotte Brontë for crying out in her pain solve that mystery of the Cross.

II

The attempt to prove from internal and external evidence that the sadness of 'Villette' is traceable to an unhappy love experience is, in my judgment, futile and inexcusable. The actual external is twisted, in order to fit it to the supposed internal, evidence; which is a fatal course in the hunt for truth.

"I returned to Brussels after aunt's death, against my conscience, prompted by what then seemed an irresistible impulse. I was punished for my selfish folly by a total withdrawal, for more than two years, of happiness and peace of mind."[1] This is the famous passage which has set the guessers at work, from

[1] 'Charlotte Brontë. A monograph.' By T. Wemyss Reid. New York: Scribner, Armstrong & Co., 1877, p. 59.

Sir Wemyss Reid to Mr. MacKay;[1] the latter gentleman using it for the base of a very elaborate structure. It is a pity that the fine dialectical skill which cut to pieces Dr. Wright's nice little romance[2] did not rest its well-earned repute at the end of that enjoyable performance; for the author himself is obliged to confess that the point is not absolutely proved, but only strongly suggested.[3]

Mr. MacKay bases his argument on what he well calls Charlotte's "element," — the depiction of the *agony* of love. "Nowhere else are to be found such piercing cries of lonely anguish as may be heard in 'Shirley' and 'Villette.' They are the very *de profundis* of love sunk in the abyss of despair."[4] He quotes her statement that she will never affect what she has not experienced. Putting the two together, the conclusion is that "the characteristic experiences recorded in her books were not gained at Haworth: there is no room for any love tragedy there."[5] In Brussels, therefore, must we search for the solution. Now, Charlotte could love only an intellectual man. M. Héger was such a man. He it was, then, whom Charlotte loved.

Mr. Nicholls and Miss Nussey, the two best and the only two living authorities, maintain that the

---

[1] 'The Brontës. Fact and Fiction.' By Angus MacKay. New York: Dodd, Mead & Co. London: Service & Paton. 1897.

[2] 'The Brontës in Ireland, or Facts Stranger than Fiction.' By Dr. William Wright. New York: D. Appleton & Co., 1893. This is the remarkable book which startled Bronteans with the astounding statement that 'Wuthering Heights' had its foundation in the family history in Ireland, and that Charlotte derived her inspiration from the same source. It was received with much applause and open-eyed wonder, but with the caveats of the thoughtful. For its complete confutation, see Mr. MacKay's book, above mentioned.

[3] MacKay, p. 73. [4] *Ib.*, p. 41. [5] *Ib.*, p. 45.

particular reason for Charlotte's anxiety at this time was a dread of leaving her father to the unchecked temptations of a "too festive curate."[1] After her first return from Brussels, she writes that she has felt for some months that she ought not to be away from him;[2] and later: "Whenever I consult my conscience, it affirms that I am doing right in staying at home, and bitter are its upbraidings when I yield to an eager desire for release."[3] But this filial feeling is not enough for Mr. MacKay, on the ground that she returns to Haworth after a stay in Brussels of only *one* year, when the father was speedily rescued; whereas it was for *two* years that she suffered this unhappiness. The visit to the confessional is mentioned; the extravagant thanks to Mary Taylor for her advice to leave Brussels,[4] and the grief at parting with Héger[5] are urged as illuminating indications of the truth of the hypothesis. The cessation of the correspondence with Héger, through the intervention of his wife, is made much of.

Turning to the novel, "we are surprised to find how absolutely Charlotte accepts M. Héger as her *beau idéal*."[6] All of her heroes have a dash of the pedagogue. Helstone, Louis Moore, Crimsworth are "merely paler copies of the same original." Charlotte's vision was haunted by this figure. Note, too,

---

[1] Shorter, p. 109. [Since this was written, Miss Nussey has died.]
[2] "You will ask me why. It is on papa's account; he is now, as you know, getting old, and it grieves me to tell you that he is losing his sight. . . . I felt now that it would be selfish to leave him (at least as long as Bramwell and Anne are absent) in order to pursue selfish interests of my own. With the help of God I will try to deny myself in this matter and to wait." Gaskell, p. 278.
[3] Gaskell, pp. 325, 326.   [4] MacKay, p. 59.
[5] Gaskell, p. 278.   [6] MacKay, p. 63.

"the frequency of love scenes between master and pupil in these works." Even the theme of 'Jane Eyre' is similar in its picture of a woman's love for a man who belongs to another woman. She could not make 'Villette' end happily as she did the other books, because, while "the lovers in her other books were composite characters," having "no absolute originals in real life," Paul Emmanuel was too real to her to permit her imagination to wed him to Lucy Snowe,—in other words, herself. Mr. MacKay even lays her poems under an embargo to help the point. Where did she get that intimate knowledge of love? What was the "irresistible impulse"?

One ought not to be compelled to say that it is not because Charlotte Brontë will sink in our esteem if we accept this as a solution, that we shrink from accepting it.[1] On the contrary, as Mr. MacKay well points out, she will rise, if such a process is possible with one who already occupies the highest place there. It is not a question of shrinking. The simple fact is, the point is not proved. That she suffered this "total withdrawal of happiness" for two years, whereas, by returning to Haworth at the close of the first year, the happiness should, under ordinary circumstances, have been restored, is, with all due respect, pettifogging. If her conscience was touched by leaving her father at such a time, knowing what a conscience it was, we may rest assured that the mere

---

[1] In her defence of Miss Brontë, Mrs. Terhune goes quite too far in speaking of this as a "malodorous scandal" ['Charlotte Brontë At Home.' By Marion Harland. G. P. Putnam's Sons, New York and London, 1899, p. 164], which it never was, even in the eyes of those who support the view here contested; and she is altogether unjustified in her suggestion that M. Héger's part was that of "a gallant *intriguant*."

fact of his reform upon her return would not quiet it. Every time she might think of it, it would prick her, no matter whether for one year or for ten. And this severe conscience would undoubtedly relieve itself in extravagant language to one who, like Mary Taylor, pointed out to her her plain duty.

Of course she grieved at parting with Héger, her one kind and sympathetic friend at the pensionnat, for whom, undoubtedly, she had a warm affection. And of course Mme. Héger objected to her correspondence with him. For was it likely that the original of Mme. Beck would regard a correspondence with the original of Lucy Snowe with favor? As for the similarity of her heroes, that is because of her realism. She only affected what she had experienced. Her intellectual experience lay in Brussels, and was affected more by M. Héger than by any other man. It was a narrow experience: what more natural than that he should form a type for her, when she had so few originals to choose from? Much of her experience in her formative period was spent in governessing; and the slavery of the life, and its hopelessly loveless social degradation, were burned into her consciousness. She could more easily fashion her imagination upon the unrequited loves of women in her position than upon any other theme. Without doubt, the peculiar unfitness of the Brontës for such a life made it more intolerable to them than to most girls forced by untoward circumstance to leave their homes. Often, indeed, the homes they go into are more comfortable than those they leave. But the social inequalities were made very prominent to Charlotte, and she is fairly entitled to ask the question: How can a great man like Rochester care for a poor unknown nobody like me, Jane Eyre? How can I, Louis Moore, a pauper and a dependant, honorably make love to a rich lady like Miss Keeldar? Does it follow, because she asked herself these questions, out of the depth of her experience in similar positions, that they are merely pale reflections of an actual passion she once entertained for a married man in Brussels? The fact that he was married is a sufficient indication to me that she did not love him in this way, so long as there are no direct proofs to the contrary.

And as for the "irresistible impulse," is not too much made of it? Do we not all of us suffer from irresistible impulses at times?—the impulse to leave a dull home for scenes of activity, for example? The impulse for change of scene is, in fact, one of the most irresistible in nature, and one which will override conscience, common sense, and all the other virtues beginning with " C."

It is so easy to find reasons in a writer's life to explain a writer's work; and it is so particularly easy in Miss Brontë's case to read between the lines that we have fallen into the impertinent habit of reading into them. Let me offer a few intrinsic reasons on the contrary side. The acme of one stage of Lucy's sufferings is her visit to the confessional, of which much is made by the supporters of this hypothesis. But that occurred before her love for Paul Emmanuel had awakened. Again, why not attempt to deduce from her treatment of Dr. John that she was in love with *his* well-known original also, George Smith? Why were his letters so precious to Lucy? To be sure, she disclaims, "with the utmost scorn, every sneaking suspicion of what are called warmer feelings," and says that women never entertain them when "to do so would be to commit a mortal absurdity." She admitted there was no hope in that case; yet there was all the more a struggle between the feelings and the reason (so keen was the struggle that she invariably capitalizes the powers, incarnating them like classic fates). It was his nature to be affectionate, she argues. He was to her what the nectarine is to the bee that feeds on it. "Is the sweet-briar enamoured of the air?" This proves to her that he does not love her with a wooer's love; but it does not prove that she does not love him: the most that it proves is that her sturdy reason will not allow her to indulge in any foolish hopes concerning it. She sums it up to Paulina thus:

"I'll tell you what I do, Paulina . . . *I never see him.* I looked at him twice or thrice about a year ago, before he recognized me, and then I shut my eyes; and if he were to cross their balls twelve times between each day's sunset and sunrise, except from memory I should hardly know what shape had gone by. . . . I mean that I value vision, and dread being struck stone blind." It was best to answer her strongly at once, and to silence forever the tender, passionate confidences which left her lips sweet honey, and sometimes dropped in my ear — molten lead.

It is demonstrated that the barrier her reason — that deadly reason! — erected between them would have been broken down had Dr. John manifested a lover's passion. So why not, I repeat, find in that history the history of Lucy Snowe's original? It seems to me quite as valid as the other.

But why, in all seriousness, should we forget that Charlotte Brontë is a novelist? Because, more than any other, she wrote herself and her friends into her fictions, they do not cease to be fictions. Her character is there; not necessarily every detail of her actual life. She was a lonely woman, thrice lonely at the time of this 'Villette;' and Lucy Snowe echoed the cry that went up from her desolate heart. I think every sympathetically observing man of middle age must number among his acquaintances many women who more or less vaguely convey the notion to his masculine understanding that there are locked up in their bosoms many sentimental confidences to which the key would not be hard to find. Charlotte Brontë had scornful words to utter on feminine outpourings such as these:

As far as I knew them, the chance of a gossip about their usually trivial secrets, their often very washy and paltry feelings, was a treat not to be readily forgone.

She was too reserved, too proud, too maidenly, to be guilty of such confidences herself; and her sentiment (which, because it was true and not false, because it was based on an ideal longing for real affection in a loveless environment, became to her a passion consuming) went into what she thought was impersonal fiction; as a composer may throw into music what he would not talk of among his fellow-men. Her life was a vacuum, which passionate nature abhorring, sent its own passion into to fill. It is the passion of passion which breathes in ' Villette; ' not the picture of any particular passion in her experience, but passion's self.

But might she not possibly have been in love with him? Why, certainly: just as she might possibly have entertained a hopeless passion for Louis Napoleon or the Prince Consort. I cheerfully confess my inability to read the secrets of her heart, and I take joy in that inability.

III

Why was she sad? No one who has read the biography need ever ask the question. Mrs. Gaskell has been charged by later writers with drawing too sombre a picture, but Mr. Shorter's book merely intensifies the gloom.[1] " Nothing happens at Haworth,"

---

[1] It is the highest tribute to Mrs. Gaskell's work that so much of it stands after the winnowing of Mr. Shorter. The two books should be read together, Mr. Shorter completing what Mrs. Gaskell began; and the student desirous of the facts of Miss Brontë's life need read none of the other biographies, except Sir Wemyss Reid's; although the Brontë enthusiast will read them all. [He will take particular pleasure, also, in the article 'In The Early Forties,' by Sir George Murray Smith, in the *Critic* for January, 1901. It is like a voice from the tombs to hear the Dr. John of 'Villette' tell his reminiscences at this late date.] Mr. Shorter's individual book and his annotations of Mrs. Gaskell's 'Life' are invaluable additions to the subject: his conscientiously gathered collection of letters, added to those published by Mrs. Gaskell, and in some places correcting them, throws the fullest light on the life of the Brontës. Mrs. Gaskell's mistakes of fact were not so many as were her errors of judgment in writing too frankly of the living; and the book is one of the best proofs extant of the impossibility of a final biography written at a near period to the death of the subject. The solitary advantage of writing at such a period is that valuable impressions vivid then, and facts remembered then, may pass away and be forgotten later. The only remedy would seem to be to write soon after death, and to put away the writing until such time as the future will permit for the rectification of the inevitable errors and the publication of the proved facts.

Mrs. Gaskell's book was resented in Yorkshire as an unfriendly picture from a Lancashire standpoint. Yet her object was merely to show that Charlotte herself held the same views; that certain of her Yorkshire characters were but exemplifications of the Yorkshire saying which Miss Brontë quoted her: "Keep a stone in thy pocket seven

writes Charlotte, "nothing at least of a pleasant kind."[1] The only happiness there ever was in the Haworth vicarage was in the early days. The loneliness of the physical surroundings, the constraint imposed upon a willing affection by an unsympathetic father, the torments of a brother's depravity, then loneliness once more — the utter loneliness of death.

The purpose in going to Brussels was to fit her for the management of a school. When she had by conscientious painstaking so prepared herself, with Héger's diploma in her hands, stating that she was capable of teaching French and was proficient in the best methods of instruction for the conduct of a school, notwithstanding her great desire to carry out this plan, she is nevertheless called away from all these fruits of victory by duties at Haworth. "With the help of God, I will try to deny myself in this matter and to wait." That was, in itself, a sufficient reason for sorrow in the home-going. She was giving up a cherished scheme, and the "irresistible impulse" which drew her to Brussels against her conscience may very well have been the fervent desire to complete her course so that she could at once embark upon her life work, notwithstanding the ever-present consciousness that her father's weakness stood in the way of its consummation.[2]

---

year; turn it, and keep it seven year longer, that it may be ever ready to thine hand when thine enemy draws near" [p. 12]. Mary Taylor says the book is not so gloomy as the truth. [Shorter, p. 22.]

[1] Gaskell, p. 327.

[2] It was not teaching that wore her out. Jane Eyre finds pleasure in the school at Morton. Lucy Snowe declines Mr. Home's offer to treble the salary she receives from Mme. Beck if she will become the companion of his daughter. "I declined. I think I should have declined had I been poorer than I was, and with scantier fund of re-

There were other griefs at the time: Martha Taylor's death, Mary Taylor's going to New Zealand, which was equivalent to death — but who shall explain all the causes for depression in sensitive human nature? Like all susceptible minds, hers had premonitions: her "conscience" was probably stirred by such. After her return, finding Bramwell in his sad plight, she writes: "When I left you I was strongly impressed with the feeling that I was going back to sorrow."[1] It has been sufficiently proved that Bramwell's fall had nothing to do with the tragic tone of his sister's life in Brussels. But it is merely a chronological point, after all: the fall occurred after the return to Haworth, *but before the writing of 'Villette.'* Her letters relating to Bramwell form an abundant evidence of its effect upon her, if any proof were necessary on such a subject. With one whose public writings were so closely a transcript of her private feelings, who can doubt that that fall added its tinge of sorrow to the gloom? That all the gloom, or, indeed, the major part of it, was due to this cause, we cannot think, for with all her melancholy, Charlotte had a sturdy common-sense which could delib-

---

source, more stinted narrowness of future prospect. I had not that vocation. I could teach; I could give lessons; but to be either a private governess or a companion was unnatural to me. Rather than fill the former post in any great house, I would have deliberately taken a housemaid's place, bought a strong pair of gloves, swept bedrooms and staircases, and cleaned stoves and locks in peace and independence. Rather than be a companion, I would have made shirts and starved . . . I was no bright lady's shadow." Compare this with the subtle analysis of her deficiencies in her letter to Mr. Williams of May 12, 1848. [Shorter, pp. 375 *seq.*] It was the dependent life of a *governess* which appalled her, and for which she had the same hatred as Mary Wollstonecraft.

[1] Gaskell, p. 205.

erately put out of sight, though not without fearful wrenchings, all that interfered with her convictions of right and wrong. The more yielding spirit of Anne was the most completely crushed by this spectacle, and in 'The Tenant of Wildfell Hall' we have, so far as I know, the one instance in the literature of fiction of a book written in an intensely abhorrent mood, as a religious duty, — with not only no artistic satisfaction with the theme, but with an anguished shrinking from it. Not even Emily could have succeeded under such genetic restraints, much less Anne with her sweet mediocrity. As for Charlotte, there is a mixture of disgust in her references to Bramwell, which saved her from the paralyzing influences his misconduct wrought upon the youngest of the sisters. What has become a basilisk to natures whose zeal is unchecked by discretion, the Ithuriel spear of stronger spirits transforms into its original shape.[1]

The Reverend Patrick Brontë, A. B.,[2] was not altogether unlike that father of another famous woman

---

[1] See p. 51.

[2] The origin of the name has never been explained. "In the register of his birth his name is entered, as are the births of his brothers and sisters, as Brunty and Bruntee; and it can scarcely be doubted, as Dr. Douglas Hyde has pointed out, the original name was O'Prunty." [Shorter, p. 29.] The name was variously spelled Brunty, Bruntee, Bronty, Branty. [The Brontë Society's Publication, Pt. III.] Mr. Shorter's guess that the spelling 'Brontë' came with the dukedom of that name conferred upon Lord Nelson in 1799, is a clever one; but although Miss Brontë knew of course the identity of the names, she refers to it as a mere accident. If her father, or some one else, had purposely conformed the spelling to Lord Nelson's title, I think she was ignorant of it. She appeared, indeed, to be singularly unconcerned about her ancestors, there being no reference to the subject in her correspondence. Mr. Brontë was doubtless struck by the high-sounding Greek name, suggesting perhaps 'Boanerges' to his ministerial mind, and thenceforth adopted it.

who has recently been made better known to us. We may easily discount as unsubstantiated gossip some of the episodes which Mrs. Gaskell chronicles, without materially modifying our estimate of his character.[1] It is a little too much to ask us to believe, as Mr. Shorter does, that the old man's passions were thoroughly aroused "for once and for the only time in his life"[2] when Mr. Nicholls asked him for his daughter's hand. I have a little sympathy with the grim old tyrant's contempt for the quaking curate, but no reasonable excuse can be offered for the violence of his outbreak. Such violence does not come late in life; it echoes former tempests.

The children suffered from his idiosyncrasies, which are traceable, after the manner of idiosyncrasies, to a general poverty of liberal knowledge on subjects the secrets of which are not far to seek for open-minded conscientiousness. Mr. Brontë's views on education, for example, were really a lack of views; and he strove in moments of active practice to atone for hours of neglect. Just how much of Mrs. Gaskell's "gossip" Mr. Shorter would throw out is not evident; he would probably exclude the testimony of the nurse who tended Mrs. Brontë concerning the father's Spartan (or, considering both the vegetable and the man, should we say Irish?) prohibition of aught but potatoes for the children's dinner. But Miss Nussey supports it, and hers is the only author-

---

[1] Miss Nussey contributed an article to *Scribner's* for May, 1871, which is an exceedingly interesting addition to Bronteana, and it has generally been overlooked. The origin of the pistol-firing stories may be found here. Miss Nussey says that every morning Mr. Brontë discharged the load which was entered the night before. See also Shorter's note to Gaskell, pp. 52 *seq*.

[2] Shorter, p. 474.

Her Passion

itative voice on the subject. "For years," she says, "they had not tasted animal food."[1] Mary Taylor also writes that Charlotte never touched it at Roe Head.[2] And we find it hard to forgive him for allowing Charlotte and Emily to return to Cowan's Bridge after the deaths of Maria and Elizabeth. The dry egoist was wrapped up in his invalid's seclusion; and the all-sufficient proof of the want of sympathy between the children and their father is that their writing was done in secret, and divulged only when the knowledge could not longer be kept from him.

But very little sympathy can be felt for such troubles of a man as arise from a too numerous progeny; and pious references to the authority of Scripture as to the blessedness of quiversful may safely be met by the equal authority of Psalm xvii. 14. A wife sacrificed to excessive motherhood is not a pleasant spectacle to contemplate.[3]

We have seen that his blindness was a cause of sorrowful anxiety to Charlotte. We know with what dutiful obedience was borne his senseless opposition to her marriage. We know how tenderly his whims were humored and his wishes anticipated. And we may be certain that a part of the gloom is due to his cold privacy and uncertain temper. We see his reflection in Mr. Helstone.[4]

---

[1] *Scribner's*, May, 1871.
[2] Gaskell, p. 104.
[3] See 'Rousseau.' By John Morley, vol. i., pp. 124–125.
[4] Mr. F. A. Leyland, in an elaborate two-volume work ['The Brontë Family. With special reference to Patrick Bramwell Brontë.' London: Hurst and Blackett, 1886], has attempted the defence of both father and brother. In regard to Bramwell, as Mr. Birrell characteristically remarks, "he fails to interest those who, to employ an American figure, 'have no use' for that young man." He fails to interest because he fails to convince; and the whole pitiful story had

Our easy-jogging optimism, fostered by pleasant surroundings, and drawing its springs principally from the negative virtues, if not sometimes from the positive vices, finds it not difficult to lay the charge of morbid fancies against those whom the stars in their courses seem to fight. There was much to foster such fancies in the life of Charlotte Brontë: the conditions were ripe for melancholy. She had, in the first place, that kind of constitutional ill-health which takes the backbone out of a certain kind of men, and makes of them a certain kind of saints. The physical conditions of a life, both past and present, must be taken into account in the summing up. The parsonage was undoubtedly very often too cold for health, to say nothing of comfort. Once she excuses the illegibility of her writing on the plea that her fingers are numb with cold;[1] and much of the ill-health is undoubtedly traceable to the stone steps which the shivering family had to go up and down many times a day. Think of what a Yorkshire winter meant in such a house to children in whom inherited weakness only needed slight encouragement to develop into incurable disease. Little wonder that the letters form a dark, continuous diary of bronchitis, toothache, loss of appetite, cold, coughs, consumption, death.

That microscopical handwriting of the early years

---

much better been left untold. All that the two volumes contain which is really a contribution to our knowledge of the subject could have been condensed into a short magazine article; and the portentous bombast and effeminate fancy of the verses which have been here so painstakenly collected serve no other purpose than to emphasize the mean absurdity of the rumor that Bramwell, and not Emily, was the author of 'Wuthering Heights.' See also Mr. Francis H. Grundy's 'Pictures of the Past,' London, 1879.

[1] Shorter, p. 408.

Her Passion

must be taken into the account. Of those youthful productions thirty-six have come down to us, containing about 700,000 words. That would make about seven large octavo books of ordinary type, of three hundred pages each. She crowded 35,000 words on eighteen pages; which is equal to one hundred pages, ordinary type! Every sufferer from overstrained eyesight will credit these performances with a good part of the ill-health which followed.

They had no other children for playmates, and their influence upon one another was intensified by this cross-breeding of the family intellect, so to speak. There is no record of children's books in the family library, which, indeed, is to be reckoned an asset of happiness, when we recall what children's books were in that day. At the same time, knowing what they are in this day, and how they influence youthful minds, we can fancy what the lack meant.

Her physical torments pursued her to the foreign city. The demon of cold, indeed, seemed fated to follow her wherever she went. She complains they have no fires in the pensionnat,[1] and says at another time: "During the bitter cold weather we had through February and the principal part of March, I did not regret that you had not accompanied me. If I had seen you shivering as I shivered myself, if I had seen your hands and feet as red and swelled as mine were, my discomfort would just have been doubled. I can do very well under this sort of thing; it does not fret me; it only makes me numb and silent; but if you were to pass a winter in Belgium, you would be ill."[2] And while speaking of Brussels, it seems appropriate to mention the other drawbacks to her hap-

[1] Gaskell, p. 274.   [2] *Ib.*, p. 262.

piness there, each of which added its weight to the sadness of 'Villette.'

Emily was not with her on this second visit. When not occupied with her duties she was as absolutely alone as if she had been on a desert island. "I get on here from day to day in a Robinson-Crusoe-like sort of a way, very lonely, but that does not signify."[1] "Brussels is indeed desolate to me now. I am completely alone. I cannot count the Belgians anything. It is a curious position to be so utterly solitary in the midst of numbers. Sometimes the solitude oppresses me to an excess. One day lately I felt as if I could bear it no longer. . . . One day is like another in this place. I know you, living in the country, can hardly believe it is possible life can be monotonous in the centre of a brilliant capital like Brussels; but so it is. I feel it most on holidays, when all the girls and teachers go out to visit, and it sometimes happens that I am left during several hours quite alone, with four great desolate school-rooms at my disposition. I try to read, I try to write; but in vain. I then wander about from room to room, but the silence and loneliness of all the house weighs down one's spirits like lead."[2]

The obtuseness and riotous disorder of her Belgian pupils were a sore trial to her spirit, and the Jesuit atmosphere was poison to her free English breath.

> The *grandes vacances* began soon . . . when she was left in a great deserted pensionnat, with only one teacher for a companion. This teacher, a Frenchwoman, had always been uncongenial to her; but, left to each other's sole companionship, Charlotte soon discovered that her associate was more profligate, more steeped in a kind of cold,

[1] Gaskell, p. 264. [2] *Ib.*, p. 273.

systematic sensuality, than she had before imagined it possible for a human being to be; and her whole nature revolted from this woman's society. A low nervous fever was gaining on Miss Brontë. She had never been a good sleeper, but now she could not sleep at all. Whatever had been disagreeable, or obnoxious, to her during the day, was presented when it was over, with exaggerated vividness to her disordered fancy. . . . In the dead of the night, lying awake at the end of the long, deserted dormitory, in the vast and silent house, every fear respecting those whom she loved, and who were so far off in another country, became a terrible reality, oppressing her and choking up the very life blood in her heart. Those nights were times of sick, dreary, wakeful misery; precursors of many such in after years.

In the daytime, driven abroad by loathing of her companion and by the weak restlessness of fever, she tried to walk herself into such a state of bodily fatigue as would induce sleep. So she went out, and with weary steps would traverse the Boulevards and streets sometimes for hours together, faltering and resting occasionally on some of the many benches placed for the repose of happy groups, or for solitary wanderers like herself. Then up again — anywhere but to the pensionnat — out to the cemetery where Martha lay — out beyond it, to the hills whence there is nothing to be seen but fields as far as the horizon. The shades of evening made her retrace her footsteps — sick for want of food, but not hungry; fatigued with long continued exercise — yet restless still, and doomed to another weary, haunted night of sleeplessness. She would thread the streets in the neighborhood of Rue d'Isabelle, and yet avoid it and its occupant, till as late an hour as she dared be out. At last, she was compelled to keep her bed for some days.[1]

From the letters she wrote from Brussels, and from 'Villette,' we know that this is not exaggerated. The

[1] Gaskell, pp. 270 *seq.*

frightful monotony of her existence under these surroundings is surely sufficient to account for the pervasive melancholy of the story, and the homesickness was of the acutest sort.

But there was one consuming fire of pain in her life which in its biting fierceness was alone sufficient to lead her into the valley of the shadow; and that was the death of her sisters. Whatever of brightness, whatever of joy, whatever of the glad zest of existence there was in her career drew its inspiration from the sunshine of their companionship; and when this was withdrawn there ensued that death-in-life which she has so deathlessly celebrated. Of Emily she writes: "You must look on and see her do what she is unfit to do, and not dare to say a word — a painful necessity for those to whom her health and existence are as precious as the life in their veins. When she is ill there seems to be no sunshine in the world for me. The tie of sister is near and dear indeed, and I think a certain harshness in her powerful and peculiar character only makes me cling to her more. . . . Above all, never allude to . . . the name Emily when you write to me."[1] "I hope still, for I *must* hope — she is dear to me as life. If I let the faintness of despair reach my heart I shall become worthless."[2] Then, when it was over: "Life has become very void, and hope has proved a strange traitor; when I shall be able again to put confidence in her suggestions, I know not: she kept whispering that Emily would not, *could* not die, and where is she now? Out of my reach, out of my world — torn from me."[3]

Upon her return from Anne's funeral, she writes: "I left Papa soon and went into the dining-room: I

---

[1] Shorter, p. 167. [2] *Ib.*, p. 174. [3] *Ib.*, p. 176.

shut the door — I tried to be glad that I was come home. I have always been glad before except once — even then I was cheered. But this time joy was not to be the sensation. I felt that the house was all silent — the rooms were all empty. I remembered where the three were laid — in what narrow, dark dwellings — nevermore to reappear on earth. So the sense of desolation and bitterness took possession of me. The agony that was to be undergone and was not to be avoided, came on. . . . The great trial is when evening closes and night approaches. At that hour we used to assemble in the dining-room — we used to talk. Now I sit by myself. . . ."[1] She knows that "Solitude, Remembrance, and Longing" — that trinity of grief — are to be her sole companions from that day on.

Turn, now, to the novels:

It flashes on me at this moment how sisters feel toward each other. Affection twined with their life, which no shocks of feeling can uproot, which little quarrels only trample an instant that it may spring more freshly when the pressure is removed; affection that no passion can ultimately outrival, with which even love itself cannot do more than compete in force and truth. . Love hurts us so: it is so tormenting, so racking, and it burns away our strength with its flame; in affection there is no pain and no fire, only sustenance and balm.

The sympathetic reader of Miss Brontë's novels can put his finger on the first passage written after the sharp agony of Emily's death, — so burned into the fibre of her being was its vital impress:

[1] Gaskell, p. 421.

... she spent the night like Jacob at Peniel. Till break of day she wrestled with God in earnest prayer. Not always do those who dare such divine conflict prevail. Night after night the sweat of agony may burst dark on the forehead; the supplicant may cry for mercy with that soundless voice the soul utters when its appeal is to the Invisible "Spare my beloved," it may implore, "heal my life's life. Rend not from me what long affection entwines with my whole nature. God of heaven — bend — hear — be clement!" And after this cry and strife, the sun may rise and see him worsted. That opening morn, which used to salute him with the whisper of zephyrs, the carol of skylarks, may breathe as its first accents from the dear lips which color and heat have quitted:

"Oh! I have had a suffering night. This morning I am worse. I have tried to rise. I cannot. Dreams I am unused to have troubled me."

Then the watcher approaches the patient's pillow, and sees a new and strange moulding of the familiar features, feels at once that the insufferable moment draws nigh, knows that it is God's will that his idol shall be broken, and bends his head, and subdues his soul to the sentence he cannot avert and scarce can bear.

As she confessed later, it was dreary work after that: the only persons in the world who understood her were no more. And how lonely the lonely moors! how still the still house! how much more like Death's self the symbols of death under the windows!

So, when the time for 'Villette' came, it was composed in a loneliness which cast long shadows across the page. "I have sometimes desponded and sometimes despaired because there was none to whom to read a line, or of whom to ask a counsel. 'Jane Eyre' was not written under such circumstances, nor were two-thirds of 'Shirley.' I got so miserable about it, I could bear no allusion to the book."[1] "I am now again at home," she writes Mr. Williams. "I call it home still, much as London would be called London if an earthquake would shake its streets to ruins."[2] "I used rather to like Solitude," she makes Moore write, "to fancy her a somewhat quiet and serious, yet fair nymph; an Oread descending to me from lone mountain-passes; something of the blue mist of hills in her array, and of their chill breeze in her breath — but much also of their solemn beauty in her mien. . . . Since that day I called S. to me in the school-room . . . since that hour I abhor Solitude. Cold abstraction — fleshless skeleton — daughter — mother — and mate of Death!" That came from Charlotte's heart of hearts. Here was a love that went down so deep that its roots got entangled in the deeper ones of friendship.

With the possibilities of ultimate utter helplessness before them, in the event of the father's death, his narrow stipend ceasing with his allotted time on earth, we can easily imagine the desolate images of the future called up by his continuous ill-health in that home which was the scene of so many noble endeavors. For, notwithstanding the spiritual barrenness of old Brontë, and the congenital dissimilarity between father and daughters, Charlotte's dutiful care of him provided an escape from intolerable tedium; and what would have become of her had he died before her? And so we have, as flowing from her, not dreary experiences only, but still more dreary anticipations, the sadly realistic picture of the unmated which readers of these novels will not soon forget. The pathetic

[1] Gaskell, p. 592. [2] Shorter, p. 201.

portraits of Miss Mann and Miss Ainley are what she sees the future has in store for her. It is not the dread of being a single woman, but of being a lonely woman, all her life, that thrills her with mournful musings, and discloses heart-burning disquietudes. After she feels that she is safe from the worst features of a solitary existence, she can write:

Lonely as I am, how should I be if Providence had never given me courage to adopt a career — perseverance to plead through two long weary years with publishers till they admitted me? How should I be, with youth past, sisters lost, a resident in a moorland parish where there is not a single educated family? In that case I should have had no world at all: the raven, weary of surveying the deluge, and without an ark to return to, would be my type. As it is, something like a hope and motive sustains me still.[1]

But the raven came very near to her, notwithstanding. Well did Mrs. Gaskell choose, in selecting a motto for her fly-leaf, that cry of Aurora Leigh, —

> Oh, my God,
> . . . Thou hast knowledge, only Thou,
> How dreary 't is for women to sit still
> On winter nights by solitary fires,
> And hear the nations praising them far off.

Now, these things being so, is it necessary to hunt for a particular love experience in Brussels to account for the particular love story in 'Villette'? May not the outward and visible signs of a known, be made, after the manner of symbols, to hide and mystify the inward and spiritual graces of an unknown, personality? The immense loneliness of a spirit, tossed and pounded on the rocks by tumultuous grief, cried out in the

[1] Shorter, p. 395.

night-time of its desolation, — cried out from her bed, her "miserable bed, haunted with quick scorpions," — cried, and "with no language but a cry," for the natural life, which is the reverse of loneliness and wreckage, — the blessed life of a home where love is, and her divine handmaidens.

IV

This, joined to her unworldliness, is, I believe, the chief cause of the absence of wit in her novels. Suffering is sometimes the mother of wit, as with Heine; but with the more spiritual sort its bitterness does not warp the mind into aphorism. In the old original sense of "Wisdom" Charlotte Brontë had wit, for that is the clearest mark of elemental genius; but her passion was too deep and her life too unspotted from the world, — too simple, in a word, to admit the worldly wisdom which we generally mean by "wit." There is a grim humor in some of her characterizations (as in Miss Ainley's attitude towards the curates, as if they were "sucking saints," in contrast with her own experimental knowledge to the contrary); but she could not work up humorous situations. Think what Jane Austen would have made out of the encounter of Donne with the dog Tartar! There is the gross material of humor, rather than the mined product. She had the capacity to realize, not the power to develop, — the sense, not the expression. The white light of her passion fills the room: we cannot distinguish the furniture.

I have referred to Miss Brontë's delineations of children under the head of her realism. There is another reason why they failed. The child pictures are, no doubt, truthful, unless her intensity unwittingly deepened the colors, as intensity is liable to do. Her favorite characters, like herself, have a capacity for suffering, and she probably read some of the feeling of her own young life into Polly's, making it supersensitive beyond the limits of common experience. It was not love for children that made her tender of Georgette, nor was it latent motherhood: it was not the child she loved, but Love. It was a drop of water, and she was dying of thirst.

The truth is, children and animals (they go together) did not enjoy a natural place in her thought. She had to individualize too sharply or to pass by too carelessly; and, although her conscience would not allow any slipshod work, from this painful lack of vital concern there results either a too particular emphasis or a too hazy view. Contrast her description of Paul Emmanuel's dog —

He . . . gave many an endearing word to a small spanieless (if one may coin such a word) that nominally belonged to the house, but virtually owned him as master, being fonder of him than of any inmate. A delicate, silky, loving, and lovable little doggie she was, trotting at his side, looking with expressive attached eyes into his face; and whenever he dropped his bonnet-grec, or his handkerchief, which he occasionally did in play, crouching beside it with the air of a miniature lion guarding a kingdom's flag —

with the picture of another bachelor's dog, Bartle Masset's Vixen, in 'Adam Bede':

The moment he appeared at the kitchen door with the candle in his hand, a faint whimpering began in the chimney corner, and a brown-and-tan-colored bitch, of that wise-looking breed with short legs and long body, known to an unmechanical generation as turnspits, came creeping along the floor, wagging her tail, and hesitating at every other step, as if her affections were painfully divided between the hamper in the chimney corner and the master, whom she could not leave without a greeting.

"Well, Vixen, well then, how are the babbies?" said the schoolmaster, making haste towards the chimney corner, and holding the candle over the low hamper, where two extremely blind puppies lifted up their heads towards the light, from a nest of flannel and wool. Vixen could not even see her master look at them without painful excitement: she got into the hamper and got out again the next moment, and behaved with true feminine folly, though looking all the while as wise as a dwarf with a large old-fashioned head and body on the most abbreviated legs.

See how George Eliot vitalizes such scenes, — George Eliot, who, by the way, would never have employed the word "spanieless." It is not more than pretty as it stands in Charlotte Brontë: George Eliot would have made it beautiful.

It may seem a small matter, but it points a moral. For the absence of a quality frequently means the engrossing presence of some other quality. Miss Brontë could give only a troubled attention to the little comforts and enjoyments, the straggling sunshine in the corners of a life, the joys of minor possessions, and the pleasures of that abundant existence surrounding all mankind. She was absorbed in a large passion which consumed the thought which might otherwise have been given to details.

She never posed the passion; it was hidden under the mantle of fiction. There was no hysterical diary for the literary executor to exploit. She was the very opposite order of being from Marie Bashkirtseff, for whose outpourings she would have expressed unmitigated scorn. But she suffered all the more for the penting up.

V

'Wuthering Heights' is an absolutely unique book. Charlotte has been denominated, though foolishly, the foundress of the "governess novel." It is quite impossible to fit Emily into a class. In the 'Professor,' although the narrator is seemingly of the male, we know, before we have turned a dozen pages, that the author is of the female, gender. Not so in 'Wuthering Heights,' where even the oaths are men's oaths in the mouths of men.[1] Crimsworth's " My God's " do not fool us for a moment, and the attempt at what she doubtless fancied distinctly male imagery, as when she makes the professor repulse Hypochondria " as one would a dreaded and ghastly concubine coming to embitter a husband's heart towards his young bride," are amusing failures. It was an almost superhuman task, indeed, for a woman like Charlotte Brontë to portray in the first person her idea of masculine power, the unconscious subtle essence of her womanhood almost of necessity changing the value of the paints. The result is, as I have suggested before, an

[1] There are many instances of women authors sinking their identity so successfully as to completely baffle the investigator of sex; but I know of only one instance where a male author has metamorphosed himself into the female narrator of his story with such consummate charm as to cause the reader to rub his eyes and ask if it be possible that a man could have written thus. I refer to the 'Sir Percival' of Mr. Shorthouse.

evidence of her genius; for with a lesser writer the altered values would have negatived the portrait into colorlessness: with her, the genius burnt through the crudities, and merely heightened the colors beyond their proper tones.[1]

Emily's masterpiece is without type, and yet it swells with form. It is pure insight, of imagination all compact; and its revelation is of the lightning's flash. It sweeps like a tornado, it burns like a sirocco. To this wonderful vestal, as icy pure as Artemis, came the most terrible vision of mortal love ever vouchsafed to human genius. In all likelihood she knew nothing of Goethe's "elective affinities;" yet here they are in this marvellous book. Just as in nature a power inherent in atoms will cause two of differing natures to rush together to form a new combination, so in human nature do the spirits "rush together" by the compulsion of a similar mysterious force. That is Love, glittering, transcendent; and it is not the chemical purity of the idea which makes 'Wuthering Heights' a dreaded book, that being more or less dimly recognized in all truly noble love stories; but it is, besides the dazzling conception of this analogy, — dazzling things being painful things, — the *milieu* which offends. Had the *dramatis personæ* been of the familiar types, the "elective affinities" would have accomplished their predestined ends without any jar or smoke. But precisely be-

---

[1] I feel that it is a little unfair to criticise the 'Professor,' as Miss Brontë did not authorize its publication. We have it, however, and no Brontë lover is other than glad, for, notwithstanding its evident mistakes, it contains some of Currer Bell's best work. Nay, its errors emphasize the growth of her powers, as seen in the subsequent volumes. The chief error is due to this attempt at emptying herself into a male consciousness, — an impossible feat for such a woman.

cause that is a common occurrence, it behooved this terrible virgin to set the atoms free in an opposing atmosphere, to show inevitable passion clashing against inevitable fate, and on characters the most unfitted to control their natures torn by the conflicting powers.[1]

The wildest Yorkshire gapes in the story; the atmosphere is of the unconquerable moors: but Heathcliff and Catherine are not of that or any other special earth, but of the universal. The reason for not marrying Heathcliff is given in Catherine's statement of this strongly felt "affinity":

"I've no more business to marry Edgar Linton than I have to be in heaven; and if the wicked man in there had not brought Heathcliff so low, I should n't have thought of it. It would degrade me to marry Heathcliff now; so he shall never know how I love him; and that, not because he's handsome, Nelly, but because he's more myself than I am. Whatever our souls are made of, his and mine are the same; and Linton's is as different as a moonbeam from lightning, or frost from fire."

It is her purpose to make this very clear.

"I cannot express it: but surely you and everybody have a notion that there is or should be an existence of yours beyond you. What were the use of my creation if I were

---

[1] The nearest approach to such a "possession" by the "affinities" since Miss Brontë's day that I have met with is Mr. Phillips' passage in 'Paola and Francesca':

> "O God, Thou seest Thy creatures bound
> Together by that law which holds the stars
> In palpitating cosmic passion bright;
> By which the very sun enthrals the earth,
> And all the waves of the world faint to the moon.
> Even by such attraction we two rush
> Together through the everlasting years."

entirely contained here? My great miseries in this world have been Heathcliff's miseries, and I watched and felt each from the beginning: my great thought in living is himself. If all else perished and *he* remained, *I* should still continue to be; and if all else remained, and he were annihilated, the universe would turn to a mighty stranger: I should not seem a part of it. My love for Linton is like the foliage in the woods: time will change it, I'm well aware, as winter changes the trees. My love for Heathcliff resembles the eternal rocks beneath: a source of little visible delight, but necessary. Nelly, I *am* Heathcliff! He's always, always in my mind; not as a pleasure, any more than I am always a pleasure to myself, but as my own being."

Love is not really blind. If it does not seem to see faults, it is because it sees through them. Catherine knew Heathcliff's faults well enough, and with the usual Brontë genius, her creator avoided that error of minor writers, of covering a lover's perceptions as with a mantle, presumably on the theory that love is a form of insanity. There is insanity galore, one might say, in the wild talk of the people of 'Wuthering Heights;' but they never commit the supreme folly of confusing love with ideality. Catherine knows that Heathcliff is the reverse of anything good, and she warns the infatuated Isabella against him.

"I wouldn't be you for a kingdom, then!" Catherine declared empathically; and she seemed to speak sincerely. "Nelly, help me to convince her of her madness. Tell her what Heathcliff is: an unreclaimed creature, without refinement, without cultivation: an arid wilderness of furze and whinstone. I'd as soon put that little canary into the park on a winter's day, as recommend you to bestow your heart on him! It is deplorable ignorance of his character, child, and nothing else, which makes that dream enter your head. Pray don't imagine that he conceals depths of benevolence and affection beneath a stern exterior! He's not a rough diamond — a pearl-containing oyster of a rustic: he's a fierce, pitiless, wolfish man. I never say to him, 'Let this or that enemy alone, because it would be ungenerous or cruel to harm them;' I say, 'Let them alone, because *I* should hate them to be wronged;' and he'd crush you like a sparrow's egg, Isabella, if he found you a troublesome charge. I know he couldn't love a Linton; and yet he'd be quite capable of marrying your fortune and expectations: avarice is growing with him a besetting sin. There's my picture: and I'm his friend — so much so that, had he thought seriously to catch you, I should perhaps have held my tongue and let you fall into his trap."

This was not jealousy, but downright friendliness and truthfulness, and the good Mrs. Dean confirms it, — not that it needs confirmation to any who read Heathcliff's history.

But the point is that, notwithstanding all this damnatory evidence, she loves him, and he, her. It is a pure love, too, and there lies the wonder of it, — a chemically pure passion. It is not the love of the classics, for that was passion of the baser sort, and impure. There is, on the contrary, no plotting, no contrivance of lust, in the design. The affinities clash, and the horrid turmoil of the book is the noise of the clashing; but why do they clash? Because they meet moral law. They dash against it as the sea against a rock-bound coast; but the coast is safe. The story is thus no picture of immorality, using that word in its customary narrow sense: were it merely that, it would not have its supreme claim upon our consideration.

On the other hand, it is not Christian love, either, for it cannot be used by way of illustrating the thirteenth chapter of the First Epistle to the Corinthians. The idea of Christian knighthood —

> I could not love thee, dear, so much
> Loved I not honor more —

is necessarily absent. It is love, neither pagan nor Christian; simply the chemical situation in its direct form, common in all ages and creeds. It is the essence of love — love *in esse* — but not love refined by Christianity; the mother liquor, not the developed potency. It is not immoral, but un-moral; not anti-Christian, simply non-Christian. Pagan love is really not love at all; Christian love is love clarified. This is love's substance, fulfilling essential laws. It is pure passion, not passionate impurity, — a new thing, not to be found in Shakspere, and a great and immortal conception.

The book has caused grave misgivings, and even Charlotte, in her beautiful preface, doubts its tendency. Ought such books to be written? it is asked. Ought it to thunder and lighten? No, they ought not to be written except by Emily Brontës. The like of it never was, is not, and never will be until a new Emily Brontë appears. Until then we need have no anxieties, for neither the class that gloats over d'Abruzzio nor the class that gapes over Marie Corelli will ever be attracted by it.

The author extends the picture beyond death. Catherine, dying, believes that when Heathcliff suffers she will suffer, too, he on the earth, she under ground. Heathcliff was in her soul; and his torture following is because of this separation. Yet the revelation made to him after her death proves that her spirit lingers still on the earth awaiting his, that they may depart together, even as their bodies will melt into one in the one grave which he has ordered. This teasing presence, driving Heathcliff mad because of its insubstantiability, may not be a comforting thought to the reader, but it is better than Catherine's of suffering *in* the grave; and as it comes as a revelation to the man after, as if to contradict that belief of the woman before, death, it may stand as the final earthly stage in the history of the "affinities."[1]

Charlotte had this thought of possession, too; it is a part of the family inspiration; it is a gleam of genius, inexplicable, heaven-sent. "Nelly, I *am* Heathcliff!" It is the apotheosis of passion; and the passion is not as it is vulgarly conceived, — not in its popular secondary sense, — but is the apotheosis of law. The law has its fullest play in the hardest of circumstances: hence the passion, which means suffering.

That is not all. The statement often made that there is no gleam of light in this dark book, nothing but gloom and despair, — no heaven above its hell, — is carelessly wrong. The awakening of a rational affection between the younger Catherine and Hareton, as the story closes, is all the more beautiful because of the preceding horrors. Emily's genius was not in the least like Poe's or Hoffmann's; its nearest relative, out of her own family, in literature, is Hawthorne. There was no delight in her working over the horrors;

[1] Mrs. Ward, in her brilliant introduction to 'Wuthering Heights,' traces its "horrors" to German Romantic influences. It may be so, in part. Yet there is the same essential difference between Emily and Hoffmann that there is between Charlotte and George Sand; and the mystery of the primal power of each sister is left unsolved by the discussion, which covers rather accidents than fundamentals.

their depiction was not a *tour de force*. They were simply the result of the conflict of the warring powers in her theme. They did not exist of or for themselves. And although the intensity of their portrayal causes them to remain in the memory after other things are forgotten, we should remember, too, that Heathcliff's hate against the Earnshaws is in the end defeated by this same love which has haunted him throughout the years. "It will be odd if I thwart myself," he muttered; "but when I look for his father in his face, I find *her* every day more." The close of the book is the Victory of Love. Heathcliff saw in that love a fresh picture of his own, and dies with it on his vision. He dies in a strange, weird happiness; and the peaceful sunset presages a beautiful dawn for those who remain.[1]

---

[1] The author of 'Wuthering Heights' is remembered also because of those valiant lines which ring yet their iron cadences:

>   No coward soul is mine,
> No trembler in the world's storm-troubled sphere.
> . . . .
>   Vain are the thousand creeds
> That move men's hearts: unutterably vain;
>   Worthless as withered weeds
> Or idlest froth amid the boundless main.
> . . . .
>   There is not room for Death
> Nor atom that his might could render void:
>   Thou — THOU art Being and Breath,
> And what Thou art may never be destroyed.

Some of Anne's verses may be found in old-fashioned "Evangelical" hymnals. Charlotte's are forgotten. It is strange that one possessed of such a lyrical gift should not have naturally taken to its supreme form; but so it was. Emily was the only poet in the family.

Mr. Brontë's account of the answers of the children to his test questions at a time when Emily was not over five years old, fits in with the character as we know it later. The question put to her was what the father should do with Bramwell when he was naughty, and her answer was: "Reason with him, and when he won't listen to reason, whip him." [Gaskell, p. 59.] "She should have been a

"Nelly, I *am* Heathcliff." I have said that Charlotte had this sense of possession also, and I take it, as exemplified in both the sisters, to be a spark of the vital fire. Observe how often Charlotte uses the word "suit" in this complementary sense of chemical force. In 'Shirley' alone it occurs at least a dozen times. Louis Moore notes that Caroline would *suit* Robert with her lamb-like ways; *his* wife must have something of the leopardess in her. Of Shirley he thinks: "If I were king, and she the house-maid that swept my palace stairs, across all that space between us my eye would recognize her qualities; a true pulse would beat for her in my heart, though an unspanned gulf made acquaintance impossible." "It delights my eye to look on her: she *suits* me," is the summing up. Even to serve a passing whim the word ministers to the same idea. When Martin ruminates over his proposed adventure with Caroline, he finds its justification thus: "If she behaves well and continues to *suit* me, as she has suited me to-day, I may do her a good turn." Again: "Well did Mr. Yorke like to have power and use it: he had now between his hands power over a fellow-creature's life: it *suited* him." Louis Moore, in writing down the scene of his proposal, says that Shirley bade him rise from his knees. "I obeyed: it would not have *suited* me to retain that attitude long." Robert comforts Caroline with the assurance that he feels that his mother-in-law and he will *suit*. Louis *feels* Shirley

man, a great navigator," said M. Héger. She was a great navigator, and only a girl. To think she scarcely received a word of praise for this! Sydney Dobell's, as I have said, was the first. But it came after the moors had ceased to weave their magic webs over their virgin slave. And oh, the pity of it, my brothers!

No coward soul *was* thine, thou bright, brave Vestal of the moors!

"in every sentient atom of his frame." That is the crowning glory of the love of Rochester and Jane. "You are my sympathy," he says. "My bride is here," he says, "because my equal is here and my likeness." "Jane suits me: do I suit her?" he asks. "To the finest fibre of my nature, Sir." That is one of the subtlest passages in English literature. The eight words are an octave of perpetual delight, for they peal ever joyous, ever true, to the inward sense of the Eternal Fitness.

VI

Her religious faith stands half-way between the independence of Emily and the piety of Anne. She conformed more to the ecclesiastical requirements and traditions than Emily, who would not teach in the Sunday-school; but hers was not that perfect peace which passeth understanding, and under whose mantle the gentle Anne rested. Emily bore her fate with fortitude; Anne, hers with resignation; Charlotte, hers with a mixture of the two. Emily was unflinching, Anne was patient, Charlotte was both. Christianity did not possess her as it did Anne; on the other hand, she was not defiant, like Emily. I do not think she found much comfort in her religion, for the Anglican faith of her day was of a somewhat barren substance. She did not, at least, get the comfort out of it which Eugénie de Guérin got out of her faith, although the outward conditions of their lives were somewhat similar. The "Evangelical Counsels" are not prominently preached in "Evangelical" circles; and the Frenchwoman found in objective "good works" a vent for subjective distress.

But Miss Brontë was not really "Evangelical" in the partisan sense. She confesses, in 'Villette,' that she sees no essential difference between Lutheranism, Presbyterianism, and Episcopacy; and neither did the judicious Hooker, for that matter. "I smile at you again," she writes, —

> I smile at you again for supposing that I could be annoyed by what you say respecting your religious and philosophical views; that I could blame you for not being able, when you look amongst sects and creeds, to discover any one which you can exclusively and implicitly adopt as yours. I perceive myself that some light falls on earth from heaven — that some rays from the shrine of truth pierce the darkness of this life and world, but they are few, faint, and scattered, and who without presumption can assert that he has found the *only* true path upwards?[1]

Lucy Snowe had no desire to turn Paul Emmanuel from the faith of his fathers, although we know what she thought of that faith: "I thought Romanism wrong, a great mixed image of gold and clay; but it seemed to me that *this* Romanist held the purer elements of his creed with an innocency of heart which God must love."

Such an honest-thinking woman could not assume an air of dilettante coquetry with such phases of belief as appeal to the æsthetic rather than the rational faculties. The splendor of Rome did not dazzle those clear eyes. She was not impervious to the incense; but she saw the loose morality, the conniving at lies, the net of involved spiritual complexities, on the other side of it all. She was not narrowly prejudiced against the Roman Catholic religion; but the Anglo-

[1] Shorter, p. 389.

Saxon in her revolted against the maudlin elements of that faith which were evident to her; and she could not reconcile the indirect and sometimes dishonest means employed to bring about desirably good results, with her inherited and instinctive open, honest, and direct methods. It was not so much a hatred as it was a contempt for what seemed to her Yorkshire independence blank idolatry. "They are at their idolatrous *messe*," she writes. The resounding glory of *securus judicat orbis terrarum*, which awoke converting echoes in Newman's heart, was as a tinkling cymbal in her ear,— the "circle of the earth" being construed in her tongue into "the ruddy old lady of the seven hills."

Yet she was no partisan of a persecuting sect, going about with its detestable Procrustean furniture. Her fancy was free enough to make grave heads shake on orthodox shoulders. She did not take everything on faith. She makes Shirley charmingly non-committal on the vexed subject of the Athanasian creed, and she condemns this symbol, *in propria persona* as, " profane."[1] That her dislike of Rome is not an exclusive prejudice is shown by the similarity she makes Lucy Snowe discover between the little book which Paul Emmanuel has put in her desk for her spiritual comfort and "certain Wesleyan Methodist tracts I had once read when a child; they were flavored with about the same seasoning of excitation to fanaticism." She judged the religion by the lives of the people who professed it, having the highest authority for the application of the test. Unfortunately, this condemns the Protestants, too.

Charlotte had plenty of that most uncommon sense

[1] Shorter. p. 407.

known as common. Emily obstinately refused all medicines, as though they interfered with her friend, Nature. Charlotte was willing to try homœopathy, to save her sister's life. Emily rejected society; Charlotte submitted to its tortures. There was, too, as a beautiful adjunct to this (and, indeed I think, it is naturally joined to a true common-sense) a simple-mindedness which a careless reader of her life might not apply to her.

No one will gather, I hope, from what I have said on this subject, that Miss Brontë was not what is usually called "an earnest Christian," for that would be doing an injustice to a conscientious follower of right paths as construed in the pre-eminently Christian sense. Truly, she has the intense feminine idea of what the right path is: "The right path is that which necessitates the greatest sacrifice of self-interest, which implies the greatest good to others."[1] The cautious male moralist, while applauding the last half of this definition, would amend the first half by inserting the word "sometimes," for he would be bound to acknowledge that certain self-interests may accomplish more good than their sacrifice.

She passionately held that domestic endearments are the best things in the world. Her piety was sufficiently "orthodox," but was not of the kind which blinds either the level gaze of common-sense or the pure sight of other than heavenly visions,— unless the visions of a home where love is are also heavenly. The arguments of St. John with Jane are of the family group of Romney Leigh's with Aurora,— the theme of the poem, the general pressure of social work (called forth by the bitter need of it) against the individ-

[1] Gaskell. p. 212.

ualistic urgency of a separative art, taking on more familiar features in Miss Brontë's hands, in that it sets forth the call on the faithful to sacrifice themselves for foreign missions, as opposed to the clear voice of the heart to stay at home. For "art," with Charlotte Brontë, read " heart." Rochester was still in England: foreign missions will remain foreign to her.

Resignation is what she teaches; but resignation is a very different thing from Content. What we long for with anguished yearnings, in the "undiscovered country," is Content, which, on earth, under the name of Resignation, is merely a negative virtue too often, to which, with hopes blighted and passions crushed, we cling with despair and not with patience. But to satisfy, there must be more than this: Content must be a thrilling force, a life-giving power. Then, indeed, "Contentment will be great riches." Resignation represents the pathetic side of Receptivity, and Miss Brontë's attitude towards it is peculiarly feminine. Here again the weather symphony chimes in with the moral quality. She tells us in 'Villette,' that she fears a high wind because that demands a painful exertion of strength, "but the sullen downfall, the thick descent of snow, or dark rush of rain ask only resignation."[1]

This resignation is the nearest she can attain on earth to the heavenly content. She is its prose-poet. The crucial struggles of her heroines are due to the ever-present conflict with temptation, as Christianly conceived. And her Christianity makes them trium-

---

[1] In a letter from Anne, published in *Hours at Home*, August, 1870, Emily's views on a prevailing east wind are recorded: " Emily considers it a very uninteresting wind." Note the personal touch, as if the wind were a neighbor dropped in from Keighley.

phant. Only, not with peace. She makes her fictional self cry out: "From my youth up Thy terrors have I suffered with a troubled mind." But she holds in check all rebellious feelings, and the passion is deep because of the restraint. Only, not with peace! There would be less resignation if there was more peace. All the more credit, then, to the valiance of the struggler.

But when she rises above all mists of earth, when her wing flashes in the blue, skirting the dizzy heights, we see the heavens opened and hear the heart-beat of the stars.

This hag, this Reason, would not let me look up, or smile, or hope; she could not rest unless I were altogether crushed, cowed, broken-in, and broken-down. According to her, I was born only to work for a piece of bread, to await the pains of death, and steadily through all life to despond. Reason might be right; yet no wonder we are glad at times to defy her, to rush from under her rod, and give a truant hour to Imagination—*her* soft, bright foe, *our* sweet Help, our divine Hope. We shall and must break bounds at intervals, despite the terrible revenge that awaits our return. Reason is as vindictive as a devil; for me she was always envenomed as a stepmother. If I have obeyed her, it has chiefly been with the obedience of fear, not of love. Long ago I should have died of her ill usage, her stint, her chill, her barren board, her icy bed, her savage, ceaseless blows, but for that kinder Power who holds my secret and sworn allegiance. Often has Reason turned me out by night, in mid-winter, on cold snow, flinging for sustenance the gnawed bones dogs had forsaken; sternly had she vowed her stores had nothing more for me — harshly denied my right to ask better things. . . . Then, looking up, have I seen in the sky a head amidst circling stars, of which the midmost and the brightest lent a ray sympathetic and attent: a spirit softer and better than human Reason has ascended with quiet flight to the waste, bringing all round her a sphere of air borrowed of eternal summer; bringing perfume of flowers which cannot fade, fragrance of trees whose fruit is life; bringing breezes pure from a world whose day needs no sun to lighten it. My hunger has this good angel appeased with food, sweet and strange, gathered amongst gleaming angels, garnering their dew-white harvest in the first fresh hour of a heavenly day; tenderly has she assuaged the insufferable tears which weep away life itself, kindly given rest to deadly weariness, generously lent hope and impulse to paralyzed despair. Divine, compassionate, succorable influence! When I bend the knee to other than God it shall be at thy white and winged feet beautiful on mountain or on plain.

Temples have been reared to the sun, altars dedicated to the moon. Oh, greater glory! To thee neither hands build nor lips consecrate; but hearts through ages are faithful to thy worship. A dwelling thou hast, too wide for walls, too high for dome,—a temple whose floors are space, rites whose mysteries transpire in presence, to the kindling, the harmony of worlds!

Sovereign complete, thou hadst, for endurance, thy great army of martyrs; for achievement, thy chosen band of worthies. Deity unquestioned, thine essence foils decay!

This is the very naked flaming soul of genius. Analysis is helpless in its midst. For there is no mechanical prism, however subtly fashioned, that can catch its fierce white light; no cunning chemistry that can divide into spectral rays that light that never was on sea or land.

Like all strong writers, Miss Brontë draws frequently from the Old Testament. "It is like an encampment of the forest sons of Anak," says Caroline of Nunnwood. The ash trees of this famed forest are "stately as Saul," a strange, strong simile. She likens herself to Jael, Sisera being her unbidden longings. We have seen how she lays Eve under contribution. When she saw Lawrence's portrait of Thackeray, her first words were, "And there came up a lion out of Judah," in characteristic contrast to her father, whose sole remark was that it was a puzzling head.

When she writes of the sunrise, whose "herald breeze" fans the expectant traveller's cheek, opening "a clear vast path of azure, amid clouds soft as pearl and warm as flame," do we not catch some faint glimpse of what is meant by the "outgoings of the morning"?—as when perchance, standing on some sea-bitten coast in the gray interval preceding dawn, Nature, sweet commentator, unfolds the significance of "the dew of Thy birth is of the womb of the morning." And she is terrible when Nature sounds her rallying bugle call. When God lets loose His thunder, when "storms the welkin rend," she makes us bow before Him who maketh the clouds His chariot, who walketh upon the wings of the wind.

VII

When she finally did marry Mr. Nicholls, did she love him? The most that we can say is that she esteemed him, that she had an affection for him. It was not an ideal marriage, but how many marriages are? It was a happy one in a negative way, and there is no reason to suppose that it would have ceased to be so. There was no passion in it, nothing approaching the loves of her fictional characters.

Mr. Shorter criticises Mrs. Gaskell for her treatment of Mr. Brontë; but his own picture of Mr. Nicholls is not of the most flattering sort; and Mr. Nicholls was alive when Mr. Shorter wrote, as was Mr. Brontë when Mrs. Gaskell wrote, the main point in much of the criticism against the latter. That he was tremendously in love with Charlotte, there can be no doubt; what her admirers complain of is the lack of manliness in its manifestations. That is not a pleasant picture of him, sullenly silent, refusing to eat, quaking, white with emotion, before the whole congregation when Charlotte approaches the altar for the sacrament. No wonder the stern old father called him an unmanly driveller, and no wonder the servants expressed their antipathy: all the world does not love that kind of a lover.

We will not linger on the theme. He got more than his deserts in winning this woman finally, but so also would have almost every other man: it is not every day that a Robert Browning weds an Elizabeth Barrett. And as she was not unhappy in the outcome, we need not be unduly disturbed. What concerns us chiefly, and what we have to give unceasing thanks for, is that her matchless productions antedated her marriage; for I verily believe that the day she joined hands with the Rev. Mr. Nicholls marked the close of her literary career.

VIII

And it is of the very essence of tragedy that just as her brave battles and bitter disappointments, her biting memories and giant griefs, retroceded a little in the light of new interests, — that just then her life should be transferred from the world which she had served so well, in spite of its buffets, to that other world into which her keen vision had so often penetrated before Death sealed those eloquent eyes. "Oh, I am not going to die, am I?" she calls out from her bed of pain. Like Manfred, about to take the fatal plunge, she in sharpest contrast saw the vision of actual life as only actual death can reveal it:

> Beautiful!
> How beautiful is all this visible world!
> How glorious in its action and itself!

or like Miranda, with a new world of happiness opening before her:

> O wonder!
> How many goodly creatures are there here!
> How beauteous mankind is! O brave new world
> That has such people in 't!

She spake more than any one what she felt. Her accumulated sorrows are reflected in her work. Her murmurs against Fate are tempered by her belief in God. Her sadness is sanctified by faith. The seeming paganisms of her earth-worship rise finally through the veil of Christian pantheism beyond all veils to the right hand of the Majesty on high. She bowed, she fell, she lay down, where she bowed there she fell, but under no other hammer than the hammer of her griefs, and fell to rise again. Hers was no "angry valor dashing against the awful shield of God;" rather in that shield do we see reflected the drawn face of a long-suffering woman.

We do not sit at her feet to learn the wisdoms of philosophy; rather stand we by her side and hold her hand as we would the hand of a stricken sister. The unruffled genius of a Leonardo is not given to every one — the delicacy, the elevation, the serenity, which can view this troublesome world with untroubled eyes, which can attain heights of knowledge without any sense of dizziness, and which can add to that knowledge the abundant courtesy of a culture so calm that it must seem cruel to those toiling under the Frankenstein burden. The laden ones do not reach that perfection. Had it come before her, Charlotte Brontë might have joined in Matthew Arnold's prayer:

> Calm Soul of all things, make it mine
> To feel amid the city's jar
> That there abides a peace of thine
> Man did not make and cannot mar,

but it would have been unanswered; the jar of *her* city — which was the tumult of her solitude — would have shaken to its foundations such transcendent peace.

Not hers was the easy flow and tempered finesse of Miss Austen; not hers the mastery of range within George Eliot's grasp. But for such as value the purity of *passion*, one will forever shine in a brighter light than those, for the light is the lustre eternal of elementary genius. There are many greater novelists, there are some greater women novelists. But even because of this Charlotte Brontë's place is all the more secure, as the greatest writer of pure passion in the English tongue. And it may be that this has more undying fame in it than to be the greatest writer of fiction. Certain it is that we shall never have anything like the Brontës again until like genius mates with like innocence and like loneliness, — such intensity of genius yoked with such immensity of loneliness, in the virgin forest of innocence.

GEORGE ELIOT

THE LITERATURE OF POWER AND THE CUP OF STRENGTH

GEORGE ELIOT
THE LITERATURE OF POWER AND THE CUP OF STRENGTH

A.—HER RELIGION AND PHILOSOPHY

I

EVERY zealous and well-directed effort to sound the deep stream of George Eliot's work must result in the discovery that the bed rock is Sympathy; and every faithful searcher for its source will find it arising from the springs of Altruism.

It is not simple passion, as it is with poor Charlotte Brontë, but that complex outward kinship of feeling which we call *com*passion; and which, in an intellectual being of the rarer sort, is not only the determinant of moral activities but is, preceding such activities, almost necessarily the result of high mental effort; because the natural tendency of rare intelligences is towards separation and aloofness. Indeed, it appears that such sympathy, attached to a life of creative art, must be in danger of collision with the separative qualities of pure intellectual productiveness. The art is not allowed to soar in its natural egoistic ether, chained as it is by human ties to human nature; the fellow-feeling, by its moral massiveness, directing the mind into channels which it would not otherwise take, and which run deeply charged with purposes issuing from that ever-active source — the spring of the Social Good.

The mind of George Eliot thus worked in bondage, but in a willing bondage, to a lofty ideal, and her slavery was but the livery of all thinkers whose realism is still in some measure controlled by an obtruding subjective conscience. It is the untroubled masters of the objective method — the Balzacs and Scotts — who alone are free. Only, we must not forget that, so closely have ethics penetrated to the centre of art, some kinds of servitude may be nobler than other kinds of liberty.

II

Two opposing contradictory traits emerge from a consistently intelligent sympathy: that conservatism which is the loving bond between us and our past, the threatened disruption of which fills us with sorrowful despair; and that radicalism which, true to its name, drives at the root of these conservative emotions. But so far from being contradictory in the destructive sense, their contradiction is their mutual salvation. Are they not, to use our author's own term, but the systole and diastole of human life? The rhythm of life needs this alternating contraction and expansion, this swinging of an infinite pendulum between a past and a future. Just as the photographer produces his *positive* result by his *negative* bath, so does a pure radicalism work on a necessary conservatism. And when you consider that this process which the plate undergoes before the photograph shall be perfected is *sensitization*, you will see that the simile has not been unwisely chosen.

Her Religion and Philosophy

If we think of George Eliot chiefly as a radical, we do not think of her properly. She is an artist, and therefore primarily conservative. The home influences and the influences of Mid-England scenery developed and heightened the strong feeling for the Anglo-Saxon attitude which she inherited from her father; together with a tender sensibility towards the pastoral beauty of her native Warwickshire. "But my eyes," she says, in that almost autobiographical chapter 'Looking Backward,'[1] "But my eyes at least have kept their early affectionate joy in our native landscape, which is one deep root of our national life and language." And although her growing knowledge revealed much of that old England of her affections in the dissolving light of an illusion, she insists that illusions have value. "They feed the ideal Better, and in loving them still, we strengthen the precious habit of loving something not visibly, tangibly existent, but a spiritual product of our visible and tangible selves." She often smiles, she says in this essay, at her "consciousness that certain conservative prepossessions have mingled themselves . . . with the influences of our midland scenery, from the tops of the elms down to the buttercups and the little wayside vetches."

To that remarkable man, Robert Evans, carpenter, builder, and agent of farms, must we turn to understand how much of George Eliot's conservatism is due to descent,— to Robert Evans and to his father, George Evans, likewise carpenter and builder. The father of George Eliot was sixteen years old when the

[1] In 'Theophrastus.' "There are bits in the paper 'Looking Backward' which are true autobiography."—'George Eliot's Life, as Related in her Letters and Journals; Arranged and Edited by her Husband, J. W. Cross.' William Blackwood and Sons, Edinburgh and London, 1885, vol. i., p. 4.

French Revolution broke out; and his Toryism was largely a confirming result, on the naturally conservative English mind, of the horrors of governmental disruption as seen in the logical outcome in France. Toryism meant the firm hand of Government, and "Government" was a religious symbol of peace and continuance of order.

The habit of the artistic mind naturally conforms to this system, and is indelibly fashioned to it by the impressions of its formative period. And the political aspect of the people is, with such a temperament, all but indissolubly connected with the physical aspect of the country which the people inhabit. Our author loves the old because the people love it; and she never urges that kind of newness which can find no nourishment in a cherished past. She is in this respect, true to art; for though art is constantly returning from her creative flights with new forms, these forms never contradict, if they are really her own, the saving central ideal of beauty, which is simply truth to the inward intuitive perception of proportion between mass and outline, and to the vivifying, informing spirit which is the inspiring life of the work. George Eliot is a reformer, with the Social Good as her ideal; but her artistic perception restrains her innovations from a noisy activity. Her genius broods; it is meditative.

She knew that that old England of her father's love had much of evil that had, in her day, disappeared. Yet she loved it, too, because of it she was born, and out of it was she nourished. She would not have been what she was, had it been different. She shared the common lot of being the product of a past, to which, therefore, she owed reverence.

The times, I heard, had often been bad; but I was constantly hearing of bad times as a name for actual evenings and mornings when the godfathers who gave them that name appeared to me remarkably comfortable. Altogether, my father's England seemed to me lovable, laudable, full of good men, and having good rulers, from Mr. Pitt on to the Duke of Wellington, until he was for emancipating the Catholics; and it was so far from prosaic to me that I looked into it for a more exciting romance than such as I could find in my own adventures, which consisted mainly in fancied crises calling for the resolute wielding of domestic swords and firearms against unapparent robbers, rioters, and invaders, who, it seemed, in my father's prime had more chance of being real. The morris-dancers had not then dwindled to a ragged and almost vanished rout (owing the traditional name probably to the historic fancy of our superannuated groom); also, the good old king was alive and well, which made all the more difference because I had no notion what he was and did — only understanding in general that if he had been still on the throne he would have hindered everything that wise persons thought undesirable.

Certainly that elder England with its frankly salable boroughs, so cheap compared with the seats obtained under the reformed method, and its boroughs kindly presented by noblemen desirous of encouraging gratitude; its prisons with a miscellaneous company of felons and maniacs and without any supply of water; its bloated, idle charities; its non-resident, jovial clergy; its militia-balloting; and above all its black ignorance of what we, its posterity, should be thinking of it,— has great differences from the England of to-day. Yet we discern a strong family likeness. Is there any country which shows at once as much stability and as much susceptibility to change as ours? Our national life is like that scenery which I early learned to love, not subject to great convulsions, but easily showing more or less delicate (sometimes melancholy) effects from minor changes. Hence our midland plains have never lost their familiar expression and conservative spirit for me; yet at every other mile, since I first looked on them, some sign of world-wide change, some new direction of human labor has wrought itself into what one may call the speech of the landscape — in contrast with those grander and vaster regions of the earth which keep an indifferent aspect in the presence of men's toil and devices. What does it signify that a liliputian train passes over a viaduct amidst the abysses of the Apennines, or that a caravan laden with a nation's offerings creeps across the unresting sameness of the desert, or that a petty cloud of steam sweeps for an instant over the face of an Egyptian colossus immovably submitting to its slow burial beneath the sand? But our woodlands and pastures, our hedge-parted corn-fields and meadows, our bits of high common where we used to plant the windmills, our quiet little rivers here and there fit to turn a millwheel, our villages along the coach-roads, are all easily alterable lineaments that seem to make the face of our Motherland sympathetic with the laborious lives of her children. She does not take their ploughs and waggons contemptuously, but rather makes every hovel and every sheepfold, every railed bridge or fallen tree-trunk an agreeably noticeable incident; not a mere speck in the midst of unmeasured vastness, but a piece of our social history in pictorial writing.

Our rural tracts — where no Babel-chimney scales the heavens — are without mighty objects to fill the soul with the sense of an outer world unconquerably aloof from our efforts. The wastes are playgrounds (and let us try to keep them such for the children's children who will inherit no other sort of demesne); the grasses and reeds nod to each other over the river, but we have cut a canal close by;

the very heights laugh with corn in August or lift the plough-team against the sky in September. Then comes a crowd of burly navvies with pickaxes and barrows, and while hardly a wrinkle is made in the fading mother's face or a new curve of health in the blooming girl's, the hills are cut through or the breaches between them spanned, we choose our level, and the white steam-pennon flies along it.

But because our land shows this readiness to be changed, all signs of permanence upon it raise a tender attachment instead of awe; some of us, at least, love the scanty relics of our forests, and are thankful if a bush is left of the old hedgerow. A crumbling bit of wall where the delicate ivy-leaved toad-flax hangs its light branches, or a bit of gray thatch with patches of dark moss on its shoulder and a troop of grass-stems on its ridge, is a thing to visit. And then the tiled roof of cottage and homestead, of the long cow-shed where generations of the milky mothers have stood patiently, of the broad-shouldered barns where the old-fashioned flail once made resonant music, while the watch-dog barked at the timidly venturesome fowls making pecking raids on the outflying grain — the roofs that have looked out from among the elms and walnut-trees, or beside the yearly group of hay and corn stacks, or below the square stone steeple, gathering their grey or ochre-tinted lichens and their olive-green mosses under all ministries, — let us praise the sober harmonies they give to our landscape, helping to unite us pleasantly with the elder generations who tilled the soil for us before we were born, and paid heavier and heavier taxes, with much grumbling, but without that deepest root of corruption — the self-indulgent despair which cuts down and consumes and never plants. . . .

I belong to the "Nation of London." Why? There have been many voluntary exiles in the world, and probably in the very first exodus of the patriarchal Aryans — for I am determined not to fetch my examples from races whose talk is of uncles and no fathers — some of those who sallied forth went for the sake of a loved companionship, when they would willingly have kept sight of the familiar plains, and of the hills to which they had first lifted up their eyes.

What George Eliot owes to her father you may see in Adam Bede, Caleb Garth, and Stradivarius — as, near portraiture as she ever permitted herself to go. Moral firmness, strength of purpose, conscientious painstaking, faithfulness to system, a high intelligence, a mastery of details springing from a thorough understanding of their underlying principles, a keenly developed sense of order, and a love for hard work — in this she was herself Adam Bede and Caleb Garth and her father's true child. And that eager tenderness, for the country which ever haunted her in her town surroundings was, in the mystic way of such inheritances, a reflection of those early attachments which are the warp and woof of a sensitive childhood. An affectionate memory was intensified by its associations with a companionship quite as devoted as that of Maggie's with Tom's — another hint at portraiture — and, we have reason to believe, meeting with about the same response. All of that wonderful 'Mill on the Floss' history of childhood was, spiritually, her own. There is a reference to her brother's share in her girlhood's life in the poetical heading to the fifty-seventh chapter of 'Middlemarch ;' and it shines with a sweet radiance in her poem 'Brother and Sister.'

III

The artistic nature is primarily conservative. It is also necessarily plastic. And when it is a woman's nature it lacks the fuller ideality of a man's. George

Eliot, with all her masculine power, suffers in company with all of her sisters, from this congenital — I will not say defect, but rather denial of nature. That is perhaps why no women musicians of the first rank have as yet appeared, although at the beginning of the new century there are indications that the less circumscribed life of women is beginning to find its first and finest response in music. But in that other kind of composing which we have here to consider, the innate feminine love of reality, — that is, love for an isolated object as the realization of an ideal — seems destined in the strongest of women novelists, to crowd out the continued contemplation of the ideal itself. That George Eliot is herself appreciative of this fundamental characteristic is demonstrated, in her most mature period, in the picture of Dorothea; the intense pity of her sympathy with her heroine being due to that mysterious chord of feeling between two sisters of the same mental and spiritual type. Hardly any male author of equal genius would have caused that girl to sacrifice herself so needlessly to such a pallid mistake as Casaubon. Reflecting his own ideality, just as George Eliot reflected her lack of it, he would have been content to let her linger hungering for that ideal which, in her environment, she could never find; knowing that though there be no reality, the ideal has a dynamic force in a "larger unity" than can be comprehended in any particular realization.

I did not mean to be carried so far afield, however, at this time, but to point out that the traits we learn to know as we read her books are evident in her early years, — the conservatism, the plastic enthusiasms, and that hungering need of realization which stands in the way of the "larger unity" for which she strove. Her religious surroundings at school were ultra-Evangelical, and she imbibed them as readily as she afterwards did those of the Westminster coterie. It is interesting to note that she recommends, in a letter to Miss Lewis,[1] a quotation from Young, whom she unsparingly castigates, a little later, when the new influences are at work, for the very qualities for which the quotation stands sponsor. Her religious fervor at this period was apparently able to extinguish her musical sensibilities, for in a letter on the eve of her nineteenth birthday she says, referring to an oratorio lately heard at Coventry, ". . . it is the last, I think, I shall attend. . . . It would not cost me any regrets if the only music heard in our land were that of strict worship, nor can I think a pleasure that involves the devotion of all the time and powers of an immortal being to the acquirement of an expertness in so useless (at least in ninety-cases out of a hundred) an accomplishment can be quite pure and elevating in its tendency."[2] She has no soul for

---

[1] 'Life' vol. i, p. 42.

[2] *Ib.*, vol. i., p. 44. To say that a book is good as far as it goes carries with it a shade of condemnation. Mr. Cross's 'Life' is that kind of a book. What it gives is valuable; what it withholds would have so added to its value that the reticence affects in some degree the utterance. It is a dignified silence, and is to that extent a happy contrast to the gossipy volubility which too often passes for biography; but the dovetailing process in this instance has conformed too steadily to one standard. There is no change of key, and as the key is high, the effect is a strained monotony. The biographer suffered in that his acquaintance did not date sufficiently into her early years to allow him to speak with both authority and interest in regard to them. What skill the 'Life' has — and that is very considerable — is due to the affectionate intelligence of an admiring husband; it lacks the highest skill of the trained writer and the born biographer. George Eliot's life in its fulness has never been written, nor can it ever be until the writer has in his possession all the letters which Mr. Cross

music, she says in this letter; and yet, seven years before, her music master confessed that he had no more to teach her, — her enthusiasm for the subject being of the kind reflected in her portrayal of Maggie Tulliver's experience "... her sensibility to the extreme excitement of music was only one form of that passionate sensibility which belonged to her whole nature, and made her faults and virtues all merge in each other — made her affections sometimes an important demand, but also prevented her vanity from taking the form of mere feminine coquetry and device, and gave it the poetry of ambition." Two

---

has seen fit to omit from his biography, and which, of course, if they have not already been destroyed, could be justifiably published only with Mr. Cross's permission: that time, we think, will never come. The student desirous of supplementing Mr. Cross's collection of letters should consult, among other matter, the correspondence (presumably unknown to her husband) copied in *Poet Lore*, vol. vi., — some of it over the name of 'Clematis,' given her by a girl friend, and appropriately, for it means 'mental beauty;' also Trollope's 'What I remember,' chapters xxxiv-v., and Elizabeth Stuart Phelps' paper in *Harper's*, vol. lxiv., p. 568.

She herself said, in a letter to Mrs. Trollope ['What I Remember,' p. 485]. "The best history of a writer is contained in his writings: there are his chief actions; ... biographies generally are a disease of English literature." Her life, indeed, must be studied mostly through her books, even where it differs from the books. Her father's family were too much estranged to have made their testimonies valuable, even if most of them had not already passed away. Her intellectual friends, Mr. Spencer, Mr. Harrison, Mr. Paul, the Coventry and Westminster groups, have contributed their moieties, and with that we must be content. Under the circumstances, Mr. Cross's book must remain the only authentic 'Life,' and may always be quoted without caveats, so far as the actual facts are recorded. [Since the present volume has been in type, Sir Leslie Stephen has published his monograph in the English Men of Letter Series ['George Eliot.' By Leslie Stephen. New York, The Macmillan Co. London, Macmillan Co., Ltd. 1902]. It contains no new biographical facts, although, of course, it is a valuable addition to the criticism of the subject].

years after writing this renunciatory letter, she is discovered at the Birmingham festival hysterically sobbing over the grand flow of harmonies[1] ["The mere concord of octaves was a delight to Maggie"]; and all through her life music was her principal solace and delight. Her musical evenings were those which gave her the most enjoyment, and it was at a concert that she caught her fatal cold. She was a fine performer on the piano, and had an exquisite taste. "I am very sensitive to blunders and wrong notes, and instruments out of tune," she says in a letter to Charles Lewes.[2] She knew the piano well enough to faint-praise it as a "moderately responsive instrument," and she illustrates the virile power of the violin by the "*masculine*" bow. Castanets are likened to "*crickets*." Her feeling for the nice shades of tone between instruments is shown in these one-word descriptions, as when she refers to the "*violoncello*" voice of Lady Pentreath. Indeed, who will ever forget the musical "notes" in her fiction? There is hardly a great composer of whom she has either not had some swift direct sympathetic word to say, or to whose style some indirect word perfectly fits. She took Haydn's measure, for example, thus:

"Philip burst into one of his invectives against 'The Creation,' the other day," said Lucy, seating herself at the piano. "He says it has a sort of sugared complacency and flattering make-believe in it, as if it were written for the birthday fête of a German Grand-duke."

And does not this describe the effect of 'The Messiah' on a appreciative listener? —

[1] 'Life' vol i., p. 44.   [2] *Ib.*, vol. ii., p. 135.

Her Religion and Philosophy

Caleb was very fond of music, and when he could afford it went to hear an oratorio that came within his reach, returning from it with a profound reverence for this mighty structure of tones, which made him sit meditatively, looking on the floor and throwing much unutterable language into his outstretched hands.

The terrible Klesmer — none but a keen musician could have painted the absolutely perfect picture of the Klesmers — must have been criticising Bellini when he thundered at Gwendolen:

"That music which you sing is beneath you. It is a form of melody which expresses a puerile state of culture, — a dandling, canting see-saw kind of stuff — the passion and thought of people without any breadth of horizon. There is a sort of self-satisfied folly about every phrase of such melody; no cries of deep, mysterious passion — no conflict — no sense of the universal. It makes men small as they listen to it. Sing now something larger."

And it might just as well have been Wagner that he sat down to play as —

... a composition of his own, a fantasia called *Freudvoll, Leidvoll, Gedankvoll* — an extensive commentary on some melodic ideas not too grossly evident; and he certainly fetched as much variety and depth of passion out of the piano as that moderately responsive instrument lends itself to, having an imperious magic in his fingers that seemed to send a nerve-thrill through ivory key and wooden hammer, and compel the strings to make a quivering speech for him.

This Klesmer, it appears,

... was as versatile and fascinating as a young Ulysses on a sufficient acquaintance — one whom nature seemed to have first made generously and then to have added music as a dominant power using all the abundant rest; and, as in Mendelssohn, finding expression for itself not only in the highest finish of execution, but in that fervor of creative work and theoretic belief which pierces the whole future of a life with the light of congruous, devoted purpose.

If you have felt the heaviness of Meyerbeer, you will clap your hands at this:

"He is a friend of yours, I think."
"No, no; an amateur I have seen in town: Lush, a Mr. Lush. Too fond of Meyerbeer and Scribe — too fond of the mechanical-dramatic."

Listen to Schubert's praise:

> Schubert, too, wrote for silence: half his work
> Lay like a frozen Rhine till summers came
> That warmed the grass above him. Even so!
> His music lives now with a mighty youth.

"There is no feeling," she says, "except the extremes of fear and grief, that may not find relief in music;" and she likens the love of Adam Bede to "the still rapture under the influence of autumn sunsets, or pillared vistas, or calm majestic statues, or Beethoven symphonies," losing "itself in the sense of divine mystery." Her finest similes are her musical similes. Of Esther's awakening she says, "Some hand had touched the chords, and there came forth music that brought tears." And how exquisitely the joyous pain of echoing sensibilities to a sweet convincing song is set forth in Mrs. Meyrick's plea for Mirah!

. . .

"Her voice is just perfect: not loud and strong, but

searching and melting, like the thoughts of what has been. That is the way old people like me feel a beautiful voice."

This feeling for music was for George Eliot the high sublimated essence of the mingled joy and sorrow of life, the "plash of an oar in the evening lake," the "broken echoes of the heavenly choir," the "strains that seemed to make all sorrows natural;" a spiritualizing energy and a soul of peace dwelling in the centre of a heart of storm. Finally, she emphasizes Mr. Casaubon's selfish seclusion by making him confess to a distaste for musical performance. "'I never could look on it in the light of a recreation to have my ears teased with measured noises,' said Mr. Casaubon."

And yet, under the controlling force of a religious impulse, she deliberately denies the possession of a supreme quality which had been discovered years before; so completely was her plastic nature in the grasp of that force. It is an important point, as it touches a fundamental characteristic, — her "radicalism," which was soon to supervene, being primarily due to extraneous influence, as was this pietistic period.

IV

In a letter to Miss Lewis under the date of the twelfth of August, 1840,[1] in connection with a disquisition on the Epistle to the Colossians, in which she adopts with enthusiasm the stereotyped Calvinistic term, "filthy rags," is to be found mention of the first book which had a subtile influence on the un-

[1] 'Life,' vol. i., pp. 70 *seq.*

settling of this same Calvinism, — Isaac Taylor's
'Ancient Christianity;' thus preparing the way for
the dominance of the Brays and Hennells in the following
year, although that would have had its full
effect on her under other conditions. It is to be
noted in passing merely as an interesting incident
of the accidental sort, for in the extensive list of her
reading at this time may be found a large amount of
matter easily convertible into agnostic ammunition.

Hennell's 'Inquiry,' probing into the very origin of
the beliefs which she had absorbed, had a powerful
effect upon her. It was a new kind of writing, a precursor
of the present critical freedom of investigation;
and the book was among the first of a large class to
dwell upon the *natural* history of the Jewish people;
their gradual growth being conceived as leading,
along the lines of evolutionary order, and apart from
special divine interference, to the production of Jesus.
Christianity is traced to the enthusiasm generated by
the character and career of Jesus, followed by the
accession of Gentile converts, the absorption into
the new belief of the prevailing Greek philosophy,
and the decay of the old Olympus; the Hebrew
theocracy disappearing in the religious revolution.
Jesus, under the exalted inspiration that he was the
Messiah — as the result of his schooling in the Essene
philosophy, joined with an ardent patriotism —
preached the "kingdom of heaven," confident that
divine power would make manifest his claim to
David's throne; and his teaching changed as it
became apparent that no such manifestation would
occur; the idea of a conquering Messiahship now
appearing as a glory to be reached only by suffering
and death. The belief in the Resurrection was, accord-

Her Religion and Philosophy 147

ing to this view, based on the actual disappearance of the body of Jesus, and its preaching was allowed as less harmful to the civic peace than the claims of a living Messiah.

This is the book which entered George Eliot's life at the time when the influences which intensified her Evangelicalism were melting under the stronger influences of rationalistic beliefs; and I have dwelt upon the position of the 'Inquiry' at some length to illustrate how easily a plastic nature may be fashioned by the right hand to new modes of thought of diametric opposition to the old. And while we are free to suppose that if the religion of her childhood had been of a more buoyant, more inclusive sort, the break with it would have been less severe, — had there been less of Hannah More in the old, there would have been less of Herbert Spencer in the new, — with her ready acquisitiveness, the change was in some way destined to be wrought out under any conditions; and the 'Inquiry' went home, backed by constant intercourse with the Hennell family. The book is remarkable as indicating the evolutionary method in the historical field several years before that method was firmly established by Darwin's great theory. It exchanges a natural history for a supernatural, and subjects miracles to the microscope of reason, — a process inimical to a belief which is essentially transcendental. The Germans had laboriously arrived at the same conclusions, and their most eminent champion, Strauss, thought so highly of Mr. Hennell's work that he had it translated into his language, and wrote a commendatory preface.

Her own translation of Strauss augmented this widening departure; and the picture of this enthusiastic, delicate girl toiling across that fearful morass, faithful to her aim, but sick at heart (Strauss-sick, she said she was) with her destructive task, is, I venture to believe, the most pathetic portrait in the whole sad wilderness of mistaken effort.[1] Christianity was full of poetry to her, with "its Hebrew retrospect and millennial hopes;" and this German Goliath was in method and purpose the incarnate antagonism of this embodied poetry. His 'Leben' was an epoch-making book, and every serious subsequent work on the rise of Christianity bears some relation to it; but the abnormal analytical development of his mind debarred him from that synthetic and constructive sympathy in the atmosphere of which a spirit like George Eliot's must find breathing room or die. Was there ever another picture like that of this woman bending over the dissection of "the beautiful story of the Crucifixion," nerved to what she believed to be a duty in behalf of truth by the image of that Suffering Christ over her desk — the image of Him who said He was the truth — keeping her to what she thought was the truth in widening the influence of a work destructive of that truth!

V

Do you wonder at the change? Yet it is the same Marian Evans we saw before, denying herself music on religious grounds, and talking about filthy rags. Her plastic nature is simply in another environment, and is being worked upon by other forces; her peculiar susceptibility to such forces being evidenced by

[1] The nearest approach to it that I know of is the picture of Anne Brontë at work on the 'Tenant of Wildfell Hall.'

the strong inherent dissimilarity between the underlying spiritual habits — so to speak — of such a man as Strauss, the unsympathetic, the anti-poetical and destructive, and the future author of 'Adam Bede.'

We have no record of the effect upon her of Strauss's final word of importance on religion, published in 1872; but if she read it, it must have been with regret at her impulsive connection with his earlier performance, for that final word was the word of a discredited and inconsistent negation, giving offence even to his scientific followers because of its total lack of spiritual light and because of its credulity. This was the outcome of the philosophy which moved George Eliot to the painful task of translation, a philosophy opposed to all that is best in her own system of thought. And yet — consider the marvel — there is no more honest work in the history of literature. It is the only English translation of the 'Leben,' and it stands to-day unassailed in point of scholarship. Strauss was delighted with it, saying in his preface " et accurata et perspicua; " which reminds us of George Eliot's own expressed ideal in 'Romola,' "accuracy the very soul of scholarship."

It should not be supposed that because of this plasticity, there was complete intellectual submission. That would have been impossible to a mind charged with a moral earnestness jealous of its emotional outlets. George Eliot never gave her mind, after it was once awakened, completely to any system of belief, — not even to Positivism; for although she contributed to the cause, she would not bind herself to the extent of joining with the Positivist church. It is a "note" of every high intelligence to be discerning; and to say that George Eliot was influenced by her environment to the extent of extinguishing her discernment is to deny her her undeniable prerogative, and to turn her into the company of slaves. She thought Strauss often wrong in details, and did not even consider his theory perfect, but "only one element in a perfect theory;" and her spirit shied at his lack of spirit. After all, the idea back of the translation served rather an intellectual than a moral purpose, difficult as it is to separate the two in such a mind. It had the element of curiosity in it; and coming after the 'Inquiry,' and in the Bray-Hennell surroundings, it provoked an intellect already set on new tracks to a further investigation of their direction. Finally, in connection with her work on Spinoza, it prepared the way for that other translation — the only one she published under her own name — into which she entered with a more grateful spirit, imbued as it was with beliefs which kindled her generosity and shook into full flower the budding convictions of her thought.

VI

If with all the independence belonging to a discerning intelligence of eminent power, she is nevertheless malleable to an unlovely religion and to an unsympathetic German philosophy, consider how deep was the response of her soul to this new influence; continuing, indeed, the critical method she had been following, but substituting a warm moral teaching for cold, abstract negations. Such was Feuerbach's 'Wesen,' rank its author though we must among the atheists. The translation of Spinoza's 'Tractatus' helped to develop her sceptical tendencies, which, when she came to Feuerbach, were at their highest pitch through constant association with the Westminster circle. Not that the metaphysical scheme of Spinoza, as shown in the 'Ethics,' which she took up later, influenced her deeply, for its absolute pantheism is naturally opposed to that desire to investigate the *laws* of phenomena which is the moving power of Positivism; and very early in Miss Evans's development we see this tendency towards the Positive belief. In the 'Ethics,' however, she came upon a system of morality very akin to the spirit of Positivism, which ruled all her after labors: a system of self-assertion losing itself in love of man and God, the happiness which crowns its fulfilment resting in virtue rather than in the rewards of virtue. "The God-intoxicated Spinoza," old Novalis called him, but, enthusiasms aside, we cannot escape seeing the logical outcome of pantheism to be atheism; and although in a speculative sense, pantheism may be regarded as a God-intoxication, the cold-blooded Hume was nearer the exact truth when he referred to Spinoza as "the famous atheist."

His denial of immortality placed Feuerbach, too, in the same category; but his peculiar charm for George Eliot lay in his revolt from the mere jugglery of metaphysics and in his belief that the search for truth should be grounded upon the investigation of actual phenomena,— this and the correspondence he claims to exist between the articles of Christian belief and the necessities of human nature, each belief being the creation of some natural wish. The removal of the supernatural from Christianity necessitates a natural explanation for Christian beliefs and practices; and to a generous mind such an explanation must be based on a hope amounting to conviction of the gradual upward tendency of human desire, through the efforts of those who have at heart the Social Good.

The morality of the system of Feuerbach is of this elevated order, and it found an echo in his translator. He aims always at reality. "Let us concentrate ourselves on what is real," he says, "and great men will revive, and great actions will return." "Health is more than immortality" is his doctrine,—that is, social health; and that is the chief note of George Eliot also. The doctrine of the Resurrection would be explained by Feuerbach as the embodiment of the instinct in man for the continuity and perpetuity of life; and, ethically, he would teach the value of the instinct as a part of that highest good which man creates out of his longings, and towards which he worships. But the practical atheism of his teaching was proved by its failure when applied by the German communists to their lives; its self-centred divinity necessarily excluding any moral obligation outside of self. Unfortunately for all such systems, mankind is composed of units, and the units not being for the most part full of an exalted social morality,—not units like Feuerbach and George Eliot,—each unit will eventually become a law unto itself, with an ensuing anarchy.[1]

The struggle of George Eliot was between her desire to help others by the application of an ennobling system of life, and her purely intellectual convictions. She was in the position of Kant, who strove to erect with his left hand what his right hand had destroyed; and she followed Kant's lead in her difficulty by

---

[1] Mallock's 'Is Life Worth Living?' chaps. i.-x. inc., is the unanswerable argument to all anthropocentric systems of morality.

separating the sphere of cognition from that of will. There is no God such as the Christians have believed in, but there is duty, there are moral obligations and a necessity for raising life from low to high planes. So Kant, swallowing his formula, in Carlyle's phrase, was bound to divorce duty from the sphere of cognition, the conception of duty being incognizable in his philosophy. A Kritik of *Practical* Reason had thus to follow, to make a place for the morality which the Kritik of *Pure* Reason had, metaphysically, abolished.

George Eliot's philosophy was moral, not metaphysical, because metaphysics is insensible to morality. The Social Good takes the place of God; and this was so much of a personality to her that the capital letters are justified, like Herbert Spencer's Ultimate Reality and Matthew Arnold's Something not Ourselves. The household goods become the household's God. She gives to the attributes of God the personality belonging to God, making them God, and calling God by the names of the attributes, as in her beautiful reference to the Unseen Pity. The result would be considered a kind of sublimated polytheism, if a rhetorical allowance were not made for an emotional — of course, I am using the word in its best and highest sense — writer warmed through and through with altruistic fire.

There is with her an *outer* conscience, the moral test being based on an intellectual comprehension of what is best and worst for society in each given case. In depicting Tito's first determining act in persuading himself, against himself, of his father's death, she says:

But the inward shame, the reflex of that outward law which the great heart of mankind makes for every individual man, a reflex which will exist even in the absence of the sympathetic impulses that need no law, but rush to the deed of fidelity and pity as inevitably as the brute mother shields her young from the attack of the hereditary enemy, — that inward shame was showing its blushes in Tito's determined assertion to himself that his father was dead, or that at least search was hopeless.

Further on, as the dilemma begins to press him more urgently:

Having once begun to explain away Baldassare's claim, Tito's thought showed itself as active as a virulent acid, eating its rapid way through all the tissues of sentiment. His mind was destitute of that dread which has been erroneously decried as if it were nothing higher than a man's animal care for his own skin: that awe of the Divine Nemesis which was felt by religious pagans, and, though it took a more positive form under Christianity, is still felt by the mass of mankind simply as a vague fear at anything which is called wrong-doing. Such terror of the unseen is so far above mere sensual cowardice that it will annihilate that cowardice: it is the initial recognition of a moral law restraining desire, and checks the hard, bold scrutiny of imperfect thought into obligations which can never be proved to have any sanctity in the absence of feeling. "It is good," sing the old Eumenides, in Æschylus, "that fear should sit as the guardian of the soul, forcing it into wisdom, — good that men should carry a threatening shadow in their hearts under the full sunshine; else how shall they learn to revere the right?" That guardianship may become needless; but only when all outward law has become needless, — only when duty and love have united in one stream and made a common force.

But here the difficulty of the Feuerbach revolutionists meets us again, for how is this "outward" morality, which "the great heart of mankind" makes for every man, to be applied where perceptions are not fine, as with most, and where the intellect is limited, as with all? Christianity has its outward conscience, too, in its Sinai and its Sermon on the Mount; and its inner conscience is the divine reflex, to borrow George Eliot's own phrase, of this outer. It is divine because it is a reflection of the divine, whereas an anthropocentric system (which, be it remembered, is the only system remaining after the removal of the divine) makes the divine human, because it is a reflection of the human.

VII

It is peculiarly appropriate, in a review of George Eliot's philosophy, to quote the definition of that doctrine which, more than any other, filled her life, given by the man who, more than any other, moulded it. "This is the mission of Positivism," says Mr. Lewes,[1] "to generalize science, and to systematize sociality; in other words, it aims at creating a philosophy of the sciences as a basis for a new social faith. A social doctrine is the aim of Positivism, a scientific doctrine the means, just as a man's intelligence is the minister and interpreter of life." According to Comte, the theological or supernatural phase of intellectual evolution is that in which the mind seeks *causes* for phenomena; the metaphysical that in which abstract forces are found inherent in

---

[1] Comte's 'Philosophy of the Sciences.' By G. H. Lewes. Bohn, London, 1853, section 1, p. 9.

substances; and the positive phase that in which causes are not looked for either above or in matter, but *laws*. Conditions, not theories, form the fundamental groundwork of the Positive scheme.

The fourth and last volume of Comte's 'Polity' was published in 1854, the first year of George Eliot's union with Lewes, and Lewes was an ardent admirer of the Frenchman's philosophy. In the classification of the sciences which Comte effected, Sociology is placed in the list after Biology, on the ground that the facts of human society may not be successfully studied without reference to the facts of animal life. Mr. Lewes' interest in Comte was undoubtedly due, primarily, to this scientific method, the "scientific doctrine" appealing to him as an enthusiastic student of biology, and awakening in him a curiosity to discover the intermediary relations between the various forms of life; and although he never accepted the full doctrine of Comte, and published his divergences with sufficient emphasis to sever the friendship existing between them,[1] Comte's attempt at co-ordination was nevertheless enough to rank Lewes among the Positivists.

The social doctrine as the aim of the system, of which the scientific doctrine was the preparation, dominated George Eliot's thought because it arranged the life of man — his mind, his force, his hopes and aspirations — in an order which gave the fullest scope to its beneficent play. Comte had no faith in political salvations, in righteousness made easy by parliaments, but recognized the profound truth that social excel-

---

[1] Leslie Stephen: article 'Lewes' in 'Dictionary of National Biography.'

lence must be the result of moral effort. Selfishness blocks this effort, and the social feeling blocks selfishness, egoism giving place to altruism. Intellect had been enslaved by the Church, and had naturally revolted. The feelings had been unduly exalted, and were in consequence unduly debased. Now was the intellect to serve the feelings, not in the old slavish way, but with a new glad liberty. This is religion, which in view of the illimitable network of life, must include all of that life in its scope. The great universal order which the inter-relationship of the sciences revealed was always before George Eliot; but the chief scientific value of Positivism was for her, as it was for Comte himself, in its application to human conduct.

An explanation of her charity — what I have called her compassion — is discoverable in her adoption of the Positive classification, for it taught her that a man, as a member of human society, could not be understood unless the facts of that portion of the society which constituted his environment were properly comprehended; which, in turn, were to be understood only by a comprehension of the biological conditions upon which the facts of human society rest. Before utterly condemning a man's lamentable shortcomings, therefore, we should consider several things, — environment, habit, heredity, — and should temper our judgments accordingly. But this simply afforded a scientific excuse for the religious end and aim of the philosophy, — altruism. The ruling power within the great universal order, bringing it "continually to perfection by constantly conforming to its laws" — its soul and its spirit — is Humanity, which Comte elevates to the throne of divinity, calling it "Our Providence," and "The Great Being." "This undeniable Providence, the supreme dispenser of our destinies, becomes in the natural course the common centre of our affections, our thoughts, and our actions. Although this Great Being evidently exceeds the utmost strength of any, even of any collective human force, its necessary constitution and its peculiar function endow it with the truest sympathy towards all its servants. The least amongst us ought constantly to aspire to maintain and even to improve this Being. This natural object of all our activity, both public and private, determines the true general character of the rest of our existence, whether in feeling or in thought; which must be devoted to love, and to know, in order rightly to serve, our Providence, by a wise use of all the means which it furnishes to us. Reciprocally, the continued service, whilst strengthening our true unity, renders us at once both happier and better."[1]

In other words, Comte said: Religion belongs to life. Life is, in its fullest development, Humanity. The God of religion is therefore Humanity. And while some of his scientific followers, like Littré, base their support exclusively on the first half of his work, going so far as to think that the extravagances of the reactionary last half are due to mental unbalance, the effort in the "Polity" at superstructure on a hitherto laid foundation is nevertheless apparent. It is, indeed, reactionary in so far as it has to account for the Absolute, which is excluded in the "Philosophy" as not properly subject to law, and as therefore not a subject for scientific, *i. e.*, positive, thought. But the wants

---

[1] 'System of Positive Polity' by Auguste Comte. Longmans, Green & Co., London, 1875, vol. ii., p. 53.

of man's nature must be taken into account; and so, under the same necessity which forced Kant to write his second Kritik, we have Comte's " social doctrine." It is the old story. Neither Kant nor Comte can eliminate God.

George Eliot, like Mr. Lewes, never went the full length of Comtism. Her sense of humor, no doubt, prevented her from joining the Positivist church, and she must have looked with pity upon the amazing sacerdotalism which it borrowed from the Catholics. She acknowledges it to be one-sided.[1] But it influenced her more than any other influence of her life. Writing from Biarritz in 1867, she says, " . . . after breakfast we both read the 'Politique' — George one volume and I another, interrupting each other continually with questions and remarks. That morning study keeps me in a state of enthusiasm through the day — a moral glow which is a sort of *milieu subjectif* for the sublime sea and sky;" and Mr. Cross says: "For all Comte's writing she had a feeling of high admiration, intense interest, and very deep sympathy. I do not think I ever heard her speak of any writer with a more grateful sense of obligation for enlightenment."[2] Her selective discernment rejected the ritual, the sacerdotal claims, the extraordinary pretensions to dictatorship of a thinker whose exalted motive she reverenced; and while she never consciously worshipped humanity, the animating idea of Comte's system she recognized as the best idea for men. Her books quiver with it, and all her contrasts are drawn with the intention of showing the two contending forces in interplay: egoism and altruism; the self-concentration which in ministering to personal grati-

[1] 'Life,' vol. ii., p. 139. [2] *Ib.*, vol. iii., p. 419.

fications, to the exclusion of the social good, hinders that good according to the varying degrees of its pernicious activity; and, opposed to this, the centring of the life on a sympathetic attempt towards perfecting and ever more perfecting the social good by relegating self to its proper place among the other units. Thus Casaubon plays against Dorothea, Rosamond against Lydgate, Tito against Romola, Romola against Savonarola, Sylva against Zarca, Esther and Harold against Felix and Mr. Lyon. The cold, deadening, snaky qualities of Grandcourt's egoism become repellent to Gwendolen only as the opposing warm, vivifying, sympathetic altruism of Deronda begins to stream upon her.

It was an heroic belief, for she was fighting under a standard which had no standard-bearer; and it is as fine a spectacle as that of the Spartans fighting in the shade. There was no exemplar, no Captain of salvation. The Luther she admires could not have fought thus, and the finest tribute to her Savonarola must always be that it is true to the Christian ideal of Christ, without which the historical Savonarola could not have defied the powers of darkness.

VIII

It is not quite fair to say that the sadness of George Eliot's work comes from a lack of belief in a divine Person, or from a disbelief in Christian immortality, because there are a good many "orthodox" novelists who are sad, and not a few agnostics who are merry. George Eliot did not make life sad; she *found* it so, just as the painter finds the sunset tender, and so represents it on his canvas. Furthermore, the genius of the author is engaged in the demonstration of why it is sad, and in suggesting the removal, or at least the bettering of its conditions by the substitution of sympathy for selfishness.

Egoism is sin, she says again and again; and she believes that its wages is death — the death of noble effort and strenuous moral activity, of high purpose and generous endeavor, of "the thoughts that urge man's search to vaster issues," of goodness in a world meant to be good — for so she believed — and of that love which is its essence. So far as moral purpose is concerned, what more does the Christian believe? Christianity, indeed, holds positively what Positivism holds positively, but it also holds positively what Positivism implicitly denies.

George Eliot said she would consent to have a year clipt off her life "for the sake of witnessing such a scene as that of the men of the barricades [in Paris] bowing to the image of Christ, who first taught fraternity to men."[1] In her early days at least Christian teaching did not dwell as tenaciously as it does now on the brotherhood of man. The Evangelicalism of her childhood certainly did not inculcate a knowledge of belief in, and love for, the fatherhood of God because of the brotherhood of man, through the connecting link of Christ the Elder Brother. The Suffering Christ was, on the one hand, too much of a theological idea, and, on the other, too much of a mechanical picture, to hinder the growing thought of the young century from forming new ideas of fraternity entirely freed from the theological standards

---

[1] 'Life,' vol. i., p. 179. In a letter concerning the second French revolution.

which had in large part ceased to convince. To-day there is a convergence of Christian and agnostic altruism, and their ethical standards are practically identical. It is because the fulness of Christianity, which in the inertness of those evil days — evil because inert — lay shrivelled in dry formulas, has now opened upon the Church with its beautiful humanities, with its practical enforcements to "do good and distribute," and with its benevolences, guilds, and brotherhoods as the direct outcome of its spirit.

Christianity, as Mr. Mallock has pointed out, has so permeated the thought of man that it has become "mixed" with that thought; and thinkers like George Eliot are, in spite of theoretical beliefs and disbeliefs, bound to breathe a moral air saturated with Christian principles. When Dorothea, after her night of agony, goes to Rosamond, she sinks the selfish promptings of a justifiable indignation in a large charity which lovingly discerns the evil inherent in the indignation if nourished to the exclusion of the "precious seeing" of the possibilities of allaying the troubles even of the personal cause of the indignation; and by so doing becomes the "sweet presence of a good diffused" which will bear its share in the general progress towards light and right. We instinctively say she does a *Christian* act. She suffers long, and nevertheless is kind. She does unto others as she would, in her best moments, have others do unto her. Dorothea, we are told, had ceased to pray, apparently on the ground that prayer is egotistical (as if good Christians limited their petitions to personal requests, like Bulstrode. The noblest prayer, the pre-eminently Christian prayer, Christ's own prayer, is the opposite of this[1]); but if conduct *is* three-fourths of life, then that proportion of her life is Christian. It is the other quarter which she misses, and which her creator missed.

IX

Had George Eliot's star arisen a little later, it would, I think, have shone in a clearer sky. We have seen how impressionable, how malleable she was. The doctrine of evolution was in its earliest development in her day, — the scientists of her acquaintance holding that life was the creature of organism, and therefore material and not immortal. She might, if living now, be entertaining the hope of the evolutionists who followed Darwin, that life is not the creature, but the maker of organism, — a hope entirely consistent with the hope of Christianity. We must consider George Eliot the greatest of all moralists in literature, because, in view of the terrible consequences of a materialistic conviction of life upon a naturally idealistic temperament, her emotions are stirred all the more generously by the aspect of the pain involved in the constant struggle for existence. With no faith in another, future, life to explain the purpose of that struggle, she nevertheless found a moral philosophy in the contemplation of a life of

---

[1] She herself says, in 'Daniel Deronda': "The most powerful movement of feeling with a liturgy is the prayer which seeks for nothing special, but is a yearning to escape from the limitations of our own weakness, and an invocation of all Good to enter and abide with us; or else a self-oblivious lifting up of gladness, a Gloria in Excelsis that such good exists; both the yearning and the exaltation gathering their utmost force from the sense of communion in a form which has expressed them both for long generations of struggling fellow-men."

social helpfulness which was, to all practical intents and purposes, Christian.[1]

She sees duty in the light of moral emotion, rather than in that of religious enthusiasm. But the important point is that it is duty that she sees. She was neither a Far Seer like Emerson, nor a prophet like Ruskin, nor a cold Wisdom like Goethe. She admired Emerson so much on meeting him in 1848 as to say, "I have seen Emerson,— the first *man* I have ever seen."[2] But her genius had really but little in common with a transcendentalism which, like a flying machine beyond the control of its maker, is likely to land one in a morass beyond the highways of human experience. And her feeling for others, her reverence for the reverence of others, as a part of the force spiritualizing the solidarity of mankind, would have restrained her from the occasional extravagances of Emerson, such as his "Jesus would absorb the race; but Tom Paine or the coarsest blasphemer helps humanity by resisting this exuberance of power." As for prophecy, it is nearer to the human heart to tell of actual experiences in the light of present known conditions than to foretell future conditions involving experiences not yet actual. And the danger underlying the Ruskin attitude is sufficiently indicated in the cruelly mistaken criticism of George Eliot's own work which the author of 'Modern Painters' persuaded an editor (doubtless by the magic of his name, for from scarcely another would it have been accepted) to publish.[3] Finally, as compared with

---

[1] It is significant that the last word she ever wrote was the word "affection," in her unfinished letter to Mrs. Strachey. 'Life,' vol. iii., p. 438.

[2] 'Life,' vol. i., p. 191.

[3] 'Fiction Fair and Foul,' *Nineteenth Century*, October, 1881.

Her Religion and Philosophy

Goethe, she may be said to have the wisdom which comes from experience. "Experientia docet," even though we must add, "tristiter." Goethe is her superior in a certain calm, sphynx-like wisdom, but, as he has himself said, he knew Man better than men; and he lacked the sympathy which must destroy this Olympian sagaciousness. If the humanity of George Eliot's wisdom sometimes prevented its freest exercise, it errs in high company. The wisest man who ever lived once said a foolish thing, for he said, "Everything is vanity;" whereas we who are not so wise know better. Wisdom, with a sympathetic thinker, is always seen through the *lumen humidum* of feeling. Goethe, on the contrary, saw life through dry spectacles.

X

"The idea of God," says George Eliot, in her essay against Evangelical teaching of the Cumming type, "is really moral in its influence,—it really cherishes all that is best and loveliest in man, only when God is contemplated as sympathizing with the pure elements of human feeling, as possessing infinitely all those attributes which we recognize to be moral in humanity;" and her quarrel with Dr. Cumming was precisely that his God was the opposite of this. "He is a God who, instead of adding his solar force to swell the tide of those impulses that tend to give humanity a common life in which the good of one is the good of all, commands us to check those impulses lest they should prevent us from thinking of his glory."

The God she here sketches as a possible ideal is, in reality, the God of the Christian ideal of these last times; while Dr. Cumming's divinity, so mercilessly exposed by her, is no longer a living God, because he cannot now be reconciled with noble feeling.[1] And though we must regard as illusions, George Eliot seems to say, much which has been accepted as fact, the illusions are only reprehensible when they do not fit into this sympathetic idea of God. After Harold Transome had left Mr. Lyon, on his electioneering tour, the author imagines a cynical sprite riding on one of the motes in the dusty study of the little minister, and making merry at his illusions in regard to the Radical candidate. She cannot help smiling herself, but she immediately falls to penitence and veneration.

[1] It is only certain kinds of preaching she objects to. "Yesterday, for the first time, we went to hear A. (a popular preacher). I remember what you said about his vulgar, false emphasis; but there remained the fact of his celebrity. I was glad of the opportunity. But my impression fell below the lowest judgment I ever heard passed upon him. He has a gift of a fine voice, very flexible and various; he is admirably fluent and clear in his language, and every now and then his enunciation is effective. But I never heard any pulpit reading and speaking which, in its level tone, was more utterly common and empty of guiding intelligence or emotion; it was as if the words had been learned by heart and uttered without comprehension by a man who had no instinct of rhythm or music in his soul. And the doctrine! It was a libel on Calvinism that it should be presented in such a form. I never heard any attempt to exhibit the soul's experience that was more destitute of insight. The sermon was against Fear, in the elect Christian, as being a distrust of God; but never once did he touch the true ground of fear — the doubt whether the signs of God's choice are present in the soul. We had plenty of anecdotes, but they were all poor and pointless, — Tract Society anecdotes of the feeblest kind. It was the most superficial grocer's-back-parlor view of Calvinistic Christianity; and I was shocked to find how low the mental pitch of our society must be, judged by the standard of this man's celebrity. . . .

"Just now, with all Europe stirred by events that make every conscience tremble after some great principle as a consolation

For what we call illusions are often, in truth, a wider vision of past and present realities — a willing movement of a man's soul with the larger sweep of the world's forces — a movement towards a more assured end than the chances of a single life. We see human heroism broken into units and say, This unit did little — might as well not have been. But in this way we might break a great army into units; in this way we might break sunlight into fragments, and think that this and the other might be cheaply parted with. Let us rather raise a monument to the soldiers whose brave hearts only kept the ranks unbroken, and met death — a monument to the faithful who were not famous, and who are precious as the continuity of the sunbeams is precious, though some of them fall unseen and on barrenness.

At present, looking back on that day at Treby, it seems to me that the sadder illusion lay with Harold Transome, who was trusting in his own skill to shape the success of his own morrows, ignorant of what many yesterdays had determined for him beforehand.

This inclusive brotherhood was always in her vision, and the large view of it here shown is but an extension

and guide, it was too exasperating to sit and listen to doctrine that seemed to look no further than the retail Christian's tea and muffins. He said, 'Let us approach the throne of God,' very much as he might have invited you to take a chair; and then followed this fine touch: 'We feel no love to God because he hears the prayers of others; it is because he hears *my* prayer that I love him.'"—'Life,' vol. iii., pp. 121 *seq.*

In a letter to Mrs. Ponsonby, from Hertfordshire, she says: "I prefer a country where I don't make bad blood by having to see one public house to every six dwellings — which is literally the case in many spots around us. My gall rises at the rich brewers in parliament and out of it, who plant these poison shops for the sake of their million-making trade, while probably their families are figuring somewhere as refined philanthropists or devout evangelicals and ritualists."—'Life,' vol. iii., p. 245. See also vol. iii., pp. 253-255.

The nobler preaching, like the nobler living, she had no quarrel with.

of that simple elementary feeling which stirs the pulses of a child, as surely as it awakens the desires of a man. As Tom and Maggie were setting out for their home on that desolate November morning, their youth already joined with sorrow, —

> Mrs. Stelling came with a little basket, which she hung on Maggie's arms, saying, "Do remember to eat something on the way, dear." Maggie's heart went out towards this woman whom she had never liked, and she kissed her silently. It was the first sign within the poor child of that new sense which is the gift of sorrow — that susceptibility to the bare offices of humanity which raises them into a bond of loving fellowship, as to haggard men among the icebergs the mere presence of an ordinary comrade stirs the deep fountains of affection.[1]

XI

This, then, was the religion of George Eliot. She would doubtless have preferred Positivism to have remained a controlling philosophy without its ecclesiastical development; just as Martineau wished to restrain Unitarian thinkers from uniting in a Unitarian denomination. But the universal tendency of abstract religious thought is inevitably towards outward ritual organization; and an attempt to free religious thought from the narrowness of sect resulted in the addition of a new sect with thoughts unfreed. Ideas, with George Eliot, were "strong agents" be-

---

[1] To those who are curious to learn how such new teaching as George Eliot's and George Macdonald's affect a pronounced "Evangelical" mind, it might be interesting to consult 'The Religion of our Literature,' by George McCrie. Hodder and Stoughton, London, 1875.

cause taken in a "solvent of feeling." "The great world-struggle of developing thought is continually foreshadowed in the struggle of the affections, seeking justification for hope and love." Like her Romola, she distrusted "phantoms and disjointed whispers in a world where there was the large music of reasonable speech and the warm grasp of living hands." Yet in the classical chapter in which Romola faces her lot and decides to leave Tito, the memory of the interview with her dying brother is thrust upon her, and she longs to understand the experience which guided his life, and which gave "a new sisterhood" [mark the word of fellowship] to the wasted face. This memory blends with that of Savonarola offering himself in the Duomo as a sacrifice for the people, and makes her thirst for these waters "at which men drank and found strength in the desert." She saw no visions herself, as "she sat weary in the darkness." "Revealed religion" was not revealed to her.

No radiant angel came across the gloom with a clear message for her. In those times, as now, there were human beings who never saw angels or heard perfectly clear messages. Such truth as came to them was brought confusedly in the voices and deeds of men not at all like the seraphs of unfailing wing and piercing vision — men who believed falsities as well as truths, and did the wrong as well as the right. The helping hands stretched out to them were the hands of men who stumbled and often saw dimly, so that these beings unvisited by angels had no other choice than to grasp that stumbling guidance along the path of reliance and action, which is the path of life, or else to pause in loneliness and disbelief, which is no path, but the arrest of inaction and death.

Inaction to George Eliot meant death, because it meant a selfish loneliness; and although the guidance was stumbling, it was along the path of life. The radiant visions of a transcendental faith were not hers, but hers was the "precious seeing"—"that bathing of all objects in a solemnity as of a sunset glow, which is begotten of a loving, reverent emotion." Although the choir invisible to her meant a very different thing from what was understood by the writer of ". . . the King eternal, immortal, invisible," it is a fine choir and it sings true. *Non omnis moriar*, she cries, even though I go down to dusty death, and worms eat me. "The memory of the just shall live," is the key-note of her 'Jubal.' What if the new race knew him not on his return? They were singing his music: what was he to that? She says at the conclusion of her 'Death of Moses':

> He has no tomb.
> He dwells not with you dead, but lives as law.

When Armgart's voice fails her, and her whole world — the world of art — is destroyed, she contemplates suicide. Walpurga, standing for the vast army of human beings outside that world, tells her that although her career in song is ended, she is not therefore sunk to such moral penury as that.

> Noble rebellion lifts a common load,
> But what is he who flings his own load off
> And leaves his fellows toiling? Rebel's right?
> Say rather, the deserter's.

Then Armgart, slowly awakening to the realization that there may be pain around her beside her own, complains that if there were one near her now suffering like herself and needing her for comfort, it would be worth while for her to live.

WALPURGA

One, near you? why, they throng! you hardly stir
But your act touches them. We touch afar.
For did not swarthy slaves of yesterday
Leap in their bondage at the Hebrews' flight,
Which touched them through the thrice millennial dark?
But you can find the sufferer you need
With touch less subtle.

ARMGART

Who has need of me?

WALPURGA

Love finds the need it fills . . .

So Positivism, like Christianity, sets its face against suicide, — another illustration of the fact that this system is but the *morality* of Christianity. You may partake of the largesse of nature, yet be paupers of grace. Grace holds, though nature fails.

She is remorseless where the morale is at stake, as is seen in her treatment of Savonarola, and in her unanswerable position against Young and Cumming. And she had a direct hand in removing the prevailing pietistic notion that right actions should be performed on earth because of rewards laid up in heaven.[1] "That

---

[1] As an indication of this changed feeling, it is interesting to note that the latest revised hymnal of the Episcopal church omits the hymn 'For the Apostle's glorious company,' the last stanza of which is:

> For martyrs who with rapture-kindled eye,
> Saw the bright crown descending from the sky,
> And died to grasp it, Thee we glorify.

This was hymn 186 of the previous edition. The reason given for the omission by one of the bishops of the committee of revision is that the idea of suffering the death of martyrdom in order to grasp even a heavenly crown is an idea unworthy of a virile Christianity.

is the path we all like," she says — and her picture of Maggie here contains a reminiscent hint of her own girlhood — "that is the path we all like when we set out on our abandonment of egoism — the path of martyrdom and endurance, where the palm-branches grow, rather than the steep highway of tolerance, just allowance, and self-blame, where there are no leafy honors to be gathered and worn."

But it is of the utmost importance to separate the record of her personal religious beliefs, as recorded in her diary and letters, — not intended for publication, — from the artistic work of her fictions: we must judge her from that latter absolutely, and not relatively from the other. In the letter to Dr. Allbut quoted by Oscar Browning,[1] she says: "You must perceive the bent of my mind is conservative rather than destructive, and that denial has been wrung from me by hard experience — not adopted as a pleasant rebellion. Still, I see clearly that we ought, each of us, not to sit down and wail, but to be heroic and constructive, if possible, like the strong souls who lived before, as in other cases of religious decay." Her genius was utterly opposed to all attacks upon vital current belief; not only because it was vital, and therefore ministering to the public good, but because, even though she could not sympathize intellectually with all its developments, she would not hurt those who loved and trusted her.[2] This is why she would not write

---

[1] 'Life of George Eliot,' by Oscar Browning. Walter Scott, London, 1890, p. 119.

[2] "Pray don't ever ask me again not to rob a man of his religious belief, as if you thought my mind tended to such robbery. I have too profound a conviction of the efficacy that lies in all sincere faith, and the spiritual blight that comes with no-faith, to have any nega-

reviews after the awakening of her creative nature. She had to do with humanity, which means the whole man, including the heart; reviewing was too apt to overlook the heart in the concentration of its gaze upon the head. She wished to be a religious writer because she wished to help the whole man; and only

tive propagandism in me. I have very little sympathy with Freethinkers as a class, and have lost all interest in mere antagonism to religious doctrines. I care only to know, if possible, the lasting meaning that lies in all religious doctrine from the beginning till now." — Letter to Madame Bodichon, 'Life,' vol. ii., p. 343.

"All the great religions of the world, historically considered, are rightly the objects of deep reverence and sympathy — they are the record of spiritual struggles which are the types of our own. This is to me pre-eminently true of Hebrewism and Christianity, on which my own youth was nourished. And in this sense I have no antagonism towards any religious belief, but a strong outflow of sympathy. Every community met to worship the highest Good (which is understood to be expressed by God) carries me along in its main current; and if there were not reasons against my following such an inclination, I should go to church or chapel constantly, for the sake of the delightful emotions of fellowship which come over me in religious assemblies — the very nature of such assemblies being the recognition of a binding belief or spiritual law, which is to lift us into willing obedience, and save us from the slavery of unregulated passion or impulse. And with regard to other people, it seems to me that those who have no definite conviction which constitutes a protesting faith, may often more beneficially cherish the good within them and be better members of society by a conformity based on the recognized good in the public belief, than by a non-conformity which has nothing but negatives to utter. *Not*, of course, if the conformity would be accompanied by a consciousness of hypocrisy. That is a question for the individual conscience to settle. But there is enough to be said on the different points of view from which conformity may be regarded, to hinder a ready judgment against those who continue to conform after ceasing to believe in the ordinary sense. But with the utmost largeness of allowance for the difficulty of deciding in special cases, it must remain true that the highest lot is to have definite beliefs about which you feel that 'necessity is laid upon you' to declare them, as something better which you are bound to try and give to those who have the worse." — Letter to Mr. Cross, 'Life,' vol. iii., p. 216.

in fiction can art and morality come together for such a purpose. The sadness of her novels is not, indeed, because of a loss of "Evangelical" faith. She felt, in common with all conscientious well-wishers and hard workers for an improved, the burden of an unimproved, humanity, and she felt it more intensely than most. It was largely an impersonal burden that she bore — the burden of Nineveh, the burden of the world — and it was calculated to enforce profoundly sober tones. So far as mere gloom is concerned, no portion of her life, as revealed in her letters, is so full of shadow as that early part of it which felt the torture of the Calvinistic screws. There is a general uplifting of spirit and an increasing serenity of vision as that period retrogresses. While she does not wear her religion like a prophylactic ring, her agnosticism is not militant, like Huxley's; and it appears in the novels only on the side which is the negative side of Christianity. She recognized with a satisfying fulness that philosophical intolerance is more repugnant than religious intolerance, and her hard raps are for the sects of thought, and not the sects of faith.[1] She always ac-

---

[1] "As to the necessary combinations through which life is manifested, which seem to present themselves to you as a hideous fatalism which ought logically to petrify your volition, — have they, *in fact*, any such influence on your ordinary course of action in the primary affairs of your existence as a human, social, domestic creature? And if they don't hinder you from taking measures for a bath, without which you know that you cannot secure the delicate cleanliness which is your second nature, why should they hinder you from a line of resolve in a higher strain of duty to your ideal, both for yourself and others? But the consideration of molecular physics is not the direct ground of human love and moral action, any more than it is the direct means of composing a noble picture or of enjoying great music. One might as well hope to dissect one's own body, and be merry in doing it, as take molecular physics (in which you must banish from your

knowledged the mystery that lay "under the processes." Her soul abhorred all negative propaganda; and she did not engage in that worst of futilities of making her opinions mark time with her religion, because her opinions were her religion.

Indeed, if we had to construct her religious position solely from the internal evidence of her fiction, — which is really all we do have to do, — we should place her faith in a personal God several degrees higher than we know it was, from the external evidence, so careful was she not to intrude metaphysical dogma into the place of moral sympathy. Mr. Myers has pictured in burning colors his impressions of her convictions as he walked with her, one evening, in the Fellows garden at Trinity, listening to her terribly earnest utterances as to the inconceivability of God and immortality, and the peremptory and absolute need of duty:

Never, perhaps, have sterner accents affirmed the sovereignty of impersonal and unrecompensing Law. I listened, and night fell; her grave, majestic countenance turned

---

field of view what is specifically human) to be your dominant guide, your determiner of motives, in what is solely human. That every study has its bearing on every other is true; but pain and relief, love and sorrow, have their peculiar history which make an experience and knowledge over and above the swing of atoms." — Letter to the Hon. Mrs. Ponsonby, 'Life,' vol. iii., p. 245.

"I should urge you to consider your early religious experience as a portion of valid knowledge, and to cherish its emotional results in relation to objects and ideas which are either substitutes or metamorphoses of the earlier. And I think we must not take every great physicist — or other 'ist' — for an apostle, but be ready to suspect him of some crudity concerning relations that lie outside his special studies, if his exposition strands us on results that seem to stultify the most ardent massive experience of mankind, and hem up the best part of our feelings in stagnation." — *Ib.*, vol. iii., p. 253.

towards me like a sibyl's in the gloom; it was as though she removed from my grasp, one by one, the two scrolls of promise, and left me the third scroll only, awful with inevitable fates. And when we stood at length and parted, amid that columnar circuit of the forest trees, beneath the last twilight of starless skies, I seemed to be gazing like Titus at Jerusalem on vacant seats and empty halls; in a sanctuary with no Presence to hallow it, and a heaven left lonely of a God.[1]

Yet this was not the talk of her books. There are no positive negations there. She had no controversy with faith, and she longed to satisfy "the need of those who want a reason for living in the absence of what has been called consolatory belief." So far as she had herself to reckon with, she regarded "religious exercises" as a kind of opium which she refused to take, preferring wide-awake pain to a drugged unconsciousness. But she frankly acknowledges that "there must be limits or negations" in her experience which may screen from her "many possibilities of blessedness for our suffering human nature." Where faith did not reconcile with reason, she saw not faith, but unreason; and "as a strong body struggles against fumes with the more violence when they begin to be stifling, a strong soul struggles against phantasies with all the more alarmed energy when they threaten to govern in the place of thought." And this discriminating power was of service in restraining her from that implicit acquiescence in the marvels of those modern "isms" and "ologies" which have wrecked more credulous souls of high intelligence. Her analytical tendency is sometimes

[1] *Century Magazine*, vol. xxiii., p. 62.

her misfortune, but her letter to Mrs. Stowe is an indication of its beneficent side:

Perhaps I am inclined, under the influence of the facts, physiological and psychological, which have been gathered of late years, to give larger place to the interpretation of vision-seeing as *subjective* than the Professor would approve. It seems difficult to limit — at least to limit with any precision — the possibility of confounding sense by impressions, derived from inward conditions, with those which are directly dependent on external stimulus. In fact, the division between within and without in this sense seems to become every year a more subtle and bewildering problem.

Your experience with the *planchette* is amazing; but that the words which you found it to have written were dictated by the spirit of Charlotte Brontë is to me (whether rightly or not) so enormously improbable that I could only accept it if every condition was laid bare, and every other explanation demonstrated to be impossible. If it were another spirit aping Charlotte Brontë, — if here and there at rare spots and among people of a certain temperament, or even at many spots and among people of all temperaments, tricksy spirits are liable to rise as a sort of earth-bubbles and set furniture in movement, and tell things which we either know already or should be as well without knowing, — I must frankly confess that I have but a feeble interest in these doings, feeling my life very short for the supreme and awful revelations of a more orderly and intelligible kind, which I shall die with an imperfect knowledge of. If there were miserable spirits whom we could help, then I think we should pause and have patience with their trivial-mindedness; but otherwise I don't feel bound to study them more than I am bound to study the special follies of a particular phase of human society. Others, who feel differently, and are attracted towards this study, are making an experiment for us as to whether anything better than bewilderment can come of it. At present, it seems to me that to rest any fundamental part of religion on such a basis is a melancholy misguidance of men's minds from the true sources of high and pure emotion.[1]

So little ground did she give for offence to the "little ones" that a reviewer in the *Westminster*, after her death, makes complaint that her art caused her to sympathize unduly with the old creeds, considering her abandonment of Christian dogma, and that the claims of the new creed and the new life were not directly recognized at all. But she did all she could do as an artist, both positively for the old beliefs and negatively for the new. Indeed, the most adverse criticisms of her art have been based on what has been taken as its didactic subservience to her morality; and it is subservient in the sense that the music of a mass is subservient to the idea of worship. She admires Sir Christopher Cheverel for the virility of his art enthusiasms, which places them on a *moral* plane.

"An obstinate, crotchety man," said his neighbors. But I, who have seen Cheverel Manor as he bequeathed it to his heirs, rather attribute that unswerving architectural purpose of his, conceived and carried out through long years of systematic personal exertion, to something of the fervor of genius, as well as inflexibility of will; and in walking through those rooms, with their splendid ceilings and their meagre furniture, which tell how all the spare money had been absorbed before personal comfort was thought of, I have felt that there dwelt in this old English baronet some of that sublime spirit which distinguishes art from luxury, and worships beauty apart from self-indulgence.

---

[1] 'Life,' vol. iii., pp. 160 *seq*. See also a former letter to Mrs. Stowe, on the same subject, 'Life,' vol. iii., pp. 92 *seq*.

She could not have formed new religions, in justice to her reiterated pleas for faithfulness to the old ideals. For while it is true that there is in her life a sad lack of that peculiar humility of the simple Christian which makes the wise things of the world foolish, there is nevertheless a saving modesty which prevents her rashness from running the full length of out-and-out Free Thinking.

I dislike extremely a passage in which you appear to consider the disregard of individuals as a lofty condition of mind. My own experience and development deepen every day my conviction that our moral progress may be measured by the degree in which we sympathize with individual suffering and individual joy. The fact that in the scheme of things we see a constant and tremendous sacrifice of individuals is, it seems to me, only one of the many proofs that urge upon us our total inability to find in our own natures a key to the divine mystery. I could more readily turn Christian, and worship Jesus again, than embrace a Theism which professes to explain the proceedings of God.[1]

She saw that a rationalistic creed is a contradictory impossibility; that rationalism is possible, and that a creed is possible, but not the two in combination. "Hopes," indeed, "have precarious life,"

> "But faithfulness can feed on suffering,
> And knows no disappointment."

And duty is the residuum. We see it through a light magnified by religion, because all of George Eliot's religion is in it. What makes the moral philosophies so spiritually dull is the mechanical divorce of religion from morality generally to be discovered

[1] Letter to Charles Bray, 'Life,' vol. i., p. 472.

in them, as though the two belonged to separate spheres. George Eliot's morality shines with a brilliance cast from Christianity. It is as a light permeating cathedral glass. That pale worker in the study bends not the knee in the adjoining minster, but the glow of the minster's window fills the workshop. When 'Felix Holt' appeared, a writer in a religious periodical exclaimed: "Felix's religious system, it seems to us, borrows everything from Christianity except its creed, and is represented as fulfilling the commands of the Beatitudes without looking for their blessing." That is true, and had George Eliot read it, she would have been pleased with her infringement of the rule against the reading of reviews.

She does not always see duty in the soft raiment belonging to kings' houses. She stands at times under the thunder-scarred tops of tall Sinais, and lies prone on desert sands as the storm hurtles by. The black tempest of Maggie's great temptation was thus pierced by the white light of moral truth. "A great terror was upon her, as if she were ever and anon seeing where she stood, by great flashes of lightning, and then again stretched forth her hands in the darkness."[1]

---

[1] The comparison which is sometimes found between George Eliot and Lucretius is not really a comparison, but a contrast. He was concerned with causes; she, with laws. He "denied divinely the divine;" in George Eliot's fiction there is not even the religious denial of religion. Revelation, if we come to the final analysis, has no place in the scope of phenomena viewed as working in the domain of law; and as George Eliot confines our human vision to that universe as the one most easily comprehensible, her religious influence is greater than it would have been had she been moved by "orthodox" zeal to impose a revelation upon her art, to explain supernaturally what, in art, may better be explained naturally. The Christian reader is quite capable of seeing the supernatural back of the natural, and working through it; for he believes that God is in law as well as that He is the cause of it.

Apart from ironical usage, and such places where one would naturally expect it, as in Tryan's talks with Janet, Dinah's exhortations, and Savonarola's preaching, the word 'sin' occurs less than a dozen times in her novels, and not once, I believe, in her two latest works. Taken together, George Eliot's full definition of the "exceeding sinfulness of sin" is something like this: Sin is the incurrence of a necessity for deceit, and the cause of suffering. And so diffusive is that suffering that even justice becomes a retribution spreading "beyond its mark in pulsations of unmerited pain." It is a lie against the truth of nature, and is therefore unnatural. It is a lie against the wise order of the universe, and its result is therefore disorder and discordant unhappiness. It is what makes that hard crust around the soul which can be pierced by no pitying voice. It is the cold damp vault where despair abides, and where the morning sun and sweet pure air are not felt. It is vain personal regrets indulged in to the harm of helpful activities. If it aims at particular concrete things, particular concrete consequences will follow. It is not a mere "question of doctrine and inward penitence." Its incorporate past will rise in unmanageable solidity before the eyes of the present. It is the reverse and the denial of the need of the prayer—

> Give me no light, great heaven, but such as turns
> To energy of human fellowship,
> No powers save the growing heritage
> That makes completer manhood. [1]

And on its border-land you are "harassed by assaults from the other side of the boundary."

[1] The motto of 'The Lifted Veil,' 'Life,' vol. iii., p. 195.

Now, is not this what theologians tell us the sin against the Holy Ghost is? Ought we not to be satisfied with it? It is just as much a Psalm of Life as Longfellow's, although it lacks the Christian teleology. Her grand Nemesis, with the swords in her hands, is as the faces which rise unbidden in the night; and in the solemn watches we hear the stifled cries. She echoes her sister poet's thought:

> There's not a crime
> But takes its proper change out still in crime,
> If once rung on the counter of this world.

And she construes crime to be every aim that ends with self. In spite of all the subtle efforts of Bulstrode to hide his past, that past rose before him at the moment when he thought himself the most secure; and when Arthur Donnithorne flattered himself that all was smooth sailing at last, the storm of his — as he foolishly thought forgotten — sin drove him a wreck upon the rocks. Her sinners are holden by the cords of their sins: it is as if they were in the clutch of some great sea-monster. She echoes the Scriptural emphasis that your sins will find you out. They rise incarnate in her novels and cry for vengeance, even as Baldassare rose across the sight of the dying Tito, and as the sin of Gwendolen in marrying Grandcourt rose before her in terrifying visions after his death, which she had — can there be any doubt of it? — caused.[1]

[1] Here, again, may be seen the greater fulness of Christianity, in that its doctrine of hell is but the Nemesis continued into future conditions, and arranged for such as fail to have their sins found out in this present life. We see that in many cases sins do not find out the living sinner, and yet we are told that our sins will find us out; so if not here, then somewhere else. What is hell but Nemesis? This is

Nor is she one of those fine Chateaubriands she makes Felix ridicule, who are forever shooting in the air. " Your dunce who can't do his sums has always a taste for the infinite. Sir, do you know what a rhomboid is? Oh, no, I don't value these things with limits." Whatever her hand found to do, she did it with might. Felix sees through Harold's generalities about a bridge being a good thing to make, though half the men working at it are rogues.

"Oh, yes!" said Felix, scornfully; "give me a handful of generalities and analogies, and I'll undertake to justify Burke and Hare, and prove them benefactors of their species. I'll tolerate no nuisances but such as I can't help; and the question now is, not whether we can do away with all the nuisances in the world, but with a particular nuisance under our noses."

It is this readiness to *do*, when once moved by genuine conviction that he ought to do, that saves Deronda. A little too much swaying between the infinite Good and the finite realization of that Good in himself would have ruined the character. He could very easily have been made one of those " large " souls who are ridiculous in a working-day world. As it is, he may not be considered a success from the " hustler's " standpoint; but there are other points of view than the commercial traveller's, highly important as those doubtless are. When Deronda is called, he answers; and the largeness and vagueness of the scheme makes the obedience all the more laudable;

not a doctrinal treatise, and I am not arguing for " orthodoxy." I have no mental conception of the quality or of the duration of future punishment, and I think it a waste of time to theorize about it. I merely wish to emphasize, in passing, the incompleteness of Positivism as compared with the rounded fulness of Christianity.

for, although *we* think it a mistake, *he* was willing to risk a probable failure in the light of a clear duty; which is the point at issue. We must look at it from his standpoint, not from ours. He was, at the last, "practical," although engaged in an impracticable scheme; and was so from the first, in the best sense of the word, because he acted in accordance with the promptings of a chivalric nature which did not allow itself to be confused by the every-day standards of "Society," nor, on the other hand, to be twisted into quixotic shape by too great a rebound from those standards. He is a combination of honor and common-sense; and if there was a fight on between him and Grandcourt, I should bet on Deronda.

XII

This feeling for the immediate good is strangely, and yet logically, mixed with a feeling for heredity. For distance is not measurable by time, but by radical differences in affinity; and ancestral claims are binding because they feed the feeling for and nourish the habit of a close filial reverence: they feed it and are therefore its parents. The indignation of Romola is against the treachery to her father's memory. A reconstructed Presence is to move in the old places, and it is as much a real Presence to the devout imagination as the actual presence was before to the visual eye. We are a part of it, bone of its bone, and it rules us from the grave.

George Eliot pushes the doctrine to its furthest limits. Squire Cass was hardly a man to inspire an affectionate memory; yet Nancy preserved "sacredly in a place of honor" the relics of her husband's de-

Her Religion and Philosophy

parted father, — a kind of Chinese worship, you see. It was the call from Jewish blood to Jewish blood that stirred the pulses of Deronda, although the author, foreseeing a difficulty there, turned her hero around his hard corner by making him fall in love with a Jewess; and not only that, but the sister of the man who put such an impossible burden upon him.

Without doubt, her theories of heredity are the direct result of her biological reading with Lewes; she extending, as is her wont, to the psychical the known laws of the physical. The solidarity of mankind may be preserved in its healthful order only by each unit keeping true to its intimate units; and what so intimate as the family? This is the theme of 'The Spanish Gypsy.' Silva is dominated by his past, by the " mystery of his Spanish blood; " and the attempted escape from this dominion makes the tragedy. His sudden killing of Zarca is explainable only by the reassertion of this rule, because there was nothing but hate between him and the Prior, whose death he was nevertheless thus *moved* to revenge. In leaving his place he disturbed —

> . . . the rich heritage
> Of nations fathered by a mighty past, —

a past which was a chambered Nautilus of memories, each linked with each in binding chains. Why, the very breeze and the breath of the sea are charged with them, for she chiefly thinks of the Mediterranean as " the Mid-sea which moans with memories."

Still further, the actual catastrophe is brought about by what some would say was an act of treachery; and yet fair warning was given to Silva that, under certain conditions, the secret would not be kept. These conditions were that if Sephardo, a Jew, could benefit *his own people* by using the secret in their behalf, he would not fail to do so. Loyalty to his kindred overrode loyalty to the trusting Silva, and the tragedy ensued.

Zarca is the embodiment of the contrast to Silva. He is the true unit remaining in its place. The grandeur of the conception is colossal. The ineffaceable memory of the past is all the more resurgent because it is a past of doom, despised and excommunicate; and by this past he calls Fedalma to her proper future, which she must tread "with naked bleeding feet," a future perhaps like the past —

> Where no man praised it and where no church blessed.

For my part, my sympathies are with Silva. The claims of heredity may be stretched too far. Something is due to the present as such, and the demands of the past may become too shadowy to be effectual. The tendency to variation under conditions of environment is as natural as the hereditary principle. There may be historic sympathy without historic rightness; and issue must be taken with "that Supreme, the irreversible Past." The past may be irreversible, but it is not perforce supreme, and if really dead, let it, in God's name, bury its dead. We feel that Fedalma is justified in her outburst against her father:

> Stay! never utter it!
> If it can part my lot from his whose love
> Has chosen me. Talk not of oaths, of birth,
> Of men as numerous as the dim white stars, —
> As cold and distant too, for my heart's pulse.
> . . . .

> No!
> I belong to him who loves me — whom I love —
> Who chose me — whom I chose — to whom I pledged
> A woman's truth. And that is nature too,
> Issuing a fresher law than laws of birth.

But, aside from this, the ethics of brotherhood are the only saving ethics. They teach that a wrong against another is an injury to society, to that vast solidarity which through all its vastness feels the shock of every evil deed, and trembles with delight at each impact of good. George Eliot's paper in 'Theophrastus'—'Moral Swindlers'—illuminates the needful lesson that a man's moral stature is not to be taken simply by his home life; that he may be a faithful husband and a tender father, and yet a bad public man, and effect more harm through his public misdeeds than another man of high civic virtue but of loose personal habits. She widens the view and the nomenclature of morality, and entirely removes it from the narrow limits in which that word is usually confined. She says of her imaginary Florentine in the Proem to 'Romola,' " He felt the evils of his time, for he was a man of public spirit, and public spirit can never be wholly immoral, since its essence is care for a common good."

XIII

And it is time to say that the emphasis she lays upon the wrong done to others by the careless assumption of unauthorized relations between the sexes is not the result of remorse at any false step of her own; but is intended to mark the difference between such relationships and her own, as she conceived this difference. That she erred, many believe who at the same time absolve her in their minds from all conscious wrong-doing; the barrier between her and George Sand is as the barrier between day and night. Feuerbach says, in the work George Eliot translated: "That alone is a religious marriage which is a true marriage, which corresponds to the essence of marriage-love." And she says of Jane Eyre, "All self-sacrifice is good, but one would like it to be in a somewhat nobler cause than that of a diabolical law which chains a man, soul and body, to a putrefying carcass," —a vitally interesting opinion, because it not only marks a clear distinction between George Eliot and Charlotte Brontë, but also because she considered Rochester's excuse as valid as her own.

The question is not so simple as some have supposed. The non-existence of the divorce court in 1854 was not the legal barrier to marriage between Lewes and Miss Evans, because that court requires conditions which could not have been complied with by the suing party. But her action was nevertheless a protest against what she thought was cruelly unjust legislation, or, rather, a cruel lack of just legislation. It is fair to assume that there was more of impulse in the step than she was conscious of. It is the same Marian Evans who at various stages repudiates music and gives up going to church with a suddenness that could not avoid a collision with her father. She does not appear to have blamed herself for this conflict between personal conviction and filial affection beyond the mere regret that it should have occurred; nor is there any self-blame evident for her union with Lewes, although, as we have seen, there is an ever-wakeful desire to differentiate such a union from loose and immoral connections. It is the same Miss Evans who surrendered Miss Lewis for Hennell's 'Inquiry,'—nay, who gave up an imperfect conception of Jesus Christ for an imperfect conception of Mr. Bray; and who did it with joy. Her character had developed, but her temperament had not changed.

Yet she would have warmly repudiated the charge that she had violated the sacramental nature of marriage in her union with a man whose wife was living; and she would have done so on the ground that while he was at one time joined to that wife by a solemn moral obligation, such an obligation had ceased to exist, and that the true marriage, after that cessation, was with her, Marian Evans. She did not violate a home, for there was no longer any home. Mr. Lewes' sons took the same view, and always called her "mother." She took the deepest interest in their welfare, and Charles, the only surviving son of George Lewes, became her heir.[1] Her view was that her act was against the social law accidentally in force at that time, but not against the fundamental idea of a sacred marriage tie; and she never wavered from that view. Lewes was always to her her "husband," and she insisted that her friends must so consider the relationship, or cease to be her friends.

No author has dwelt with fuller force on the binding relations of the marriage tie, notwithstanding this living protest against what she deemed an unjust law.

> She who willingly lifts up the veil of her married life has profaned it from a sanctuary into a vulgar place.

[1] Leslie Stephen: article 'Lewes,' Dictionary of National Biography.

"Marriage is so unlike everything else. There is something even awful in the nearness it brings. Even if we loved some one else better than — than those we were married to, it would be no use" — poor Dorothea, in her palpitating anxiety, could only seize her language brokenly — "I mean, marriage drinks up all our power of giving or getting any blessedness in that sort of love. I know it may be very dear, but it murders our marriage — and the marriage stays with us like a murder — and everything else is gone."

She paused. There was something else to be stripped away from her belonging to that past on which she was going to turn her back forever. She put her thumb and her forefinger to her betrothal ring; but they rested there without drawing it off. Romola's mind had been rushing with an impetuous current towards this act for which she was preparing: the act of quitting a husband who had disappointed all her trust; the act of breaking an outward tie that no longer represented the inward bond of love. But that force of outward symbols by which our active life is knit together so as to make an inexorable external identity for us, not to be shaken by our wavering consciousness, gave a strange effect to this simple movement towards taking off her ring, — a movement which was but a small sequence of her energetic resolution. It brought a vague but arresting sense that she was somehow violently rending her life in two, — a presentiment that the strong impulse which had seemed to exclude doubt and make her path clear might after all be blindness, and that there was something in human bonds which must prevent them from being broken with the breaking of illusions.

Romola went home and sat alone through the sultry hours of that day with the heavy certainty that her lot was unchanged. She was thrown back again on the conflict between the demands of an outward law which she recognized as a widely ramifying obligation and the demands of inner moral facts which were becoming more and more peremptory. She had drunk in deeply the spirit of that teaching by which Savonarola had urged her to return to her place. She felt that the sanctity attached to all close relations, and therefore pre-eminently to the closest, was but the expression in outward law of that result towards which all human goodness and nobleness must spontaneously tend; that the light abandonment of ties, whether inherited or voluntary, because they had ceased to be pleasant, was the uprooting of social and personal virtue.

She enforces her views by putting her favorite Romola into the wrong in fleeing from Tito, notwithstanding her great provocations, and by putting the rebuke on the lips of such a one as Savonarola. She is not free, he tells her, for she is a debtor. She owes the debt of a wife and of a Florentine woman. She has no right of choice. She is fleeing from the presence of God into the wilderness. How will she find good? "It is not a thing of choice; it is a river that flows from the foot of the Invisible Throne, and flows by the path of obedience." Man cannot choose his duties. Then comes that superb command of Savonarola to draw forth the crucifix she carries within her mantle. "There, my daughter, is the image of Supreme Offering made by Supreme Love, because the need of man was great." He bids her conform her life to that image, to make her sorrow an offering. And the heading of the first chapter in the next Book is "Romola *in her Place*."

The effect of the Christian teaching of Savonarola is so abiding with Romola that even when she discovers facts which would undoubtedly warrant, in the eyes of our century, absolute divorce, she determines not to attempt a second time a clandestine escape, but to come to an agreement with Tito concerning a limited separation. And yet she feels that, though the law is sacred, "rebellion might be sacred, too;" and she sees, in a flash, that her problem is essentially the same as Savonarola's, "the problem where the sacredness of obedience ended, and where the sacredness of rebellion began." So, when such an agreement with Tito as she had contemplated is found impossible, after her godfather's death, after the shock of the failure of her faith in Savonarola, when the burdens become unbearable, she flees again; and this time there is no arresting voice, and no blame on the part of any reader.

She questioned the justness of her own conclusions, of her own deeds: she had been rash, arrogant, always dissatisfied that others were not good enough, while she herself had not been true to what her soul had once recognized as the best. She began to condemn her flight: after all, it had been cowardly self-care; the grounds on which Savonarola had once taken her back were truer, deeper than the grounds she had had for her second flight. How could she feel the needs of others and not feel above all the needs of the nearest?

But then came reaction against self-reproach. The memory of her life with Tito, of the conditions which made their real union impossible, while their external union imposed a set of false duties on her which were essentially the concealment and sanctioning of what her mind revolted from, told her that flight had been her only resource. All minds, except such as are delivered from doubt by dulness of sensibility, must be subject to this recurring conflict where the many-twisted conditions of life have forbidden the fulfilment of a bond. For in strictness there is no replacing of relations: the presence of the new does not nullify the failure and breach of the old. Life has lost its perfection: it has been maimed; and until the wounds are quite scarred, conscience continually casts backward doubting glances.

We all know how the struggle ended.

The only "separations" in her novels are the separations of spirits made bitter, but through their bitterness sublime, by the galling chains which fasten in marital faithfulness. Who ever than Lydgate, than Dorothea, better fulfilled the awful words of the service which bound them "for better, for *worse*"? I do not know of any finer picture of a wife than the picture of Mrs. Bulstrode as she stands over the poor, beaten, irretrievably disgraced husband, and though ruined in his ruin, falling with his fall, her intense pride quenched in the quenched light of his, says to that broken idol, "Nicholas, look up!"

If we could only view it objectively, and apart from necessarily binding standards, we should have to acknowledge her union with Lewes as a true "inward" marriage. No two persons were ever more happily mated. While his critical suggestions may have occasionally interfered with the freest scope of her art, his acute cleverness yielded unquestioned acquiescence to all that was essential in her genius. It was, thus viewed, an ideal union, his mental sprightliness keying her to effort, and her moral earnestness stirring hitherto unawakened depths in him. He was her willing slave in every good sense. Each of her books acknowledged the indebtedness:

each is dedicated, in terms of constant affection, to her " husband."

Her marriage to Mr. Cross did not indicate a change of view in regard to the importance of legality and regularity in the marriage bond, which, as we have seen, she emphasizes with power in her writings, but merely that the union with Lewes would have been blessed by Church and State if she could have had it so. That it was not so blessed, she seems to say, was because of the cruel neglect of legislation, for which, in a more perfectly regulated State, room would be found, and to which neglect her " outward " conscience rose superior. It is the most positive proof in her career of the fallibility of any " outward " conscience which has not the universal sweep of exceptionless divine command, in the absence of which all other standards, however seemingly just, must clash. The result of her example demonstrates with convincing clearness the grand overtopping excellence of God-given over man-derived laws of conduct. The " outward " conscience does not, and never will, conform to any one rule in any two men unless it conform to one standard above them both, and beyond their human touch. It is not as if the divine law were a fetish, as if it were apart from all human understanding, to be followed blindly and sullenly by a frightened, awe-struck people; it is precisely the law, the only law, which the " outward " conscience represents. It ought not to be surprising that George Eliot failed to grasp that vital fact at the solemnest moment of her life, because the fact had passed, with the rest of her Christian belief, into the limbo of discarded faith. With her, it was not rebellion against God's law, because she did not believe that the law was God's in that it did not conform, in this given case, to the essential moral idea of God. She can only reason it out. The Christian's act of faith transcends reason. Not that the Christian is unsupported by reason, but the faith remains with those who lack the reason, and is supported by that which is above it.

That is all, I believe, that can be said for her, and it is a good deal, because it is all that can be said for one who was guided by no low motives, and who could honestly justify her course to her conscience. Perhaps in the last analysis, one must qualify that word "honestly;" for she loved much, and love is a casuist. It is easier to formulate philosophy for others than to abide by it ourselves; her Romola is truer than herself. But no genuine, generous student of her life ever for the smallest fraction of a second doubted her purity. It is hard for some to understand that because there is illegality there is not perforce an amour. Only once or twice did she break her silence in regard to this union, her letter to Mrs. Bray, soon after its formation, being intended as a sufficiently full explanation:

> If there is any one action or relation of my life which is, and always has been profoundly serious, it is my relation to Mr. Lewes. . . . Light and easily broken ties are what I neither desire theoretically nor could live for practically. Women who are satisfied with such ties do *not* act as I have done. . . . From the majority of persons, of course, we never looked for anything but condemnation. We are leading no life of self-indulgence, except, indeed, that, being happy in each other, we find everything easy. We are working hard to provide for others better than we

provide for ourselves, and to fulfil every responsibility that lies upon us. Levity and pride would not be a sufficient basis for that."[1]

And it speaks volumes for the recognition of her moral weight in the most thoughtful society of her country that its leaders — women as well as men — agreed to overlook the irregularity of the connection. It was not because of her genius, — at least, not because of that alone, for it is not presumable that the Rector of Lincoln and his wife, Mr. Goschen, Jowett of Balliol, the Hollands, would have received George Sand into their homes.

We cannot justify her course, because we are Christians; we must account for it, for the same reason.

XIV

We have seen how she tries to understand the spirit of Dino's monasticism, but her sympathies are enraged at his abandonment of Bardo. That fine old pagan complains that his son's ideas *elude* argument. There is, indeed, something evasive in even the weakest forms of religion, before which even the strongest moral philosophy is helpless. And even a philosophy that implicitly denies a Christian immortality, "in moments high," when "space widens in the soul," will stand mute and wondering before the reaches of the soul into the life beyond. Although Dorothea had ceased to pray, she cries out to her dead husband, "Do you not see *now* that I could not submit my soul to yours?"

[1] 'Life,' vol. i., p. 327 *seq.* See her remarks on the Byron incident, 'Life,' vol. iii., p. 100.

To sum up: was she a Christian? No, because she had lost faith in a personal Christ. Was she a theist? No, because, she had lost faith in a personal God. That is, No, to both these questions, as a philosopher; but — and this only concerns us — as a writer of fiction, Yes, for is she not the immortal creator of Mr. Tryan, whose memorial is his fervent faith? and of Savonarola, whose doctrine of submission is the doctrine of all the blessed saints? and of Dinah, whose life is a sacrament? Was there a contradiction, therefore, between her private philosophy and her public work? Yes, because in the latter she was, like all creators, divinely possessed; whereas philosophy is not creation, but reason; is not hot, but cold; is not mystic, but positive, even though Positivism be negative; has naught to do with the feelings, except as they are controlled by the intellect; is not, to conclude, sympathetic.[1] Does her philosophical negation make her writings irreligious? No, because she does not allow her personal views to influence her art; because she is all the more intensely religious by reason of her lack of religion; because she finds more religion in life than many find life in religion; because every positive word she has uttered is for Virtue and against Vice, is a shield for Truth, and against Deceit. Was she an optimist? No, she was too intellectually honest. Was she a pessimist? No,

---

[1] "My function is that of the *æsthetic*, not the doctrinal teacher — the rousing of the nobler emotions, which make mankind desire the social right, not the prescribing of special measures, concerning which the artistic mind, however strongly moved by social sympathy, is often not the best judge. It is one thing to feel keenly for one's fellow-beings; another to say, 'This step, and this alone, will be the best to take for the removal of particular calamities.'" — Letter to Mrs. Peter Taylor, 'Life' vol. iii., p. 300.

she was too careful of others. What was she? She was a "meliorist," pierced by "that thorn-pressure which must come with the crowning of the Sorrowful Better because of the Worse." She was a moralist of the finest fibre. Her books are standards set on high for all men to follow in righteousness and true holiness. And although she occasionally writes from "Grief Castle on the River of Gloom, in the Valley of Dolour," she has a strong message of peace, of comfort, and of courage.

B.—HER ART

I

In the sphere of art, Wordsworth and Dante influenced her the most closely.

We have so completely entered into Wordsworth's labors that his works do follow him as a matter of course in our undisputed basic conceptions of art; and it is only by an effort of the historic imagination that we can understand the revolutionary controversy their promulgation caused in the first year of the past century. All that he contended for was naturalness, and all that he contended against was its opposite. And where could naturalness have freer play than among people living in simple surroundings?

If we agree with Wordsworth that humble incidents may be dignified in poetry by the imagination, and that their true dignity, in poetic diction, is not only not fitly expressed, but thoroughly spoiled by artificially ornamental language, it follows that the thesis applies with more than equal force to prose. Wordsworth's argument was in defence of a theory of poetry; but as it was based on a theoretically accepted standard of prose, its acceptance had the joyous result of improving the style of prose as well. The most exciting novels of incident, to-day, which are at the same time works of art, are, notwithstanding the spur they apply to the craving for the extraordinary, not therefore " gross and violent stimulants " such as the "degrading thirst after outrageous stimulation" which, Wordsworth rightly charged, the taste of his day produced, one hundred years ago, in "frantic novels, sickly and stupid German tragedies, and deluges of idle and extravagant stories in verse."

Like Wordsworth, George Eliot strove to reproduce the emotional motive kindling her imagination, as opposed to the more vulgar method of arbitrarily choosing a theme, and working at it like a cobbler over a pair of shoes. Even in her "Evangelical" days she expresses her delight at meeting in Wordsworth so much of her own feeling; and this response she continued to enjoy throughout her life.

The indebtedness to Dante is equally great, and for somewhat similar reasons. There is, in fact, a peculiar similarity between the Florentine and the English laureate in their veracious representations and their discriminating perceptions. Her study of the Italian poet was profound. In the powerful paper in 'Theophrastus' directed against the false testimonials men give themselves for what is mistaken as a high imagination, and what is, in reality, "a ready activity in fabricating extravagances such as are presented by fevered dreams," she calls Dante to witness that this supposed imaginativeness is nothing but confusion resulting from a defective perception. "These characteristics are the very opposite of such as yield a fine imagination, which is always based on a keen vision, a keen consciousness of what *is*, and carries the store of definite knowledge as material for the construction of its inward visions. Witness Dante, who is at once the most precise and homely in his reproduction of actual objects, and the most soaringly at large in his imaginative combinations." And witness herself also.

Deronda, setting out to find Mirah's relatives, is, for a while, sickened by the coarse surroundings of his field:

He went often rambling in those parts of London which are most inhabited by common Jews: he walked to the synagogues at times of service, he looked into shops, he observed faces,— a process not very promising of particular discovery. Why did he not address himself to an influential Rabbi or other member of a Jewish community, to consult on the chances of finding a mother named Cohen, with a son named Ezra, and a lost daughter named Mirah? He thought of doing so — after Christmas. The fact was, notwithstanding all his sense of poetry in common things, Deronda, where a keen personal interest was aroused, could not, more than the rest of us, continuously escape suffering from the pressure of that hard, unaccommodating Actual, which has never consulted our taste and is entirely unselect. Enthusiasm, we know, dwells at ease among ideas, tolerates garlic breathed in the middle ages, and sees no shabbiness in the official trappings of classic processions; it gets squeamish when ideals press upon it as something warmly incarnate, and can hardly face them without fainting. Lying dreamily in a boat, imagining oneself in quest of a beautiful maiden's relatives in Cordova elbowed by Jews in the time of Ibn-Gebirol, all the physical incidents can be borne without shock. Or if the scenery of St. Mary Axe and Whitechapel were imaginatively transported to the borders of the Rhine at the end of the eleventh century, when in the ears listening for the signals of the Messiah, the Hep! Hep! Hep! of the Crusaders came like the bay of bloodhounds; and in the presence of those devilish missionaries with sword and firebrand the crouching figure of the reviled Jew turned round erect, heroic, flashing with sublime constancy in the face of torture and death — what would the dingy shops and unbeautiful faces signify to the thrill of contemplative emotion? But the fervor of sympathy with which we contemplate a grandiose martyrdom is feeble compared with the enthusiasm that keeps unslacked where there is no danger, no challenge — nothing but impartial midday falling on commonplace, perhaps half-repulsive, objects which are really the beloved ideas made flesh. Here undoubtedly lies the chief poetic energy, — in the force of imagination that pierces or exalts the solid fact, instead of floating among cloud-pictures. To glory in a poetic vision of knowledge covering the whole earth, is an easier exercise of believing imagination than to see its beginning in newspaper placards, staring at you from a bridge beyond the corn-fields; and it might well happen to most of us dainty people that we were in the thick of the battle of Armageddon without being aware of anything more than the annoyance of a little explosive smoke and struggling on the ground immediately about us.

"Falsehood is so easy, truth so difficult," she says. She will draw no griffins with exaggerated claws and wings, but, if possible, a real unexaggerated lion. This is what she finds to admire "in many Dutch paintings which lofty-minded people despise," — this "precious quality of truthfulness." They are "faithful pictures of a monotonous homely existence," and therefore nearer the life of the majority than a life of exciting activity.

Paint us an angel, if you can, with a floating velvet robe, and a face paled by the celestial light; paint us yet oftener a Madonna, turning her mild face upward, and opening her arms to welcome the divine glory; but do not impose upon us any æsthetic rules which shall banish from the region of Art those old women scraping carrots with their work-worn hands, those heavy clowns taking holiday in a dingy pothouse, those rounded backs and stupid, weather-beaten faces that have bent over the spade and done the rough work of the world, those homes with their tin pans, their brown pitchers, their rough curs, and their clusters of onions.

And at the very time she was writing these words in 'Adam Bede,' Millet, unknown to her, was starving in Barbizon! It was as if he had heard her voice across the sea and strove to do her bidding.

She carries out in her novels the principles she advocates in her essay on Riehl. She gives us pictures of true peasantry, as she claims, English painters do not, — such pictures as those of Teniers and Murillo. If our sympathies are to be expanded they must be based on realities, as when Wordsworth sings the reverie of 'Poor Susan.' Falsification in art dealing with the life of the people is pernicious because it turns the attention away from a serious regard of their real joys and sorrows. What is wanted is a natural history of our social classes; and neither the doctrinaire nor the dreamer can write it.[1]

The allusion in this essay to Dickens is most important:

We have one great novelist who is gifted with the utmost power of rendering the external traits of our town population; and if he could give us their psychological character — their conceptions of life, and their emotions — with the same truth as their idiom and manners, his books would be

---

[1] The raw material of some of her after fiction may be found here. For example, she notes, in passing, Riehl's reference to the German peasants' inveterate habit of litigation, which has its parallel in England; and which may have suggested Mr. Tulliver's lawsuit, although Mr. Tulliver would doubtless resent being classed with Dandie Dinmont!

the greatest contribution Art has ever made to the awakening of social sympathies. But while he can copy Mrs. Plornish's colloquial style with the delicate accuracy of a sun-picture, while there is the same startling inspiration in his description of the gestures and phrases of "Boots" as in the speeches of Shakspere's mobs or numskulls, he scarcely ever passes from the humorous and external to the emotional and tragic, without becoming as transcendent in his unreality as he was a moment before in his artistic truthfulness. But for the precious salt of his humor, which compels him to reproduce external traits that serve, in some degree, as a corrective to his frequently false psychology, his preternaturally virtuous poor children and artisans, his melodramatic boatmen and courtesans, would be as noxious as Eugene Sue's idealized proletaires in encouraging the miserable fallacy that high morality and refined sentiment can grow out of harsh social relations, ignorance, and want; or that the working-classes are in a condition to enter at once into a millennial state of *altruism*, wherein every one is caring for every one else, and no one for himself.[1]

Everything false in Dickens is the opposite of something true in George Eliot. The great humorist would have made much of the picture of Warner weaving on and on in his cabin, — would have made it a companion picture to his Madame Defarge, always knitting and seeing nothing. George Eliot,

[1] See also her review of 'Hard Times' in the Belles-Lettres column of the *Westminster*, Oct., 1854, p. 604, in which remonstrance is recorded that the author neglected a rare opportunity to portray the inner life of the great labor movement in the north of England for the comparatively unimportant exhibition of the evil effects of an education which subordinates the finer feelings to the intellect, — a system of education which existed only in Dickens's imagination. In this she unconsciously prognosticates her own great fame in 'Felix Holt.'

whom I shall presently try to prove a finer humorist than Dickens, was too much occupied with the psychical Warner to linger on the pictorial.

II

No art can meet with a satisfying recognition that is not true to known conditions, — not, of necessity, experimentally known, but appealing to a universal intuitive apprehension. The best art is, therefore, that which meets the most readily with this recognition. It must be true to nature, as we say, and hold in check the tendency of the subjective bias to "improve," on an imperfect nature, — so imperfect that the compelling force of the art would seem to be the removal of the imperfections. The best art is the best imitation of an instinctively known nature; and the subtlest appreciation of its display, in such a picture, for example, as the horror of Macbeth in the banquet scene, is shown, not by our exclamation, "How sublime!" but by our exclamation, "How natural!"

The judgments even of professional critics have been too often of the snap variety to pause at the word "unnatural," which has thus been rashly written down where the word "unusual" should have stood. If we can rightly say, "How unnatural!" upon a work, that work, in the rightness of that criticism, is not a work of art, and cannot live. One would be the happy, or perhaps unhappy, possessor of an almost superhuman vision into the inter-relationship of cause and effect who could settle whether truth to nature is the result of a well-directed devotion to a moral purpose, or the power which moves the intelligence into framing the moral concept into accord with a universal consciousness of right. The trueness of George Eliot's art will stand either test; and its convincing qualities are dubious only when the concept is emphasized with an enthusiasm which excludes a due consideration of the surrounding circumstances, which are thus felt not to be given their fairest play. Just as Wordsworth failed to convince chiefly in the poems where he pushed his concept beyond the point of universal intuitive recognition, so George Eliot failed only where some great doctrine absorbed her attention with a too cruel insistence, as in her treatment of heredity in 'The Spanish Gypsy.'

Even on such dangerous ground her general truthfulness saves her from some of the errors she has been charged with. The Hebrew note in 'Daniel Deronda' has raised a chorus of dissent; and it is a little as if she had planned to arrange her scale without the use of accidentals. But let the unwary critic who standeth where George Eliot has slipped beware lest he fall where George Eliot stands firm. The scene between Deronda and his mother has been used as a part of the argument against the whole "unnatural" Jewish scheme; yet in 'The Life and Writings of Isaac Disraeli' may be found a situation so nearly identical that one of two things is certain: either George Eliot used that situation representatively, or the creation of the situation in her book is an evidence of marvellous intuition into the possibilities of racial feeling.

Except under this occasional dominance of a theory, she had that nice perception of fitness without which mere power remains ineffectual. If Romola seems to you cold, the impression is a correct reflection of a finely true conception. She is made cold with a purpose; nay, the author *finds* her cold, just as the miner finds his gold yellow. She is the embodiment of what is noblest in the Florentine spirit. Florence is a serious city — the city of Dante and Savonarola. The daughter of Bardo was brought up in the sternest austerity of the Stoic philosophy, and she fits into the *ingenia acerrima Florentina* which chilled Tito's warmly sensuous spirit:

"There is something grim and grave to me always about Florence," said Tito. . . . "and even in its merriment there is something shrill and hard — biting rather than gay."

III

Are there any really successful historical novels, with the subjective element in control? Does not the subjectivity control the history? It is a most intricate question, and it cannot be decided out of hand. Certain is it that the earnestness of one's study of a past era may not prepare one for its exact representation, and that the most conscientious effort to represent its spirit is apt to be tinctured with a modern spirit. Under a dominant idea, this possibility will become almost a certainty. But who can free one's self, when the working stuff of one's thought is the disjecta membra of moral philosophies, from injecting into a past what belongs to the present? And who shall say with certainty that a Florentine of the fifteenth century could not guide his life with some ethical method not so different, after all, from that of a later time? The fear of the Church, the dread of hell, the awards of heaven, are not enough to explain the Savonarola of history; and George

Eliot's explanation is at least not proven to be antihistorical. It knits us to a past when we are made to feel that the same grand purposes which rule us ruled it; and a conception is not damnable because it is a nineteenth-century exposition of a fifteenth-century fact, so long as the real exposition is hidden in the fall of years, and can be approximated only by a sympathetic imagination, which must be guided in some degree by the facts of the present.

'Romola' may be 'Middlemarch' in ancient Florentine garb, but only in the nearness of a great moral idea which may have its forerunners in a previous age, though the manner of approach be different. At least two things which are apparent in all George Eliot's work are especially notable in this: a thorough preparation for her task, and a minute carefulness of detail in working it out. She conceived the idea of 'Romola' when in Florence in 1860; and following the advice of the French bishop to his clergy to let a text *rot* in the mind before preaching from it, she let her imagination play on the concept for more than a year before putting pen to paper. The list of the books she read covers the complete bibliography of the period, and she read them in the original, — not only such writers as Villari and Sismondi, but Dante and Savonarola, Boccaccio and Politian. She made a study of the topography of Florence, and examined the costumes of the period in the British Museum. She put herself in the way of acquiring the learned slang of a Renaissance city and the alley-talk of its mobs by reading 'La Mandragola' (twice) and 'La Calandra,' — she whom her critics (how many of them, by the way, could read the originals whence *she* drew her colors?) charged with a lack of contemporaneousness. She said that she began 'Romola' a young, and finished it an old, woman, so terribly did it plough into her brain.[1] And whether anachronistic in motive or not, it contains none of the usual anachronisms which mar the historical novels which are the mere result of cramming. She reflects the actual forms of speech. The Italian characters always address Politian by his Italian name, although when she speaks it is 'Politian.' She refers to Tito lifting his cap to Romola as an unusual sign of reverence at that time. A less careful writer, in describing the atrium of the Piazza dell' Annunziata might — and probably would — have fallen into the error of including the surrounding cloisters and the frescoes of del Sarto in the description, which George Eliot knows were not then existing. These are little things, but it is the painfully gathered mickle of detail that makes the muckle of a noble result. Right was thy judgment, O Strauss! — "et accurata et perspicua": "accuracy, the very soul of scholarship."[2]

[1] 'Life,' vol. ii., p. 352. See also Trollope's 'What I Remember,' chapter xxxv.

[2] To paint with authority such a character as Lydgate, she read, among other books, Renouard's 'History of Medicine,' Cullen's 'Life,' Gall's 'Anatomy,' Carpenter's 'Comparative Physiology,' 'Heroes of Medicine;' diversifying these studies with Nisard's 'History of French Literature,' Drayton's 'Nymphidia,' Grote, Aristophanes, Theocritus, Owen, Plato, and 'Macbeth.' Before writing 'Felix Holt' she read Bamford's 'Passages from the Life of a Radical,' Mill, Comte, Blackstone, English histories of the reign of George III., the 'Times' for 1832-3, and the Annual Register for 1832. She read the Bible to get the proper tone for Lyon's talk, and consulted Mr. Harrison for law points. Jacobs says she must have read, before writing the Jewish chapters in 'Daniel Deronda,' Gratz's 'Geschicte der Judea,' in ten volumes, Jehuda Halevi, Spinoza, 'The Book of Light' (the Cabalistic Book) Sohar, and Maimonides. Was there ever another such?

I do not know that angels fear to tread where the Scotch dialect flourishes, — although I think they might, — but George Eliot refrains from rushing into those brambles. She describes and imitates only what she is wholly familiar with. She understands the speech of North Staffordshire and the neighboring parts of Derby, and she does not hesitate to use it in 'Adam Bede.' But she is not so sure of Scotch, and is filled with caution as she approaches it. "I think it was Mr. Craig's pedigree only that had the advantage of being Scotch, and not his bringing up, for except that he had a stronger burr in his accent, his speech differed little from that of the Loamshire people around him." It is well sometimes to beat the literary devil around the bush; and this is an instance not only of the cautiousness which accompanies the scholarly habit of accuracy, but also of the honesty which rejects what is not strictly its own. We always feel, in reading George Eliot, that what she gives us is the genuine coin of the realm earned by hard work; the kind of confidence we feel in a doctor who has taken an honest degree. Even one who might dispute her theory would take without question her facts; and a continued reliance upon the truthfulness of her perceptions gradually persuades many to put credence in her moral system also. At all events, one is convinced that she has as much right, and the same kind of right, to talk about philosophy as Captain Marryat has to talk about the sea.[1]

---

[1] What the critic of the *Edinburgh Review* said of 'Felix Holt' may be said of all her works: "'Felix Holt' has some of the defects of ordinary novels, but ordinary novels have none of the merits of 'Felix Holt.'"

Just how much of an experimental knowledge is requisite for an artistic presentation of value is a question I will leave to the "nice geographers" whose objections to 'The Tempest' are based on the general proposition that it is n't so. An intelligent cabinet-maker said, when 'Adam Bede' appeared, that nobody but a cabinet-maker could have written it. It was the finest possible tribute to that accuracy of perception for which our author stood, but it was a cabinet-maker's criticism; and to apply it in general would be to rob her of the divining-rod of genius — which is insight — and to place in her hand instead the reporter's detective camera. She did not have to frequent taverns to know what went on at the Rainbow, and yet the Rainbow scene has been well called Shaksperean.

There are indeed no portraits after the 'Clerical Scenes,' only hints and broken bits of portraiture. The persecution of Tryan was based on an actual occurrence, but the details were her own. The evening at Mordecai's club was undoubtedly suggested by a similar experience of Mr. Lewes, but there are philosophical alterations, for Lewes' man was a disciple of Spinoza, and Mordecai was his opponent. She said in regard to 'Adam Bede,' "There is not a single portrait in the book, nor will there be in any future book of mine."[1] Even in her dialect she aimed at giving a general physiognomy rather than a close portraiture; and one might wish that the Scotchmen could be prevailed upon to adopt the same liberal terms with their readers.

To be general without generalizing; to be broad

---

[1] 'Life,' vol. ii., p. 117.

and generous, yet exact and true; to build a high tower of observation on a firm rock of knowledge, — that is art, and that is George Eliot.

IV

She is true, too, in those nuances of feeling which mark off one mode of life from another. She makes her gardener in 'Mr. Gilfil's Love Story' find in the Gothic architecture something intelligible because of its symbols drawn from his own profession.

"Howiver, I'll noot deny that the Goothic stayle's prithy anoof, an' it's woonderful how near them stoon-carvers cuts oot the shapes o' the pine-apples an' shamrucks an' rooses."

When Adam Bede in his old age recalls the memory of Mr. Irwine's pastorship, he defends his lack of spirituality with similes drawn from his old trade of carpentry:

"He did n't go into deep speritial experience; and I know there's a deal in a man's inward life as you can't measure by the square, and say do this and that 'll follow, and do that and this 'll follow."

He is asked if Mr. Ryde did not preach more about the spiritual part of religion than Mr. Irwine.

"Eh! I knowna. He preached a deal about doctrines. But I 've seen pretty clear ever since I was a young un, as religion 's something else besides doctrines and notions. I look at it as if the doctrines were like finding names for your feelings so as you can talk of 'em when you 've never known 'em, just as a man may talk o' tools when he knows the names, though he's never so much as seen 'em, still less handled 'em."

And Mrs. Poyser's pleasure in seeing this same Mr. Irwine Sunday after Sunday is a part of that large general pleasure we all instinctively feel in a harmonious familiar picture.

"It's summat-like to see such a man as that i' the desk of a Sunday! As I say to Poyser, it's like looking at a full crop o' wheat or a pasture with a fine dairy o' cows in it; it makes you think the world's comfortable like."

Mrs. Poyser's wit is not only rare, it is the native wit of a Staffordshire farmer's wife; and its rarity no more interferes with its nativeness than the superior quality of the Hall Farm cheeses interferes with the equally natural failures of the Britton establishment near by. There is no humor in Mrs. Poyser's speech; it is all wit. Because humor calls for reflective and deliberative characteristics absolutely uncharacteristic of Mrs. Poyser and her class.

The "scorching sense of disgrace" which the Hall Farm felt at Hetty's fall is more severely voiced by Poyser than by his wife, to the surprise of a good many besides Mr. Irwine. People who relieve a nervous irritability by keen speech on trivial things are apt to be awed by the shadow of vital events, and the nervousness works off in a sympathy which enlists against all that affects the peace of the sufferer. Mrs. Poyser's silence is similar to that of Aunt Glegg, whose sharp tongue might be looked to for a vigorous wagging against Maggie, instead of which it becomes Maggie's defender.

Caterina, in the hands of some latter-day and almost all former-day novelists, would have been forced into suicide by the necessitous art of melodrama. But George Eliot's art knows better. Caterina never thought of suicide. Her nature was too tender and too timid to allow her anger to settle into anything more active than mourning. This is the art "close to nature" because based on a knowledge of human nature.

Perhaps the finest example of this wonderful correlation of her art to the standards of nature is the scene of the betrothal between Adam and Hetty. To call it 'The Betrothal,' as the author does in the heading to the chapter, is a part of the art, for it is a part of the evasive mockery of the human concrete conditions, which interfere with the realization of the divine abstract conditions, which we would like to make human.

"I could afford to be married now, Hetty. I could make a wife comfortable; but I shall never want to be married if you won't have me."

Hetty looked up at him and smiled through her tears, as she had done to Arthur that first evening in the wood, when she thought he was not coming, and yet he came. It was a feebler relief, a feebler triumph she felt now, but the great dark eyes and the sweet lips were as beautiful as ever, perhaps more beautiful, for there was a more luxuriant womanliness about Hetty of late. Adam could hardly believe in the happiness of that moment. His right hand held her left, and he pressed her arm close against his heart as he leaned down towards her.

"Do you really love me, Hetty? Will you be my own wife, to love and take care of as long as I live?"

Hetty did not speak, but Adam's face was very close to hers, and she put up her round cheek against his, like a kitten. She wanted to be caressed; she wanted to feel as if Arthur were with her again.

Hetty was not false to Adam; she was simply true to herself. She was true to her nature, and Adam was true to his; and it was the truth of her feeling that was the deception of the truth of his. What more can art do?

V

One infallible sign of creative art is that it enters with enthusiasm into the subtleties of its creations. It does not follow that because there is enthusiasm there is genius. It may be that in the composition of 'Aurelian' and 'Serapis' their authors felt a glow they thought divine, but which seems to their readers but the heat of the midnight oil; and it might be supposed that George Eliot, who burned so much of this oil, would have suffered, too, from dimness of vision. She did not prepare for 'Romola,' however, as the schoolboy prepares for an exam. The text rotted in her mind, and when she came to create she created with enthusiasm because she knew her substance, and was thrilled with joy whenever it revealed its possibilities; just as an engineer, let us say, is delighted with each new manifestation of speed in the engine he has constructed. We are prepared for the note in her diary, "Killed Tito in great excitement." [Fancy, if you can, Mr. Ebers saying, "Killed Cambyses in great excitement."] That reveals the Promethean spark, and strikes off 'Romola' from the historical novel class into a class not to be judged by the standards of mere accurate research.

That she thoroughly enjoyed her dramatic situations is shown by the fine outbursts with which she filled them. When the black marks become magical to Baldassare, as the moonlight falls on the page of Pausanias, which, an hour before, had suggested nothing to him, but which now conjured up a world, all the vibrations of memory are shocked into re-awakened activity, the chill of age falls away like a broken chain, and he is ready to shout with almost delirious delight in his new-found power. "*The light was come again, mother of knowledge and joy!*" It is like a great crash of keys at the end of a Wagnerian theme.

VI

Her essay moves in a broad, dignified style from a concept well thought out to its appropriate finish. We are taken into its secret at the start, and given a hint of the outcome early in its progress. Our minds are soon keyed to the proper pitch; and the climax is, for the most part, legitimately reached. The style is like the angel of dawn described in the Proem to 'Romola,' travelling with "broad slow wing." At its best it is a grand largo in open diapason.

There is, it is true, an occasional anti-climax, as the reprieve of Hetty at the gallows, which an artist like Mr. Hardy, for example, would have avoided, as witness the end of 'Tess.' But that is out of regard for our feelings; and her Nemesis, awful as it is, is tempered with mercy. A realist is always in danger of extending a story to an end not demanded by its setting, but in agreement with some likely possibility of actual experience. It is quite natural that Adam should marry Dinah, but the real Finis is in the Stoniton jail. I cannot agree, however, with the opinion that the tragedy of Maggie and Tom should have been spared us. Maggie's life was a series of sacrifices. Her mistakes were all of the impulsive sort. The theme opened with a sister's love. It ends with that love, in a noble impulse, and in a crowning sacrifice. It is the deep-sounding return at the end of the symphony to its rich beginning. As for 'Deronda,' the question is not so easily settled; but if the Hebrew note is true, the legitimate outcome is the wedding journey to the East; and the anti-climax would have been reached only by a picture of Daniel's experiences there. It would have been a little too much, though, to have asked us to look on at Mirah, sitting at a window in Jerusalem, with her little hands folded, waiting Deronda's return from his daily business of re-establishing the temporal power of the Jews. And so far as the history of Gwendolen is concerned, which is vastly more important than the history of Deronda and Mirah, the end of the novel is true to life, for she has her spiritual awakening just as she is left alone to carry it out.

At all events, George Eliot never relies on her climax to save her story, and that is the main point. She is a sensational writer in the right sense. She does not keep her climax up her sleeve. Her tenors do not expire singing high C's. There is seldom any straining for effect, and when the effect is terrible it is because it is natural. What Maggie wakens to on the boat with Stephen is " the plash of water against the vessel, and the sound of a footstep on the deck, and the awful starlit sky." How could the fearfulness of her position be better expressed, — the natural emphasizing the supernatural?[1]

VII

A very bad name has gradually become attached to the idea of rhetoric. The art of persuasion is naturally the art of special pleading, and the mere beauty of language has been employed to dazzle the convictions. Words are weapons, and weapons may be used basely. Yet all living art must be rhetorical, — that is, it must persuade through the beauty of proportion, of temper, of form, of matter, of truth; and fine thoughts deserve fine dress. The quarrel of literature with the rhetoricians is that they put poor thoughts in fine dress, like a kitchen wench decked with jewels. George Eliot is not afraid of large language. She has no nervous dread of having her rhetoric misunderstood; where the canvas requires splendor, she has the joy of the true artist in splashing it on. If you are to persuade a perverse generation that beauty is truth and truth is beauty, you must emphasize the truth by emphasizing the beauty.

Pure rhetoric, indeed, is a simple thing: it is but the gold found by the touchstone, which little instrument has the equal power of rejecting all that is not gold, but looks like it. Descriptive strength of a high order is impossible without it; but the gifted artist uses it only to heighten an effect which could not be

[1] The Introduction to 'Felix Holt' is a microcosm of a large part of what is valuable in George Eliot, being an excellent example at once of her conservatism, her humor, her ethics, her pathos, and her method of germinating the plot.

otherwise handled without loss of power. The difference between a delicate water-color and a deep-toned encaustic is precisely the difference between the sketch of Dinah Morris at the opening of 'Adam Bede' and the tragic coloring of Hetty towards its close:

It was one of those faces that make one think of white flowers, with light touches of color on their pure petals.

It was the same rounded, pouting, childish prettiness, but with all love and belief in love departed from it — the sadder for its beauty, like that wondrous Medusa-face, with the passionate passionless lips.

Antithesis, which is perhaps the deadliest of rhetorical weapons, was easy to George Eliot, but she uses it sparingly on account of its inherent possibilities of misdirection. She is really a master of both epigram and aphorism, yet is not reckoned as an epigrammatic or aphoristic writer, because she conscientiously avoids dangerous ground. No English author save Shakspere is more quotable.[1] There is hardly a field in religion, philosophy, science, art, that she has not illuminated; and yet in the application of her thought to any subject, it is observable that it is the solid worth of the thought that attracts rather than the glitter of the apothegm. An aphorism is often nothing more than a witty truism: what George Eliot contributes is truth.

[1] Some years ago I set out to make a George Eliot Calendar, the plan being to record the anniversary of some event of interest with each day, and fitting to that an appropriate quotation. Before finishing the work I found that I had a sufficient number of events to fill out calendars for three years — *i. e.*, 1100 slips — and this without any repetition; and that the quotations fitted into them with the greatest possible ease, with enough left over for still another year.

She enlarges the borders of thought more than she makes to glisten some thought already well defined. Like Dr. Holmes, who condemns certain lightnesses of speech, and yet shows that he can himself indulge in fooling like other mortals, by putting in the mouth of "the young fellow they call John" what he straightway proceeds to punish in *propria persona* as the Autocrat, George Eliot shows herself capable of the epigram by putting it in the mouths of her witty characters; it is for the most part confined to her dialogue. Take such a passage as —

Under every guilty secret there is hidden a brood of guilty wishes, whose unwholesome infecting life is cherished by the darkness. The contaminating effect of deeds often lies less in the commission than in the consequent adjustment of our desires — the enlistment of our self-interest on the side of falsity; as, on the other hand, the purifying influence of public confession springs from the fact that by it the hope in lies is forever swept away, and the soul recovers the noble attitude of simplicity.

Rochefoucauld, it is certain, would have put that into the form of a maxim; but she is too anxious not to be misunderstood on a subject of such weighty importance to crowd into an inch what can only be fairly stated in an ell. That brilliant Frenchman would have struck out the "most often" in George Eliot's sentence, "The touchstone by which men try us is *most often* their own vanity," thus increasing its proverb-like quality, but lowering its careful wisdom. She criticises Novalis, in 'The Mill on the Floss,' for his "questionable" aphorism "Character is destiny," on the ground that it is not the whole of our destiny; and towards the close of the book she says:

All people of broad, strong sense have an instinctive repugnance to the men of maxims; because such people early discern that the mysterious complexity of our life is not to be embraced by maxims, and that to lace ourselves up in formulas of that sort is to repress all the divine promptings and inspirations that spring from growing insight and sympathy. And the man of maxims is the popular representative of the minds that are guided in their moral judgment solely by general rules, thinking that these will lead them to justice by a ready-made patent method, without the trouble of exerting patience, discrimination, impartiality— without any care to assure themselves whether they have the insight that comes from a hardly earned estimate of temptation, or from a life vivid and intense enough to have created a wide fellow-feeling with all that is human.

It is but another indication of her honesty. Her judgment is sound because it keeps always in view the wrongs possible through haste. Her wit does not blind her wisdom.

Her style has no tricks. You may look in vain for traces of the alliterative habit, for example, in her prose work. She is content with the plain " said " in her reports of conversation, and never employs " remarked," " replied," "laughed," " smiled," " insinuated," like the novelists who seem to think it necessary to indicate in some such way the *tone* of the speech, which should be sufficiently clear from its body. She puts no tags on her tones; the dialogue explains them. I do not know that she was influenced by Thackeray, and she has left a record of her dislike to 'Esmond;'[1] but her form is most at fault when it is Thackerayean, as in the opening paragraphs of the seventeenth

---

[1] 'Life,' vol. i., pp. 296 *seq.* But see, per contra, 'Life,' vol. ii., p. 351.

chapter of 'Adam Bede,' and the fourth paragraph of the ninth chapter of 'Deronda;' for although her style is as leisurely as one charged with feeling can be, it does not easily lend itself to the let-me-link-my-arm-in-yours-and-talk-it-over-as-we-saunter-down-the-street method of the mighty satirist. A chorus is now and then a little tiresome. "Does it seem incongruous to you," she asks," that a Middlemarch surgeon should dream of himself as a discoverer?" No, no more incongruous that he should hail from Coventry than from London; why ask? But this never became a mannerism, and was always prompted by a loving zeal to set an action or a character in just the right light.

"Nice distinctions are troublesome;" she says in 'Amos Barton.' "It is so much easier to say that a thing is black than to discriminate the peculiar shade of brown, blue, or green to which it really belongs." The speech is figurative, with the point of the application in the plea for a careful judgment of character; but it may be taken in its literal force as well. Remembering the reference to Dante in her 'Theophrastus' essay, and her contention for the necessity of correct perceptions if we are to build a palace of delight which shall be something more than a pack of cards, a study of her fiction convinces one that she carried out in her own work what she commends in another's. She is almost always a clear writer. Her descriptions in her journal are a sufficient evidence of a keenly developed perceptive ability, encouraged and fostered, no doubt, by her scientific investigations with Lewes. Among her recollections of the Scilly islands are their *rectangular* crevices, *cubical* boulders, *oval* basins. The easiest thing in

Her Art

the world to be hazy about is the precise *form* of a thing. This is why George Eliot is fine in minute delineations: she knows the difference between shapes, and can distinguish shades. She is not satisfied with telling us that old Mrs. Dempster has beautiful white hair. The picture does not hang in that large gallery of our memory labelled " old ladies with beautiful white hair ": there is a special salon for it. She is separated from the other old ladies because her hair is "of that peculiar white which tells that the locks have once been blond." " You saw at a glance that she had been a *mignonne* blond." If we find this perceptive sharpness a little burdensome here and there as for instance, in —

And the slow absent glance he cast around at the upper windows of the houses had neither more dissimulation in it, nor more ingenuousness, than belongs to a youthful well-opened eyelid with its unwearied breadth of gaze; to perfectly pellucid lenses; to the undimmed dark of a rich brown iris; and to a pure cerulean-tinted angle of whiteness streaked with the delicate shadows of long eyelashes,

it is perhaps because we are ourselves not trained to exact descriptions.

I wonder how many "lovers of nature " can picture it with precise fidelity. It is the highest of gifts to have the power to reproduce a scene on paper and at the same time to make it poetical; the rhetorical tendency will in most cases destroy the precision. The principal charm of Tolstoi to critical readers is his revolt from extravagant rhetoric to the plain truths of description; but the result may often be bareness, a puritanical exaggeration of the opposite of what was revolted from. George Eliot never forgets that beauty belongs to art; that a scene in nature which has beauty must be beautifully reproduced; that the poetry of nature must be expressed poetically; but with all this the saving truth that an exact description and a poetical description must go hand in hand, that the most exact is the most poetical, and the most poetical the most exact. The very genius of Christmas burns in the words describing Tom's holidays; the hoar spirit of old England floats through them, — aye, and of old Time, too.

Fine old Christmas, with the snowy hair and ruddy face, had done his duty that year in the noblest fashion, and had set off his rich gifts of warmth and color with all the heightening contrast of frost and snow.

Snow lay on the croft and river-bank in undulations softer than the limbs of infancy; it lay with the neatliest finished border on every sloping roof, making the dark-red gables stand out with a new depth of color: it weighed heavily on the laurels and fir-trees till it fell from them with a shuddering sound; it clothed the rough turnip-field with whiteness, and made the sheep look like dark blotches; the gates were all blocked up with the sloping drifts, and here and there a disregarded four-footed beast stood as if petrified "in unrecumbent sadness;" there was no gleam, no shadow, for the heavens, too, were one still, pale cloud — no sound or motion in anything but the dark river, that flowed and moaned like an unresting sorrow. But old Christmas smiled as he laid this cruel-seeming spell on the outdoor world, for he meant to light up home with new brightness, and give a keener edge of delight to the warm fragrance of food: he meant to prepare a sweet imprisonment that would strengthen the primitive fellowship of kindred, and make the sunshine of familiar human faces as welcome as the hidden day-star.

The joy of winter, and also its pain, the hush of nature, the glow of the season, its mystery and its charm, are there; and yet the picture of the snow-covered fields is as realistically true to what we see every winter as its poetry is true to our inward loving sense. The sentiment does not warp the reality. It is a rare and notable gift.

Ask the returned driving party what they have seen along the high-road, and you will be answered by a chorus of glittering generalities. "Such a lovely view!" "Such a grand stretch of mountains!" "Such beautiful wild flowers!" "Such a wonderful lake!" Particularize they cannot; they do not remember what they saw at certain points; the result of the day's experience is a hazy, jumbled sense of pleasure, with a total absence of the specialized rational joy of the observer. But if George Eliot were of the party, and you had the power of drawing her out, she would tell you quietly, and in a corner by yourself:

The ride . . . lay through a pretty bit of midland landscape, almost all meadows and pastures, with hedgerows still allowed to grow in bushy beauty and to spread out coral fruit for the birds. Little details gave each field a particular physiognomy, dear to the eyes that have looked on them from childhood; the pool in the corner where the grasses were dank and trees leaned whisperingly; the great oak shadowing a bare place in mid-pasture; the high bank where the ash-trees grew; the sudden slope of the old marl-pit making a red background for the burdock; the huddled roofs and ricks of the homestead without a traceable way of approach; the gray gate and fences against the depths of the bordering wood; and the stray hovel, its old, old thatch full of mossy hills and valleys, with wondrous modulations of light and shadow, such as we travel far to see in later life, and see larger but not more beautiful. These are the things that make the gamut of joy in landscape to midland-bred souls — the things they toddled among, or perhaps learned by heart standing between their father's knees while he drove leisurely.

It is not too much to say that the possession of this faculty made George Eliot a fine critic. I use the word advisedly. Her essays rank with Arnold's, as may be proved by comparing the article of each on Heine. Turn over the Belles-Lettres columns of the *Westminster* from July, 1855, to October, 1856, and note with what insight and ready appreciation of merit, with what admiration for what is admirable, and with what skill at the detection of false notes the then obscure Miss Evans wrote those necessarily hurried reviews. That she refused to acknowledge them in her collected essays is merely another proof of that critical exclusiveness which would have nothing but the best perpetuated, and does not interfere with the enjoyment which their positive excellence carries to this day. I allude in another place to the interest attached to her critique of 'Hard Times' discovered in these old files; and, remembering the unjust remarks of Ruskin on her 'Mill on the Floss,' it is worth while to notice that in her paper on 'Modern Painters,'[1] she employs a catholic breadth quite the opposite to *her* critic's prejudices. Her object, she maintains, — and it is the object of all her criticisms, — is to care more to know what the author says than what other people think he ought to say. She simply laughs at the peculiarly Ruskinian Preface, where the papal

[1] *Westminster Review*, April, 1856.

promulgation is uttered forth that the author is incapable of falling into an illogical deduction. "We value a writer not in proportion to his freedom from faults, but in proportion to his positive excellences,—to the variety of thought he contributes and suggests, to the amount of gladdening and energizing emotions he excites." She has the three essential characteristics of the fine essayist: penetration of vision, clearness of expression, sympathy of judgment.[1] She told Kate Field that she wrote reviews because she knew too little of humanity; and the paper on Lecky was the only one composed after her creative period had set in. She left injunctions that no pieces printed by her prior to 1857 should be republished,[2] and she carefully revised all the work of her Westminster days the republication of which she sanctioned. This hesitancy about reviewing is a marked characteristic of our author, indicative as it is of her honorable caution about dealing with a subject which had, in all likelihood, not engrossed her attention with

---

[1] No student of her work ever joins in the usual dispraise of 'Theophrastus,' as that book carries us into her workshop, as it were, and we see the artificer surrounded by her tools. Each essay has a clearly defined end, which is pursued with vigor and humor; and each essay contains also the germ of a story which, you feel, could be well worked out if the author had the time. Without 'Theophrastus' we should not have the whole of George Eliot. It is folly to resent a book of essays from the pen of a novelist; concerning such things as are treated in 'Theophrastus,' the best novelist ought to make the best essayist, just as Salvini's papers on certain matters of the stage have a peculiar claim which the closest student of the drama who is nevertheless not an actor could not possess. "A book," says Mr. Birrell, in one of his delightful touch-and-go papers, "which we were once assured well-nigh destroyed the reputation of its author, but which would certainly have established that of most living writers upon a surer foundation than they at present occupy."

[2] See Preface to 'Essays' by Charles Lee Lewes.

the same force as it had the author's, and in her judgment of which, therefore, she was liable to err. And we have no reason to complain of the cessation of her essays, because that meant the continuation of her fiction, the blaze of which has dimmed our eyes to the earlier work. The criticisms must not be omitted, however, in any comprehensive review of her life.

For the same reason, she would not read reviews of her own books; which is an indication, in turn, of another interesting phenomenon,— a strength of will sufficient to cope with and subdue a natural curiosity. It takes character to deliberately shut one's eyes to what is printed about one. Think of George Eliot calmly refusing to read all criticisms,[1] and then think

---

[1] George Eliot's prejudice, of course, was directed against the hopelessly mistaken criticism which puts every creation of art into the procrustean bed of a preconceived and obstinately maintained theory; and which can never enter sympathetically into phases not experimentally known to its puny self. And yet her sense of humor might have been fed by some of the amusing stuff written of her work. The classification of Ladislaw as "a worthless Bohemian" would have been an offence in her nostrils; and it puts the writer on the dry-as-dust plane of Casaubon without Casaubon's excuse. But the magazine which contains that hit-or-miss characterization also offers the profound suggestion that we acquiesce in Celia's marriage to a baronet because of our perhaps unconscious prejudice in favor of county families over tradespeople; which prejudice explains why we view as a mésalliance the marriage of Rosamond to the grand-nephew of a baronet, although Celia is no better than Rosamond! Here is substance for mirth, and a little reading of this sort of thing would have done George Eliot no harm.

The peculiarly feminine idea of *mission* — not that all male authors are free from it — was intensified in her by a supersensitive dread that the message would be misunderstood; and her fears could be removed, or at the best minimized, only by the loving care of her companion's censorship. Her tolerance did not include a welcome to the hostile reviewing of work she brought forth with pangs of honest labor. *Her* books were *her* children, and the critics were stepmothers.

of Charlotte Brontë weeping over the *Times'* brutalities at her publisher's breakfast-table!

This clearness condenses into a single happy word at times, which does duty for a sentence. There is a perfect picture in her metaphorical adjective describing Casaubon's "*sandy*" absorption of his wife's care. Fred Vincy is in the "*pink-skinned*" stage of typhoid fever; in almost everybody's else hands he would have been "trembling on the verge" of it. A "*violoncello*" voice is a novel inspiration for "barytone," and a "*chiaroscuro*" parentage is a stroke of genius. The sense of Baldassare's weakness pressed on him like a "*frosty*" ache. Mr. Vincy's florid style is contrasted with the "*Franciscan*" tints of Bulstrode. "*Ethereal* chimes" is worthy of Charlotte Brontë. Her dramatic sense prompted the sure adjective at critical moments. As the French army approached Florence, the dark grandeur of the moving mass overwhelmed the onlookers with its "long-winding *terrible* pomp." And there is fine recklessness, suitable to a wild acceptance of the future as a result of a delirious pleasure in the present, in her "*hell-braving* joy."

She is not afraid to use a word usually stamped as vulgar if circumstances justify. "There was something very fine in Lydgate's look just then, and any one might have been encouraged to *bet* on his achievement." That is just the right word; none other would do at all. She employs "kick" and "roast" in the same manner. She is fortunate in her choice of words with the prefix *un*,— as "unapplausive audience," "uncherishing years;" although "unfecundated egg" is perhaps unnecessary, as the more recognizable "unfruitful" (she does not mean "unhatched") would have answered. "Otherworldliness" is not her invention, Lewes having used it in his 'History of Philosophy,' and, it may be, others before him.

One has the frequent feeling, in reading George Eliot, that in this happy selective ability the one correct word is found to describe what must otherwise be described only by circumlocution, and that no synonym could have been used without weakening the picture. Mrs. Poyser's dairy is described as "a scene to sicken for with a sort of *calenture*" in hot and dusty streets. "Fever" would have been altogether too tame and too generalizing. If a cruel fate has ever kept you close to a stifling office through an oppressive summer, and if before your aching eyeballs have passed mocking visions of children playing in meadows, and wide ocean sweeps, *then* you know what a word in due season this "calenture" is,—that tropical delirium which drives sailors to hurl themselves into the sea, which seems to them a grassy field. If you know your George Eliot, your sickening for the country at such a season will be heightened by recollections of her "gleams and *greenth* of summer." What other word would so vividly represent the *living* green for which you long? "Verdure," after that, sounds almost as unreal as Mrs. Henry Wood's "pellucid tear of humanity."

Her exactness is shown in such a description as "*minim* mammal," which is more scientifically precise than "most minute mammal." Mr. Chubb wore so much of the mazarine color of the Whig candidate at the Treby election that he looked like a very large "*gentianella*." That flower is not so well known to most of us as the gentian, of the same family, and which other writers would have used in its place. But the gentian lacks the intense blue which the author meant to convey, and which no flower but the gentianella does convey, in connection with size.

She is not a constant neologist, like De Quincey, and her invention of new, or employment of forgotten, words has not always the immediately appreciated value of that master, who uses "parvanimity" and "dyspathy" with a reason difficult to apply to George Eliot's "innutrient," with a choice already at hand between "innutritive" and "innutritious." She shares the rewards, however, as well as the penalties, of the fearless, as may be noted by the quotation of this sentence from her works in all the dictionaries, in illustration of the underscored word: "Has any one ever pinched into its *pilulous* smallness the cobweb of prematrimonial acquaintanceship?"

In her descriptions of the varying moods of nature, the functional power of the adjective is especially noticeable. A sky has that "*woolly*" look which comes before snow. She speaks of the "*dewy*" starlight as a "*baptismal*" epoch. The still lanes on a bright spring day are filled with a "*sacred silent* beauty like that of fretted aisles." The snow falls from the laurels and fir trees with a "*shuddering*" sound. (You see it falling, and then close your eyes to listen for the dear familiar sound.) Gwendolen was married on a "*rimy*" morning in November. The sunlight stealing through the boughs plays about Tito and Tessa "like a *winged* thing."

These lyrical strokes are not all: the broad chestnotes of nature are sounded also. Surely it is as if Lablache were once more singing "In diesen heil'gen Hallen" to hear

... the solemn glory of the afternoon, with its long swathes of light between the far-off rows of limes, whose shadows touched each other.

And the spirit-music of Maggie in the Red Deeps listening " to the hum of insects, like the tiniest bell on the garment of Silence," and watching " the sunlight piercing the distant boughs as if to chase and drive home the truant heavenly blue of the wild hyacinths " comes, as it were, from the echo organ in the roof of some dim cathedral.

Similes are made striking in George Eliot by the beautiful symmetry she discovers between the fact described and the corresponding fact in nature. Worldly faces at a funeral " have the same effect of grating incongruity as the sound of a coarse voice breaking the solemn silence of night." The rough brother in 'The Lifted Veil' is lost to fine influences, which are as little felt by him " as the delicate white mist is felt by the rock it caresses." In the eloquent belief of Mordecai, the heritage of Israel lives in the veins of millions " as a power without understanding, like the morning exultation of herds." The rustle of the silk garments of the syndics on the pavement " could be heard like rain in the night."

And how happy in her choice of names! *Adam Bede* — the father of men, and the father of English history; suggesting original strength and primal power. We can see the red deep earth in her *Loamshire*, and can feel the quivering slants of sunlight through the *Red Deeps*. We, too, are " in love with moistness," as we stand with George Eliot leaning over the bridge on the February afternoon on which Maggie's story opens. " How lovely the little river is, with its dark, changing wavelets! It seems to me like a living companion while I wander along the banks and listen to its low, placid voice as to the voice of one who is deaf and loving." The little river is the *Ripple*. *Fedalma* means "fidelity," and gives in a name the explanation of a character. The cold aristocracy of family glitters with the right frostiness in *Grandcourt*. One would have to think a long time before improving on such fine old Jewish names as *Deronda, Charisi, Kalonymos;* and *Casaubon* hints at scholarly seclusion. She was not afraid of novelty, either, because *Gwendolen* appears in 'Deronda' for the first time in English fiction.[1]

VIII

George Eliot was the reverse of a pedant. She had no regard for futile learning, as her treatment of Casaubon shows; and her seemingly pedantic use of scientific words, now and then, is but the accidental overflow of her vast reading. Luke, the miller, is "subdued by a general mealiness, like an *auricula*" — the fruit of her zoölogical studies by the seaside with Lewes. She makes "*laches*" stand for "negligence" (having Macaulay's authority there), and "*opoledoc*" for "liniment;" "*præterite*" for "past," and "*loobies*" for the better known "gawks" or "lubbers." A type is spoken of as presenting a "brutish *unmodifiableness*." Jermyn wishes to "*smoothen*" the current of talk, which is unnecessarily Old English; and "*contradictiously*" is grafted upon an obsolete adjective.

[1] It is possible that Mr. Kipling got a hint for a catching patronymic from the Mrs. Gadsby who is mentioned incidentally in 'Daniel Deronda' as the yeomanry captain's wife; just as his "That's another story" was borrowed from Sterne.

But what is really the matter with the "*dynamic*" glance of Gwendolen, which has raised such a hubbub? The word was seized with peculiar power at a time when electricity was revealing new possibilities of energy ; and the idea of force production, of a disturbed equilibrium, of energy not static but in active motion, could not be completely emphasized by any other term. Nor have we any quarrel with her " systole and diastole," either in 'Middlemarch,' when applied to rational conversation, or in 'Deronda,' when applied to blissful companionship. And who but a purist would object to the humorous dash she gives to the word "*chancy*," — her invention, I believe, in this significance of " untrustworthy" and which she used more than once, as, *e. g.*, " By a roundabout course even a gentleman may make of himself a chancy personage." She forgets, once in a while, that her readers may not be as learned as herself; but this is a compliment which it is ungracious in us to fling back at her,— as much of a compliment as when she supposes us sufficiently acquainted with literature to accept without question her metaphors of " Laputan," " Mawworm," and " Harpagons."

Even granting a needlessly complex term here and there, it is interesting to note how she herself pokes fun at those who use the same word without the same intelligence. She seems, for example, to be rather fond of "*energumen*," and it may be that she wishes to defend its proper use in holding the editor of the *Trumpet* up to ridicule for playing with edged tools, which should be handled only by trained workmen:

In a leading article of the *Trumpet* Keck characterized Ladislaw's speech at a Reform meeting as "the violence of an energumen — a miserable effort to shroud in the brilliancy of fireworks the daring of irresponsible statements and the poverty of a knowledge which was of the cheapest and most recent description." "That was a rattling article yesterday, Keck," said Dr. Sprague, with sarcastic intentions. "But what is an energumen?" "Oh, a term that came up in the French Revolution," said Keck.

Some of her seeming pedantry, indeed, is altogether humorous, as when she refers to Dempster's "preponderant occiput and closely clipped coronal surface," — a jesting glance back at the days when she discussed phrenology with Mr. Bray. Her Darwinian reading is shown in her reference to Molly carrying a large jug, two small mugs, and four drinking cans, all full, as an interesting example of the "prehensile" power of the human hand, and in her jolly talk about Bob Jakin's big thumb — a "singularly broad specimen of that difference between the man and the monkey." And, just as we saw while considering her religion, a difference between her private views and her artistic expressions, so we find more pedantry in her letters to friends than in her novels. We need not ask which is the real George Eliot. There is always in letter-writing of the subjective sort an individualistic pressure which may easily turn the large language of generous art into a narrowing expediency. In view of her public work, however, there is no need to concentrate the gaze on such of her private letters as Mr. Cross has seen fit to select from the materials at his command. They are only a partial portrait; the full picture is the other.

But what is most remarkable is that her trained skilfulness in the fields of investigation goes hand in hand with the rapture of her most ethereal fancies. The same George Eliot who wrote —

Certain seeds which are required to find a nidus for themselves under unfavorable circumstances have been supplied by nature with an apparatus of hooks, so that they will get a hold on very unreceptive surfaces. The spiritual seed which had been scattered over Mr. Tulliver had apparently been destitute of any corresponding provision, and had slipped off to the winds again, from a total absence of hooks —

could speak of an emotion passing over the face "like the spirit of a sob."

Nobody denies her occasional obscurity. A good many readers have echoed to the heading to the opening chapter of 'Daniel Deronda' Dolfo Spini's perplexed cry, "It seems to me no clearer than the bottom of a sack," although George Eliot was under the double difficulty there of conveying a thought which should be the excuse for beginning a story just where she did — a very unusual place, namely, in the middle of it, serving her roast before her soup — and of conveying this in her favorite pastime of a style imitative of another author. "Moment-hand," in "His mind glanced over the girl-tragedies that are going on in the world hidden, unheeded, as if they were but tragedies of the copse or hedgerow, where the helpless drag wounded wings forsakenly, and streak the shadowed moss with the red moment-hand of their own death," has given commentators some trouble. But I am weak enough to think the sentence fine in its illustrative suggestion of unutterable pathos in the fate of tender human beings, so unheeded that it can only be likened to a shot bird in the forest,—

its death a thing hidden from the great outside-world, and forgotten at the *moment* of its consummation.

But there are no purposely invented Meredithian darknesses; and meeting her obscurity, one has the sensation of inevitableness, not of teasing deceit. You guess that Browning is playing with you; you know that George Eliot is not.

And her friends must acknowledge that there is some dry reading in her fiction, as, for example, the chapter, 'A Learned Squabble' in 'Romola.' The talk of the Club in 'Deronda' is hard, but it has the value of a background to Mordecai's ideas, emphasizing the tremendous odds against them. When she nods, it is over some deep learning, for she was a very learned woman. The dead languages were not dead to her. She could say with Tito that she had rested in the groves of Helicon and tasted of the fountain of Hippocrene. It was no slippered ease, with a pipe, a decanter, and an encyclopædia within reach. It was not so much a desire for learning with her as it was a passion for knowledge. And it was a down-to-date knowledge.

After waiting for the note to be carried to Mrs. Bulstrode, Lydgate rode away, forming no conjectures, in the first instance, about the history of Raffles, but rehearsing the whole argument, which had lately been much stirred by the publication of Dr. Ware's abundant experience in America, as to the right way of treating cases of alcoholic poisoning such as this. Lydgate, when abroad, had already been interested in this question. He was strongly convinced against the prevalent practice of allowing alcohol and persistently administered large doses of opium; and he had repeatedly acted on this conviction with a favorable result.

She could say of herself, as Mordecai said of himself: "I know the philosophies of this time and of other times; if I chose I could answer a summons before their tribunals."

This profundity was not wholly due to her intellectual grasp, but was, it must be reiterated, in large part the result of her conscientiousness. She had what she says Mr. Stelling, Tom Tulliver's teacher, had not, a "a deep sense of the infinite issues belonging to every-day duties." The number of her volumes is not large. Seventeen years elapsed between 'Adam Bede' and 'Daniel Deronda,' and five years between her two latest fictions. For the same reason that she refused to write reviews after the beginning of her creative period, she declined her share of all those flattering proposals of publishers anxious for the appearance of great names on their advertisements. She said "no" to Macmillan's offer to write the 'Shakspere' for his 'Men of Letters' series, although none could have done it better. She put up with Smith's offer of £7,000, instead of the £10,000 guaranteed for the publication of 'Romola' in *Cornhill*, because the acceptance of the larger sum would have necessitated a speed which she would not undertake in justice to the solemnity of her subject. And though she became rich through her works,[1] she was herself an

---

[1] It is pleasant to know that she became a wealthy woman. There is no complete record of her earnings, but it is apparent that she was treated most generously by her publishers, whose vision was not narrowed to superfine distinctions existing between legal and ethical claims, but, on the contrary, was of such noble breadth that the two became merged. £800 were the stipulated terms for 'Adam Bede,' together with the copyright for four years. Later, Blackwood paid her, voluntarily, at different times, £400 and £800, with the surrender

example of Felix Holt's doctrine to put away the desire to be rich.[1]

She takes her time in observing, and she observes thoroughly. Most tourists give half a day to Goethe's town; but compare the scholarly leisure of '*Three Months* in Weimar' with the slap-dash, hit-or-miss reportorial speed of the special correspondent in '*The West* from a *Car* Window'—not one town, but the whole West at sixty miles an hour![2]

IX

The poetry of observation, of description, of narration, is necessarily contained in a long-swinging line; and George Eliot adopts as her most uniform

---

of the copyright. Altogether she probably received over $300,000 from her works, and not less than $100,000 from the sale of 'Middlemarch' and 'Daniel Deronda' alone. As indicative of the value of reputation, the *Atlantic Monthly* gave her £300 for her poem, 'Agatha,'—an enormous sum for a piece which would probably have been returned, with the thanks of the editor, to any unknown or little-known writer.

[1] Charlotte Brontë *could* not write faster; George Eliot *would* not.

[2] It is perhaps hardly necessary to say that she was, *toto cœlo*, removed from the blue stockings. After her intellectual revolt from evangelicalism we find her recording her detestation of the Hannah More type of woman, classifying it with singing mice and card-playing pigs. For "Woman's Rights" she has the most cutting of all contempts—the contempt of absolute silence. She would have been amazed at some of the later demands of the "new woman," and she would have shrunk from the publicity of many of its advocates; for, with all her mental boldness, she was a timid, which is to say a true, woman. [Jowett wrote, on hearing of her death: "*Elle était plus femme* and had more feminine qualities than almost any woman I have ever known." 'Life and Letters of Benjamin Jowett,' vol. ii., p. 181.] Yet she always advocated any plan looking towards a real advance for her sex, favoring, for example, the petition that women should have legal rights to their own earnings and founding the George Henry Lewes studentship at Cambridge, for original research in physiology, for men *and* women.

verse the ten-syllabled heroic iambic metre. It is the metre of epic as well as of dramatic movement,— the metre of 'Paradise Lost' and the 'Task,' as of 'Hamlet' and 'Tamburlaine.' She is really an epic poet, as the consideration of her *largo* prose might suggest, and she borrows the dramatic form merely for convenience. Critics have pointed out defective lines in 'The Spanish Gypsy;' but (although she had authority for purposely irregular verses[1]) to my mind its greatest defect is its uniformity, its continuous flow, its lack of irregularities. Marlowe's 'Faust' and Jonson's 'Alchemist'— to take two examples of a dramatic poem — contain defective lines, but they occur in the passionate speech of the *dramatis personæ*, as if the thought were too impetuous to be confined within the limits of prosody; which was the feeling, doubtless, which led Shakspere to put some of his uncontrollably turbulent talk into prose. But the wild speech of Silva's final outburst against Zarca is as easy to scan (except for a false accent on the word "Zincalo," which she discovered later and apologized for) as the most gently tempered descriptive passages. And yet, to do her full justice, much of Othello's madness is transcribed in even measures also.

Ladislaw (in whom there is, perhaps quite unconsciously, a good deal of Lewes, and of whom George Eliot is very fond) defines in his swift way what poetry is:

> To be a poet is to have a soul so quick to discern that no shade of quality escapes it, and so quick to feel that discernment is but a hand playing with finely ordered variety

[1] 'Life,' vol. iii., p. 56.

on the chords of emotion — a soul in which knowledge passes instantaneously into feeling, and feeling flashes back as a new organ of knowledge.

She does not precisely fulfil this definition herself, for her knowledge is too elaborately painstaking to pass *instantaneously* from one state to another. She had the poetic insight to see what poetry is, but not the perfected gift of utterance to body forth its realization. The rapturous vision of faith is absent; and what we hardly missed in the prose we notice the omission of in the poetry. Compare her 'Jubal' with Mrs. Browning's 'Seraphim:' there is a Good Friday in her calendar, but no Easter Day. The apocalyptic flight is not necessary in prose fiction, but Positivism in poetry leadens the wings. The lyrics in 'The Spanish Gypsy' are admirable imitations of correct forms, but lack the inspiration of the born lyrist.

But here a general protest against the spirit of much modern criticism may perhaps safely be entered. A work of art is too often judged by an arbitrarily assumed standard. The particular book is fitted to the general rule, and found wanting or not wanting, as the case may be. If the rule is "Art for art's sake," and the book enforces certain moralities, it is condemned on the plea that morality has no place in art. It is a green-grocer's parcel-tying style of criticism. We must come to our studies without prejudice if the result is to be chronicled without malice. A work of art is good or bad, not because it balances the scale on the other side of which is laid the weight of our theories, but because it accomplishes or fails to accomplish what it sets out to do. Every such work has one aim — Beauty. It may be merely a physical, an objective, a romantic beauty; or it may be moral beauty. Why should Handel be condemned because he is not Beethoven, and Strauss because he is not Handel? Great tragedians have essayed with success such characters as Petruchio and Benedick. One's enjoyment of Mr. Irving's Mathias does not conflict with the delight of his Jingle. Now, if Handel should compose a waltz, or Strauss attempt a Ninth Symphony; if Booth should come from his grave to act Rip, or if Jefferson should put on the inky cloak of Hamlet, a large part of the critical world would say that the waltz ought to be left alone because its composer had once written 'The Messiah;' that the symphony was beneath contempt because Strauss had hitherto done nothing but waltz; that Booth and Hamlet were so inextricably mixed, the one with the other, that it was folly to ask us to concentrate our attention on something new; and as for Jefferson, well, he must be crazy. But that is not criticism. There is no harm in comparisons, — nay, they are inevitable. But the final question must be — to return to our subject — *not:* Is George Eliot a failure in poetry because she is not a failure in prose; but, Does she accomplish her poetical purpose? And for the same reason, we do not say that George Eliot should never have written 'Middlemarch,' just because she once wrote 'Silas Marner.' To be fair, we must judge 'Middlemarch' positively, just as if 'Silas Marner' had never been written; it stands, as does every work of art, of itself. It is more than unfair, and it is ungenerous, to ask for repetitions. When a writer like George Eliot ceases to produce Silas Marners, it is a sign that she has passed beyond the control of the genius which guided her through that stage into the control of another. She hath done what she could, in the past. Let there be no reproach in our regret that it is past.

The chief and final thing to ask of any poem, as of any prose work, is nobility of thought. In the long run we forget the imperfections of form and design, and remember only that; as we recall at the close of a day's journey the beauties of the landscape, in the recollection of which all sordid features fade away. All the poets nod at times, — not only Homer. We forget the nodes of form in remembering the loops of thought. Ought we not to be a little ashamed of ourselves? Do we not, in our hypercritical moods, too often place ourselves where Felix Holt's scorn fairly reaches us?

"It comes to the same thing; thoughts, opinions, knowledge, are only a sensibility to facts and ideas. If I understand a geometrical problem, it is because I have a sensibility to the way in which lines and figures are related to each other; and I want you to see that the creature who has the sensibilities that you call taste, and not the sensibilities that you call opinions, is simply a lower, prettier sort of being — an insect that notices the shaking of the table, but never notices the thunder."

We spend too much time in talking about the type of a book, and not enough on what the type conveys to us. George Eliot may not be, technically, a poet, and she may not be, strictly speaking, a prose-poet. But she is a poet, nevertheless, in the broad sense of a possession of susceptibilities to poetic emotion, and an endowment of imaginative creation in forms of eloquent beauty. The author of this was a poet:

> The grey day was dying gloriously, its western clouds all broken into narrowing purple strata before a wide-spreading saffron clearness, which in the sky had a monumental calm, but on the river, with its changing objects, was reflected as a luminous movement, the alternate flash of ripples or currents, the sudden glow of the brown sail, the passage of laden barges from blackness into color, making an active response to that brooding glory.

Indeed, the whole character of Mordecai is poetically conceived and wrought; and she says, in one of the notes she left in her commonplace book, that the time we live in is "prosaic to one whose mind takes the prosaic stand in contemplating it;" implying that its real poetry may be sought for, as it was by Mordecai, away from its sordid meannesses. "Feeling is energy," she says; and she is one of the priestesses of feeling, discharging her office through poetic energy.

A great deal of 'The Spanish Gypsy' will live, even though she did write poetry "with her left hand." It will live because of its inherent nobility of thought, or its pathetic beauty, or its melody, tuned to nature's tones, or to all these in combination; such lines, for example, as —

> What times are little? To the sentinel
> That hour is regal when he mounts on guard.

>   The maimed form
> Of calmly joyous beauty, marble-limbed,
> Yet breathing with the thought that shaped its lips,
> Looks mild reproach from out its opened grave

Her Art

At creeds of terror; and the vine-wreathed god
Rising, a stifled question from the silence,
Fronts the pierced Image with the crown of thorns.

But when they stripped him of his ornaments
It was the bawbles lost their grace, not he.

                        The bawbles were well gone.
He stood the more a king when bared to man.

                           I thought he rose
From the dark place of long-imprisoned souls
To say that Christ had never come to them.

                          I thought his eyes
Spoke not of hatred — seemed to say he bore
The pain of those who never could be saved.

                           He is of those
Who steal the keys of snoring Destiny
And make the prophets lie.

Speech is but broken light upon the depth
Of the unspoken.

                         Say we fail!
We feed the high tradition of the world.

The saints were cowards who stood by to see
Christ crucified: they should have flung themselves
Upon the Roman spears and died in vain, —
The grandest death, to die in vain, — for love
Greater than sways the forces of the world.

O love, you were my crown. No other crown
Is aught but thorns on my poor woman's brow.

Can we believe that the dear dead are gone?
Love in sad weeds forgets the funeral day,
Opens the chamber door and almost smiles, —
Then sees the sunbeams pierce athwart the bed
Where the pale face is not.

                        Shall he sing to you?
Some lay of afternoons, some ballad strain
Of those who ached once but are sleeping now
Under the sun-warmed flowers?

                        Juan, cease thy song.
Our whimpering poesy and small-paced tunes
Have no more utterance than the cricket's chirp
For souls that carry heaven and hell within.

                        Now awful Night,
Ancestral mystery of mysteries, came down
Past all the generations of the stars,
And visited his soul.

He could not grasp Night's black blank mystery,
And wear it for a spiritual garb, creed-proof.

Vengeance! She does but sweep us with her skirts,—
She takes large space, and lies, a baleful light
Revolving with long years, sees children's children,
Blights them in their prime.

                        O great God!
What am I but a miserable brand
Lit by mysterious wrath!

The deepest hunger of the faithful heart is faithfulness.

New-urged by pain he turned away and went,
Carrying forever with him what he fled —
Her murdered love — her love, a dear wronged ghost
Facing him beauteous 'mid the throngs of hell.

                        I said farewell:
I stepped across the cracking earth and knew
'T would yawn behind me.

And these lines —

Her Art

>   Two angels guide
> The path of man, both aged and yet young,
> As angels are, ripening through endless years.
> On one he leans : some call her Memory,
> And some Tradition; and her voice is sweet,
> With deep mysterious accords : the other,
> Floating above, holds down a lamp which streams
> A light divine and searching on the earth,
> Compelling eyes and footsteps.   Memory yields,
> Yet clings with loving check and shines anew
> Reflecting all the rays of that bright lamp
> Our angel Reason holds.   We had not walked
> But for Tradition; we walk evermore
> To higher paths, by brightening Reason's lamp —

have always reminded me, both in the swing of the verse, and in the contrasts between two clamorous demands, of the famous appeal of Ulysses:

> Time hath, my lord, a wallet at his back.

I protest, then, against reiterated emphasis on faults which no one denies, and a style of criticism which deals with the approaches to a subject rather than with the subject itself. A tyro, for example, sees the necessity of putting comic scenes into prose, and appreciates the superiority of the Falstaffian revelry, for this reason among others, to the scene at the inn where Juan teases Lopez. 'The Spanish Gypsy' is a narrative poem, and carelessly defies dramatic unities and historical probabilities for the sake of an ethical principle. It was not written for the stage. We would stare at Shakspere writing his stage directions in verse, as a part of the text; but we only smile and pass on at George Eliot's—

> Enter the duke, Pable, and Annibal,
> Exit the cat, retreating towards the dark.

We might say that the dramatic end of the poem is the death of Zarca and the seizing of Silva by the infuriated Gypsies; but that would have cut out the doxology from the hymn and the peroration from the sermon. And it is curious that the dramatic faults of an imperfect dramatist should approximate in some respects to the dramatic faults of a supreme dramatist; for does not Shakspere continue 'Hamlet' after all interest ceases, namely, after Hamlet's death? The play ends, dramatically, with Horatio's "Good-night, sweet prince;" and the prompt-book so understands it, for it rings down the curtain before Fortinbras and other people we care nothing about have a chance to distract our attention from a stage where lie the dead bodies of the real actors in the drama. You see, it is only the critics who never transgress the unities. Is it not a pity that they do not write a drama once in a while to show us what really correct form is like?

It has been abundantly proved, however, that George Eliot has dramatic power of a high order. The scenes descriptive of the meetings of Baldassare and Tito illustrate it,— on the Duomo steps, at Tessa's hiding-place, in the Rucellai gardens, in the final clutch on the river's bank. I have quoted the language of the scene describing the dying glory of the afternoon as Deronda approached Blackfriars bridge in his wherry, as an example of her poetical gifts; it is equally indicative of a dramatic feeling of rare intensity. For all that brooding splendor is but the setting to a supreme spiritual glory about to descend, like that other, upon this man. He lifts his eyes, as he fastens the top button of his cape, and sees on the bridge — " brought out by the western light into startling distinctness and brilliance " — Mordecai.

It was the face of Mordecai, who also, in his watch towards the west, had caught sight of the advancing boat, and had kept it fast within his gaze, at first simply because it was advancing, then with a recovery of impressions that made him quiver as with a presentiment, till at last the nearing figure lifted up its face towards him, — the face of his visions, — and then immediately, with white uplifted hand, beckoned again and again.

The paths meet; let the heavens burn. "The prefigured friend had come from the golden background . . . this actually was: the rest was to be." It was no accidental meeting; Mordecai had been waiting for it for five years.

"But now look up the river," said Mordecai, turning again towards it and speaking in undertones of what may be called an excited calm, — so absorbed by a sense of fulfilment that he was conscious of no barrier to a complete understanding between him and Deronda. "See the sky, how it is slowly fading! I have always loved this bridge: I stood on it when I was a little boy. It is a meeting place for the spiritual messengers. It is true — what the Masters said — that each order of things has its angel: that means the full message of each from what is afar. Here I have listened to the messages of earth and sky; when I was stronger I used to stay and watch for the stars in the deep heavens. But this time, just about sunset, was always what I loved best. It has sunk into me and dwelt with me — fading, slowly fading; it was my own decline. It paused — it waited, till at last it brought me my new life — my new self — who will live when this breath is all breathed out."

"We boldly deny," says Mr. Jacobs of this scene, "we boldly deny greater tragic intensity to any incident in Shakspere."[1]

[1] *Macmillan's*, vol. xxxvi., p. 101.

There is, indeed, a close psychical kinship between Shakspere and George Eliot, which remains after you have subtracted the difference between his age and hers. For, notwithstanding the modern subtlety evident in the portrayal, her Bulstrode is far more Shaksperean than Dickens's Pecksniff or Molière's Tartuffe; because, though the subtlety be modern, it *is* subtlety, and there is no subtlety at all in those other hypocrites. But there *is* subtlety in Shakspere's hypocrites,— in Claudius, for example. She is Shaksperean, too, in the management of separate sets of people, even where the inter-connections are slight. It relieves the mind and the eye to see a crowded stage; it withdraws the attention from a too monotonous concentration on the main theme. Like a large historical painting, it shows the multifariousness of life; and it is the means of introducing comedy. It is as true of her as it is of Sheridan that her minor are as real as her major characters. There are no lay figures. To let one example stand for many, Philip Debarry is as fine as a portrait by Lawrence.

She follows the great master, or perhaps we should say she follows the sure instinct of the dramatist, in putting relatively slight particular events into strong contrast with the grand sweep of general events,— so illustrating the apparent littleness of the special world as compared with the real bigness of the outside world.

While this poor little heart was being bruised with a weight too heavy for it, Nature was holding on her calm inexorable way in unmoved and terrible beauty. The stars were rushing in their eternal courses; the tides swelled to the level of the last expectant weed; the sun was making brilliant day to busy nations on the other side of the swift earth. The stream of human thought and deed was hurrying and broadening onward. The astronomer was at his telescope; the great ships were laboring over the waves; the toiling eagerness of commerce, the fierce spirit of revolution, were only ebbing in brief rest; and sleepless statesmen were dreading the possible crisis of the morrow. What were our little Tina and her trouble in this mighty torrent, rushing from one awful unknown to another? Lighter than the smallest centre of quivering life in the water-drop, hidden and uncared for as the pulse of anguish in the breast of the tiniest bird that has fluttered down to its nest with the long-sought food, and has found the nest torn and empty.

Mr. Tulliver's prompt procedure entailed on him further promptitude in finding the convenient person who was desirous of lending five hundred pounds on bond. "It must be no client of Wakem's," he said to himself; and yet at the end of a fortnight it turned out to the contrary, not because Mr. Tulliver's will was feeble, but because external fact was stronger. Wakem's client was the only convenient person to be found. Mr. Tulliver had a destiny as well as Œdipus, and in this case he might plead, like Œdipus, that his deed was inflicted on him, rather than committed by him.

Could there be a slenderer, more insignificant thread in human history than this consciousness of a girl, busy with her small inferences of the way in which she could make her life pleasant? — in a time, too, when ideas were with fresh vigor making armies of themselves, and the universal kinship was declaring itself fiercely; when women on the other side of the world would not mourn for the husbands and sons who died bravely in a common cause, and men stinted of bread on our side of the world heard of that willing loss and were patient: a time when the soul of man was waking to pulses which had for centuries been beating in him unheard, until their full sum made a new life of terror or of joy.

What in the midst of that mighty drama are girls and their blind visions? They are the Yea or Nay of that good for which men are enduring and fighting. In these delicate vessels is borne onward through the ages the treasure of human affections.

Reference has been made, as an indication of good honest art, to her habit of hinting at the outcome of her story at or near its beginning. The depths of Tito's future deceit are sounded by that wise forecaster, Piero di Cosimo, on the first day of his career in Florence. We see the tragic possibilities surrounding the Tullivers in the careless, boyish talk of Tom and Bob Jakin. Shakspere, once more, plunges *in medias res*, and into the end of things, too. The tragedy of 'Hamlet' hangs on what Hamlet does, and what he does depends upon what the Ghost tells him to do; so the Ghost enters Act I., Scene 1. Finally, she is Shaksperean in the proximity of her tragedy and comedy; sufficient examples of which are the Rainbow tavern scene, the talk at the Genoese wharf after Grandcourt's death, and the contrast between Mordecai and little Jacob Cohen. It is all profoundly true to life.

If her dramas were more technically dramatic, they would lose in psychic value. They are for the closet. Her contemplative outweighed her dramatic powers because she was not merely a dramatist.

X

Whatever one may think of 'Daniel Deronda' after 'Adam Bede,' the disappointment is not, or ought not to be, due to the transfer of the scene to city life and the manners of county people. A sufficient hint was given in that earlier work of an ability to portray refinement, in the sketch of the Irwines, which should have prepared all intelligent readers for its fuller display in later books. George Eliot knew "Society." Her observation was not limited to the middle and artisan classes, nor was her discriminative enthusiasm kindled only by her passion for the country. She had also an intellectual companionship with the city, and with that which corresponded to it in county houses. The inside history of some of the adverse criticism of 'Daniel Deronda' would make interesting reading, painful as it might be to those who look for such generous comradeship among literary folk as of necessity excludes jealousy at the invasion of one field by a master of another. Any reasonably calm view would lead one to suppose that the skill which could carve out an Adam Bede and a Silas Marner would be equally successful with a Sir Hugo or a Mr. Van der Noodt; and would justify the expectations that the art which is shown in devising the conversation of the tenants at Arthur's birthday party would be just as much at home in reporting the give-and-take talk of the upper class across Grandcourt's mahogany. Her success in this department developed rapidly, and never deteriorated. Captain Wybrow and Miss Assher are drawn with a somewhat uncertain hand, but at the very next stroke she rises to the full possession of power in the Irwines; unlike poor Miss Brontë, whose Ginevra Fanshawe is as bad as her Blanche Ingram. It is another proof of her remarkable observation that she not only gives to each of these sharply defined extremes its appropriate language, but shades most delicately the difficult differences between county manners and the style of the middle class. There is no mistaking the provincial atmosphere of the men Mr. Brooke had invited to his table; and no careful reader would ever suppose that Mr. Brooke himself, with all his commonplaceness, belonged to that set.

XI

Who ever entered more deeply into the moods of her characters than George Eliot? At the 'Adam Bede' period she was as far removed from the religious influences of her childhood as she ever was; and yet it was George Eliot who drew that sweet Wesleyan saint, Dinah Morris. The very passion of religious outpouring pulses in her exhortations, and the pleading in the prison with Hetty is a grand night-wrestle with God. If there is a classical literature of prayer, the prayers in 'Adam Bede' belong to it.

The character of Kalonymos, in 'Daniel Deronda,' has always seemed to me an excellent example of this sympathetic power of entrance into mental attitudes not her own; and its consideration next to the paragraph dealing with Dinah will, in addition, indicate the multifariousness of her genius. Kalonymos is the type of the faithful high-class, but not vividly religious, Jew; with the steady gaze of the fatalist, and taking opinions as he took the shapes of trees; loving freedom, but not thinking of his people's future. He told Deronda that when travelling in the East he liked to lie on deck and watch the stars: the sight of them satisfied him, and he had no further hunger. "And almost as soon as Deronda was in London," the author says at the end of the interview, "the aged man was again on shipboard, greeting the friendly stars without any eager curiosity." It is an effective touch — that fine old Kalonymos watching his stars, and it is quite apart from other touches. We may not recognize his counterpart among our present acquaintances, yet we instinctively feel the truth of it all; and when we do meet him we shall recognize him.

In a widely sympathetic nature, responsive to influences from unusual as well as customary surroundings; or in a mental habit of calm, sane, open-eyed, unemotional receptiveness, like that of Kalonymos, who takes nature at her word, without asking any questions, — who has an affection rather than a love for nature; or, again, in a fundamentally religious constitution, whose depths may be stirred profoundly, but only by profound causes, — in all such there is no dread of the supernatural. The Kalonymos class, satisfied that it is a part of the celestial order, would receive its manifestations with a cool enjoyment and a fearless curiosity; and with the other two a sense of wonder and a feeling of awe would completely swamp all vulgar manifestations of alarm. We cannot fancy Dinah Morris *frightened* at a thunder storm. One of the most telling strokes in the portraiture of Gwendolen Harleth is the *terror* she feels when the supernatural touches her. There is no depth in her to correspond with the depth in the phenomenon; no deep answering to deep. It is as if a great tornado struck a duck-pond, — its piteous shallowness bared to the lightning's flash.

Not only in the general symmetry of her characters, but in the tender side-lights she throws upon their varying moods from the many-angled mirror of her sympathy, does she satisfy the anxious expectations of art. Do we ever stop to consider what the word "sympathy" stands for in all its fulness? To cultivate it, says Ruskin, "you must be among living creatures and thinking about them;" and that means not only an intellectual effort to comprehend them, but that quick understanding of another's feeling which seems like a sudden warm pressure of the hand — a sympathy without criticism, almost without speech. George Eliot so understood Romola's mood when she pictured her setting forth on the day of the procession with Brigida: "Romola set out in that languid state of mind with which every one enters on a long day of sight-seeing purely for the sake of gratifying a child or some dear childish friend."

C. — HER SYMPATHY: FURTHER CONSIDERED

I

It is time to examine a little more narrowly into the texture of this sympathy, which she wore, not as fine clothes or jewelry, but as a necessary garment for warmth.

It is a fine thing to be able to show how a despicable character has, perhaps by some mysterious inheritance, or by the sure working out of some hidden law, a bent or twist which circumstances will mould along the line of a resistance made the least by these conditions. The growth of Tito's duplicity was like the rising tide. He had borrowed from falsehood, and he had to pay the debt by further borrowings. George Eliot makes no weak apologies, and is not one of those fools who make a mock at sin by calling bitter sweet and sweet bitter. She subtly removes him more and more from her sympathy and ours, or rather, let us say, he removes himself from a sympathy which would still wistfully follow him if it might; and yet without dogmatism, without undue emphasis or passion, she makes it evident that Tito's troubles come largely from an innate love of reticence. It was an impulse, acting unconsciously at the beginning: concealment was easy to him. "He would now and then conceal something which had as little the nature of a secret as the fact that he had seen a flight of crows." It does not lessen the despicability of the character, viewed objectively, and it does not call for much waste of pity viewed subjectively; but it does widen our sympathies with glimpses into dark unopened chambers where one must grope blindly to find the key of escape. George Eliot makes us hate the sin for a long time before we begin to hate the sinner, so insidious is this growth of reticence into falsehood, and so subtly does it blend with his pleasure-loving nature, which finds it easier to lie than to bear burdens under the truth. He is a lovable fellow, even after he has begun to deceive, and we are kept hoping that he will find the courage to retrace his steps. Such good looks, such pleasant manners, such winning address, such sweet amiability — surely Apollo will not turn into an evil god! But the canker grows and grows, until in one of those grand climacteric moments which carry within them all the mockery of the past and all the tragedy of the future, he stands before Romola, not in the fair Grecian shape which won her, but "in his *loathsome*[1] beauty," *his* attractiveness, *her* curse.

Of all hopeless cases of sympathy one would say the case of the miser was the most hopeless. Yet no one can ever read 'Silas Marner' without thinking that perhaps there are extenuating circumstanes for all the other misers also. And what is there accomplished in an idyll is more laboriously traced forth in the complicated history of Mr. Bulstrode. The piti-

---

[1] "Twenty letters of twenty pages do not display a character," says Taine, in his chapter on Richardson, "but one sharp word does."

ableness of his position is allowed to disturb the security of our scorn only so far as a sympathetic analysis of his temperamental peculiarities tempers our desire to see the heaviest punishment inflicted. The dangerous doctrine is not taught that a man is not to be held responsible for the unforeseen consequences of his actions; what is enforced is the difficulty of deciding how far he is to be held responsible. The honest force of righteous indignation is nowhere minimized in George Eliot's work, but is, on the contrary, applauded; and yet there is a gentle insistence of "Judge not," because there may be some hidden fact which if known would alter the judgment. The glory of such magnanimity shines the more steadfastly in that while it is easy to find excuses for vices akin to our own, and for such as are somewhat loosely classed as "amiable," it requires sympathy of an heroic fibre to shadow forth natural causes for unnatural vices, and to attempt an understanding of one spiritually one's opposite. As George Eliot is, of all novelists, the most strenuous in emphasizing the beauty of altruism, it would be natural to expect a coldness of feeling towards the unloveliness of egoism. But it is a part of her reverent attitude towards this same Social Good that she should be eminently just to all, — including therefore those opposed to the Social Good: hence her sympathy with those most naturally repugnant to her sympathy. I do not know of such a mental attitude, proceeding from such a moral purpose, in any other novelist.[1]

---

[1] The fairness resulting from an honest, intelligent sympathy is clearly illustrated in her defence of Byron against the pietistic cant of Cumming. In her essay against that preacher's doctrines she repudiates with noble scorn the charge that Byron's "dying moments"

Thus she makes it apparent that Mr. Bulstrode's way of explaining dispensations would have been deceitful only to an idealized self,—that is, to a self freed from egoistic fetters: in view of those fetters, it was a genuine method because egoism does not affect the sincerity of beliefs: "rather, the more our egoism is satisfied, the more robust is our belief." He is wrapped in the atmosphere of a doctrine which admits of the view that the depth of a particular sin is "but a measure for the depth of forgiveness." If sin is egoism, in the bad sense and with all that may logically flow from its uncontrolled possession of a man, a religious system which may be twisted into a feeder for this egoism is to be taken into consideration. Mr. Bulstrode was in the grasp of such a system. He was a hypocrite, yes, but it was a doctrinal hypocrisy; and that is of a kind that can only be understood, and then only partially, by an understanding of the doctrine. The "outer" conscience, with its concrete warnings, is likely to be swallowed up in the "inner" conscience of abstract formulas: bad deeds are excused by a "sense of pardon." George Eliot does not mean to say that doctrines are responsible for sins. A man may use his religion for a cloak of maliciousness. But she delicately shows how "mixed" the sinner's motives are likely to be when the sinner is a certain kind of a "professing Christian."

were spent in writing a certain recklessly hopeless poem; rejoicing that, on the contrary, the poet's "unhappy career was ennobled and purified towards its close by a high and sympathetic purpose, by honest and energetic efforts for his fellow-men." Yet by turning to the passage referred to in the footnote to p. 196, it will be seen that this generous tribute is in the face of a general and fundamental dislike of Lord Byron's character.

Nor does she make Bulstrode wish to continue in sin that grace may abound. He would have echoed St. Paul's "God forbid!" to that; and yet that is what he actually did. He used his wealth — such, for instance, as he got through investments in the dyes which rotted Mr. Vincy's silk — for the exaltation of God's cause; "which was something distinct from his own rectitude of conduct." Vincy was, in Bulstrode's view, one of God's enemies, in that he was a worldly man: he was to be used, therefore, as an instrument in Mr. Bulstrode's hands for the glory of God, through wealth wrung from Vincy, who would not have used it for God's glory.

Mr. Bulstrode had from the first moments of shrinking, but they were private, and took the form of prayer. "Thou knowest how loose my soul sits from these things — how I view them all as implements for tilling Thy garden rescued here and there from the wilderness." It was easy for him to settle what was due from him to others by inquiring what was God's intention in regard to himself. He was not a coarse hypocrite. "He was simply a man whose desires had been stronger than his theoretic beliefs, and who had gradually explained the gratification of his desires into satisfactory agreement with those beliefs."

But, that we may not charge his hypocrisy against his "Evangelical" creed, in the flattering belief that our own creed, for example, if it does not happen to be "Evangelical," would have saved him, George Eliot points out, with her wide-eyed sanity of vision, that we are all occasional hypocrites of this sort, and that Bulstrode's implicit reasoning is not peculiar to his sect. "There is no general doctrine which is not capable of eating out our morality if unchecked by the deep-seated habit of direct fellow-feeling with individual fellow-men."

The two night scenes with Raffles are a most marvellous revelation of insight into the motive force of this subconsciousness of desire warping the soul from its true course. Bulstrode was bound by conscience to obey Lydgate's behest not to give his patient liquors of any sort. All through the first night his prayers for Raffles are colored by wishes which can only be accomplished by Raffles's death. Then the apologies for those wishes: Who was Raffles? Why should such a useless, miserable creature live to torture him, Bulstrode, God's servant, and wreck all his plans for God's glory? Ah, yes, but it was dreadful to think of his dying so impenitent. Well, were not public criminals impenitent, and did they not have to die? If Providence should award death to this private criminal, as the law did with the public criminals, surely there was no sin in contemplating it as desirable. Lydgate might have made a mistake. He was human. None of the other doctors in Middlemarch would have prescribed in that way. Perhaps the opposite course of treatment was the correct one. No, no. He will obey Lydgate's orders. He will separate his intentions from his desires. But if the orders are not valid? Piteous, piteous conflict!

Then the day comes, and with it Lydgate. Raffles is pronounced worse. Lydgate prescribes opium in case of prolonged sleeplessness, and is most minute in his directions as to the point at which the doses should cease. He also reiterates his orders against alcohol. The next night — the fatal night — arrives. Bulstrode is too weary for further watching, and turns the case over to the housekeeper; but forgets to tell her when the doses of opium must cease. An hour and a half elapses. He starts to make good the omission — and stops. Perhaps she has already given him too much. He hesitates a long time. Raffles can be heard moaning and murmuring. As there was still no sleep, perhaps Lydgate's prescription had best be disobeyed. He turns away from the sick man's room. Presently Mrs. Abel raps at his door. Cannot she give the poor sinking creature some brandy? Bulstrode does not answer; the struggle is going on within him. Mrs. Abel, who knows nothing of Lydgate's prohibition, pleads strongly for the stimulant. Still silence. "It's not a time to spare when people are at death's door," cries Mrs. Abel, in her ignorant pity. He gives her the key of the wine-cooler. . . . At six o'clock he rises and spends some time in prayer. He visits Raffles, and finds him in his last agony. He hides the almost empty opium phial and the brandy bottle; and Lydgate, on his arrival, is forced to the conclusion that his treatment was a mistake. That is all. It was virtually murder; the diseased motive acting "like an irritating agent in his blood."

II

A book full of human nature must be more or less full of human sin. We know George Eliot's definition of sin, and we know why she deals with it, and how. She widens the scope of morality in fiction, by extending the word "sin" to something beyond the infraction of one of the commandments, as if no grief could ever flow from less evident aspects of wrong-doing. It is not difficult to fancy how George Sand would have dealt with Maggie and Stephen. Our sympathies are much more subtly moved, however, by the picture of Maggie, not sinning in a way which would indicate, among other things, a vulgar lack of inventive imagination on the part of the author, but undergoing self-imposed expiation for an injustice done another in thought, not deed, — an expiation made sublime by the fact that it involves a public condemnation such as would have been called forth by the sin of deed; Maggie's public having every reason to suppose that the sin of deed had been committed.

Perhaps her intense sympathy does lead her into an occasional weakness. Her tenderness in the treatment of folly grows, like other used faculties, and a little out of proportion, now and then, to the other faculties.

> "Continual harvest wears the fruitful field."

In one of her poetical headings she says:

> " Pity the laden one: this wandering woe
> May visit you or me; "

and she extends her pity to the woe-causer. She is as sorry for Tryan as for Tryan's victim. Mr. Irwine, it seems to us, is almost too pitiful for Arthur. Arthur is more favorably considered than Anthony in 'Mr. Gilfil,' and yet he is of the same stripe. The Poysers, one feels, ought really to have left the neighborhood, as they wished to do, to make the Nemesis complete. But then, as we have seen, her Nemesis has *some* healing in her wings. It is a deep question, and it may be that she errs on the safe side.

The treatment of Dorothea is clearly an indication, however, of a faculty used to excess, for the reader fails to give his sympathy into the keeping of the author's; which, when the reader is in general sympathy with the author, — when he is a sympathetic reader, in short, — suggests, at least, a false note somewhere. The character is built on a sure foundation; namely, the lack of complete ideality in woman; but the superstructure is not convincingly true. "All Dorothea's passion was transferred through a mind struggling toward an ideal life; the radiance of her transfigured girlhood fell on the first object that came within its level." Exactly; but was Casaubon within the level of any such girl as Dorothea? His letter of proposal is nothing more than a bid for an amanuensis. Can it be supposed that a girl like that would not see through such language, — would not feel insulted by the suggestion that their introduction came at a moment when he most needed help for the completion of a life's plan? He is proposing marriage to her, but he is thinking of himself and his book on fish deities and things. The "meanness of opportunity" is what galled Dorothea, but that is a kind of meanness felt by all whose ideals are higher than their surroundings; and it is difficult to conceive of any genuine girl regarding that semi-petrified mummy as in any way a realization of an ideal.

In the concluding chapter of the story, Dorothea is pictured as living happily with Ladislaw, and yet the general opinion seems to be that, spiritually, her marriage with that attractive Bohemian was her *second* mistake. The author acknowledges that it was not ideally beautiful. And she maintains that her first mistake could not have happened if "Society" had not smiled on such propositions. But Dorothea's society did not smile on it. Brooke said all he could for Chettam, although what Brooke said on any subject was not much to the purpose, and she would not have had Chettam, no matter who had spoken for him. Her sister is filled with horror at the thought of the marriage. She has been ridiculing Casaubon before Dorothea, unconscious of her engagement; and when that is announced she is awed with a sense of doom. "There was something funereal in the whole affair, and Mr. Casaubon seemed to be the officiating clergyman, about whom it would be indecent to make remarks." When Chettam hears of the engagement he exclaims — as do all of us — "Good God! It is horrible!" Mrs. Cadwallader's view is that the great soul which Dorothea has discovered in Casaubon is really a great bladder for dried peas to rattle in; and as for Mr. Cadwallader, why should he interfere? It was surely none of his business. George Eliot's horses have run away with her, for once. In the first place, Casaubon is too evident a bag-of-bones to win the warm esteem of any Dorothea; and in the second place, Dorothea's story closes in great happiness, notwithstanding the author's intention to make it plain that it ought not to, in the light of ideal longings. It is a double failure, — the result of an overworked sympathy.

III

Her extensive feeling is shown by her frequent use of the word 'poor': it is 'poor Tom,' 'poor Rosamond,' 'poor Mr. Casaubon,' where we think of the adjective as primarily applicable in a very different sense. But this, again, may be the non-possession in us of that wide horizon of hers. At least, she does not allow us to have any gross misconceptions as to the cause of sin; being careful to point out, for example, that Stephen's fault was not hypocrisy, but something much more subtle. "For my part, I am very sorry for him," she says of Casaubon; and for her reason she gives us a picture of a scholarly scrupulousness made egoistic by an absence of emotion, a denial of inspiration, and a total lack of humor. Why should we not pity him, too, — this pallid Casaubon — a little — just a little — bit? What she really thought of Casaubon's magnum opus is expressed in Dorothea's revolt and Ladislaw's contempt; and in another book as follows: "the heaping of cat-mummies and the expensive cult of enshrined putrefactions." Yet her own sense of humor inspires her to discern, even in herself, the minor shades of faults which in their unshaded intensity glare in him. She is not tainted with the common error of confusing sympathy with respect. She has no respect for Casaubon's work, as such, but much sympathy with him in the light of his environment. "I have some feeling for Dr. Sprague," she says. "One's self-satisfaction is an untaxed kind of property which it is very unpleasant to find depreciated."

Sympathy tempers the judgment, and the chief intellectual result is fairness. Savonarola's refusal to interfere with the execution of Bernardo was a particularly heinous offence in George Eliot's eyes, and her great fairness is nowhere better shown than in her continued sympathy with the friar after that downfall in her esteem. It is only the Grandcourts she cannot help with her compassion, and that through no fault of hers, — them and the "moral swindlers" she fulminates against in 'Theophrastus;' and even those we can fancy brought within the range of her painstaking thought when placed in the artistic setting of fiction.

Mr. Hutton says of Rosamond Vincy: "This exquisitely painted figure is the deadliest blow at the commonplace assumption that limitation in both heart and brain is a desirable thing for women that has ever been struck."[1] And the education of a young lady in her day (has it changed so very much since, in our fashionable "seminaries"?) encouraged such limitations. Like the rest of us, Rosamond is partially the product of her environment. The woman who could break Lydgate's heart could nevertheless be the flower of Mrs. Lemon's school, "where the teaching included all that was demanded in the accomplished female, even to extras, such as the getting in and out of a carriage." "Propriety" was her bugaboo, and Mrs. Lemon taught it as earnestly as Arnold taught Latin and Greek. Taste she was mistress of, and there her powers ceased. She is the kind of young lady who smiles little in society, because the smile reveals dimples which she thinks unbecoming; who is ashamed of her good mother's use of such words as "tetchy" and "pick;" who feels that she might have been happier if she had not been the daughter of a Middlemarch manufacturer; and who is hit off to a nicety by her brother Fred, who tells her that the word "disagreeable" does not describe the smell of grilled bone to which she objects, but a sensation in her "little nose associated with certain finicking notions which are the classics of Mrs. Lemon's school." So

[1] 'Essays on Some of the Modern Guides of English Thought in Matters of Faith,' by Richard Holt Hutton. Macmillan, London, 1887.

Rosamond, too, is taken into the broad bosom of George Eliot's sympathy, and we are made to see that a lamentable deficiency in the educational system must be fairly weighed as important evidence in the final judgment of a character whose native narrowness could only be removed by an altogether different system. Mrs. Lemon and the general arrangement of things which permits Mrs. Lemon to exist are partially responsible. Not all our pity must go to Lydgate.

IV

If George Eliot asks us to enter with her into a sympathetic understanding of the mental conditions of people who are neither her favorites nor ours, and who stand in the way of the happiness of the favorites, she does not, on the other hand, fail to point out the faults in those favorites which help to make the unhappiness possible. She has not, it is true, the modern trick of disparaging the personal appearance of her heroes and heroines, and she does not deprecate their "irregular features," nor apologize for their lack of beauty. She is sufficiently in love with her Esthers and Romolas and Dorotheas to think them beautiful, and to make us think so, too. She is chiefly occupied, however, with the more important business of illustrating their moral shortcomings; and they are ethical, rather than æsthetic heroines.

Thus Lydgate, of whom, I think, George Eliot is the most fond of all her heroes, has a fundamental fault,— a flaw in a base otherwise nobly strong, and which causes the downfall of the statue. If he had only married Dorothea! IF: precisely: the whole tragedy of the universe is held in that one little word. There is just a thread of coarseness in Lydgate's attitude towards women,— a thread as common to men of intellect and chivalry as a still coarser fibre is to men of lower grade; it is the tendency to exalt mere outward grace to a pinnacle the rarified atmosphere of which only grace of the inward and spiritual sort can bear. Lydgate, with all his cleverness and worth, is not capable of gauging such a character as Dorothea's; although Ladislaw, who has been quite an unnecessary grief to Dorothea's admirers (for he is really a fine fellow), has the essential necromancy which Lydgate, his superior in most things, lacks. He is afraid of Dorothea: "a little too earnest," he thinks. "It is troublesome to talk to such women. They are always wanting reasons, yet they are too ignorant to understand the merits of any question, and usually fall back on their moral sense to settle things after their own taste." But of Rosamond he thinks: "She is grace itself; she is perfectly lovely and accomplished. That is what a woman ought to be: she ought to produce the effect of beautiful music." "Notwithstanding her undeniable beauty," Miss Brooke is found wanting in that she does not fill his idea of *adornment*, which, to his notion, is the first necessary qualification in a wife. She did not possess the "melodic charm" for him that the other woman did. "She did not look at things from the proper feminine angle. The society of such women was about as relaxing as going from your work to teach the second form, instead of reclining in a paradise with sweet laughs for bird-notes, and blue eyes for a heaven." So, although his point of view is far from being the same as Mr. Chichely's, what he sees is not dissimilar; that coursing gentleman confessing, "Between ourselves, the mayor's daughter is more to my taste than Miss Brooke." And thus Lydgate got his bird-notes and his blue eyes,— got them with a vengeance; and the paradise that he reclined in was the chair he flung himself into that day when the Quallingham letter came; checkmated by the utter insensibility to all true values of that "perfectly lovely and accomplished" product of Mrs. Lemon's fashionable school. This masculine vice (which takes hold of the Lydgates as well as the Chichelys) of blindness to psychical, in the neighborhood of physical, grace, and which deceived this particular Lydgate into thinking the physical was but the outward and visible part of something lovely inward and spiritual, was the cause of his wasted energy and the wreck of his noble ambitions. "*This* is what I am thinking of; and *that* is what I might have been thinking of." And the man who had dreamed of discoveries which would have revolutionized medical treatment finally writes a treatise on gout — of all things in the world — and calls his wife his basil plant,—"a plant which had once flourished wonderfully on a murdered man's brains."

What has been said about George Eliot's perceptive qualities, joined to what has been said about her conscientious avoidance of generalities, is perhaps the sufficient evidence of a peculiarly logical order of mind in which synthesis follows in beautiful sequence upon analysis. First of all, she *observed*, — she gave a close attention to the things she was to write about; and observation "is the great instrument of discovery in mind and matter" because it is the instrument of the analytical method. The percept, let us say, is Tom Tulliver. Like all other objects, he stands before us in a complex state. How can we best understand what is simple in Tom, resolve him from his complexities into his elements? We must separate him from the other characters, — from Mr. Riley among the others. Mr. Riley enters Tom's life at a very important period, being called in by Mr. Tulliver for advice concerning Tom's schooling. He recommends Mr. Stelling, without a sufficient knowledge of his acquirements. Stelling was the son-in-law of Timpson, and Riley was kindly disposed towards Timpson. He did not know of any other schoolmaster whom he had any ground for recommending in preference to Stelling; why, then, should he not recommend Stelling? It is chilling to have no opinion when your opinion is asked; and if you are to give it at all, it is stupid not to give it with an air of conviction. Riley knows no harm of Stelling. He wishes him well, especially as he is the son-in-law of Timpson. He recommends him, therefore, and then he "begins to think with admiration of a man recommended on such high authority." There was no plot for self-interest in the advice. The idea of pleasing Timpson by serving Stelling was one of those "little dim ideas and complacencies" which enter without forethought into a brain stimulated by a snug open fire and such open-handed hospitality as Mr. Tulliver was famous for. His "immovability of face, and the habit of taking a pinch of snuff before he gave an answer made him trebly oracular to Mr. Tulliver." On this highly imperfect evidence, poor Tom (we cannot avoid the "poor," after all) is subjected to a treatment of instruction resulting only in unhappiness and heaviness of spirit, and Mr. Tulliver is made to sacrifice money he ought to save.

It is, in itself, a most subtle analysis of Mr. Riley's mental attitude, but it is here introduced to illustrate the author's method of separating the influence of the environment in order to show what this particular Tom might have been with Mr. Riley eliminated. Hence our sympathy with Tom — a spiritually hard and unyielding character, but demanding pity, nevertheless, as well as Maggie. The author says, as it were: Put yourself and all your friends in Tom's place, and the result would be the same.

Like all creators, she must be more than an analyst, or she would be no more than a scientist, and an incomplete one at that. On the contrary, we have a *system* in George Eliot, because her synthesis is founded upon her analysis. Art is constructive, and construction is essentially synthetic. While laws are the result of discovered facts, the artist derives subsequent facts from the laws, which is deduction, — the process of synthesis. It is an axiom of philosophy that the analysis must be exact, else the synthesis will not be legitimate. We have seen how exact her analysis is. There is, to be sure, such a thing as pure imagination, which is synthesis without analysis; but George Eliot's imagination, like Wordsworth's and Dante's, is not of that order. Her deduction was based on induction, her synthesis on a precedent analysis, *because of her sympathy with her subject.* There are certain known characteristics of Lydgate and Rosamond, and the artist's business is to show us the tragic facts resulting from these clashing laws of character. By tracing the motive to its source, she forces upon us an attitude of judicial fairness. It is a noble thing to be fair-minded. We ought not to blame a stream for its muddiness. Perhaps there is a mud spring that is responsible. And then what caused the spring to be muddy? Tom Tulliver as we know him is the joint result of the different tendencies acting upon him and in him. The tendencies have been decomposed, and a general principle has evolved. He is studied in the light of the principle, and we have the special case. One must be a logician to do it rightly, and one must be a poet to do it wisely.

The delineation of Machiavelli, in 'Romola,' is a good illustration of this mental process. George Eliot was thoroughly familiar with the works of the Italian in the original, which is a different sort of knowledge from that derived from translations. She knew the times also. The result is a most interesting sketch of a character which she makes attractive without minimizing the qualities we associate with that name; or, it would be more correct to say, without omitting hints of those qualities, because the portrait is of Machiavelli in his youth.

His conversation is tinctured with the peculiar flavor which we should naturally expect in the future author of 'The Prince.' He admires Soderini's attack upon Pieroda Bibbiena because both the offence and its punishment are beneficial to Soderini. He says at another time, in illustration of this Machiavellian idea: "Many of these half-way severities are mere hot-headed blundering. The only safe blows to be inflicted on men and parties are the blows that are too heavy to be avenged;" and when Cennini says that is Satanical, he laughs and replies that Satan was a blunderer who made a stupendous failure. "If he had succeeded we should all have been worshipping him, and his portrait would have been more flattered." He measures "men's dulness by the devices they trust in for deceiving others." His clear natural vision penetrates the political mistakes of Savonarola, and he points out with cool incisiveness the fatal points in the friar's position. But he lacks the vision which belongeth not to the natural man, and fails to fathom the spiritual grandeur of Savonarola. He is always contrasted pleasantly with the merely spiteful cynics like Francesco Cei and Ceccone. When Cei sneers at Politian for praising both Savonarola and Alexander, Machiavelli laughs and says, " A various scholar must have various opinions," — the cynicism of intellect versus the cynicism of sheer ill-will. His refined irony is always used as a buffer, in 'Romola,' to some grosser kind. There is a winsome magnanimity in him, in fact, for, though suspicious of Tito, and a little jealous of his success, he defends him against the venom of Cei's gossip about the stolen jewels: " You forget the danger of the precedent, Francesco. The next mad beggarman may accuse you of stealing his verses, or me, God keep me, of stealing his coppers." And yet he is not above thinking Savonarola capable of false prophesyings, nor does he blame him for them except that they are not wise prophesyings also, as the times were on his side, and he might have done something great. The grand charcoal sketch of Savonarola in this novel reveals faults as well as virtues; but because Machiavelli's natural cleverness was unable to comprehend the complexities of the faults, it could not pierce the depth of the virtues. The analysis is so fine that one exclaims, "That is the real Machiavelli!" And the case is interesting because the synthesis is not only based on a true analysis, but is illuminated also by the historical imagination.

V

The makers of the best of modern English dictionaries have thought so well of Fred Vincy's definition of a prig that they have included it among the examples under that title. "A prig," says Fred, "is a fellow who is always making you a present of his opinions." He is, of necessity, a kill-joy and a nuisance; a jest for enemies and a burden for friends. And he is of no use whatever in the world, unless as a test for saintship in others; for to put up with him charity must suffer very long and be most exceeding kind. It was like old Thackeray to say that his Esmond was a prig; but he was, in reality, nothing of the kind. Thackeray held the common view that if you stood stoutly for virtue and truth, and did not yield now and then to the weaknesses of the majority, you were a bit too good for mortal companionship. It is a thoroughly worldly view, because Thackeray was a thorough man of the world. But surely that is not priggishness? If it is, then all the strong souls that have ever lived, all the reformers and all the martyrs, and all who have not been afraid to look Wrong in the face and say, "You are Wrong," and to look Right in the face and say, "You are Right," have been prigs; and the only persons who are not prigs are the easy-going creatures we meet every day, who do what most men and women do for no other reason than that most men and women do it. If there is anybody in this vale of tears who is wholly irreproachable, you may be sure that he is the one man in the universe who is wholly modest: if he is conscious of the fact, it follows that he is not irreproachable. The trouble with most "irreproachable" people is that they are unapproachable also.

Daniel Deronda is, therefore, most decidedly, not a prig. His chief weakness is sympathy ["you have a passion for people who are pelted, Dan"], which is the chief thing a prig is deficient in. A prig is an egoist. Deronda was always doing, or thinking about doing, something for others. He did not smoke himself, but he carried a cigar case in his pocket, the contents of which he offered his friends, upon occasion. A prig would have pointed out to his tobacco-consuming acquaintances the evils of the habit, illustrating the beauty of abstention with edifying references to himself. Lydgate is not a prig, because his occasionally pragmatical talk is not prompted by a consuming self-love, but by a self-consuming love for his profession; and his anger is stirred, not because his coworkers do not agree with him, but because of their stubborn and harmfully stupid opposition to all reform. A physician who happened at the same time to be a prig would not have acknowledged at Raffles' death that he had, after all, made a mistake. Your real prig never makes mistakes.

As for Felix Holt and Adam Bede, more allowance must be made, because of their humbler stations in life, conversational self-restraint being not only a matter of grace but of gentle breeding also. If Deronda and Lydgate had talked with the outspokenness of those two worthies, they could hardly have escaped this opprobrious title, which has been carelessly given them by some. But to bestow it upon the honest wrath of the radical and the righteous bluntness of the strong young carpenter is to take narrow views. Felix expressly tells Esther that he does not think himself better than others, that he does not blame others for not doing as he does; but that he is nevertheless determined not to get entangled in affairs where he " must wink at dishonesty and pocket the proceeds, and justify that knavery as part of a system that" he " cannot alter." He sees that the old Catholics were right with their higher and lower rule, and that he is called upon to accept the higher. To some men appears " the strong angel with the implacable brow," and on his awful lips are written Goethe's words, " Renounce! Thou must renounce!" Felix Holt was one of those men. He says he will not be rich; it is not his inward vocation. " Thousands of men have wedded poverty because they expect to go to heaven for it, but I wed it because it enables me to do what I most want to do on earth." And yet he fairly acknowledges that " some men do well to accept riches." Now, a prig, in dwelling on the superiority of his self-denial, would not have made this positive assertion that others *do* well in doing something that he was himself above doing: he would have said "others *may* do well," with a hesitating accent on the conditional word. Felix is not addressing his working-men, remember, but pleading among the birches with the woman he loves, whom he is trying to raise from the plane of taste to the plane of thought, and who finally is raised by contact with his noble mind. His notion about cravats is merely the exaggerated emphasis which a soul-stirring, mind-convincing, life-binding theory will lay upon details. It is a very great book, this 'Felix Holt,' because it throbs with the vivifying truth that a man should stay in his place to accomplish his purpose; and differentiates for all time a genuine and a fictitious, a moral and a political, radicalism. Felix belongs to the people. God has given him gifts. He intends, please God, to use them for the people. Who cares whether he wears cravats or not?[1]

Scepticism has its advantages. In unexpected ways it is the servant of an exalted ideality in its searching distrust of "practical" measures which fail to touch the hidden sores. 'Felix Holt' is a political novel in the best sense, in which sense it is, with the exception of 'Alton Locke' and 'Les Miserables,' the only political novel in existence. Its politics are subordinated to a philosophical idealism. Its hero is a literal radical because he aims at a literal reform. One has only to contrast the talk of the trades-union speaker at the Duffield hustings with Felix's ringing charges to understand this vital distinction. The one wants power through the ballot; the other carefully distinguishes between ignorant and instructed power, and shows that the ballot, under existing circumstances, would only increase the misery. What he is aiming at is to force public opinion, "the greatest power under heaven," into proper views of the labor problem, knowing that without that the ballot is a mere mischief-maker. Class elevation is the desideratum,—moral conversion, not political change. Herein is the Comptist faith, once more, and the faith of all moral enthusiasts as

---

[1] When one remembers the starched towels men wrapped around their necks in those days and called them cravats, one is ready to acknowledge that there may have been more of common-sense than stubbornness in Felix's position.

against the mechanical legislative efforts of Saint-Simonism and worse.

With this should be read the expansion of the idea in the 'Address to Working-men by Felix Holt,' printed in the 'Essays;' where, basing the argument on the recognized principle of Trades-unionism, the author proves that society can only prosper when its members consider the general good as well as their own. This 'Address' covers the Reform of '67, while the story belongs to the stirring days of '32. The 'Address' is a postscript, emphasizing what the novel sets forth; and its publication shows that its author did not intend the latter to be merely a vivid picture of a certain period: with her usual thoroughness, she made that merely the *milieu* for ideas covering all periods. That 'Felix Holt' did not close in a blaze of victory is not because of any heavy-hearted despair as to the ultimate triumph of justice: such a tone would have been foolishly optimistic in the light of observation. Moral changes come slowly, and are not generally discernible in any one lifetime.

Here is George Eliot's radicalism,—a pure radicalism, a radical radicalism;[1] having the strong support of a thinker like John Stuart Mill, who always maintained that the ballot alone would not serve. See how such radicalism is really conservatism, in that while striking at the root of acknowledged evil, it aims at conserving what is good in the old, in preserving it from a less complete radicalism, which would in destroying it only give birth to a worse new. See the true artist nature at work with the nature of the real

---

[1] Unlike her Spike, in 'Theophrastus,' to whom the epithet was applied very unfairly, "as he never went to the root of anything."

radical. The book might just as well have been called 'Felix Holt the Conservative.'

Contrasted with Harold's political radicalism, what Felix advocates is as gold with dross. Compared with Esther, refined as we see her at last by Felix, Harold and his social superiority are the vulgar realities, not the absence of cravats in Felix's bureau; and as mistress of Transome Court, this woman would have ranked below the wife of Felix Holt.

It is an important point, because if George Eliot's strongest characters are really prigs, how can we sympathize with her sympathy for them? Indeed, there is only one prig in these fictions, and that is Tom Tulliver. It is natural for the average boy of strong integrity and with a love of justice in him to be a prig; for such a boy is, almost inevitably, an egoist, inasmuch as he has not reached the age of opinions toned down by extenuating circumstances. Tom Tulliver is the natural boy, — perhaps we should say the natural Anglo-Saxon boy, of high courage and true, brave principles, with a lingering touch of the savage, and blind to all subtle distinctions between shades of Right and Wrong. It is a part of the fineness of George Eliot's art that he should be made a prig — he would not be typical else; and this emphasizes once more the claim that Daniel Deronda is not, and never was, a prig, because in the sketch of his early years, there is a notable absence of this characteristic bullyragging of boyhood. He was distinguishable from the average boy, in other words, by the absence of priggishness, which is the characteristic of typical boyhood.

VI

This strength of entrance into the hearts of others through the door of sympathy is effected with tender-footed sureness where the tread is most apt to be either too heavy or too light. It is a pity that George Eliot never wrote a book for children, because she understood them, — this childless woman. She could stoop to their intelligence without lowering her own; she could unbend and yet stand straight. Witness the delightful Garth children, and the scene at the Vincy's New Year party, when Mr. Farebrother " dramatized an intense interest" in Mary's story of Rumpelotiltskin, and preached his little sermon against cakes, how they were bad things, especially if they were sweet and had plums in them, — a little to Louisa's alarm, who " took the affair rather seriously." We have often to apply the word " Shaksperean " to phases of George Eliot's power; in her portrayal of child-life she surpasses Shakspere. Her boys and girls are not a lump sum ticketed " children," like a dozen specimens of a certain species of beetle in a natural history collection; but are just as much individualized as are her adults. Harry Transome, for example, is as different, in his petty, spiteful cruelties, from Tom Tulliver in his young English savagery, as the fathers of each are different; and one sees at once the insight of Lady Debarry's remark that Harry was not the child of a lady. The 'Mill on the Floss' is the one complete idyll in literature of this world of childhood, this microcosm of a world, with an order and growth of its own, repaying a loving study with

Her Sympathy

views into depths which, alas! are not often sounded at later stages.

Through the children our hearts are opened to the elders, just as they are in "real life," as we say, — as if a fine novel was not real life. The magician waves her wand at the outset over Mr. Gilfil:

Thus in Shepperton this breach with Mr. Oldinport tended only to heighten that good understanding which the Vicar had always enjoyed with the rest of his parishioners, from the generation whose children he had christened a quarter of a century before, down to that hopeful generation represented by little Tommy Bond, who had recently quitted frocks and trousers for the severe simplicity of a tight suit of corduroys, relieved by numerous brass buttons. Tommy was a saucy boy, impervious to all impressions of reverence, and excessively addicted to humming-tops and marbles, with which recreative resources he was in the habit of immoderately distending the pockets of his corduroys. One day, spinning his top on the garden-walk, and seeing the Vicar advance directly towards it, at that exciting moment when it was beginning to "sleep" magnificently, he shouted out with all the force of his lungs, "Stop! don't knock my top down, now!" From that day "little Corduroys" had been an especial favorite with Mr. Gilfil, who delighted to provoke his ready scorn and wonder by putting questions which gave Tommy the meanest opinion of his intellect.

"Well, little Corduroys, have they milked the geese to-day?"

"Milked the geese! Why, they don't milk the geese; ye 'r silly!"

"No! dear heart! why, how do the goslings live, then?"

The nutriment of goslings rather transcending Tommy's observations in natural history, he feigned to understand the question in an exclamatory rather than an interrogatory sense, and became absorbed in winding up his top.

"Ah, I see you don't know how the goslings live! But did you notice how it rained sugar-plums yesterday?" (Here Tommy became attentive.) "Why, they fell into my pocket as I rode along. You look into my pocket and see if they did n't."

Tommy, without waiting to discuss the alleged antecedent, lost no time in ascertaining the presence of the agreeable consequent, for he had a well-founded belief in the advantages of diving into the Vicar's pocket. Mr. Gilfil called it his wonderful pocket, because, as he delighted to tell the "young shavers" and "two-shoes" — so he called all little boys and girls — whenever he put pennies into it, they turned into sugar-plums or gingerbread, or some other nice thing. Indeed, little Bessie Parrot, a flaxen-headed "two-shoes," very white and fat as to her neck, always had the admirable directness and sincerity to salute him with the question, "What zoo dot in zoo pottet?"

With such an auspicious opening, we could have found it in our hearts to have forgiven the old parson any number of faults.

Mrs. Holt, in a flash, becomes something more to us than a humorous mass of foibles by the motherly longings awakened by Felix's attitude towards little Job Tudge.

"Where does Job Tudge live?" she said, still sitting, and looking at the droll little figure, set off by a ragged jacket with a tail about two inches deep sticking out above the funniest of corduroys.

"Job has two mansions," said Felix. "He lives here chiefly; but he has another home, where his grandfather, Mr. Tudge, the stone-breaker, lives. My mother is very good to Job, Miss Lyon. She has made him a little bed in a cupboard, and she gives him sweetened porridge."

The exquisite goodness implied in these words of Felix impressed Esther the more, because in her hearing his talk had usually been pungent and denunciatory. Looking at Mrs. Holt, she saw that her eyes had lost their bleak northeasterly expression, and were shining with some mildness on little Job, who had turned round toward her, propping his head against Felix.

"Well, why shouldn't I be motherly to the child, Miss Lyon?" said Mrs. Holt, whose strong powers of argument required the file of an imagined contradiction, if there were no real one at hand. "I never was hard-hearted, and I never will be. It was Felix picked the child up and took to him, you may be sure, for there's nobody else master where he is; but I wasn't going to beat the orphin child and abuse him because of that, and him as straight as an arrow when he's stripped, and me so fond of children, and only had one of my own to live. I'd three babies, Miss Lyon, but the blessed Lord only spared Felix, and him the masterfulest and the brownest of 'em all. But I did my duty by him, and I said, he'll have more schooling than his father, and he'll grow up a doctor, and marry a woman with money to furnish — as I was myself, spoons and every thing — and I shall have the grandchildren to look up to me, and be drove out in the gig sometimes, like old Mrs. Lukyn. And you see what it's all come to, Miss Lyon: here's Felix made a common man of himself, and says he'll never be married — which is the most unreasonable thing, and him never easy but when he's got the child on his lap, or when — "

"Stop, stop, mother," Felix burst in; "pray don't use that limping argument again — that a man should marry because he's fond of children. That's a reason for not marrying. A bachelor's children are always young; they're immortal children — always lisping, waddling, helpless, and with a chance of turning out good."

"The Lord above may know what you mean! And have n't other folks' children a chance of turning out good?"

"Oh, they grow out of it very fast. Here's Job Tudge, now," said Felix, turning the little one round on his knee, and holding his head by the back; "Job's limbs will get lanky; this little fist, that looks like a puff-ball, and can hide nothing bigger than a gooseberry, will get large and bony, and perhaps want to clutch more than its share; these wide blue eyes that tell me more truth than Job knows, will narrow and narrow, and try to hide truth that Job would be better without knowing; this little negative nose will become long and self-asserting; and this little tongue — put out thy tongue, Job " — Job, awe-struck under this ceremony, put out a little red tongue very timidly — "this tongue, hardly bigger than a rose-leaf, will get large and thick, wag out of season, do mischief, brag and cant for gain or vanity, and cut as cruelly, for all its clumsiness, as if it were a sharp-edged blade. Big Job will perhaps be naughty — " As Felix, speaking with the loud emphatic distinctness habitual to him, brought out this terribly familiar word, Job's sense of mystification became too painful: he hung his lip, and began to cry.

"See there," said Mrs. Holt, "you 're frightening the innicent child with such talk — and it 's enough to frighten them that thinks themselves the safest."

"Look here, Job, my man," said Felix, setting the boy down and turning him toward Esther; "go to Miss Lyon, ask her to smile at you, and that will dry up your tears like the sunshine."

"The question of beauty," says Emerson, "takes us out of surfaces to thinking of the foundations of things. The tint of the flower proceeds from its root." The foundation of 'Silas Marner' is the beauty of a sweet human interest filling a heart made vacant by the destruction of what that heart held dear, and which, base as it was, it had clung to in the death of affection brought about by a treachery which its simplicity accepted as the knell of all human intercourse and love. And the change is wrought by a little child. "And a little child shall lead them."

I once heard a physician say that a child's illness calls for more science and skill than an adult's, because the symptoms must be discerned without verbal hints from the patient. In George Eliot we repose the kind of faith we place in the old family doctor whom we call in when anxious about the baby's health. One feels that there will be no mistake in diagnosis, and that right treatment will follow. Dorothea's hands were "powerful, feminine, maternal." Mark the ascending emphasis: it describes George Eliot's attitude towards children; and hence the mother's instinct in this woman, who never was a mother, except in the sense that Felix Holt was a father.

She went on willingly, singing with ready memory various thing by Gordigiani and Schubert; then, when she had left the piano, Mab said, entreatingly, "Oh, Mirah, if you would not mind singing the little hymn."

"It is too childish," said Mirah. "It is like lisping."

"What is the hymn?" said Deronda.

"It is the Hebrew hymn she remembers her mother singing over her when she lay in her cot," said Mrs. Meyrick.

"I should like very much to hear it," said Deronda, "if you think I am worthy to hear what is so sacred."

"I will sing it if you like," said Mirah, "but I don't sing real words — only here and there a syllable like hers — the rest is lisping. Do you know Hebrew? because if you do, my singing will seem childish nonsense."

Deronda shook his head. "It will be quite good Hebrew to me."

Mirah crossed her little hands and feet in her easiest attitude, and then lifted up her head at an angle which seemed to be directed to some invisible face bent over her, while she sung a little hymn of quaint melancholy intervals, with syllables that really seemed childish lisping to her audience; but the voice in which she gave it forth had gathered even a sweeter, more cooing tenderness than was heard in her other songs.

"If I were ever to know the real words, I should still go on in my old way with them," said Mirah, when she had repeated the hymn several times.

"Why not?" said Deronda. "The lisped syllables are full of meaning."

"Yes, indeed," said Mrs. Meyrick. "A mother hears something like a lisp in her children's talk to the very last. Their words are not just what everybody else says, though they may be spelt the same. If I were to live till my Hans got old, I should still see the boy in him. A mother's love, I often say, is like a tree that has got all the wood in it from the very first it made."

"Is not that the way with friendship, too?" said Deronda, smiling. "We must not let mothers be too arrogant."

The bright little woman shook her head over her darning.

"It is easier to find an old mother than an old friend. Friendships begin with liking or gratitude — roots that can be pulled up. Mother's love begins deeper down."

Probably Mr. Brooke, were he brought into the talk at this point, would say: "Well, but dogs, now, and that sort of thing. I had it myself, that love of dogs. I went a good deal into that at one time. But a man can go too far. Too far, you know." I certainly do not wish to go too far in pursuit of any theory, nor to substantiate any theory from unsubstantial facts. But would not my medical friend be justified in extending his belief in the finer science needed for the treatment of children to the so-called dumb animals, and find the science requisite there equally fine? Veterinary surgery seems to have gone down in the general moral wreck with everything connected with kennels and stables, and one rarely hears of a horse doctor leading a cotillon. But there ought to be no grander profession in the world; and it fits in with the Positivist belief to care for living things considered positively, and not relatively in regard to some future life. Mr. Buchanan tells of the indignation with which George Eliot once met his reference to the necessarily short life allotted to her splendid bull-terrier, as if it were cruel to deny to the lower what we affirm of the higher animals.[1] At all events, I am sure that her love for dogs sprang from the same source as her love for children; and what makes her domestic scenes so complete is her inclusion of this noble friend of man among the familiar pictures of her country life.

---

[1] 'A Look Around Literature,' pp. 218 *seq*. But reports of conversations — especially such conversations — should always be read with some doubt as to precise accuracy. Memory is notably tricky, and in the heat of controversial talk much is struck off which would be modified if the thought of perpetuity in print were considered. If only tones, gestures, laughter, tears could be reported! Without them as interpreters, the text remains imperfect.

There are several well-known dogs in fiction, — notably Bill Sikes's Bull's-eye and the noble staghound of 'The Talisman,' to say nothing of the immortal Rab. But nearly every character of George Eliot's making is intimately associated with this "friend of man."

The last time I made my journey through the novels I kept tally of the number of dogs desiring my further acquaintance there; and unless I have overlooked some of them, there are fifty-five, divided as follows: eight spaniels, three bull-terriers, four terriers, three bloodhounds, three setters, two bulldogs, one sheepdog, two shepherds, two Newfoundlands, two King Charles, two pointers, two water-spaniels, one pug, two maltese, one turn-spit, two black-and-tans, one deerhound, one staghound, one Blenheim, one retriever, one St. Bernard, one mastiff, one half-mastiff, half-bull, one unspecified "Fido," one mongrel, one black cur, belonging to the gypsies, in 'Mill on the Floss,' and five other undesignated animals. Am I not safe in venturing the assertion that there is no category in any other writer even faintly approaching this?

And the same cleverness is shown in the invention, or, let us say, the discovery, of their names, as we saw before when considering their masters. The solemn mastiff of mine host in the 'Spanish Gypsy' is appropriately called Seneca, and Mary Garth's black-and-tan answers when you address him as Fly. Mr. Brooke's St. Bernard is Monk, and the deerhound is Fleet. A King Charles suggests Minny, and Mumps seems natural to any dog Bob Jakin might own. She is full also of indirect references. She confesses to the same kind of sympathy for ungainly people that she has for mongrels: the finely bred dogs any one can love. Caterina is represented as following Gilfil like a Blenheim spaniel trotting after a large setter. Gwendolen wheels away from Lush as if he had been a muddy hound. Maggie is on the watch — don't you see her? — like a skye-terrier; and in another place, is " shaking the water from her black locks like a skye-terrier escaped from his bath." Hans Meyrick is humorously reminded by the child Jacob, in relation to Mirah, of dogs that have been brought up by women and are manageable by them only.

She enters into their thoughts, — that is, she interprets what seem to be their thoughts, with a sympathy which brings laughter and tears. Mr. Gilfil's loneliness is shared with no other society than that of the brown old setter, Ponto, "who, stretched out at full length on the rug with his nose between his forepaws, would wrinkle his brows and lift up his eyelids every now and then, to exchange a glance of mutual understanding with his master." When Caterina started out on her journey to Mosslands, she was met at the door by "Rupert, the old bloodhound stationed on the mat, with the determination that the first person who was sensible enough to take a walk that morning should have the honor of his approbation and society."

As he thrust his great black and tawny head under her hand, and wagged his tail with vigorous eloquence, and reached the climax of his welcome by jumping up to lick her face, which was at a convenient licking height for him, Caterina felt quite grateful to the old dog for his friendliness. Animals are such agreeable friends. They ask no questions; they pass no criticisms.

And the last touch in the death scene of Anthony is given to this grand old Rupert. Sir Christopher is hurrying as fast as he can to where the body of Anthony has been found, and where the dog already is beside it. "He comes back and licks the old baronet's hand, as if to say 'Courage!' and is then down again snuffing the body."

Rupert was there, too, waiting and watching; licking first the dead and then the living hands; then running off on Mr. Bates's track, as if he would follow and hasten his return, but in a moment turning back again, unable to quit the scene of his master's sorrow.

Faithful unto death!

What a charming introduction to Mr. Irwine's home, which we are invited to enter, very softly, "without awaking the glossy brown setter who is stretched across the hearth, with her two puppies beside her; or the pug who is dozing with his black muzzle aloft like a sleepy president"! The setter's name is Juno, and presently we see her wagging her tail "with calm, matronly pleasure;" and when Arthur comes in, mingled with the confusion of greetings and handshakings are "the joyous short barks and wagging of tails on the part of the canine members of the family, which tells that the visitor is on the best terms with the visited." The Poysers' chained bulldog performs "a Pyrrhic dance" as the parson and the captain leave the farm-yard, his peculiar bulldog frame of mind at such an intrusion being expressed by "furious indignation." Adam's Gyp is one of the characters in the story, and it is noticeable that he does not bark, but howls, at the mysterious rapping at the door, the night of old Bede's death. None but a close student of dogs would have mentioned that.

George Eliot has a very deep feeling for this "dumb" animal, who is not dumb at all.

"Poor dog!" said Dinah, patting the rough gray coat; "I 've a strange feeling about the dumb things, as if they wanted to speak, and it was a trouble to 'em because they could n't. I can't help being sorry for the dogs always, though perhaps there 's no need. But they may well have more in them than they know how to make us understand, for we can't say half what we feel with our words."

The finished fascination of his air came chiefly from the absence of demand and assumption. It was that of a fleet, soft-coated, dark-eyed animal that delights you by not bounding away in indifference from you, and unexpectedly pillows its chin on your palm, and looks up at you desiring to be stroked — as if it loved you.

And she makes them enter into your feelings for the moment, as a dog always will if you give him half a chance.

The sun was already breaking out; the sound of the mill seemed cheerful again; the granary doors were open; and there was Yap, the queer white-and-brown terrier, with one ear turned back, trotting about and sniffing vaguely, as if he were in search of a companion. It was irresistible. Maggie tossed her hair back and ran downstairs, seized her bonnet without putting it on, peeped, and then dashed along the passage, lest she should encounter her mother, and was quickly out in the yard, whirling round like a Pythoness, and singing as she whirled, "Yap, Yap, Tom 's coming home!" while Yap danced and barked round her, as much as to say, if there was any noise wanted he was the dog for it.

Her dogs are always true to their best dog-nature, even when her men and women are not true to their best human nature.

Snuff, the brown spaniel, who had placed herself in front of him, and had been watching him for some time, now jumped up in impatience for the expected caress. But Godfrey thrust her away without looking at her, and left the room, followed humbly by the unresenting Snuff, — perhaps because she saw no other career open to her.

When Lydgate, in one of those involuntarily awkward actions assumed in angry moods, "stooped to beckon the tiny black spaniel," that wise creature "had the insight to decline his hollow caresses."

Yes, and artistically true, too. Mrs. Transome's sleepy old and fat Blenheim is as appropriate to her as the fine black retriever who guards Mr. Transome (and who barks "anxiously," another fine touch of observation of an *aged* dog) is to him; and one cannot think of the sporting parson uncle without thinking at the same time of the black and liver-spotted pointers over whom he shot. "Little Treby had a new rector," she says, near the close of the book, "and more were sorry besides the old pointers." You see, the dogs come in among the final touches, as they should. The King Charles puppy belonging to little Harry, "with big eyes, much after the pattern of the boy's," is as much a part of the boy as his clothes, to say nothing of the black spaniel Moro, whom he dragged about, tied to the seat of a toy wagon, "with a piece of scarlet drapery round him, making him look like a barbaric prince in a chariot." The contrast of dogs is as clever as that of the other characters.

Moro, having little imagination, objected to this, and barked with feeble snappishness as the tyrannous lad ran forward, then whirled the chariot round, and ran back to "Gappa," then came to a dead stop, which overset the chariot, that he might watch Uncle Lingon's water-spaniel run for the hurled stick and bring it in his mouth. Nimrod kept close to his old master's legs, glancing with much indifference at this youthful ardor about sticks, — he had "gone through all that;" and Dominic walked by, looking on blandly, and taking care of both young and old.

Presently Mrs. Holt, with little Job, advances upon this group.

She courtesied once, as if to the entire group, now including even the dogs, who showed various degrees of curiosity, especially as to what kind of game the smaller animal Job might prove to be, after due investigation.

Bob Jakin declares he's getting so full of money he must have a wife to spend it for him. "But it's botherin', a wife is; and Mumps might n't like her." When Stephen struck the deep notes which represent the tread of the heavy beasts in 'The Creation,' Minny, the King Charles, —

who had intrenched himself, trembling, in his basket as soon as the music began, found this thunder so little to his taste that he leaped out and scampered under the remotest *chiffonière*, as the most eligible place in which a small dog could await the crack of doom.

"Happen you'd like Mumps for company, Miss," he said, when he had taken the baby again. "He's rare company, Mumps is; he knows iverything, an' makes no bother about it. If I tell him, he'll lie before you an' watch you — as still — just as he watches my pack. You'd better leave him a bit; he'll get fond on you. Lors, it's a fine thing to hev a dumb brute fond on you; it'll stick to you, and make no jaw."

Just as our hatred of Sikes is heightened by his treatment of Bull's-eye, so is the refined cruelty of Grandcourt made more loathsome by the trouble he takes to torment his "pets."

Mr. Grandcourt had drawn his chair aside so as to face the lawn, and with his left leg over another chair, and his right elbow on the table, was smoking a large cigar, while his companion was still eating. The dogs — half a dozen of various kinds were moving lazily in and out, or taking attitudes of brief attention — gave a vacillating preference first to one gentleman, then to the other; being dogs in such good circumstances that they could play at hunger, and liked to be served with delicacies which they declined to put into their mouths; all except Fetch, the beautiful liver-colored water-spaniel, which sat with its forepaws firmly planted and its expressive brown face turned upward, watching Grandcourt with unshaken constancy. He held in his lap a tiny maltese dog with a tiny silver collar and bell, and when he had a hand unused by cigar or coffee-cup, it rested on this small parcel of animal warmth. I fear that Fetch was jealous, and wounded that her master gave her no word or look; at last it seemed that she could bear this neglect no longer, and she gently put her large silky paw on her master's leg. Grandcourt looked at her with unchanged face for half a minute, and then took the trouble to lay down his cigar while he lifted the unimpassioned Fluff close to his chin and gave it caressing pats, all the while gravely watching Fetch, who, poor thing, whimpered interruptedly, as if trying to repress that sign of discontent, and at last rested her head beside the appealing paw, looking up with piteous beseeching. So, at least, a lover of dogs must have interpreted Fetch, and Grandcourt kept so many dogs that he was reputed to love them; at any rate, his impulse to act just in this way started from such an interpretation. But when the amusing anguish burst forth in a howling bark, Grandcourt pushed Fetch down without speaking, and depositing Fluff carelessly on the table (where his black nose predominated over a salt-cellar), began to look to his cigar, and found, with some annoyance against Fetch as the cause, that the brute of a cigar required relighting. Fetch, having begun to wail, found, like others of her sex, that it was not easy to leave off; indeed, the second howl was a louder one, and the third was like unto it.

"Turn out that brute, will you?" said Grandcourt to Lush.

There is no domestic scene without them; they are a part of the landscape. The first thing that Dorothea discovers, looking abroad on the dawning day after her night of anguish, is the shepherd with his dog.

And not only dogs. Bob Jakin is described as regarding Maggie "with the pursuant gaze of an intelligent dumb animal with perceptions more perfect than his comprehension." It is not only the "bouquet of young faces" around the Meyrick's tea-table that we are invited to inspect. There is Hafiz, the cat, "seated a little aloft, with large eyes on the alert, regarding the whole scene as an apparatus for supplying his allowance of milk."

Let us close with this bit of domesticity:

Eppie was now aware that her behaviour was under observation, but it was only the observation of a friendly donkey, browsing with a log fastened to his foot—a meek donkey, not scornfully critical of human trivialities, but thankful to share in them, if possible, by getting his nose scratched; and Eppie did not fail to gratify him with her usual notice, though it was attended with the inconvenience of his following them, painfully, up to the very door of their home.

But the sound of a sharp bark inside, as Eppie put the key in the door, modified the donkey's views, and he limped away again without bidding. The sharp bark was the sign of an excited welcome that was awaiting them from a knowing brown terrier, who after dancing at their legs in a hysterical manner, rushed with a worrying noise at a tortoise-shell kitten under the loom, and then rushed back with a sharp bark again, as much as to say, "I have done my duty by this feeble creature, you perceive;" while the lady-mother of the kitten sat sunning her white bosom in the window, and looked around with a sleepy air of expecting caresses, though she was not going to take any trouble for them.

VII

Although we know from her letters[1] that George Eliot did not regard the clergy, as a class, with extraordinary affection, her fairmindedness was not warped from a generous consideration of such of them as individually came within the scope of her creations. She purposely picked out the best; and whatever weaknesses they have are all on the side of humanity, are the weaknesses they share with laymen, and are not particularly the vices of a sect,—which

[1] 'Life,' vol. i., p. 31.

would have made them objects of ridicule rather than subjects for sympathy. She makes their weaknesses fit into the scenery; and to be able to do that is a gift of God. Bnt she probes far deeper than that; for with all their amiability, they are not — the best of them — weak men, but firm and strong upon occasion. They rise to their opportunities; they meet the crises like true priests.

That rich Velasquez portrait of Mr. Irwine is the speaking likeness of the genial gentleman, dignified by natural grace and the gentleness of birth, which we like to associate with the other rich belongings of the Established Church. Mr. Irwine lived before the days of " Settlements " and guilds, and perhaps would not have been happy amidst the busy activities of a latter-day city parish. But he was of more real usefulness in the quiet rusticity of his setting than his successor, Mr. Ryde, who was, without doubt, more " zealous," but who, in the language of Mrs. Poyser, "was like a dose of physic. He gripped you and worried you, and after all he left you much the same." And the faces of the people of Broxton and Hayslope did not brighten at the approach of Mr. Ryde, as they did when Mr. Irwine met them on the highway. They learned a good deal more about doctrines from Mr. Ryde, but less about feelings; and the farmers did not look forward to their Sundays with the pleasure they had when Mr. Irwine " filled the pulpit," and talked to them about the things they understood.

" Mr. Ryde was a deal thought on at a distance, I believe, and he wrote books; but as for mathmatics and the natur' o' things, he was as ignorant as a woman. He was very knowing about doctrines, and used to call 'em the bulwarks of the Reformation; but I've always mistrusted that sort o' learning as leaves folks foolish and unreasonable about business. Now Mester Irwine was as different as could be: as quick! — he understood what you meant in a minute; and he knew all about building and could see when you'd made a good job. And he behaved as much like a gentleman to the farmers, and th' old women and the laborers, as he did to the gentry. You never saw *him* interfering and scolding, and trying to play th' emperor. Ah! he was a fine man as ever you set eyes on; and so kind to's his mother and sisters. That poor sickly Miss Anne — he seemed to think more of her than of anybody else in the world. There was n't a soul in the parish had a word to say against him; and his servants stayed with him till they were so old and pottering he had to hire other folks to do their work."

"Well," I said, "that was an excellent way of preaching in the week-days; but I dare say, if your old friend Mr. Irwine were to come to life again, and get into the pulpit next Sunday, you would be rather ashamed that he did n't preach better after all your praise of him."

"Nay, nay," said Adam, broadening his chest and throwing himself back in his chair, as if he were ready to meet all inferences, "nobody has ever heard me say Mr. Irwine was much of a preacher. He did n't go into deep speritial experience; and I know there's a deal in a man's inward life as you can't measure by the square, and say 'Do this and that 'll follow,' and 'Do that and this 'll follow.' There's things go on in the soul, and times when feelings come into you like a rushing mighty wind, as the Scripture says, and part your life in two a'most, so as you look back on yourself as if you was somebody else. Those are things as you can't bottle up in a 'do this' and 'do that;' and I'll go so far with the strongest Methodist ever you'll find.

That shows me there's deep speritial things in religion. You can't make much out wi' talking about it but you feel it. Mr. Irwine did n't go into those things: he preached short moral sermons and that was all. But then he acted up pretty much to what he said; he did n't set up for being so different from other folks one day, and then be as like 'em as two peas the next. And he made folks love him and respect him, and that was better nor stirring up their gall wi' being over-busy. . . . I began to see as all this weighing and sifting what this text means and that text means, and whether folks are saved all by God's grace, or whether there goes an ounce o' will to 't was no part o' real religion at all. You may talk o' these things for hours on end, and you 'll only be all the more coxy and conceited for 't. So I took to going nowhere but to church, and hearing nobody but Mr. Irwine, for he said nothing but what was good, and what you 'd be the wiser for remembering. And I found it better for my soul to be humble before the mysteries o' God's dealings, and not be making a clatter about what I could never understand. And they 're poor foolish questions, after all; for what have we got either inside or outside of us but what comes from God? If we' ve got a resolution to do right, he gave it to us, I reckon, first or last; but I see plain enough we shall never do it without a resolution, and that 's enough for me."

Yet when the tragedy of the story rises in overflowing tide upon Adam, Irwine rises with it, and saves Adam from the drowning.

Her disagreeable clergymen, like this Ryde, and Mr. Tyke, in 'Middlemarch,' are mentioned only incidentally, and do not figure in the story, except as foils to the agreeable ones, like Irwine and Farebrother. No one knew better than himself that Farebrother was far from being a model priest.

He does not scruple to play whist for the money which he needs; which, though not thought ill of in the days of Peel, is not what one expects of an exemplar in any day. Yet his very failings help towards his appreciation of the faults of others; and a young man like Fred Vincy can go to him for advice and direction, who would nervously shrink from a "father confessor" who had learned everything about sin, not in life, but in a theological seminary. Could anything be finer than the picture of this high-toned, delicately organized Farebrother swallowing his own feelings and going to Mary Garth in behalf of a fellow not worthy to tie his shoestrings? Almost any boy in Middlemarch would have said of Farebrother, had you asked his opinion, that he was a tip-top fellow and a brick; and a boy's opinion of a parson is not to be despised.

She is equally fair to all her clergymen. There is the broad, tolerant Cadwallader, who thought no evil of Casaubon, because he was allowed to thrash his stream, and in whose study might be found, not tomes of Augustine, but all the latest fishing-tackle; who always saw the joke of any satire against himself, and who was an all-round good fellow. Even Stephen Guest speaks well of the high-Church incumbent, Kenn.

"I say anything disrespectful of Dr. Kenn? Heaven forbid! . . . I think Kenn one of the finest fellows in the world. I don't care much about the tall candlesticks he has put on the communion-table, and I should n't like to spoil my temper by getting up to early prayers every morning. But he's the only man I ever knew personally who seems to me to have anything of the real apostle in him — a man who has eight hundred a year, and is contented with deal furniture and boiled beef because he gives away two-thirds of his income. That was a very fine thing of him — taking into his house that poor lad Grattan who shot his mother by accident. He sacrifices more time than a less busy man could spare, to save the poor fellow from getting into a morbid state of mind about it."

Because this noble-minded woman loved goodness rather than any of the forms of goodness. You think of high motives, and not of high Church, when you think of Kenn; just as you think of what is best in Evangelicalism, as part of what is best in all parties, rather than what is typically "Evangelical," when you think of Tryan; and as you think of earnest striving for purity in the dissenting doctrines of Lyon, rather than the peculiar kind of purity associated with the idea of Puritanism; and just as, finally, in regarding Dinah Morris, you do not think of the beauty of Methodism, but of the beauty of holiness. Her only partial failure among clergymen is Gwendolen's uncle, who is a little too much influenced by county superstitions. Even he can rise nobly to his opportunities, but he should have looked more closely into Grandcourt's past. He is a little too worldly, even for a worldly clergyman; and this very worldliness might have prevented Gwendolen's mistake better than the innocence of a less knowing priest.

George Eliot did not care for the Jews especially, as such, although she thought them a fine old race, like the Florentines.[1] She was fired with the idea of

---

[1] As such, indeed, they were nothing to her, and the gypsies were less than nothing ['Life,' vol. i.,'pp. 172 *seq.*] It is a narrow criticism that finds fault with the gypsies in her poem because of their dissimilarity from the known article. They do not stand there for photo-

nationality; and she failed, in 'Daniel Deronda' and the 'Spanish Gypsy,' to see that Christianity was intended to swallow nationality in universality; that there was to be nothing in the new dispensation but new creatures — not new nations. Judaism is necessarily tribal; there can be no converts to it. You may be converted to Christianity; you must be born into Judaism. But conversion is a new birth. There is really no good reason why Lady Mallinger should provoke a smile by her suggestion that there was a society for the conversion of the Jews, except that most of Lady Mallinger's remarks were regarded as foolish, and that there is little tangible evidence that that society ever accomplishes anything. If the creator of Daniel Deronda had been inspired by a convincing Christianity, she would have grafted her hero's sentiment for his hereditary people onto a Christian base. Yet Deronda, it should be remembered, did not renounce Christianity. He acknowledged that it, too, had claims upon him. It is open to the imagination that his final belief was not fundamentally opposed to a religion that had been born anew, out of Judaism, under a standard destined to absorb all religions.

Mordecai's doctrine is a sublimated Erastianism, a high-keyed nationalism resting upon a politico-moral, rather than on a religious basis. "Deronda," we learn, "like his neighbors, had regarded Judaism as a sort of eccentric fossilized form which an accomplished man might dispense with studying and leave to specialists." But George Eliot, after her usual manner, re-

graphic reproductions of a type, but are arbitrarily chosen as possible examples of truth to a national ideal. The actual gypsy is sketched in the 'Mill in the Floss.'

gards it from the standpoint of a Jew who still believes in his people; and she makes Deronda anxious to feed his new interest by studying it from the inside. Mr. Jacobs says there is a notable array of Jews in 'Daniel Deronda,'[1] and the book awoke the keenest sympathy among learned rabbis; which certainly is a better proof that she wrote understandingly of them than the adverse criticism of those who have never approached, and can never approach, the field from any other than an anti-Jewish, or, at the best, a non-Jewish position. Think what we will of the futility of the main idea of the story, the character of Mordecai stands out in breathing colors; and we are made to pity the abject hopelessness of his visions by the coarse unbelief of his surroundings. Is it not, for example, one of those over-shrewd mistakes of criticism to point out that the author erred in allowing Cohen to transact business on the eve of the Sabbath? Did she not purposely make him do so by way of emphasis on the infinite distance between the sordid conditions in the life of the typical money-making, money-lending Jew and the visions of her Mordecai — between those who held the ancient forms divorced from their spirit, and those who breathed the spirit which animated the forms? It seems, in truth, as though she viewed the theocracy of the Hebrews as on the same level with the nationalism of the Italians, and asks for them not a Messiah, but a Mazzini; and it is a little typical that Mordecai himself is not orthodox: his quotations are not from the Old Testament, but from later writers. Still, the great tribute to the story is that eminent Jews to-day are endeavoring to establish in the East what Mordecai died with visions of in his throbbing brain,

[1] *Macmillan's*, vol. xxxvi., p. 101.

VIII

George Eliot's wit, as I have said, is distributed among her characters: she washes her hands of it, so to say, and makes Mrs. Poyser and Mrs. Cadwallader stand for sponsors. It is different, however, with her humor; because the essential nature of humor agrees with such exquisite fitness with the deliberative qualities of her art that the portrayal is, in its sympathetic fulness, almost necessarily humorous.

Humor is a part of sympathy; it is sometimes its last touch; and it is connected with love through its kinship to pity. Wit flashes, humor glows; wit hurts, humor soothes; wit is serious, humor gambols; wit is swift, humor lingers; wit is direct, honest, open; humor is vague, sly, wandering; the weapon of wit is the rapier; humor has no weapon, but its shield is sympathy. Wit may be the mere product of a keen intelligence; the leisurely qualities of humor make it a relative of intellectual culture. Hence it is natural that most of George Eliot's own talk, as distinct from the talk of her characters, should be humorous rather than witty. Take, for example:

> Mr. Barton was not at all an ascetic. He thought the benefits of fasting were entirely confined to the Old Testament dispensation.

> . . . when Lady Assher, Beatrice, and Captain Wybrow entered, all with that brisk and cheerful air which a sermon is often observed to produce when it is quite finished.

The conversation is sometimes quite literary, for there is a flourishing book-club, and many of the younger ladies have carried their studies so far as to have forgotten a little German.

Nothing like "taking" a few bushes and ditches for exorcising a demon; and it is really astonishing that the centaurs, with their immense advantages in this way, have left us so bad a reputation in history.

The woman who manages a dairy has a large share in making the rent, so she may well be allowed to have her opinion on stock and their "keep," — an excuse which strengthens her understanding so much that she finds herself able to give her husband advice on most other subjects.

The possession of a wife conspicuously one's inferior in intellect is, like other high privileges, attended with a few inconveniences, and among the rest, with the occasional necessity for using a little deception.

He was unmarried, and had met all exhortations of friends who represented to him that a bishop — *i. e.*, the overseer of an Independent church and congregation . . .

Mr. Brooke felt so much surprise that he did not at once find out how much he was relieved by the sense that he was not expected to do anything in particular.

. . . their opponents made use of the same writings for different ends, finding there a strong warrant for the divine right of kings and the denunciation of those who, like Korah, Dathan, and Abiram, took on themselves the office of the priesthood which belonged of right solely to Aaron and his sons, or, in other words, to men ordained by the English bishops.

"An odd man," as Mrs. Muscat observed, "to have such a gift in the pulpit. But there's One knows better than we do," — which in a lady who rarely felt her judgment at a loss, was a concession that showed much piety.

. . . the Franciscans, who loved mankind, and hated the Dominicans.

She was a great reader of news, from the widest-reaching politics to the list of marriages; the latter, she said, giving her the pleasant sense of finishing the fashionable novels without having read them, and seeing the heroes and heroines happy without knowing what poor creatures they were.

. . . the philanthropic banker, . . . who predominated so much in the town that some called him a Methodist, others a hypocrite, according to the resources of their vocabulary.

They were saved from the excesses of Protestantism by not knowing how to read.

Many of her opinions, such as those on church government and the character of Archbishop Laud, seemed too decided under every alteration to have been arrived at otherwise than by a wifely receptiveness.

People who live at a distance are naturally less faulty than those immediately under our own eyes; and it seems superfluous, when we consider the remote geographical position of the Ethiopians, and how very little the Greeks had to do with them, to inquire further why Homer calls them "blameless."

The end of Brooke's pen is a "thinking organ;" so she appropriately says: "His pen found it such a pity . . ."

Humor calls for reflective rather than purely sentimental characteristics. Not only in her power to delve below the surface, but in her self-restraint, in the deftness of her touch, in her admirable discretion, is she the superior of Dickens, who is too often a mere sentimentalist. George Eliot has not the trick of repeating, which the great humorist uses past all forbearance. She has, so far as the outward aspects of her humor are concerned, the Dickens stroke at its best, without any of its exaggerations. Her Mr. Brooke, her Trumbull, all her minor characters in 'Middlemarch,' are bodied forth humorously, each with some characteristic, but never tiresomely reiterated note. She is a high, not a low, comedian, like Dickens. The memory of Trumbull, trimming his outlines, and uttering grandiloquent sentences, remains with the reader as perfect a bit of portraiture as the recollection of Silas Wegg, although the auctioneer occupies the stage not one-quarter the amount of time the other worthy holds it. Dalton, the Donnithorne's coachman, appears only once or twice, in 'Adam Bede':

"The cap'n's been ridin' the devil's own pace," said Dalton the coachman — whose person stood out in high relief, as he smoked his pipe, against the stable wall — when John brought up Rattler.

"An' I wish he'd get the devil to do's grooming for 'n," growled John.

"Ay; he'd hev a deal hamabler groom nor what he has now," observed Dalton; and the joke appeared to him so good that, being left alone upon the scene, he continued at intervals to take his pipe from his mouth in order to wink at an imaginary audience, and shake luxuriously with a silent, ventral laughter; mentally rehearsing the dialogue from the beginning, that he might recite it with effect in the servants' hall.

The creator of Sam Weller would have been so delighted with this Dalton that in his hands we should have had, instead of that single winking, many repetitions before many imaginary audiences, just as Grandfather Smallweed throws a pillow at Mrs. Smallweed whenever he looks at her, and as Mr. Bounderby never appears upon the scene without traducing the devoted mother whom he has miserably pensioned off. Had the hint been given to Boz to illustrate the mental attitude of Caleb Garth by punctuating his talk with Scriptural diction, the temptation would have been irresistible, and that worthy man could not have opened his mouth without recalling to our memories the prophets of olden time. Once is sufficient to George Eliot, and it is done with so sure a hand that it is sufficient for us also.

"Pooh! where's the use of asking for such fellows' reasons? The soul of man," said Caleb, with the deep tone and grave shake of the head which always came when he used this phrase — "the soul of man, when it gets fairly rotten, will bear you all sorts of poisonous toadstools, and no eye can see whence came the seeds thereof." It was one of Caleb's quaintnesses, that in his difficulty of finding speech for his thought, he caught, as it were, snatches of diction which he associated with various points of view or states of mind; and whenever he had a feeling of awe, he was haunted by a sense of biblical phraseology, though he could hardly have given a strict quotation.

Mary Garth is always hiding her emotion back of her humor, and her humor never takes the same form twice. Brooke is a high comedy portrayal of rare quality,— a character distinct from all others, minutely faithful in details and not in the least exaggerated. The comic element does not reside in a constant repetition of the same words, but in his uniform manner of repeating various words. Contrast —

"Quite right, Ladislaw; we shall make a new thing of opinion here," said Mr. Brooke. "Only, I want to keep myself independent about Reform, you know: I don't want to go too far. I want to take up Wilberforce's and Romilly's line, you know, and work at Negro Emancipation, Criminal Law — that kind of thing. But of course I should support Grey."

"If you go in for the principle of Reform, you must be prepared to take what the situation offers," said Will. "If everybody pulled from his own bit against everybody else, the whole question would go to tatters."

"Yes, yes, I agree with you — I quite take that point of view. I should put it in that light. I should support Grey, you know. But I don't want to change the balance of the constitution, and I don't think Grey would."

"But that is what the country wants," said Will. "Else there would be no meaning in political unions or any other movement that knows what it's about. It wants to have a House of Commons which is not weighted with nominees of the landed class, but with representatives of the other interests. And as to contending for a reform short of that, it is like asking for a bit of an avalanche which has already begun to thunder."

"That is fine, Ladislaw: that is the way to put it. Write that down, now. We must begin to get documents about the feeling of the country, as well as the machine-breaking and the general distress."

"As to documents," said Will, "a two-inch card will hold plenty. A few rows of figures are enough to deduce misery from, and a few more will show the rate at which the political determination of the people is growing."

"Good: draw that out a little more at length, Ladislaw. That is an idea, now: write it out in the Pioneer. Put the figures and deduce the misery, you know; and put the other figures and deduce — and so on. You have a way of putting things. Burke, now — when I think of Burke, I can't help wishing somebody had a pocket-borough to give you, Ladislaw. You 'd never get elected, you know. And we shall always want talent in the House: reform as we will, we shall always want talent. That avalanche and the thunder, now, was really a little like Burke. I want that sort of thing — not ideas, you know, but a way of putting them."

with his speech from the balcony of the White Hart:

"I am a close neighbor of yours, my good friends — you 've known me on the bench a good while — I 've always gone a good deal into public questions — machinery, now, and machine-breaking — you 're many of you concerned with machinery, and I 've been going into that lately. It won't do, you know, breaking machines: everything must go on — trade, manufactures, commerce, interchange of staples — that kind of thing — since Adam Smith, that must go on. We must look all over the globe: — 'Observation with extensive view,' must look everywhere, — 'from China to Peru,' as somebody says — Johnson, I think, The 'Rambler,' you know. That is what I have done up to a certain point — not as far as Peru; but I 've not always staid at home — I saw it would n't do. I 've been in the Levant, where some of your Middlemarch goods go — and then again in the Baltic. The Baltic, now."

The author of Pickwick found himself, too soon in his career, in the unfortunate condition of all successful humorists, in that, in meeting from an unreasonable public a demand far beyond the possibility of even excellence in the supply, he was forced into the position of a professional fun-maker, — a sort of literary Barnum. And while it is not disparaging to Dickens to say that he does not belong to the same class with George Eliot, any more than it is disparaging to Hogarth to say that he does not belong to the same class with Van Dyck, it is nevertheless true that the best humorists are not the professional ones. Strange as it may seem, a humorist ought to be a grave person. Not only is a little nonsense now and then relished by the gravest men, but the relish gets its grace from the gravity. Humor is an appreciation of incongruities, and this involves wisdom, — a quality sadly lacking in most of our comic writers.

IX

Every writer of strength has attempted to represent the feeling of sympathy between the nature outside of us and the nature within us, — that "pathetic fallacy" by which we read nature in the tones of the mind. If you visit the sea-shore heavy-hearted with grief, the ocean has its andante movements for you; if in joy, its allegro: yet it is the same ocean. The dreary monotony of Dorothea's existence is thus shadowed forth to her by the outlook from her boudoir:

Mr. and Mrs. Casaubon, returning from their wedding journey, arrived at Lowick Manor in the middle of January. A light snow was falling as they descended at the door, and in the morning, when Dorothea passed from her dressing-room into the blue-green boudoir that we know of, she saw the long avenue of limes lifting their trunks from a white earth, and spreading white branches against the dun and motionless sky. The distant flat shrank in uniform whiteness and low-hanging uniformity of cloud. The very furniture in the room seemed to have shrunk since she saw it before: the stag in the tapestry looked more like a ghost in his ghostly blue-green world; the volumes of polite literature in the book-case looked more like immovable imitations of books.

But, as if fearing that we might place too much stress upon this personal construction of nature, we are particularly warned in another place that the great mother is impersonal, too, and that its objectivity is not to be charged at will by man's subjectivity:

The eighteenth of August was one of those days when the sunshine looked brighter in all eyes for the gloom that went before. . . . And yet a day on which a blighting sorrow may fall upon a man. For if it be true that Nature at certain moments seems charged with a presentiment of one individual lot, must it not also be true that she seems unmindful, unconscious of another? . . . There are so many of us, and our lots are so different: what wonder that Nature's mood is often in harsh contrast with the great crises of our lives?

Because of her predominant humor (which is another way of saying, because of her predominant sympathy) George Eliot is an ironist rather than a satirist. A mind capable of vast indignation, yet checked by culture, is apt to find its outlet in that tempered form of sarcasm to which we have given the name of irony: the scorn compounds with the humor; the sense of the ridiculous weds the sense of What is Right.

These narrow notions about debt, held by the old-fashioned Tullivers, may perhaps excite a smile on the faces of many readers in these days of wide commercial views and wide philosophy, according to which everything rights itself without any trouble of ours: the fact that my tradesman is out of pocket by me is to be looked at through the serene certainty that somebody else's tradesman is in pocket by somebody else; and since there must be bad debts in the world, why, it is mere egoism not to like that we in particular should make them instead of our fellow-citizens. I am telling the history of very simple people, who had never had any illuminating doubts as to personal integrity and honor.

She is a master of ridicule, but, save in rare instances, an avoider of derision. Hers is not the "indignatio sæva" of Swift. There is only good nature in her imitation of the Wolffian school of critics:

As to the origin of this song, whether it came in its actual state from the brain of a single rhapsodist, or was gradually perfected by a school or succession of rhapsodists, I am ignorant. There is a stamp of unity, of individual genius, upon it, which inclines me to the former hypothesis, though I am not blind to the consideration that this unity may rather have arisen from that consensus of many minds which was a condition of primitive thought, foreign to our modern consciousness. Some will perhaps think that they detect in the first quatrain an indication of a lost line, which later rhapsodists, failing in imaginative vigor, have supplied by the feeble device of iteration:

others, however, may rather maintain that this very iteration is an original felicity, to which none but the most prosaic minds can be insensible.

In this connection, it is amusing to watch the flight of her Parthian arrow at those who claimed for that remarkable personage, Mr. Liggins, the authorship of 'Adam Bede':

He . . . produced a work on the 'Cultivation of Green Crops and the Economy of Cattle Feeding' which won him high congratulations at agricultural meetings; but in Middlemarch admiration was more reserved: most persons there were inclined to believe that the merit of Fred's authorship was due to his wife, since they had never expected Fred Vincy to write on turnips and mangelwurzel.
But when Mary wrote a little book for her boys, called 'Stories of Great Men, taken from Plutarch,' and had it printed and published by Grip & Co., Middlemarch, every one in the town was willing to give the credit of this work to Fred, observing that he had been to the University, "where the ancients were studied," and might have been a clergyman if he had chosen.
In this way it was made clear that Middlemarch had never been deceived, and that there was no need to praise anybody for writing a book, since it was always done by somebody else.

A sense of humor is, after all, the principal form of common-sense. Moreover, it is the saving sense which distinguishes common from vulgar sense, and is as remarkable for what it hinders as for what it does. Among other things, it prevents an author from sprinkling his pages with villains. "Plotting covetousness," says George Eliot, "and deliberate contrivance, in order to accomplish a selfish end, are nowhere abundant but in the world of the dramatist: they demand too intense a mental action for many of our fellow-parishioners to be guilty of them." There are, strictly speaking, no villains among her leading characters. Tito does not set out to be one; his is not a predetermined villainy; it comes late, and is not so much the result of acute maliciousness as it is of complexities brought about in large part by love of ease and softness of temper. He does not wish harm to others; he wishes good to himself so steadfastly that, in the exclusiveness of this passion, the harm to others follows. It all depends on the sense of obligation, — an all-essential sense which Tito neglects, not because of active malice, but of irksomeness under the burden which the obligation lays upon his pleasure-loving nature. He is driven into malice only by the circumstances of his deceit; which is quite different from the Iago point of action. Raffles and Lapidoth are more dead-beats than villains. Dunstan Cass is lost sight of early in the story, and Dolfo Spini is too stupid in his wickedness to merit the title. The primal fire of Grandcourt's villainy is burnt out when the story opens, and the base plotters in 'Romola,' are, like the disagreeable clergymen, kept in the background.

X

The novel is the youngest of the arts of writing, and its superlative force lies in its inclusion of the older ones. It is able to present what is essential in

Bacon and Kant to myriads who never read philosophy in the abstract. Its form permits it to grasp subtle aspects of living truths which even a twentieth-century Shakspere could not enforce in drama. Its clothing of prose allows an extension of delineation not possible in any readable style of verse. Think, then, of the power of the novelist learned in philosophy, with the dramatic instinct, and possessing all the weapons of a prose armory. Raise that thought to the conception of the use of such a power in behalf of all suffering men and women, and George Eliot stands revealed as its realization. Cervantes, Scott, Fielding, even such lesser lights as Goldsmith and Le Sage, are placed before her; but unless we hold our vision at the range of manners, and prefer to consider the playful buoyancy of imagination superior to its spiritual depth, we must exalt George Eliot, with all her faults, to a position not yet reached by any other.

Hers was an ardent age, — the age of a new birth in science, with wide-spreading results in art; the age of 'Modern Painters,' and 'Sartor Resartus,' and of a Tennyson rebellious against all commonplace acceptances. She knew Fielding's place, just as she knew Dickens's, and was glad to take a holiday with him as she might.

A great historian, as he insisted on calling himself, who had the happiness to be dead a hundred and twenty years ago, . . . glories in his copious remarks and digressions as the least imitable part of his work, and especially in those initial chapters . . . where he seems to bring his arm-chair to the proscenium and chat with us in all the lusty ease of his fine English. But Fielding lived when the days were longer (for time, like money, is measured by our needs), when summer afternoons were spacious, and the clock ticked slowly in the winter evenings.

Surely all other leisure is hurry compared with a sunny walk through fields from "afternoon church," as such walks used to be in those old leisurely times, when the boat, gliding sleepily along the canal, was the newest locomotive wonder; when Sunday books had most of them old brown leather covers, and opened with remarkable precision always in one place. Leisure is gone — gone where the spinning-wheels are gone, and the pack-horses, and the slow wagons, and the peddlers who brought bargains to the door on sunny afternoons. Ingenious philosophers tell you, perhaps, that the great work of the steam-engine is to create leisure for mankind. Do not believe them; it only creates a vacuum for eager thought to rush in. Even idleness is eager now — eager for amusement; prone to excursion trains, art museums, periodical literature, and exciting novels; prone even to scientific theorizing, and cursory peeps through microscopes. Old Leisure was quite a different personage; he read only one newspaper, innocent of leaders, and was free from that periodicity of sensations which we call post-time. He was a contemplative, rather stout gentleman, of excellent digestion, of quiet perceptions, undiseased by hypothesis; happy in his inability to know the causes of things, preferring the things themselves. He lived chiefly in the country, among pleasant seats and homesteads, and was fond of sauntering by the fruit-tree wall, and scenting the apricots when they were warmed by the morning sunshine, or of sheltering himself under the orchard boughs at noon, when the summer pears were falling. He knew nothing of week-day services, and thought none the worse of the Sunday sermon if it allowed him to sleep from the text to the blessing—liking the afternoon service best, because the prayers were the shortest and not ashamed to say so; for he had an easy, jolly conscience, broad-backed like himself, and able to carry a great deal of beer or port wine — not being made squeamish by doubts and qualms and lofty aspirations. Life was not a task to him, but a sinecure; he fingered the guineas in his pocket, and ate his dinners, and slept the sleep of the irresponsible; for had he not kept up his charter by going to church on the Sunday afternoon?

Fine old Leisure! Do not be severe upon him, and judge him by our modern standard; he never went to Exeter Hall, or heard a popular preacher, or read 'Tracts for the Times,' or 'Sartor Resartus.'

Of course one feels the strain in such an atmosphere, and it is for relief that critics fall back on the "fine old leisure" of the previous age.

Fielding, as a *character*, was not a new force in literature, although the nature of his work was deliciously so. He belongs to the Samuel Johnson type of man, — blunt, honest, prejudiced, rough in judgment, but tender of heart; and he is followed, at a a more or less respectful distance, by the Levers, the Lovers, and the Marryats. He is, next to Cervantes, the most complete of the comic Homers. His wide sympathies are reckoned among the proofs of his greatness, but can they be seriously compared with the minute conscientiousness of George Eliot's? Are they not merely a boisterous goodfellowship, a bluff heartiness of liking for downright English traits of outspokenness, which carries with it a corresponding hatred for the opposites? The fine qualities of Tom Jones are emphasized by the contrasting mean qualities of Bilfil, — by the qualities of a hypocritical sneak and coward. All the sympathy is for the major, there is none for the minor, figure. But we know how George Eliot treats hypocrisy in Bulstrode, and how her contrasting color is not wholly black because what it is contrasted with is not wholly white. It seems to me that her method is the more subtly humorous as well as the more deeply sympathetic; the humor getting its flavor from the sympathy.

Those others were, first, story-tellers, then delineators of character. They had great art and much sympathy; and the enjoyment they gave was hearty, direct, and simple. Judged by the standards themselves set, before George Eliot's day, George Eliot's work fails; but as combining poetical insight, religious feeling, philosophical breadth, humorous portrayal, and a deep loving sympathy, that work stands apart, not only by reason of its positive qualities, but as pointing the way to all future art of the highest worth — the art which has to do with the most abundant life.

She has invention. Some of her plots are quite complicated. But she was the first to illustrate the overwhelming importance of the relationship of the men and women of a story to the natural history of all men and women — her world the microcosm, the world outside the macrocosm. This was science; it was the correlation of forces; it was Comtism, if you please; but it was life. The mere device of plot is mere cleverness, compared with the power to develop the embryonic principles of life in the blessed sunlight of eternal law. It is not as if she placed the natural history of mankind on a plane superior to and apart from the history of her hero and heroine: violently would that have divorced her philosophy from her art, and translated her from a George Eliot, to be known forevermore as the creator of 'Adam Bede' and 'Silas Marner,' back to the obscure essayist of the *Westminster Review*. She probed — as no one before her did — far deeper than that. She showed that romance, so far from dying in the new light, took on deeper colors; that the inter-relationship of cause and effect, desire and will, the I and the Other than I, not only afforded scientific phenomena, but by the grasp it had on the human heart and conscience, was composed of the very passionate inmost soul of poetry, — of the stuff of its creation and the breath of its life. She did not reduce romance to a science; nor was it her mission to illustrate the romance of science. The mystery of life is not explained in her works. There is no Be-All and End-All system dreamt of in her philosophy. But her greatness is that she subordinates the finite parts to the infinite whole; and her music, though cradled in pain, is a true music of the spheres.

JANE AUSTEN
"THE EXQUISITE TOUCH"

JANE AUSTEN
"THE EXQUISITE TOUCH"

A. — HER PLACE

I

It is not, and yet again it is, because the three authors whose names adorn these pages happen to have been women that they are the subjects of our thought. This is not an attempt to add another volume to the large library of female appreciations. These names would the rather stand as a protest against that peculiar frivolity of criticising a woman's work in the light of her gender. But beyond this lies a fundamental truth, which prompts the general recognition of congenital differences in sex, which manifest themselves in the colors or forms of the work accomplished. The sexes are spiritually as well as physically complementary. A good woman novelist must have something of a man in her, for she must have judgment and strength: a good male novelist must have something of a woman in him, for he must have sympathy, which tempers judgment and justifies strength.

The wise critic, however, will not repeat the error of Lewes in dwelling on the differences so long that the more notable similarities are lost sight of: he will simply acknowledge the force of the differences when, as in the case of our present study, they are evident, and will not regard them in any fanciful way as dividing into permanent separate camps the intellectual conceptions of men and women. Each of these women is chosen because she stands a determinate quality in literature; and the three are considered in one book, not because together they form an interesting study of the distinctly feminine nature of these qualities, but because each of the qualities is of supreme importance in itself: yet none of these would have filled her place had she not had the essential characteristics of her sex; hence it is, indirectly and yet fundamentally, because of the womanhood that the subjects attract our notice. Guizot confessed that he found French and German fiction too artificial for his taste, and commended the English novels as more natural, " particularly those written by women." And of Miss Austen he says, one must go back to the great Athenian age for a parallel.[1] Scott, writing of the portraiture of actual society, thinks the women " do this better."[2] With men there is "too much attempt to put the reader exactly up to the thoughts and sentiments of the parties." Upon these dicta, — the grave historian and the splendid romancer, the austere thinker and the enthusiastic poet each emphasizing the undeniable point — we fall back for our

[1] 'Lady Susan, the Watsons.' With a Memoir by the Nephew, J. E. Austen-Leigh. Boston: Little, Brown, & Co., 1899, p. 293.
[2] 'Memoirs of the Life of Sir Walter Scott,' by J. G. Lockhart, Esq., Edinburgh: Adam and Charles Black, 1878, p. 618. Sir Walter was always complimentary to the ladies. " Miss Lucy Aikin tells a pretty story," says Mrs. Ritchie, in her ' Book of Sibyls,' " of Scott meeting Mrs. Barbauld at dinner and telling her that it was to her he owed his poetic gift." He said that Miss Edgeworth's Irish tales gave him his hint for the Waverleys, and even praised Mrs. Charlotte Smith's now forgotten novels, including them in his 'British Novelists.'

support in claiming that it is not as woman's work that we wish to regard Miss Austen's, Miss Brontë's, and George Eliot's, even though much of that which makes the work notable is distinctively womanly.

II

Charlotte Brontë was a voice crying in the wilderness, — crying for pain, crying unrestrained. It was the first note of pure personality — pure in every sense — heard in our literature; and it was the more startling because it was a woman's voice. George Eliot felt this passionate emotion in a larger way. The sympathetic tendencies of her thought were gradually developed until the personality of emotion was absorbed into a generalized sympathy, and the passion passed into compassion. She thus became the first (if not in time, at least in power) of altruists in fiction, — the first to give the fullest expression to that throbbing sense of the painful pressure of universal life upon the individual conscience which is now felt by all upon whom her message has fallen. Miss Austen's right of admittance to this fellowship, bearing its own unassailable credentials, we hope to make plain in the present essay.

III

We shall perhaps the better understand both Miss Brontë and George Eliot by considering the other lady out of her chronological order, and it is not without purpose that this place has been reserved for her. If we were to yield to the voice of the charmer — and so it always sounds when Mr. Birrell calls — this relegation would be for the same reason that the bishop is made to march at the end of the procession, namely, that the first shall be last; for Mr. Birrell concludes his monograph on Charlotte Brontë thus:

"It would hardly be safe to name Miss Austen, Miss Brontë, and George Eliot as the three greatest women novelists the United Kingdom can boast, and were one to go on and say that the alphabetical order of their names is also the order of merit, it would be necessary to seek police protection, and yet surely it is so.

"The test of merit for a novel can be nothing else than the strength and probable endurance of its pleasure-giving capacity. . . . To be read always, everywhere, and by all is the impossible ideal. Who fails least is the greatest novelist. A member of the craft may fairly enough pray in aid of his immortality, his learning, his philosophy, his width of range, his depth of passion, his height of feeling, his humor, his style, or any mortal thing he can think of; but unless his novels give pleasure and are likely to go on giving pleasure, his grave is dug, and sooner or later, probably sooner, will be occupied by another dead novelist.

"Applying this test, we ask — what pleasure-giving elements do Miss Austen's novels now possess which they will not possess a century hence? None! If they please now, they will please then, unless in the meantime some catastrophe occurs to human nature, which shall rob the poor thing of the satisfaction she has always hitherto found in contemplating her own visage. Faiths, fashions, thrones, parliaments, late dinners, may all fade away: we may go forward, we may go back; recall political economy from Saturn, or Mr. Henry George from New York: crown Mr. Parnell King of Ireland, or hang him high as Haman: but fat Mary

Bennet, the elder (*sic*) Miss Bates, Mr. Rushworth, and Mr. John Thorpe must always remain within call, being not accidental, but essential figures." [1]

But if the reasons brought forward in the foregoing studies for the supremacy of Miss Austen's successors are valid, this preference of Mr. Birrell's will be regarded merely *as* a preference — which is quite apart from a critical estimate; and we shall find other than ritual reasons for putting Miss Austen last.

This present is, indeed, the "strenuous life." The personal yet noble cry of Charlotte Brontë, and the

> . . . pulses stirred to generosity
> In deeds of daring rectitude

of George Eliot are living forces to-day, which, because of the later disturbances, does not feel the calm air of Miss Austen's time. Miss Austen had to do with manners; we have advanced to methods. She was content with picturing the life she saw; we search for the philosophy which will explain it. Her view was from the level of her own age; ours from that of all the ages. Yet the very laxity of her day was in part the reason for the energy of this, and we cannot hope to even approach a comprehension of the full purpose of the last half of the nineteenth century until we have considered the apparent lack of purpose of the last half of the eighteenth. We have reserved Miss Austen, then, that in studying her works, with the more modern "notes" of her successors still ringing in our ears, we may more clearly understand the great differences between that time

[1] 'Life of Charlotte Brontë,' by Augustine Birrell. London: Walter Scott, 1887, pp. 175-176.

and this and find therein their partial explanation. And as Miss Austen's name is associated with the lighter things of life, may not the consideration of her in this place be offered as a dessert after the more solid courses which have preceded?

IV

Just as Charlotte Brontë's and George Eliot's were new voices in literature, so also was Jane Austen's. The earlier novelists were the successors of the Essayists. Now, the Essayists were, first and last, moralists. They meant to rebuke the vices of an age become hideously corrupt through the subjection of those whose office is, by its nature and by the terms of its commission, to rebuke vice, to the class which could thus feed unchecked on what went unrebuked. The social position of the lower clergy in the first half of the eighteenth century was somewhat below that of the upper servants in a great man's house.[1] Forced to consort with the basest elements of society, they, who should have been the champions of moral living, were no better than their companions. As for their superiors in the Church, they were either themselves a part of the aristocratic class and submerged in its coarse depravities, or were so closely attached to it as not to be able to influence it from any vantage point of morality; and were, when not them-

---

[1] The innocence of Abraham Adams, Fielding says, was not so remarkable "in a country parson" as it would have been "in a gentleman who had passed his life behind the scenes;" thus recognizing the clear distinction of that time between the class to which even a learned parson like Adams belonged and the class of "gentleman."

selves actively vicious, at least negatively so in their cold and ineffectual worldliness. Every reader of the *Spectator* will remember Addison's picture of the country parson of that time at his best, — Sir Roger de Coverley's domestic chaplain:

"My chief Companion, when Sir Roger is diverting himself in the Woods or the Fields, is a very venerable Man who is ever with Sir Roger, and has lived at his House in the Nature of a Chaplain above thirty years. This Gentleman is a Person of good Sense and some Learning, of a very regular Life and obliging Conversation. He heartily loves Sir Roger, and knows that he is very much in the old Knight's Esteem, so that he lives in the Family rather as a Relation than a Dependant. . . . As I was walking with him last Night, he asked me how I liked the good Man, whom I have just now mentioned? and without staying for my Answer told me, That he was afraid of being insulted with Latin and Greek at his own Table; for which reason he desired a particular Friend of his at the University to find him out a Clergyman rather of plain Sense than much Learning, of a good Aspect, a clear Voice, a sociable Temper, and, if possible, a Man that understood a little of Backgammon. . . . At his first settling with me, I made him a Present of all the good Sermons which have been printed in *English*, and only begg'd of him that every *Sunday* he would pronounce one of them in the Pulpit. Accordingly, he has digested them into such a Series, that they follow one another naturally, and make a continued System of practical Divinity.

"As Sir Roger was going on in his Story, the Gentleman we were talking of came up to us; and upon the Knight's asking him who preached to-morrow, told us the Bishop of St. *Asaph* in the Morning, and Dr. South in the Afternoon. He then showed us his List of Preachers for the whole

Year, where I saw with a great deal of Pleasure, Archbishop *Tillotson*, Bishop *Saunderson*, Doctor *Barrow*, Doctor *Calamy*, with Several living Authors who have published discourses of Practical Divinity. . . . A Sermon repeated after this Manner, is like the Composition of a Poet in the mouth of a graceful Actor.

"I could heartily wish that more of our country Clergy would follow this Example; and instead of wasting their Spirits in laborious Compositions of their own, would endeavor after a handsome Elocution, and all those other Talents that are proper to enforce what has been penned by greater Masters. This would not only be more easy to themselves, but more edifying to the People."

For this same parson at his worst, we have only to refer to the novelists who succeeded Addison, whose Trullibers and Thwackums and Jack Quicksets, and the knavish curate who figures in Chapter IX. of 'Roderick Random,'[1] and the clerical gentlemen we are invited to look upon at the Visitation dinner in Letter LVIII. of the 'Citizen of the World,' and such "ministers" as the splay-footed, tobacco-stained priest called upon to read the marriage service over Harriet Byron, and the "buck parson" who, in 'Belinda,' first taught my Lord Delacour to drink, are, one would say after reading Bishop Burnett's unprejudiced testimony, not exaggerated delineations.

---

[1] This "young fellow in a rusty gown and cassock," with an exciseman for a partner, is soon perceived to be a sharper at cards, stripping the opponents "of all their cash in a very short time." "I did not at all wonder," says Roderick, "to find a cheat in canonicals, this being a character frequent in my own country; but I was scandalized at the indecency of his behavior and the bawdy songs which he sung." The whole chapter, introducing as it does, one of the upper clergy ("this rosy son of the Church") is a striking commentary on the times.

This corruption, permeating society, deadened all spiritual life, and fastened upon the eighteenth century the low-water mark of materialism. Vice among the robust Northern races, taking on its coarser forms, becomes a sin against taste, as well as a transgression against morals, and on this score the urbane Addison attacked it in his Essays. The vulgarity, the rowdyism, these scandalous indecorums, and the graceless foppery of all this profligacy, he set himself against; and it is a clear indication of the unspiritual atmosphere of the time that its chief moralist should, in his metrical criticism of the poets, never rise beyond the standpoint of taste. He who was beyond all else polished finds damning qualities in Chaucer because of his "*un*polished strain;" and this is the criticism in which he disparages Spenser and makes no mention at all of Shakspere. Addison was the high priest of Conventionalism, and was the true son of an age which could make " manners, good breeding, and the graces," of more consequence than honor and justice, in the calm language of Lord Chesterfield to his son. But the *Spectator* undoubtedly had a civilizing influence, and deserves the reputation it enjoyed of " making morality fashionable." That it was a calculating morality, of the sort later exemplified in Benjamin Franklin, is due to the fact that with good taste and manners as the main lever, it was impossible to have lifted it beyond a practical level in a materialistic age. Addison measures the loftiest flights by a standard of imagination in which *form* regulates all the by-laws. He thinks Sin and Death of too chimerical an existence to be proper actors in an Epic poem. Even his famous Hymn does not lift up, it simply pleases; it addresses itself to our fancy as a kind of poetical appendage to Butler's Analogy; and Haydn's tune, to which it is usually sung, connects it in our thought with Philip Wakem's criticism of that master's 'Creation,'—"sugared complacency and flattering make-believe, as if it were written for the birth-day fête of a German grand duke." Indeed, a Bolingbroke of his day might have said to its author what that satirical statesman later told Whitefield, on hearing him preach in Lady Huntingdon's drawing-room,—that "he had done great justice to the Divine attributes in his discourse." Although powerfully moved (moved but not overwhelmed, in Taine's phrase) by his greatest simile of the angel who "rides in the whirlwind and directs the storm," we can never quite dissociate the picture from that other picture of Thackeray's, representing this good angel flying off with Mr. Addison and landing him in the place of Commissioner of Appeals as his reward for writing the party poem which contained this valiant simile.

An age whose finest product is Addison, and whose prose had more poetry in it than its poetry,[1] must in the lower forms of its phenomena afford much ground for the moralist. This ground the Essayists occupied to good effect. And as in dealing with objectionable qualities, these qualities must be represented, a later reading of the reforming literature is liable to be distasteful to those who live in an age in which the reforms are in operation. Miss Austen's outburst

[1] Even as late as Goldsmith, the poetry had not been divorced from the formalism. The 'Vicar' has more poetic charm (in that it has more simple nature) than its author's most celebrated poem, which still represents the stiffness of the age by such lines as—

> But now the sounds of population fail;
> No cheerful murmurs fluctuate in the gale.

against the *Spectator* in 'Northanger Abbey' has puzzled some who too exclusively associate the Essays with the urbanity of Addison, and whose regard for the delightful Sir Roger causes the less admirable portions to be overlooked. It will be remembered that Miss Austen is defending her trade in attacking the habit of novelists of " degrading . . . the very performances to the number of which they are themselves adding. . . . Alas! if the heroine of one novel be not patronized by the heroine of another, from whom can she expect protection and regard?" If a young lady, she says, is detected reading a novel, she will affect indifference and momentary shame, but will be proud if caught with a volume of the *Spectator* in her hand, " though the chances must be against her being occupied with any part of that voluminous publication of which either the matter or manner would not disgust a young person of taste; the substance of its papers so often consisting in the statement of improbable circumstances, unnatural characters, and topics of conversation which no longer concern any one living; and their language too frequently so coarse as to give us no very favorable idea of the age that could endure it."

This is interesting, not only as emphasizing Miss Austen's personal taste, but also as pointing to the fact that the age "that could endure it" she at least thought was passed. Her strictures would seem to indicate that a new age had come in. Though a larger view might have been taken of the subject, Miss Austen was right in her charge that the Essayists were coarse. It is almost always a frivolous and very frequently a vulgar company we have to travel with through their pages, and the interest is literary and historical, rather than living and spontaneous, in all those dissections of beaux' hearts and ritual directions for the proper exercise of fans. But the same criticism might be applied to Juvenal, and Miss Austen would have enjoyed that author still less. That she did not inveigh against coarseness in Richardson, who carried on the didactic purpose of the Essayists, is because she so gladly recognized in his great synthetic skill the same power that moved her to construct, that had Lamb's summing up been known to her, that "the keynote of the whole composition is libertine pursuit," "the undivided pursuit of lawless gallantry," she would not have allowed the truthfulness of the complaint to have interfered with the enjoyment of the work. 'Pamela, or Virtue Rewarded,' — the sub-title shows the moral purpose. The novelist's aim in 'Clarissa' is elaborately set forth on the titlepage: "Clarissa: Or, The History of A Young Lady: comprehending The Most Important Concerns of Private Life: And Particularly Shewing the Distresses That May Attend The Misconduct Both of Parents and Children, In Relation to Marriage."[1]

The eighteenth century was an outspeaking age, and in the department of manners the change for the better was so gradual that it was not until its very close that it became remarkable, — a change for which, on its literary side, Miss Austen herself was mainly responsible. But the point is that a moralist in a coarse age, reflecting its predominating characteristics by having them as the subjects of his discussion, must either weary the readers of future ages through constant repetitions of unattractive scenes

[1] See also the Preface and Postscript.

(which is the fault of Richardson, and is what Miss Austen objects to in the *Spectator*), or must make the scenes themselves alluring, which was accomplished by Fielding. Although I fancy that gentleman had his tongue in his cheek when he wrote of 'Tom Jones' that it contained nothing which could "offend even the chastest eye," still, by the grace of satire, and by his enormous comic power in the delineation of human weaknesses, he is, with all his animal coarseness weighing against the estimate, ranked properly with the moralists. The age did not consider him coarse. One young lady can write to another of 'Joseph Andrews' that it has a "surprising variety of nature, wit, morality, and good sense," and that it is "peculiarly charming" because of its "spirit of benevolence."[1]

V

Miss Burney has been called the creator of the family novel. Using that faculty of observation on which all true realism must be built, and which is first noticeable in the pages of the *Spectator*, and is later developed to a high degree by Richardson and Fielding, she presents her public with a chastened set of characters, whose actions, for the first time in a chronological course through English fiction, may be read aloud without expurgations and without

---

[1] 'A Series of Letters between Mrs. Elizabeth Carter and Miss Catherine Talbot,' etc., London: Printed for F. C. and J. Rivington, 1808, vol i., p. 16. This is the "Mrs. Carter" who was so celebrated for her extraordinary learning, the chief result of which was her translation of Epictetus,— a learning, however, which did not exclude an almost equally notable piety.

blushes. 'Evelina' was published in 1778, some sixty years from the date of the *Spectator*, and thirty-six from 'Joseph Andrews,' and the question arises, is this change in tone due to a feminine delicacy, or is it the reflection of a real change in manners and morals? A chivalrous desire to associate the two ideas, Woman and Purity, in letters, is unhappily defeated by recollections of Mrs. Behn and Mrs. Haywood; and a glance at the times will show that the habitual grossness of the century had not materially improved. Miss Burney's comparative mildness probably owes its origin to a refinement which is to be found among women in all ages, notwithstanding these typical exceptions.

We have touched on the coarse looseness of the early part of the century to denote the difficulties in the way of any subtler art in its closing years; for this viciousness, growing by what it fed on, increased in the dead weight of its materialism until its utter lack of principle, its graceless infamy, its brutal hardness, its almost cannibal grossness, would make one cry out that religion was dead in England in the eighteenth century, did not one remember that religion never dies, and that if it should die, it would not be religion.

In 1786 there were nearly two hundred offences on the statute book punishable by death. Even to receive a stolen pocket-handkerchief might be made a capital offence. Pope's verse —

And wretches hang that jurymen may dine —

applied to the latter quarter of the century also; for although suits in chancery were spun out over many years, in criminal cases — as if human life were less valuable than civil property — the trial was generally compressed into a single day. Women were still whipped publicly through the streets. In 1789 persons were burned at the stake for crimes for which we now give ten years' imprisonment, and school children were allowed holidays to see executions. For petty debts men languished in prison for life. The keystone of commercial existence was the African slave trade. As late as 1828, Lord Shaftesbury saw the insane in " mad houses " chained to straw beds and left from Saturday to Monday without the care of their keepers. It was not until 1771 that the law was repealed which condemned a prisoner who refused to plead on a capital charge to death by weights laid on the breast.[1]

An age so publicly careless of human life, so monstrously perverted in the general principles of law and equity, must necessarily be an age of private social corruption and ugly indelicacy. To the active vice of the early years of the century was now added the accumulated grossness of the Hanoverians, mixed with the stupid limitation of wisdom to all things material. The novel of manners naturally reflected these characteristics, and it is to Miss Burney's credit that so much of them is handed down to us in a way that sufficiently denotes the age, without the unbridled license of her masculine predecessors. For the first time we see the possibilities and the attempts of prof-

---

[1] See Lecky's 'History of England in the Eighteenth Century,' vol. i., pp. 245 *seq.*, and vol. vi., pp. 541 *seq.*, and the authorities there quoted; also Mr. Russell's chapter 'Social Ameliorations,' in his 'Collections and Recollections;' and biographies of Shaftesbury and Howard.

ligacy rather than the high-noon picture of vice actually triumphant. She, too, is a moralist and has a distaste for the immoralities which she describes. But she shares with Richardson, and with all who fall short of the highest art, the failure to make that art so compellingly great that it will, on the one hand, not be pushed aside by its own creations (and be thus defeated by the means intended for its victory) and, on the other, not lend its own proper beauty to the enhancing of what, without such aid, would appear to all healthy eyes as improper and hideous. We are not now concerned with this latter fault, as it marks too nearly that decadence of art which has always set in after some great golden age, signifying that initial stage of a decline, after a long life upon the heights, when art begins to be cultivated, not to make its subject beautiful, but to minister selfishly to itself. There were no heights in the days of our eighteenth-century realists; and the best of them were beginning a new ascent, with many missteps and huge difficulties to overcome, to an elevation under whose grateful shade we still take refuge in the poems of Wordsworth.

Such was the age still extant when Jane Austen wrote, with a public taste to coax with her delicate flavors which had been fed for innumerable years on those rude meats which nourish the animal at the expense of the spiritual in man, as well as that later fondness for highly spiced condiments first prepared in the 'Castle of Otranto.' Until we reach Miss Austen we do not meet with realism wholly devoid of offence (for Miss Burney's mildness is only comparative), and she is the first novelist who combines with this a living interest, which makes the smallness of her scale, forced on her by her omissions, a positive merit.

On the point of taste alone — a word we shall have to make frequent use of in our consideration of Miss Austen — the superiority of 'Pride and Prejudice' and 'Emma' to 'Evelina' and 'Cecilia' is everywhere manifest. The atrocious behavior of Captain Mirvan towards Madame Duval has no counterpart in the younger lady's fiction, who cannot allow Emma's momentary ill-humored wit at the expense of Miss Bates to go unrebuked. There is nothing in the six books of Miss Austen like the adventure of Evelina with the creatures, male and female, of the Marylebone Gardens, that night of the fireworks. Only a trace of the swearing habit of the day may be found in our author. "Good God!" with Miss Burney is as common as the "Mon Dieu!" of a Frenchman, and even Lord Orville cannot announce breakfast without calling upon divinity to witness; while, as an Irishman might put it, every time Miss Larolles opens her mouth a "Lord!" pops out. Even Miss Edgeworth makes her women profane, or at least one of them, Mrs. Freke; and as for her men, the language of Sir Philip Baddely might be used as a swearing dictionary. In regard to drinking, contrast the mild solitary instance of Mr. Elton with Miss Edgeworth's Lord Delacour, who could "drink more than any two-legged animal in his majesty's dominions." It would have been impossible for Miss Austen to have described such a cruel scene as the two young rakes in 'Evelina' arrange for their jaded amusement in compelling two old women, over eighty years of age, to run a foot-race for a bet. Mrs. Goddard occasionally leaves her neat parlor to "win or lose a few sixpences by" Mr. Woodhouse's "fireside." That is all,—a mere touch. Per contra, in Miss Edgeworth's Mrs. Luttridge, we see the vice emphasized.[1]

So much for her restraint in picturing the grosser forms of the life of the times, which was partially due to her actual unacquaintance with them, and a conscientious realism which deterred her from portraying what she did not experimentally know; but still more, to a native delicacy which shrank from all coarseness and vice. Because of their broader brushes, we gain from Miss Burney and Miss Edgeworth a wider view of the day than from Miss Austen, and the works of the latter would be incomplete without hints from the former; and yet, such is the nicety and the truthfulness of her art, there is more verity in her limited portraiture than in the more comprehensive exhibits of the others.

VI

"There is no way," says Herbert Spencer, "of distinguishing those feelings which are natural from

[1] How prevalent it was may be learned from Horace Walpole's letters. See in particular his letter to the Earl of Strafford, in 1786, vol. viii., p. 73: "At the end of the century three titled ladies, Lady Buckinghamshire, Lady Archer, and Lady Mount-Edgcombe, were so notorious for their passion for play that they were popularly known as 'Faro's Daughters,' and Gilray published in 1796 a caricature representing two of them as standing in the pillory, with a crier and his bell in front. This was in consequence of what was said by Chief Justice Kenyon, in a case that came before him in 1796, when he said, with reference to the practice of gambling: 'If any prosecutions of this nature are fairly brought before me and the parties are justly convicted, whatever be their rank or station in the country,—though they should be the first ladies in the land—they shall certainly exhibit themselves in the pillory.'"—'Novels and Novelists of the Eighteenth Century,' by William Forsythe. New York: D. Appleton & Co., 1871.

those which are conventional, except by an appeal to first principles." And it might be added that an age which loses sight of first principles is *unprincipled*, as well as unnatural. Hence the grossness of this age we are considering, which makes its formalism so peculiar. There are by Miss Austen's time the opening notes of new voices, aiming at these first principles. Cowper and Burns have come. It is real nature that we see once more in Cowper, who was the first to criticise Pope (in whom was gathered up the quintessence of the formal) on the ground that he —

> Made poetry a mere mechanic art,
> And every warbler has his tune by heart.

Guided by the same standard of judgment as Addison, Pope thought Dryden the greatest because the smoothest of poets. Disguise it to our consciences by whatever literary chicanery we may invent, the fact is that Christianity has changed the standards of art by its infusion of ethics. Much of the talk about the separation of art and ethics is futile because the latter has so quietly and so insidiously charged the atmosphere of life that the art which is true to life cannot but partake of that atmosphere. An ethical emphasis, therefore, should not be regarded as a differentiation from, but as a representation of, art, other things being equal. Christianity has established a perfect reciprocity between nature and grace, between art and ethics. What is simply non-moral in Theocritus, because simply natural, is, in his paraphraser Dryden, immoral, because of the altered atmosphere; and Pope's ever-straining aim at finish made him, although a realist, unreal; and, like his master, the pseudo-classicism of his work, mixed with a native pruriency of thought, resulted in a body of indelicate imagery which will forever exclude it from the best poetry of the world.

While Cowper breaks away from this formal standard, we do not find in him, or in the poets before him, more than a simple feeling for nature. The deepest note he touches is the noble poem on his mother's picture, the receipt of which stirred a real affection to real poetry, which still moves us to real sympathy. "The meek intelligence of those dear eyes" looks at us as it did at him; which is, I think, the best proof of the living quality of the emotion. To appreciate how Cowper had advanced on the mechanical conventionalisms of the day, compare this poem with one on a similar subject by his friend and biographer, Hayley. Poor Hayley's filial love was probably as deep as Cowper's, but we weep with the one and do not weep with the other. The adjective's the thing. The ages of conventionalism are weak in adjectives, and Hayley can think of no better word to describe the ocean rolling under a vessel tossed by a fearful storm than "indignant." And yet we do not find in Cowper the passionate love for, the high communings with, Nature which come later. We have in Cowper and Crabbe, in Thomson and Gray, a series of objective moralizing pictures, pleasingly new and pure, with a comment running along with the sentiment, and in the degree in which it is unduly emphasized, interfering with the completeness of the charm. Cowper's ideal of bliss was an evening at Olney, with Mrs. Unwin and Lady Austen purring about the tea-kettle.

> Fireside enjoyments, homeborn happiness,
> And all the comforts that the lowly roof

Of undisturbed retirement, and the hours
Of long uninterrupted evening knows.

This is also the Vicar's thought: "What thanks do we not owe to heaven for thus bestowing tranquillity, health, and competence! I think myself happier now than the greatest monarch upon earth. He has no such fireside, nor such pleasant faces about it." When the storm arises outside, there is no fierce Brontean joy in its demoniac fury. Mrs. Unwin pours another cup of tea, and Lady Austen suggests a new canto to the 'Task,' in which the wild bluster of the outdoor night shall be contrasted pleasantly with the cozy indoor comfort of blazing logs and blissful companionship. Nor has the day of "eager thought" yet come in its fulness —

"Leisure is gone — gone where the spinning-wheels are gone, and the pack-horses, and the slow wagons, and the peddlers who brought bargains to the door on sunny afternoons. Ingenious philosophers tell you, perhaps, that the great work of the steam engine is to create leisure for mankind. Do not believe them; it only creates a vacuum for eager thought to rush in. . . . Old Leisure . . . was a contemplative, rather stout gentleman, of excellent digestion, of quiet perceptions, undiseased by hypothesis: happy in his inability to know the causes of things, preferring the things themselves."

or Goldsmith would disturb the peaceful reflections of his good Vicar with a few troublesome thoughts about the social conditions beyond his fireside. The poor were being observed, but objectively. Their miseries were noted by Crabbe, but there was no plan of social helpfulness in his design, and no philosophical or ethical reach in his poetry.[1] No better idea of the complete change of attitude in this respect can be gained than by contrasting Crabbe's "hoary swain" with Mr. Markham's 'Man with the Hoe.' The passion for humanity had not yet developed; but it was something to have the facts recognized which in due time awakened the enthusiasm. So, although the Rev. Mr. Crabbe did not care so very much for the poor of the two livings he so rarely visited, he is sufficiently sorry for their wretchedness to observe them from a distance, and to make reflections. This "exercise of the internal sense" is to bear fruit in time. Reflection comes after observation, and observation had only lately had its new birth. The search for causes, the effort to substitute a good new for a bad old, the probing of evil prompted by a loving hope in the high possibilities of all mankind, — this had not yet begun.

The democratic song of Burns had little or no immediate influence on the society which we are considering: it was only the milder feeling of Cowper and Crabbe, of Thomson and Gray, of Goldsmith and Young, which reflected the premonitions of the dawn which came with Wordsworth. It was still the ornamental age, still an age lacking the highest forms of imagination, still content with fancy. And further, apart from its choicest springs, it was still the downright age, and, in a way, a hopeless age, for Satire is frequently the last stage of hopelessness. A lack of im-

---

[1] It is only just to note, however, that the essay on prisons which Goldsmith puts in the mouth of his unhappy Vicar is in full accord with the enlightened views of modern reformers, and that in his prose preface to 'The Borough,' Crabbe condemns what has since been legislated out of existence in our best alms-houses, — the promiscuous herding of the sexes in such places.

agination precluded optimism, and without optimism there can be no reform. The depths of coarseness which are sounded in Smollett's works, for example, — are they not merely echoing notes of hoarse, pitiless voices around him? Is he not simply Crabbe extended into prose, his coarser nature less gently moved, a Hogarth in fiction, who, feeling the meanness, perpetuates it for a warning; and, stopping at realism, not endowed with power to draw the opposing virtues, presents too unrelieved a picture of the vice? Here is the moralist again, not differing in character, only differing in manner, from the Essayists.

VII

We can best approach the positive study of Miss Austen by a little further comparison with the elder lady. And here again, let me say, it is not primarily because the two are of one sex that I thus group them, but because Miss Austen is pre-eminently the novelist of manners, and the manners of the age had, between herself and Fielding, been most typically described by Miss Burney.

First, in their attitude towards the " lower classes." Miss Austen has been called narrow because she limited her view to her own class. But when the sympathies are not sufficiently extended to gather into their scope objects which, away from those sympathies, have no interest, and are perhaps antagonistic, it is the part of wisdom and good taste to leave them alone. Jane Austen's omissions were not due to a wilful disobedience to some heavenly vision; they were nothing more than the absence of fruit because no seed had been sown. It was simply a denial of nature; and to be true to such a denial is as fine an art as is the opposite art which compels its votaries to be true to it. We have only to recall Miss Burney's Branghtons and her Mr. Smith to become grateful to Miss Austen for *her* "narrowness," and to appreciate the difference between that and the sort which throws contempt upon what does not belong to itself. Better even contemptuous silence than contemptuous speech. With all her superiority to her great predecessors in the matter of refinement, Miss Burney shares in the weakness of her age — which is the weakness of all brutal ages — in holding up for purposes of ridicule manners and customs below the level of her own. Her plan is to make them contemptible, which is the very word her good clergyman, Mr. Villars, uses concerning them. It was the age of the whipping-post and the stocks, and this is their reflection in literature. There are three ways of treating a class whose habits and tastes are different from those of the readers the author has in mind: not to treat it at all, which was Miss Austen's method; or to accentuate the vulgarities, and thus widen the difference between it and other classes by the addition of disgust to the sum of the comic effect, and this was Miss Burney's way; or to let sympathetic take the place of supercilious laughter, — to laugh with, instead of at, the children of one's fancy, and thus to bear a more human relation to them, — more that of a father, less that of a stepfather. "Put yourself in his place" is a form of *noblesse oblige* which had not yet made itself manifest in fiction, — the sensibility to appreciate the values of standpoints other than one's own, and from those standpoints to humorously criticise one's own. It was reserved for Dickens to first draw the life of the "lower classes" with both sympathy and humor; and there is nothing in the later nineteenth-century attitude of art towards those classes which would not add to the lessening of the gap of a proper mutual understanding between master and servant, the employer and the employed, the sons of leisure and the sons of toil. But if Miss Austen does not reach beyond her times after this sympathy, she at least rises above them in abstaining from a ridicule which, considering its origin, is as vulgar as the vulgarity it discloses.

And yet how keen is Miss Austen's contempt when the occasion justifies it! Nowhere else is her swift wit so well employed as when piercing some affected extravagance, or some indecorous vulgarism. In all her books there is not a single page of broad comedy; the wit is as subtle as frost-work, the humor as delicate as dew. She is always the gentlewoman, apparently unconscious of, because consciously refusing to see, coarse colors. There is a look of disdain, a quick lifting of the eyebrows, a shooting glance from the hazel eyes, and it is done.

She is the very impossibility he would describe, if indeed he has now delicacy of language enough to embody his own ideas.

He was a stout young man of middling height, who, with a plain face and ungraceful form, seemed fearful of being too handsome unless he wore the dress of a groom, and too much like a gentleman unless he were easy where he ought to be civil, and imprudent where he might be allowed to be easy.

Elinor agreed to it all, for she did not think he deserved the compliment of rational opposition.

This capacity for restraint places her strongest heroines on secure levels with able men without subtracting from their feminine charm; for restraint in speech is supposed to be an intellectual faculty given in its superior excellence only to the stronger sex. Yet Elinor is here akin to the gentleman Mr. Hamerton tells us of, who never disputed with his French mother-in-law because of the known futility of the outcome: when, because accustomed to use '*Algérie*' and '*Afrique*' as convertible terms, she would maintain, for example, that the Cape of Good Hope belonged to France because Africa belonged to France, he would cheerfully reply, "*Oui, chère mère. Vous avez raison.*"

Indeed, the position of women is so much firmer with Jane Austen than with Miss Burney that we must attribute the difference to a finer conception rather than to any change in manners that may have crept in in the few years between the two. The full power of restraint is now used for the first time in fiction. It is not only because Miss Austen's scenes are removed, for the most part, from the contamination of the "great world" that her heroines are not offered the surprising facilities of falling into scrapes that fascinated the attention of Miss Burney. She knew that world, at least through books, and we can fancy her reading the current fiction with an easy smile on her lips as she detects some exaggerated "sensibility," and inwardly compares it perhaps with the simple proud standard of her own "sense." The "world" which touched Evelina in the person of Sir

Clement Willoughby gets toned down to the "world" which touches Fanny Price in the person of Henry Crawford. In passing to Miss Austen we leave the old familiar situation, in which, to the "inexpressible confusion" of the heroine, the hero drops "on one knee" in the act of his declaration; the heroine meantime "scarcely breathes," the "blood forsakes her cheeks," "her feet refuse to sustain her." Then the hero "hastily rises" (with his one knee) and "supports" her to a chair, "upon which she sinks almost lifeless." It was her ladylike delicacy, her feeling for proportion, her distaste for faults against taste, her conceptions all constantly checked and challenged by a never-failing sense of humor that discovered the false "sensibility," in the place of which she set up the true.

Consider the occasion of this outburst: "'Deny me not, most charming of women,' cried he, 'deny me not this only moment that is lent me, to pour forth my soul into your gentle ears,'" etc., etc. Sir Clement has hurried Evelina into a carriage away from the others of her party and given the driver a wrong direction in order to press his suit with a girl who grows more and more frightened as she realizes the situation. One would suppose that the infinite cunning and pertinacious plotting to accomplish the one object which apparently ever animated the breasts of the eighteenth-century "men of the world" would, in this case, have been wise enough to avoid the absurdity of expecting success over timidity by employing means of a particularly terrifying nature. Mackenzie's 'Man of the World,' which may be taken as a summing up of the characteristics of the eighteenth-century conception of its Lovelaces and its Sir Clement

Willoughbys (this latter, however, being but a pale feminine reflection of the article), is a very different person from what we mean when we use the term; and thanks, first of all, to Miss Austen that the difference exists. Think, madam, of your daughter "pursued" by some modern Sir Thomas, who thinks that he can best commend his gentility to her gentleness, and mollify the dislike which he feels she has for him, by such moderate and pacifying conduct as driving her, against her will, away from the only place where she will be safe, and seizing that of all moments to urge his claims. And this the "only moment" that is "*lent*" him! Unsuitability of situation and speech is generally marked by the unnaturalness of both. So we smile contentedly when we hear Sir Clement, about this time, addressing Evelina: "My dearest life, is it possible you can be so cruel? Can your nature and your countenance be so totally opposite? Can the sweet bloom upon those charming cheeks, which appears as much the result of good-humor as of beauty," etc., etc.

In Miss Burney's novels, gentlemen address young ladies in the street without introductions, and without any rebukes from accompanying chaperons. Every man seems to have been at liberty to insult every woman, and before we arrive at the last of our dear Evelina's adventures, we have wondered many times where were the police. These adventures, it is true, cease to alarm us as we proceed, for we come to a certain comforting knowledge, based on exceptionless examples of past experience, that at the supreme moment Lord Orville will appear, and sighing will melt away in joy. I got into a little habit, when standing on the brink of one of these climaxes, of betting with myself that the next words would be, "just then who should come in sight but Lord Orville!" and I always won the bet.

Yet this is the book that Burke sat up all night to finish, and over whose Mr. Smith, Johnson exclaimed, "Harry Fielding never drew so good a character!"[1] It was great, for the times; and, as we have said, such an improvement morally on the preceding fiction as to fairly win for its author the domestic title she enjoys. But it was a simple age in its standards, or the great vogue of 'Evelina' would not have been possible. It went through four editions in one year;[2] and when Mr. Austen wrote his publisher about 'Pride and Prejudice,' he referred to the manuscript as likely to make a book of the same size as this, which was still, now some nineteen years since its first appearance, the most talked-of novel in print. I doubt if there is a publisher on the green earth to-day who would receive its like; whereas, supposing the twentieth-century counterpart of 'Northanger Abbey' were, to-morrow, presented to any discriminating house, a repetition of the Bath episode would be equally impossible to realize in one's fancy. This is because Miss Austen struck the modern note, as well as that of her own time. She was natural; and up to the limit she purposely set herself, one sees in her work a true reflection of that time. But its grosser extravagances are suggested rather than dwelt upon; hints take the place of delineations; the particular is referred to the general, and the universal corrects the individual. So

---

[1] 'Diary and Letters of Madame D'Arblay, edited by her Niece.' London. Published for Henry Colburn by his Successors, Hurst & Blatchett. 1854. vol. i., p. 63.

[2] See original preface to 'Cecilia.'

an old-time heroine may for the first time appear before the critical eyes of a new-time girl without awakening risibilities; and whatever oddities of her century may cling to her have the effect of emphasizing the quaintness, without in the least widening the lines of divergence between the periods.[1]

So only the gravest literary persons read Richardson and Miss Burney and Miss Edgeworth to-day. Is there a single man of letters of your acquaintance under sixty years of age who can lay his hand upon his heart and swear that he has read *all* of Richardson?[2] Is there one among them who has read the *four* novels of Miss Burney? Is not this the first intimation to some that there are four? 'Evelina,' yes;

---

[1] This kinship to the modern idea is very evident in all her letters. One of the specimens given by Mr. Austen-Leigh to indicate "the liveliness of mind which imparted an agreeable flavor both to her correspondence and her conversation" is the following trifle which she hit off upon hearing of the marriage of a certain middle-aged flirt with a Mr. Wake:

> "Maria, good-humored and handsome and tall,
> For a husband was at her last stake;
> And having in vain danced at many a ball,
> Is now happy to jump at a Wake." — *Memoirs*, p. 260.

This sounds as if it had been written for last week's comic paper; and her more serious essays in prose suggest, one hundred years before her time, the light and graceful style of Miss Repplier.

[2] It is difficult to see how it could be done to-day without stimulants. Nothing but a sense of the importance of an acquaintance with the "father of the English novel" [he should more properly be called the father of the English realistic novel, as the more general title is, by rights, Defoe's] saves the student, to whom very likely, it is an intolerable bore on account of the reiteration *ad infinitum;* which is not variations on one theme, but a constant pounding of one note through endless volumes. Think of the size of it: there are about one million words in 'Clarissa,' which makes the work more than five times bigger than the longest of Miss Austen's, which is about the size of the average novel of the day.

'Cecilia,' perhaps; but, honestly now, 'Camilla'? and 'The Wanderer'? On the other hand, who that has ever read and appreciated one of Jane Austen's novels has not immediately read all the others? Nay, are they not among the immortal few that we read again and again?

VIII

It must be acknowledged, however, that they are not read by very many, and that they have never been "popular." They have not the human clutch of Miss Brontë's work upon the heart, and do not sound the depths of the spirit like George Eliot's. It is far more difficult to find reasons for the dislikes of non-literary readers than it is to find reasons for the likes of their opposites; but we shall probably not be far wrong if we attribute the popular neglect of Jane Austen chiefly to the absence of passion in her books. Her avoidance of the high lights of others resulted in too tame a color scheme to please the majority, who, in the long run, do not care for the mere novel of character, unless passionately conceived. She is too quiet for those whose definition for all peaceful things is "stupid," and who fail to distinguish the varying degrees of quietness. And it should be noted that she never was a "popular" novelist; which suggests that the "people" have about the same standard of likes and dislikes in each generation, although they may be at any time moved by some strange power controlling them against their will. Miss Austen's genius was not of that compelling kind. But it had the lasting qualities which proved it to be genius, and which, sooner or later, provokes discovery, and gathers to itself a constantly increasing discernment. Herein lies the essential difference between Miss Austen and Miss Burney, that, whereas the latter was immensely popular, she is not read to-day — in other words, she has fallen from her popularity — Miss Austen, no more popular then than now, has never suffered such an eclipse; but among the discerning, from then till now, her fame has been constantly increasing. And it is a legitimate hope that this number will so continue to increase as to finally merge the "discerning" into the "popular."

"Popular" pedestals are naturally insecure: Miss Austen's fame is safe, partly because it never rested upon one.

IX

It is astonishing how slowly this appreciation grew, and how little the rare quality of the work was recognized during her lifetime. I do not know of any equal neglect elsewhere; her case is singularly apart from others.

Jane Austen's life has always been regarded as peculiarly free from the besetting cares of the author; and if a life without a history is a happy one, hers was indeed the happiest of all. It is a pleasant story of domestic peace that her chief biographer tells,[1] and there is scarcely a murmur to

---

[1] 'The novels of Jane Austen. Lady Susan, the Watsons. With a Memoir by her Nephew, J. E. Austen-Leigh.' Boston: Little, Brown, & Co., 1899. This is the second edition, a valuable addition to which is the cancelled chapter of 'Persuasion.' The first edition (London, Bentley, 1870) contains less matter, and does not include the stories. The Memoir is a thin volume, dignified, tender, and in excellent taste; and, with Lord Brabourne's book, forms the source of the inspiration

break the secluded quiet from beginning to end. It was apparently a family that lived entirely to itself, — related, indeed, to great personages, as any one may discover who chooses to puzzle through Lord Brabourne's genealogies, but with an acquaintance limited to the society of its own rural neighborhood. With the exception of the father's death, there was no break in the contented circle until Jane herself was called away; and the gentle shadow of Cassandra's lost love, and the financial troubles of Henry, near the close of Jane's career, were the only clouds upon the almost unbroken prosperity of that long summer day of her life. There seems to have been no desire on the part of her father to enlarge his acquaintance; and his sons, like himself, cultured but retiring men, remained content in their narrow stations; this habit of privacy pertaining even to that brother who rose to the highest rank in the British navy; for, though dying full of honors, we have to search the official records for our knowledge of his distinguished services. I cannot agree with Mr. Adams that the lack of recognition which we have noticed is devoid of pathos, on the ground that she received as much as the taste of the age would allow, or induce her to expect.[1] I think there is an exceeding pathos in those years of waiting, she knowing instinctively, all the time, her strength; and her father's responsibility for the gaps between writing and publishing has not been suffi-

---

of the subsequent biographies, some of which are not much more than synopses of the novels; the one critical exception being Prof. Goldwin Smith's monograph ('Life of Jane Austen,' by Goldwin Smith. London, Walter Scott, 1890). [All references to Mr. Austen-Leigh's book in this Study relate to this edition.]

[1] 'The Story of Jane Austen's Life,' by Oscar Fay Adams. Chicago: A. C. McClurg & Co., April, 1891, pp. 13, 14.

ciently pointed out. Instead of sending the manuscript of 'Pride and Prejudice' to Cadell, he *writes* about it. As the author was entirely unknown, the publisher, wearily recalling, no doubt, the many manuscripts he had received from young lady aspirants in country towns, entertaining visions of repeating Miss Burney's success, naturally puts the proposition to death by return of post; and 'Pride and Prejudice' is not published until sixteen years later. The Reverend George Austen is not the first "handsome proctor" who, settled in some sleepy parish, lets his wits grow fat at the expense of his family's credit; and his greatest punishment is that he did not live to know that his daughter was a recognized author, for not one of her books came out in his lifetime. If we are visited in the land of shadows with an accusing knowledge of our omissions on earth, perhaps it was his lot to mingle his grief with her regret that he was not with her to enjoy the fruition of a work which, by a more strenuous effort on his part, might have been accomplished before the separation.

There seems, indeed, to have been a lethargy about that country parsonage life, a conservatism grown into an almost fatalistic habit. "Lethargy" is about the last word one would apply to Jane Austen's quick perceptions and ready wit; but the effort to publish was constantly arrested by a kind of sleeping-sickness, — periods of inactivity hindering the fulfilment of terms of industry. There were, as we have said, sixteen years between the writing and the publishing of 'Pride and Prejudice.' 'Sense and Sensibility' was not printed until fourteen years after it was begun. 'Northanger Abbey' was written five years before it was prepared for the press, and then reposed, forgotten and unclaimed for several years longer in the safe of a Bath publisher. She began two stories which she never finished, and she finished one which she never published. Two of her novels, one of which was the earliest sold, she did not live to see in print. These facts are not set forth complainingly, — for as *we* possess the happy outcome, it is a matter of no moment, now, — but by way of illustrating the advantage on the side of those whose inward call is hurried by the outward circumstance. There was too much affluence with Jane; there was no compulsion to write; it was an amusement, chiefly; she was too easily queen in her small circle. And yet the family did not exalt her, for, with all their cheerful pride in her accomplishments, they shared the unapprehension of the age as to the greatness of her distinction.

X

She lived in stirring times, but there is no trace whatever of them in her letters[1] or her books. She

[1] Mr. Austen-Leigh's biography was supplemented in 1884 by 'Letters of Jane Austen. Edited with an Introduction and Critical Remarks by Edward, Lord Brabourne.' Two vols., London, Richard Bentley and Son. The great-nephew here supplements the work of the nephew with a large collection of Jane's letters, almost all of which are addressed to her sister Cassandra. They are just such letters as one acquainted with the novels would expect; bright, humorous, full of the gossip of the neighborhood, never intended for other eyes than the sister's, and without any public interest. It is a grave question whether such letters should be published; and there can be no doubt whatever that if Jane could have fancied the possibility of such an event, she would have very indignantly forbidden it. Lord Brabourne would have served his purpose by printing, say two dozen of the best of these letters; the rest is repetition.

They are, at all events, honest, and delightfully correspond, in tone

was satisfied with the parish. Not that she was narrow in her judgments, and fancied the parish at a metropolitan eminence: it was an elegant indiffer-

and spirit, with the fiction. Compare, for example, her defence of novel reading in 'Northanger Abbey' with " I have received a very civil note from Mrs. Martin requesting my name as a subscriber to her library. . . . As an inducement to subscribe, Mrs. Martin tells me that her collection is not to consist only of novels, but of every kind of literature, etc. She might have spared this pretension to *our* family, who are great novel readers, and not ashamed of being so; but it was necessary, I suppose, to the self-consequence of half her subscribers" [vol i., p. 178]. And we see the humorous impatience which, for the public, took form in Miss Bates, here reflected in private: "The Webbs are really gone! When I saw the wagons at the door and thought of all the trouble they must have in moving, I began to reproach myself for not having liked them better, but since the wagons have disappeared, my conscience has been closed again, and I am excessively glad they are gone" [vol. ii., p. 319].

We get in these letters, in short, just what a careful reader of her books would expect. The delightful impromptu balls of the novels are the counterparts of those Steventon affairs so vivaciously described to her sister; and we prefer to associate that innocent, roguish face which Lord Brabourne has selected for his frontispiece, rather than that better known picture with the hideous cap, assumed too early by 'Aunt' Jane, with the gaieties in which she took such a prominent part, — going through twenty dances on one occasion, without fatigue; and they were not our easy waltzes, either.

But there is too much of it, and there is not the excuse for a longwinded effort which prevails when the letters present interesting views on varied topics and exchanges of opinion with distinguished correspondents. A thinker's opinions are always interesting — to thinkers. But there was a total unacquaintance with the many celebrated men of the day, intercourse with whom would have spurred her intellect into a keener atmosphere than that surrounding this exchange of family confidences. Jane was capable of criticising Kean's Shylock, but all she says to Cassandra is that she is "quite satisfied" with it [vol. ii., p. 218]. Doubtless she would have had suggestive things to say about Byron had she, like Miss Edgeworth, had Walter Scott for a correspondent, instead of the sister, to whom it is sufficient to write: "I have read the 'Corsair,' mended my petticoat, and have nothing else to do" [vol. ii., p. 222]. Nor do we get any account of those engaging details concerning the publishing of an author's famous books which adds to the interest of so many biog-

ence to things outside, not a rustic conceit, that magnified her people and place; and the place was magnified only because it happened to be the home of the people. Referring to some calamity, she exclaims: "How horrible it is to have so many people killed! And what a blessing that one cares for none of them!"[1] Yet here it is George Eliot and not Jane Austen who is the more unusual, for most of us bear the losses of others with equanimity.

This close partnership pertained even to literary matters, in which, one would suppose, the self-knowledge of her superiority would have caused a little more seclusion from her home circle and a little more widening out to her brothers and sisters of the pen. But no. She writes to an aspiring niece, about the success of whose manuscript she probably entertained critical doubts: "I have made up my mind to like no novels but Miss Edgeworth's, yours, and my own;"[2] and she generously contrasts the "strong, manly, vigorous sketches, full of variety and glow" which a nephew has submitted to her friendly criticism, with her own miniature effects.[3] If she did not consider her writing as her contribution to a family symposium, there was at least a playful and modest assumption to that effect. It is an indication of the peculiar privacy of this pleasant family that the only literary confidences

---

raphies: one would like to know, for example, how Murray came to succeed Egerton as her publisher.

And so we say that to give us two octavo volumes is a little too much. Two dozen letters would have been as good as two hundred. We do not in the least share the great-nephew's lament that the letters of his other great-aunt have been destroyed. Like Mr. Woodhouse, we like our gruel thin.

[1] Brabourne, vol. ii., p. 109.   [2] *Ib.*, vol. ii., p. 318.
[3] Austen-Leigh, p. 310.

of Miss Austen were with those children of her brothers who themselves had yearnings in the direction of letters; and it is further significant of her unassuming helpfulness and gentle affection that she conveys her criticisms in terms of such equal partnership. Those were fortunate nieces and nephews who had a Jane Austen for an "Aunt Jane," too much of whose time they unwittingly occupied with manuscripts of fiction which she must have suspected would never see the light of day, but which she nevertheless discussed with them with such ungrudging fulness.[1]

Her letters show her a thorough woman of the world, little though her world was, with such a real delight in its obvious pleasures as to shut out the considerations of the larger world outside. And yet her view is everywhere private and domestic, for the "worldly" attitude obtains in the quietest surroundings, and one may be a "man" or "woman of the world," and still care chiefly for one's own fireside. In her last immortal work, it is the dreadful solitude of Charlotte Brontë's heroine which gives the tragic touch to her portrayal. There were no sisterly confidences there, for the sisters who had been were not. On the other hand, one has only to think of Elizabeth and Jane Bennet, Elinor and Marianne Dashwood, Henrietta and Louisa Musgrove, Fanny and Susan Price, Julia and Maria Bertram, Emma and Mrs. John Knightley, to see how the sweetest relationship of their creator's life was reflected in the best of these groups, and how the worst got hints for its depiction from the

[1] One wishes that the phonograph had been in use then and employed to take down those impromptu fairy stories she continued for days to the delight of her brother's children.

contrasting shadows. It would seem that nothing beyond this domestic life moved her. The French cousin who was an inmate of the parsonage during Jane's formative period, and whose father had perished in the Revolution, was more useful in helping her get up private theatricals than in supplying the material for thoughts that were beginning to shake the world. Of Southey's 'Life of Nelson,' she says: "I am tired of Lives of Nelson, being that I never read any;"[1] and she makes it apparent that her only interest in public affairs is because of her sailor brothers' connection therewith. "This peace will be turning all our rich naval officers ashore," says Sir Walter Elliot's lawyer to him one morning. "They will all be wanting a home." That is how the abdication of Napoleon is reflected in Miss Austen's novels. No wonder that Mme. de Staël thought 'Pride and Prejudice' "*vulgaire,*"[2] — a term that has been misunderstood by some of Miss Austen's commentators. She is the very opposite of everything vulgar, as we commonly apply the word. The Frenchwoman, responsive to the ideas awakened by the Revolution — ideas furiously active in her own 'Corinne,' — could not understand the unconcern of this evidently brilliant contemporary, whose thoughts were occupied with balls and tea-drinkings and the mild flirtations of curates while Europe was seething with the activities of an awakened hope. This passionless impersonality was what aggravated Charlotte Brontë in Miss Austen, whose "mild eyes" reflected

---

[1] Brabourne, vol. ii., p. 175.
[2] 'Madame de Staël, Her Friends and her Influence in Politics and Literature,' by Lady Blennerhassett, 3 vols. London: Chapman and Hall, 1889, vol. iii., p. 455.

none of the troubles which in one way or another move most of the great writers to literary expression. Mme. de Staël, therefore, reading Miss Austen in the light of her own flame, thought 'Pride and Prejudice' "*trivial*," which is all she could have meant by "*vulgaire*."

Our author was a Gallio caring for none of these things. It might be said that she did care for them, but was clever enough to avoid the incongruity of introducing them into her peculiarly domestic scheme; and it is true that she had, in a more singular degree than most, that nice discrimination which would justify such a defence, were it not remembered that when the heart is full of a subject, that is the subject chosen for discussion. Had she been moved by the urgency of the times, as was the author of 'Corinne,' as was later the author of 'Middlemarch,' we should have had a different outcome. To be sure, it was only a faint echo of that conflict which reached the country parishes of England, still remote by reason of bad roads in an age before steam had annihilated distance.[1] Notwithstanding the change slowly coming over the face of English life and letters, it was still the dull era; the deep motives at work under the transition not yet showing effect on the surface. And while every great artist is in some way superior to his times, Miss

---

[1] It was not yet a time of general travel. We learn from Miss Burney that to reach Kensington in those days, one had to take a coach from London; and from Miss Edgeworth that there was a turnpike between Grosvenor Square and Knightsbridge. Much of the unrest of modern fiction is nursed by globe-trotting. Dorothea's awakening from restful supposition to restless realities came in Rome. Miss Austen's career was bounded by one or two countries of an England not yet disturbed by too easy facilities for escape.

Austen's superiority was not in that sympathetic strength which, seizing on a new generous idea, is able to build on it a beautiful structure of hope and love. She was a realist, with an imagination held in check by the little ironies of time and place; a domestic realist, therefore confined in her view; domestic in the purest sense, and admirable in consequence; but still, because a realist, reflecting as much of the coarseness of the time as her elegant discrimination would allow. There must be something either of philosophy, or romanticism, or æstheticism, or pure personal suffering in an author's work to make it appeal to the majority; there was none of these things in Jane Austen's, unless it was the philosophy which recommended silence where there was not sympathy, which is sometimes the wisest philosophy of all.

It is amusing to read of Mme. de Staël's desire to meet the author of 'Pride and Prejudice' rebuked by the declaration that she did not wish to be met as an author, but as a lady; and the Frenchwoman might have replied, as Voltaire did on a similar occasion, that she did not have to travel out of France to meet ladies. The episode is characteristic of the Austen privacy, and it has an interest in that it was almost the only actual opportunity Jane ever had of meeting a distinguished stranger, although the opportunity might frequently have been found but for this seclusion, which was not, on the one hand, a proud aloofness, nor on the other, due to shyness and bashful modesty, but was simply a satisfaction with existing conditions, they being very pleasant. She certainly did not rise superior to her times in her attitude towards Mme. de Staël, for her answer indicates a fear of being mistaken for a female pedant; the idea of the sexlessness of genius not yet having arisen.

XI

This lack of public spirit was not wholly due to the times, nor to the position of women then: witness the keen interest of Mrs. Barbauld concerning the Test Act, and her poem to Wilberforce. It was due rather to an isolation more mental than physical, which she did not strive to break. Recall the men who made Bath brilliant in the first years of the past century. These were they who probably met Miss Austen every fine morning on their strolls to and from the Pump Room, without ever knowing that the sprightly young woman to whom perhaps they gave a glance of careless admiration as they passed, was the author of a story having as its centre of interest that same Bath, and destined to help materially in the evolution of fiction from romantic impossibilities to conceivable realities,—a story lying forgotten at that moment in a publisher's office in that very city. And as *she* passed *them*, knowing who they were and what they had done, and knowing that she had already written three novels which ranked her as worthy of their most respectful salutations, but which, as she had made none but the most futile efforts to publish them, were, so far as that distinguished company was concerned, no better than unwritten,—as this momentarily challenged her attention, I think she must have suffered some compunctions. For I believe that she knew that her work was great. The playful references which she makes, in the letters to her sister, to her favorite creations, as if they were real personages, proves a live interest; and her resentment of the manner of the acknowledgment of 'Emma' on the part of the Prince of Wales, after, at his own suggestion, that work had been dedicated to him, showed that she was alive to slights. The First Gentleman thanked her for the *handsome* copy she had sent him; whereupon Miss Austen says: "Whatever he may think of *my* share of the work, yours seems to have been quite right."[1] She knew that her work was great, and she felt that she had a distinct call to write — of that, too, I am convinced. Indeed, one of the indications of her genius is that she responded to this call, notwithstanding the surroundings which opposed it. The pressure from without was in the contrary direction: the only excitation was from within, and it was great enough to overcome the opposition.

Yet she deliberately chose anonymity, and she was barely discovered before she died. This was not because of any isolation which convention then required of her sex. Mrs. Barbauld numbered among her friends Johnson, Fox, Priestley, and Howard. Lamb talked about her, and Rogers came to her three-o'clock dinners. She had the advantage of having Dr. Aikin for her brother. Miss Edgeworth was fortunate, too, in the possession of a father with a distinguished acquaintance. She was very intimate with the Barbaulds; the famous Dr. Beddoes was her brother-in-law; the elder Darwin, and Day, of 'Sandford and Merton' fame were her father's friends; and there is a striking chapter in her 'Memoirs' of her visit to Mme. de Genlis. "They seem," says Mrs. Ritchie, in her 'Book of Sibyls,' "to have come in for everything

---

[1] Austen-Leigh, p. 279. In a letter to her publisher.

that was brilliant, fashionable, and entertaining. They breakfast with poets, they sup with marquises, they call upon duchesses and scientific men." Both Byron and Moore thought her charming, and the Duke of Wellington composed verses in her honor.

As Mrs. Barbauld's brother and Miss Edgeworth's father assisted their relatives to widening literary experiences, so did the husband of Mrs. Opie help her; for, although he had lost his fashionable following by the time of his marriage, he had retained such powerful friends as Erskine and Sheridan. Sir James Mackintosh, Godwin, Mrs. Inchbald, Sydney Smith, Horne Tooke, knew this amiable lady, who also enjoyed the Athenian privilege of residence in Norwich. Before her retirement from the world, Hannah More was the idol of the most brilliant society of the day; and after that, Horace Walpole used to visit his "holy Hannah" at Cowslip Green. We know how Dr. Johnson made a celebrity of Fanny Burney. Mrs. Grant of Laggan writes to Mrs. Hemans, "praised by all that read you, and known in some degree wherever our language is spoken." Even Miss Mitford had a wide acquaintance. Talfourd introduced her to Macready. Charlotte Cushman played her Claudia, and Young and Charles Kemble were the actors of her hero parts. Scott and Mackenzie wrote prologues and epilogues for Joanna Baillie. Byron dedicated verses to Lady Blessington, and Lawrence painted her portrait.

But there are compensations in most situations. Miss Austen was at least unharassed by her father, whereas the best and most enduring portions of Miss Edgeworth's works are those in which her father did not interpolate, nearly all the didacticism by which she is chiefly but not justly remembered being due to his interfering zeal. Mr. Austen was a just man of unspotted reputation, whereas Miss Mitford's works were, in large part, the outcome of a bitter urgency to pay the debts of a reckless parent, the anxious hurry manifesting itself in the strained result. The unfortunate adoption of Johnson's style by Miss Burney was doubtless due to his literary sponsorship, and makes her later works unreadable.[1] [And a father's unwise zeal also hurried 'Cecilia' forward to its detriment.[2]] Mrs. Barbauld's brother apparently did not prevent his sister from falling into the same imitation in at least one of her essays, whereas Miss Austen's brothers exercised no disturbing influence upon her style, although it is evident that at least two of them enjoyed a quiet sympathy with her talent, which occasionally took the form of active, but not overbearing helpfulness. The elder brother, James, the father of her biographer, was a Varsity man, interested in literature, and showed an unobtrusive and sobering influence upon the formation of her taste. The other brother, Henry, the least worthy in character, seems to have been her chief literary adviser; and he it was who finally circumvented the Bath publisher, which, in our judgment, covers a multitude of faults; although to buy back a manuscript for the same amount for which it had been sold some years previously has been characterized by some unduly

---

[1] Goldsmith's remark to Johnson, "Dr. Johnson, if you were to make little fishes talk, they would talk like whales," is, when applied to his copiers, still more ludicrous, for the doctor's would at least not be imitation whales.

[2] Preface to 'Cecilia,' by Annie Raine Ellis. London: Geo. Bell & Sons, 1890, p. xviii.

anxious persons as sharp dealing, in that the ignorant man was kept in the dark as to the identity of the author, who had become famous since his purchase of the novel, of the surpassing merits of which he was so evidently uninformed. The transaction seems to me not only justifiable, but poetically just: some publishers get their punishment in this world.

Indeed, it may readily be maintained that the narrow but cultured environment of Miss Austen gained for her more than the fuller and socially wider lives of her contemporaries. It was a very harmonious family, bound together by cheerful affections, and with sufficient variations as to individualities to prevent monotony. Each member doubtless contributed, quite unconsciously, his share of influence; we fancy that we can see, for example, how the lively dispositions of Edward and Henry helped to replenish the vials which fed her sense of humor,—and this kind of influence is manifestly better than the actually co-operative sort when that is exercised to the harm of natural expression.

XII

Whether for good or ill, her seclusion had the certain effect of keeping her unknown and unappreciated for a long period. The *Quarterly* article of October, 1815, was the first authoritative recognition, and this but two years before her death![1] That was not only

[1] A similar interest to that surrounding the 'Jane Eyre' criticism invests this article. Mr. Austen-Leigh refers to it as from an unknown pen, and criticises it for a lack of acumen. Mr. Goldwin Smith also condemns it. Neither knew that it was Walter Scott's work, as we learn that it was from Lockhart. ['Memoir of the Life of Sir

the first, it was the only notable criticism of her books which she ever saw; and she died supposing that the small portion of the world which knew her at all held her inferior to Miss Edgeworth and Miss Burney. It was five years afterwards that Dr. Whately's article was published.[1] Then a nine years' silence, until a reviewer in the *Edinburgh* wrote: "Miss Austen has never been so popular as she deserved to be."[2] And it is interesting to note that the writer finds his reason for Miss Austen's unpopularity in her naturalness. As late as 1859 a writer in *Blackwood's* begins an essay on our au-

---

Walter Scott, Bart.,' by J. G. Lockhart. Edinburgh: Adam and Charles Black, 1878, p. 472, note.] And this unwitting criticism of Scott for a lack of sympathy is amusingly odd, seeing that it was Scott who, more than any other, gave the most generous sympathy to other writers, and was the first to speak of the "exquisite touch" of Miss Austen, as compared with his "bow-wow" strain. [Ibid., p. 614.] It is interesting to note that in Whately's contribution of five years later, reference is made to this earlier criticism, thus, "We remarked in a former number," which might lead one to suppose either that Whately himself was its author, or that the *Quarterly* editor assumed the right, by manipulating the phraseology of his writers, to bring all contributions on a given subject into uniformity. As we know from Lockhart that the former hypothesis is not true, the conclusion may be that the latter is an explanation of the arbitrary power which gave such a brutal strength to the papers of the *Quarterly*, especially as Lockhart himself hints that the style of the article "might have been considerably doctored by Mr. Gifford." Of course, the writer may have himself thus indicated his agreement with Sir Walter's opinion, the anonymous character of the *Quarterly* articles allowing such freedoms. In any case, but for Lockhart, the reference would only deepen the difficulty of authorship. And it adds to the entertainment of the situation that the very citation from Lockhart which Mr. Austen-Leigh makes (p. 289, footnote) to prove that Scott did not write the January, 1821, article is *our* authority for the assertion that he did write the October, 1815, review!

[1] *Quarterly*, vol. xxiv., pp. 352 *seq.*
[2] *Edinburgh Review*, vol. li., pp. 448-457.

thor by saying: "For nearly half a century England has possessed an artist of the highest rank, whose works have been extensively circulated, whose merits have been keenly relished, and whose name is still unfamiliar in men's mouths."[1]

If Miss Austen's admirers have been few in comparison with other novelists', they form at least a notable set; and if the acknowledgment has been tardy, it has been select. What a pity that she did not know Scott's full opinion! She did not know what Scott really thought; she had no information as to Lord Holland's appreciation;[2] she died too soon for Macaulay's praise to reach her.[3] She was not aware that Southey and Coleridge "had an equally high opinion of her merits."[4] No one was ever known to ask for her autograph. She never sat to Lawrence. No cheap edition of her novels was published until fifty years after her death, when the 'Memoirs' awak-

---

[1] Among the magazine articles on Jane Austen, let me commend in particular that of the *North British Review*, vol. lii., p. 129. An instructive paper by Mr. Adams, in the *New England Magazine*, vol. viii., pp. 594 *seq.*, contains illustrations of Steventon, Bath, Lyme-Regis, Chawton, and Winchester. Another illustrated article, with an older set of pictures, may be found in *Harper's* for July, 1870.

[2] 'Recollections of Past Life,' by Sir Henry Holland, Bart., M.D. F. R. S., etc. New York: D. Appleton & Co., 1872, p. 231.

[3] "But amidst the infinite variety of lighter literature, with which he beguiled his leisure, 'Pride and Prejudice' and the five sister novels, remained without a rival in his affections. He never for a moment wavered in his allegiance to Miss Austen. In 1858 he notes in his journal, 'If I could get materials, I really would write a short life of that wonderful woman, and raise a little money to put up a monument to her in Winchester Cathedral.'" [' Life and Letters of Lord Macaulay,' by his nephew, G. Otto Trevelyan. 2 vols. New York: Harper & Bros., 1876, vol. ii., p. 394. See also the *Edinburgh Review*, vol. lxxxvii., p. 561.]

[4] 'Memoir and Letters of Sara Coleridge,' edited by her daughter. 2 vols. London: Henry S. King & Co., 1873, vol. ii. p. 75.

ened a tardy interest. Yet of her Sara Coleridge wrote, "the most faultless of female novelists,"[1] and the great Jowett asks: "Have you thoroughly made yourself up in Miss Austen, the 'Vicar of Wakefield,' and Boswell? No person is educated who does not know them."[2] Newman read her books through yearly to improve his style, and Tennyson spoke of her as next to Shakspere.[3] She is the critic's novelist, as Spenser is the poet's poet. In a letter to Murray, Gifford praises 'Pride and Prejudice' as "a very pretty thing. No dark passages; no secret chambers; no wind howlings in long galleries; no drops of blood upon a rusty dagger, — things that should now be left to ladies' maids and sentimental washerwomen."[4] This appreciation ought not to be surprising. What the *Quarterly* dissectors could not understand was spiritual newness and the tempestuous qualities of genius. The opposite of what it condemned in Charlotte Brontë was to be discovered in Miss Austen. The evenness of manner, the lightness of touch, the unruffled temper, the freedom from exaggeration, the uniform fineness, the writing, all

---

[1] 'Memoir and Letters of Sara Coleridge.'
[2] 'Life and Letters of Benjamin Jowett, M. A.,' by Evelyn Abbott and Lewis Campbell. 2 vols. New York: E. P. Dutton & Co., 1897, vol. ii. p. 338.
[3] 'Autobiography of Henry Taylor.' 2 vols. New York: Harper & Bros., 1885, vol. ii., p. 160. In this conversation, the laureate thanks God that no letters of Jane's had been preserved. Lord Brabourne's little indiscretions must have added gloom to his closing years.
[4] 'A Publisher and his Friends. Memoirs and Correspondence of the late John Murray,' by Samuel Smiles. 2 vols. London: John Murray. New York: Chas. Scribner's Sons, 1891, vol. i., p. 282. And at that moment 'Northanger Abbey,' ridiculing these very things, was lying forgotten and unclaimed in a publisher's drawer in Bath!

unconscious, as if a French Academy was watching her, — this would delight a critic like Gifford, whose devotion to the classical ideal was, negatively, not upset by any revolutionary thoughts in the perusal of Miss Austen's fiction, and was, positively, stimulated by such perfection of form, disclosing the completest natural method. The newness of Jane Austen highly important as it was, was not a supernatural newness; it was a return to nature quite within the approving understanding of a *Quarterly* reviewer. For this reason, Miss Austen has a following of peculiar strength, although it be small in numbers; and the ability to appreciate her has come to be regarded as one of the marks of a delicate culture. "First and foremost," says George Eliot, " let Jane Austen be named as the greatest artist that has ever written, using the term to signify the most perfect mastery over the means to her end. . . . To read one of her books is like an actual experience of life. . . . Only cultivated minds fairly appreciate the exquisite art of Jane Austen."

We find her commended where we should ordinarily turn last of all for judgments on novels. In a letter quoted by Mr. Austen-Leigh, Miss Quincy refers thus to Chief Justice Marshall and Justice Story: " To them we owe our introduction to her society."[1] Even Mr. Saintsbury, who is generally rude to the ladies, says, " We shall have another Homer before we see another Jane."

And yet it is of the essence of irony that almost the only appreciation she ever received in the flesh was from the very last source whence it would be looked for. In the unpublished diary of Lord Rob-

[1] Austen-Leigh, pp. 297–298.

ert Seymour, the most decorous exploit of the First Gentleman in England, — an exploit which, as compared with others chronicled, might be held up as a model of polite behavior — is thus set forth: " At an assembly he beckoned to the poor old Duchess of Bedford across a large room, and when she had taken the trouble of crossing the room, he very abruptly told her that he had nothing to say to her." This was the royal blackguard whose " permission " to dedicate ' Emma ' to himself was necessarily regarded in the light of a command by the unfortunate authoress, who, however, got her quantum of amusement out of it in her negotiations with the entertaining Mr. Clarke. This surprising discrimination on the part of the prince has been imputed to him for righteousness. I am not so sure. Only last week I heard a young woman confess, in one breath, her equal fondness for George Eliot and Marie Corelli.

XIII

It might not be uninteresting to conclude this section of our subject with a cursory survey of the lighter manners and customs which this distinguished lady will always make to live again for us as long as her novels are read by a delighted public.

It was a day when a gentleman might use a knife to convey food to his mouth, because it was the day before silver forks. Potatoes were eaten only with the roast. A hostess did not then invite her dinner guests with the fell purpose of paralyzing them with envy at the variety of her china, which is now, we are told, the sole reason for the swift succession of courses; there was rather the housewifely pride in the superiority of her game pies and home-brewed mead. It was a day when people dined at four or five o'clock, and friends, coming thereto in a chaise and four, perhaps with postilions, stayed to tea afterwards, concluding with a supper at eleven. The elegance of the table was heightened by a hundred burning candles, and no meats were served *à la Russe*, — no, indeed, the host had to do some heavy carving. On less elaborate occasions they feasted on "cold souse," and they always died of "putrid sore throat" instead of "malignant diphtheria."

In the country districts, such as Jane Austen lived in, instead of attending meetings of women's clubs, ladies employed their spare time in spinning the thread for the household linen, for the spinning-jennies had not yet entirely taken the place of the Jennies spinning. It was a day when young ladies made use of their beaux in parliament to obtain franks for their correspondence;[1] when they paid visits of ceremony with their hands encased in muffs of gigantic size, and wearing puce-colored sarsenets; when they might appear in the street wearing simultaneously an India muslin dress and a fur boa; and when they paid morning calls in peaked caps and pelisses. But it was a day late enough for a Jane Fairfax to have a grand piano instead of a spinet.

A woman was then a "female" — to whom lavender drops were applied when she fainted, which she was doing pretty constantly — not Jane's females, however. Roads were not then "muddy," but "dirty," and pattens had not gone out. A carriage drive was

[1] Brabourne, vol. ii., p. 172.

called what it really was, a "sweep." Palmer's coaches were adding a new pleasure to life; and the tribe of stay-makers, according to a pamphleteer of 1798,[1] were "likely to be thrown into extreme distress because the female sex have thought proper to throw off their bodices." Linen was taking the place of silk, and the unpoetical shoe-string was the successor to the silver buckle.

In the higher classes, horse-racing was ousting the cock-fight from its pre-eminence as the leading diversion for idle moments. Mrs. Selwyn will not venture in a "phaeton" with a young buck as long as her will is unsigned, its height being apparently regarded as the dangerous objection: the carriages which ladies used were called "chariots." It was the day when the measured minuet was passing, probably because swords were ceasing to be worn, and to dance the minuet without getting the sword between the legs was the chief mark of distinction. The waltz had not been introduced, and as the partners were separated in the country dance, it must have been a good deal of a bore to the spirited belles of Miss Austen's time. The umbrella with which Dr. Grant rescues Fanny Price from the rain may have been his own, but a few years earlier he could not have appeared on a London street with it without having been mobbed, as the frank British public was wont to manifest its disapproval of the masculine use of a feminine article in this manner.

It was a day when gentlemen wore high-crowned hats with curved brims, the cocked hat having been dropped in '93; when they had their hair cut, like

[1] 'Essay on the Political Circumstance of Ireland under Lord Camden,' p. 89.

Frank Churchill, and ceased to powder it, — a change of fashion brought about, as Mr. Lecky supposes, by Pitt's tax on hair powder of a guinea a head; and a day when, if they followed Fox, they wore a buff, and if they swore by Pitt, a scarlet waistcoat, and when ladies dressed their hair with foxes' tails to denote their devotion to the Whig cause.[1] It was a day when Goldsmith's 'History' was considered an authority and when it was elegant for a young lady to know a little Italian, but before German was much thought of, although Lady Susan writes to Mrs. Johnson of the "*prevailing* fashion of acquiring a perfect knowledge of all languages, arts, and sciences," — mentioning German as one of the accomplishments which it is " throwing time away to be mistress of." It was still the day of stiff, angular chairs; but it is not safe to assert, either that ease of manners has come in with ease of furniture, or that the age of increasing luxuries is necessarily that of decreasing courtesy; for the literature of the times we are discussing abundantly shows that some young men were as rude then as their counterparts are now. The sofa was a sufficiently new and expensive comfort, in those days, to warrant a poem in its honor; and although we should now think the kind then used the reverse of comfortable, it ranked as such a luxury that when Jane Austen was ill, she dutifully forbore to use the only one in the house because it would be depriving her mother of its solace.

Finally, it was a day when babies were farmed out, and we shudder to think of the possibilities surrounding Jane's case; for, had she been exchanged like the babies of the comic operas, and as Evelina was

[1] *Lounger*, No. 10.

exchanged by Dame Green, where would have been the Jane Austen whom we know?[1]

[1] For full accounts of the customs and manners of the times, see Lecky's 'History,' vols. i. and vi., Fairholt's 'History of Costume,' Andrew's 'Eighteenth Century,' Wraxall's 'Memoirs,' and other authorities, not omitting the invaluable Annual Registers.

It may be interesting to learn that Miss Austen received about £700 for all her books ['A Publisher and His Friends. Memoir and Correspondence of the late John Murray,' by Samuel Smiles, L.L.D., 2 vols., London: John Murray, vol. i., p. 283]; a sum which, of course, would have been materially increased had she begun to publish earlier. To those desirous of information concerning editions: The Messrs. Bentley and Sons were regarded for some time as the authorized publishers of the novels, they having bought the copyrights some seventy years ago. This edition contains 'Lady Susan,' 'The Watsons,' and Mr. Austen-Leigh's 'Life.' It is not illustrated, except for some fine steel frontispieces, and Jane Austen pre-eminently needs illustrating. A very pretty edition is that published by Messrs. J. M. Dent & Co. with colored prints by Cook; and the set published by Macmillan, illustrated by Brock and Thomson, and with introductions by Austin Dobson, is also attractive. Messrs. Little, Brown, & Co. issue an excellent edition, including the supplementary works and the Memoir, which are omitted in the Macmillan and Dent volumes.

B. — HER WONDERFUL CHARM

I

THE simile of miniature painting which has so frequently been applied to her work is her own invention, occurring in the letter to her nephew which we have already quoted, and in which she contrasts his "strong, manly, vigorous sketches, full of variety and glow" with her own performance on the "little bit, two inches wide, of ivory, on which I work with so fine a brush as produces little effect after much labor."[1]

It is the business of a discriminating criticism to distinguish between positive faults and those negations which are incidental to a given manner. A negation is not a fault. We ought not to expect large treatments and big canvases of a genius whose forte is evidently the "two inches wide of ivory." If we have a proper sense of proportion, the "effect" will not be "little" because physically small, but will be as large, in relation to its medium, as one of the wall-covering pictures of Benjamin West.

The negations must be pointed out, however, for no one's place in history is fully comprehended until the omissions as well as the commissions are understood. Let us take the two together.

Much of the failure to properly measure Miss Austen's work is due to a misapprehension of the

[1] Austen-Leigh, p. 310.

nature of a miniature. It is not so much a question of reduced scale as it is of fineness of execution. The space is limited, of necessity; and not to wander outside the confines requires a delicate self-restraint which, constantly applied, is likely to interfere with enthusiasm: and as enthusiasm, in youth at least, is apt to destroy perspective, the restraint has — with whatever regrettable losses may flow from the checking — a strong tendency to heighten the value of the art.

"Three or four families in a country village is the very thing to work on," Miss Austen says, in one of her charming letters of advice.[1] This, as we know, was her own method, from which she never varied. She did not "create" eccentric characters, like Smollet and Dickens; there are no Lismahagos nor Mrs. Havishams in her books, but only the every-day people of an English community. Her work is immediately recognized as typical; and one feels that Mr. Elton stands for numerous clergymen whose spiritual descendants may be found to this day in every diocese. In the *Quarterly* article above referred to, Scott points out that the nature imitated by the former novelists "was, as the French say, *la belle nature*," involving an exaggerated sentimentalism. "He who paints from *le beau idéal*," concludes Sir Walter, "if his scenes and sentiments are striking and interesting, is in a great measure exempted from the difficult task of reconciling them with the ordinary probabilities of life; but he who paints a scene of common occurrence places his composition within that extensive range of criticism which general experience offers to every reader."

[1] Brabourne, vol. ii., p. 312.

But here the objection is offered that this confined view is too narrow. Madame de Staël, with her eyes on four nations, thinks this village study *vulgaire*. Miss Brontë, not finding in her any reflection of her own spiritual unrest, deems her "only shrewd and observant." It is true that the age is partially responsible for negative shortcomings. The age makes the men; but the greatest men help to make the age. Miss Austen was not supereminently greater than her times, as the greatest writers have been; but she was superior to her times, as all great writers are,— superior in her own peculiar field.

II

The brutal coarseness of the earlier years of the eighteenth century had been only partially bettered in Miss Austen's time, and the finer ideals following the transition had not yet taken full possession of many minds. It was still a day when the recollections of a Lawrence Sterne in the pulpit — in two pulpits, in fact — could be regarded with amused indifference, but not yet a day which could have understood the earnestness of a Charles Kingsley.[1] It was a day when religious observance was so rare that Admiral Francis Austen was referred to as "*the* officer who

---

[1] There could be no stronger contrast between that day and this than the fact that the drawing-room in which 'Emma' and 'Persuasion' were written is now the reading-room of a laborers' club. The idea still prevailed — Cowper's idea, Goldsmith's idea — that if God made the country and man made the town, the place for good men, and especially "men of God," was the country, — a very comfortable, snug idea indeed, and one that saved the clergy a vast deal of trouble.

kneeled at church;"[1] when mothers corrected their daughters by reading to them extracts from the 'Mirror,' and the favorite gospel was that according to Henry Mackenzie. It was also a day when livings were bought by the highest bidder, Miss Austen's father having had one of his bought for him by an uncle, and another given him by a cousin;[2] and a day when the utmost worldliness controlled all grades of the clergy. The awakening of the English conscience was of a very slow growth. Mr. Russell tells how the proposal of certain clergymen to improve themselves in their profession was met by a brother priest: "When the neighboring parsons first tried to get up a periodical clerical meeting for the study of theology, he responded genially to the suggestion, 'Oh, yes, I think it sounds a capital thing, and I suppose we shall finish up with a rubber and a bit of supper.'"[3] If there were not so many "squires in orders" as formerly, the bishop was still a prince, travelling in a coach and six, with his wife and daughters following in a humbler carriage, to mark the distinction between an apostle and his female connections. It was the day of the "Greek play bishops," — sometimes "all Greek and greediness," like Parson Lingon's. Even Sydney Smith, who could be witty at the expense of missionary efforts, finds the indifference of an Archbishop of Canterbury too much for him: "A proxy to vote, if you please, a proxy to consent to arrangement of estates if wanted; but a proxy sent down in a Canterbury fly to take the Creator to wit-

---

[1] Austen-Leigh, p. 185.
[2] *Ib.*, p. 176.
[3] 'Collections and Recollections.' By one who has kept a Diary. Harper & Bros., New York and London, 1898, p. 63.

ness that the Archbishop, detained in town by business or pleasure, will never violate that foundation of piety over which he presides — all this seems to me an act of the most extraordinary indolence ever recorded in history."[1]

It was an age of utilitarianism. Johnson's voice was still the most powerful in the land, although Johnson himself was dead. The doctor belonged to the old school, and had no affiliations with the new and brighter sympathies just dawning into life. He was the prose Pope, and he was the pope of prose, making of the *Rambler* a heavy supplement to the *Spectator*.

Yet religion was not quite dead, and a deeper note than the purely utilitarian was being occasionally struck. As early as 1739 the first foundling, and in 1769 the first Magdalen, hospital were founded. Law's 'Serious Call' had done its work, and John Wesley was embarked on his great enterprise. During Jane Austen's lifetime, the first Factory Act was passed, remedying the terrible evils of child-labor; and parliamentary inquiry into the state of the prisons had, many years previously, prepared the way for Howard's magnificent crusade. The first Sunday-school was started four years before her birth.

And as a renewed earnestness in religion is, if it be of the vital quality, always accompanied by philanthropic effort, so also, in such a day may be looked for a renascence of commercial glory and a fresh spring of poetic inspiration. This was the day which saw the introduction of the spinning-jenny and the elevation of British pottery to the dignity of a fine art. In 1785 Pitt reckoned the number of persons engaged in England in cotton manufacture at eighty

---

[1] 'Collections and Recollections,' p 60.

thousand; and in the same year we have Wedgworth's statement that between fifteen and twenty thousand workmen were employed in his potteries. The brain of James Watt was big with the birth of steam, and there were already several hundred miles of navigable canals in England.

The nature of beauty was beginning to be understood once more; and the search of it for its own sake, and for the revelations back of it, was slowly substituting for the didactic and polished artifice of Pope a kindling passion for the absolute and the veritable. Beauty passed from her service as a handmaid to her kingdom as a queen. We hear the first notes of it in Cowper and Burns, although there is a presage of the dawn in Gray and Thomson. The greatest poets of the last one hundred years were contemporaries of Jane Austen: 'Tam O' Shanter' was published in 1793; the first two cantos of 'Childe Harold' were published five years before; the 'Revolt of Islam,' the year of, and 'Endymion,' the year after, her death. This seizure *by* beauty, taking the place of the artificial employment *of* beauty, ran to its extremest length in Shelley, who fled from it as a thing which one could not gaze upon and live, and in Keats, who, crying "Beauty is truth," looked into its face and died; and this idea of subjection, not by arbitrary choice, but of natural necessity, still throbs in modern poetry, one of whose followers has thus expressed and defended it:

> The eternal slaves of beauty
> Are the masters of the world.

And the fuller and saner music of Wordsworth, gathering into itself the deep meaning of a life irradiated with intimations from "before and after," gently impressed the new Idea into a loving companionship with the poet who, in that he was not driven mad by it, was its master, and yet a beauty which, in that he did not toy with it, was his queen. It could have been said of Cowper and Crabbe — and therefore it could not have been said by them —

> A primrose by the river's brim
> A yellow primrose was to him
> And it was nothing more.

III

Now, if Jane Austen had reflected the larger impulses whose faint stirrings were beginning to be heard, she would not to-day be praised for the qualities which got their excellence from this denial. It was not from any sympathy with the poor that she admired Crabbe and playfully said she could fancy herself his wife; it was doubtless because of her pleasure in his orderly sense of observation. Not much of this newness found its way into her life. As she knew it, and as most of the people around her knew it, it was still a complacent age which had not begun to question itself very seriously; still the age of the copy-book maxim that the proper study of mankind is man; and because this study was of Man in the abstract, and not of men as brethren of one compassionable family, it was still artificial and ornamental. And yet within her sphere she rose superior to the artifice, being the first to escape from affectation without offering a brutal frankness in its stead. She became the pioneer of refined naturalness in fiction, neither Richardson, nor Fielding, nor Miss Burney, having attained that honor, and Miss Edgeworth failing to accomplish it with charm.

Hers is a true microcosm because it perfectly reflects her macrocosm, albeit the "three or four families" comprise it. She does not passionately identify herself with any of her characters; none of her books is written in the first person, and, nervously apprehensive of its possible absurdities, she is careful to avoid Richardson's and Miss Burney's error of putting the narrative into the form of correspondence.[1] On the contrary, Miss Austen is an amused looker-on in Vienna, not personally concerned, and not looking on as a student. Had Charlotte Brontë written 'Mansfield Park,' Fanny's story would have been conceived in an atmosphere of rebellion. Julia Bertram would have become Miss Ingram, and the little dependant would have suffered from her cousins what Jane Eyre suffered from the Reeds. Miss Austen, to be sure, makes us feel her pity for Fanny, and sufficiently identifies her moral support with her heroine's actions; but it is wholly impersonal, and with all the drawbacks to Fanny's happiness at Mansfield Park, the reader sees that she is happier there than she would be in any other place.[2] George Eliot would have been tempted to force Fanny back

---

[1] Mr. Villars must have devoted all his waking hours to the reading of Evelina's letters, and the consumption of time in writing such voluminous epistles would have left no time for the events they chronicle.

[2] Governesses, with Miss Austen, are not necessarily unhappy. Miss Taylor's position was an enviable one; and while there is criticism of the method of hiring them in 'Emma,' the despairing attitude of Miss Fairfax is almost wholly due to her unfulfilled engagement with Frank Churchill.

to her father's disreputable home on the plea of family duty and social helpfulness; and her unhappiness in that great author's hands would have been in the struggle between taste and duty. Miss Austen's viewpoint was not harassed by the pressure of altruistic ethics, and thus avoided the initial errors to which authors suffering under their too urgent claims are liable — errors of unnecessary sacrifice, and errors, therefore, on the artistic side, against taste. Miss Brontë's indignation frequently stands in the way of her humor, which, indeed, is her chief defect. We have seen that Tennyson ranks Miss Austen with Shakspere, and others have not stumbled at this bold assertion. Shakspere was pre-eminently great in three things: range, depth, and impersonal detachment; and the comparison undoubtedly refers only to this last quality, for in that she was certainly more Shaksperean than either Charlotte Brontë or George Eliot. That necessitates humor; and the laughter which springs from such a humor was absent in Currer Bell. George Eliot's superiority, in general, to both is her combination of the strong imagination of the one with the fine flow of humor of the other, except when her kinship of loving feeling with some great idea confused the imagination and obstructed the humor. The faults of each were faults of greatness; and Miss Austen, though more Shaksperean in her impersonal freedom, was less great because of this excellence than they.

The outside world does not press, nor the inside passion. The sanest genius knows its limitations and does not transgress them. It is not that each character is an end in itself; she had a well-defined moral scheme, and one has only to remember the contrasted sisters in 'Sense and Sensibility' to understand how thoughtless selfishness is played against considerate self-abnegation in her novels. Marianne expresses astonishment that Elinor should have known of Edward's secret engagement to Lucy for four months and kept silent. "Four months! and yet you loved him!" "Yes, but I did not love only him." If she was ever tempted — but, of course, she never was — to lengthen the links of the chain beyond the individual family to the big social family outside, she was wise to decline the invitation; for what was a mission with George Eliot would have been only an experimental *tour de force* with Jane Austen.

Hence we should not regret her "limited" view, as it is all the more perfect for that reason. If there is no attempt to reach beyond one's range, it is not a defect to be "defective" in range. She never attempted what she was unable to perform; and the French critic, looking across the Channel at the amazing precocities of children in English fiction, could not possibly include Jane Austen in his astonishment: "C'est seulement en pays protestant que vous trouverez un roman employé tout entier à décrire le progrès du sentiment moral dans une enfant de douze ans."[1]

IV

A miniaturist, with the definite object of a portrait before him, has, by reason of his reduced scale, no room for extraneous matter. Character must be

---

[1] 'Histoire de la Littérature Anglaise.' Par H. Taine, Paris: Libraire Hachette et Cie, 1895. Tome iv., p. 474.

emphasized without outside help. In no other style of work is nicety of expression, is delicacy of detail, so necessary; and, consequently, is the least failure so noticeable. There are many world-famous pictures of the heroic size which have for centuries ranked among the wonders of the world, but which, in certain minute details, may be subjected to unfavorable criticism: the grandeur of the general execution smothers the faults in the largeness of the canvas. But in the "exquisite touch," there is no escape in size, and a minor instantly becomes a major fault. Miss Austen almost never erred in this essential. There is, in the first place, no padding in her stories; there are no superfluous characters. One might say that there is a sister or two too many in some of the novels, but further consideration clearly shows a reason for each. Even Mary Bennet is necessary as an offset to the others, her pedantic nonsense adding an extra touch of comedy to the situation and heightening the contrast between the numerous kinds of foolishness that may exist in any one family. In this particular family, Mary is one of the vehicles of Mr. Bennet's irony, and thus indirectly the means of expressing the author's satire, for in 'Pride and Prejudice' the author speaks chiefly through Mr. Bennet and Elizabeth.

"What say you, Mary? for you are a young lady of deep reflection, I know, and read great books and make extracts."

They are discussing Mr. Darcy's behavior at the ball. Miss Lucas defends that particular instance of "pride." "I could easily forgive his pride," says the injured Elizabeth, "if he had not mortified mine."

"Pride," observed Mary, who piqued herself upon the solidity of her reflections, "is a very common failing, I believe. By all that I have ever read, I am convinced that it is very common indeed; that human nature is particularly prone to it, and that there are very few of us who do not cherish a feeling of self-complacency on the score of some quality or other, real or imaginary. Vanity and pride are different things, though the words are often used synonymously. A person may be proud without being vain. Pride relates more to our opinion of ourselves, vanity to what we would have others think of us."

And so we are prepared for the characteristic opinions of the members of the home circle over Mr. Collins' remarkable letter announcing his coming, in which he speaks of himself as —

" . . . so fortunate as to be distinguished by the patronage of the Right Honorable Lady Catherine de Bourgh, widow of Sir Louis de Bourgh, whose bounty and beneficence has preferred me to the valuable rectory of this parish, where it shall be my earnest endeavor to demean myself with grateful respect towards her ladyship, and be ever ready to perform those rites and ceremonies which are instituted by the Church of England. As a clergyman, moreover, I feel it my duty to promote and establish the blessing of peace in all families within the reach of my influence; and on these grounds I flatter myself that my present overtures of good will are highly commendable, and that the circumstance of my being next in the entail of Longbourne estate will be kindly overlooked on your side, and not lead you to reject the offered olive-branch. . . . If you should have no objection to receive me into your house, I propose myself the satisfaction of waiting on you and your family, Monday, November 18th, by four o'clock, and shall probably trespass upon your hospitality till the Saturday se' nnight following, which I can do without any inconvenience, as Lady Catherine is far from objecting to my occasional absence on a Sunday, provided that some other clergyman is engaged to do the duty of the day. . . . "

Mr. Bennet chuckles over the possibilities of a fresh field of amusement in this visit. "Can he be a sensible man, sir?" asks Elizabeth.

"No, my dear, I think not. I have great hopes of finding him quite the reverse. There is a mixture of servility and self-importance in his letter which promises well. I am impatient to see him."

Elizabeth is "chiefly struck with the extraordinary deference for Lady Catherine" on the part of Mr. Collins, and with "his kind intention of christening, marrying and burying, his parishioners whenever it were required." Catherine and Lydia are not interested, since for several weeks they "had received pleasure from the society" of no man who did not appear in a scarlet coat.

"In point of composition," said Mary, "his letter does not seem defective. The idea of the olive-branch perhaps is not wholly new, yet I think it is well-expressed."

We surely could not spare Mary Bennet.

V

Her sense of humor kept her safely within these narrow confines. No one ever abided by the knowledge of his limitations more consistently than did Miss Austen. To the egregious Mr. Clarke's suggestion that she should attempt the delineation of a clergyman like Beattie's minstrel, she very sensibly replies that it is quite beyond her powers. "A classical education, or at any rate a very extensive acquaintance with English literature ancient and modern appears to me quite indispensable for the person who would do any justice to your clergyman; and I think I may safely boast myself to be, with all possible vanity, the most unlearned and uninformed female who ever dared to be an authoress."[1] The irrepressible secretary to H. R. H. then proposes "an historical romance illustrative of the august house of Coburg," that gentleman having just been appointed to a chaplaincy in that house. "But I could no more write a romance than an epic poem," she says. "I could not sit seriously down to write a serious romance under any other motive than to save my life; and if it were indispensable for me to keep it up and never relax into laughing at myself or at other people, I am sure I should be hung before I had finished the first chapter."[2]

This power of self-restraint, revealing in such a very unusual degree a perception of boundaries, assures one almost in advance that, within the boundaries, the work is also critically excellent. We have a right to look for chastened expression, for a holding in check of all exaggerations, for a sweet intuitive understanding of proportions. Miss Austen is the pre-eminent mistress of taste. If order is heaven's first law, this lady must rank among the hierarchs of art, for in no other author is to be found a nicer perception of congruous beauty and a keener discernment of symmetry.

[1] Austen-Leigh, p. 270.
[2] *Ib.* p. 271.

And this is all the more remarkable in one whose extraordinary humorous perception would naturally lead her to caricature. Even her avowed burlesque on the romantic school is not exaggerated beyond the allowed limits, and she shows herself a true sister to Fielding in that her attitude towards her subject does not permit her to rest in satire, but compels her to create a positive interest in the characters aside from the types they are intended to ridicule. 'Northanger Abbey' may be farcical comedy in places, but it is never mere farce. We have already contrasted Miss Austen with Miss Burney and Miss Edgeworth, in regard to this restraining excellence of taste. No other woman writer of her time had this gift in an equal degree. Miss Ferrier, for example, must be grouped with Smollett and Dickens as a farce — or broadly comic, rather than with Jane Austen as a high-comedy, author; as may be seen by a comparison of her Dr. Redgill with Mr. Collins. There is the constant danger of unwarranted exaggeration in caricature, which is what makes the comic papers so frequently unjust. Caricature is almost always exaggeration; yet Miss Austen could burlesque with such delicate art as to avoid its objectionable qualities. She knows how to amusingly emphasize a foible without amplifications beyond the range of human probability, — a power not generally exercised by Dickens, whose Mrs. Nickleby, for this reason, is not nearly so convincing as Jane's Miss Bates.[1]

---

[1] The temptation of a too farcical portrayal is well shown is some of the pictures in the illustrated editions of Miss Austen's novels. Mr. Brock makes Mrs. Bennet look a little too like Mrs. Gamp to completely satisfy our idea of that lady, who doubtless looked wise

Miss Austen reverts to nature. The tendency of romance towards the grand style is always a reflection of the overweening artificiality of the age. In the absence of true standards, the attempt at the lofty results in the top-lofty, and instead of the heroic we get the stilted. The consequent absurdities awaken the comic geniuses, who become the saviors of art through the medium of ridicule; and — to let the greatest of them stand for all — Cervantes grows into a caricaturist because what he is satirizing is itself a caricature of nature. The outrage done on nature is avenged by nature through him. Fielding and Miss Austen are, each in his and her individual way, followers in this path, — the latter perhaps unconsciously; and what the author of 'Joseph Andrews' accomplishes with masculine coarseness, the creator of 'Northanger Abbey' brings about with refinement and taste. She is a humorist on the hither side of Caricature. "Taste" controls her, as much as "suit" controls Miss Brontë, and is the chief reason of the latter's dislike.

On each side there was much to attract, and their acquaintance so promised as early an intimacy as good manners would warrant.

The three charges she brings against Mr. Price's home are that it is the "abode of noise, disorder, and impropriety." It is not the moral unfitness of the home which disturbs her so much as the unseemli-

---

enough, though she talked so foolishly. One expects exaggerations in illustrations to Dickens, to match the exaggerations in the text. Not so with Miss Austen, and we would probably have as deep a quarrel with any picture of Elizabeth as we would have over any picture of Rosalind.

ness of the impropriety, which is simply the outcome of the noise and the disorder; and she contrasts these with the "elegance, propriety, regularity, harmony" of Mansfield Park. Fanny shrinks from introducing her father to Mr. Crawford.

He must be ashamed and disgusted altogether. He must soon give her up, and cease to have the smallest inclination for the match; and yet, though she had been so much wanting his affection to be cured, this was a sort of cure that would be almost as bad as the complaint; and I believe there is scarcely a young lady in the United Kingdoms who would not rather put up with the misfortune of being sought by a clever, agreeable man, than have him driven away by the vulgarity of her nearest relatives.

It would almost seem that "by taste ye are saved" is her sufficient gospel. It is, as we have seen, the keynote of her disapproval of the *Spectator*. Through this orderly sense she chiefly regards nature.

Her pleasure in the walk must arise from the exercise and the day, from the view of the last smiles of the year upon the tawny leaves and withered hedges, and from repeating to herself some few of the thousand poetical descriptions extant of autumn, that season of peculiar and inexhaustible influence on the mind of taste and tenderness, that season which has drawn from every poet worthy of being read some attempt to description or some lines of feeling.

VI

There were, indeed, no artists of scenery in her day; that is a more recent development. Miss Burney never describes it. Mrs. Radcliffe's highly wrought pictures are too fantastic to be called representations.

Take the following instances at random from two well-known living writers, to exemplify the modern fondness for emphasizing the illustrative value of nature in the scheme of the design:

It was four o'clock in the afternoon, and the hottest hour of the day on that Sierran foothill. The western sun streaming down the mile-long slope of close-set pine crests, had been caught on an outlying ledge of glaring white quartz, covered with mineral tools and débris, and seemed to have been thrown into an incandescent rage. The air above it shimmered and became visible. A white canvas tent on it was an object not to be borne; the steel-tipped picks and shovels, intolerable to touch and eyesight, and a tilted tin prospecting pan, falling over, flashed out as another sun of insufferable effulgence.

It was autumn, but the morning was of June. In the park beyond the ha-ha the deer lay laagered, twitching fly-infested ears. On the rail fencing the lawn from the main road, a dozen feet below, a belated fly-catcher sat and looked over the brooding vale. Far away a church spire pricked up against the blue; and through the still noon the stertorous breathing of a little pompous engine travelled noisily.

The eighteenth-century view was entirely different. Instead of a particularized picture, it contents itself with references to the "animated charms" of nature. The poets of Miss Austen's time had not yet impressed upon the prose writers the idea of its kinship with man's personal longings and griefs. Here again Miss Austen does not rise above her age. It is not enough to say that her theory of art forbade the interruption of her tale with descriptions of scenery. She is not a poetic artist; and a real absence of that passion for nature which is usually linked with a consuming personal attachment — regarding her as the soothing mother, or finding similarities between her insensibility and the cruelties of forsaking love — this real absence is the dominant cause of her emotionless attitude; for a real presence would have transformed her theory into an acceptance of nature as we see her portrayed in the later literature. The love of woods and seas is too real an emotion for any theory of art to restrain.

Miss Austen had an appreciation for scenery; she had an eighteenth-century regard, rather than a nineteenth-century love, for beauty. Her environment contributed its subduing influences, for the chalk hills of North Hants are not picturesque, and a country where the "chief beauty" is confessedly the "hedgerows" is a country where the beauty is confined. And the girl who had no keen personal disappointments to find reflecting images for in nature would doubtless have preferred the orderly slopes of her native downs to the disturbing grandeur of the Alps.

Her descriptions are never specific. A line of cliffs is simply "beautiful." Different kinds of trees in Lyme are referred to as "the woody varieties." The rocks are "romantic." Spring's progress is the "progress of vegetation." A bank is of "considerable abruptness and grandeur." The idea of comfort — Cowper's idea — is dominant. The beauty of the situation of Mr. Knightley's farm is apparently felt, but what is emphasized is that it is "favorably placed and sheltered;" and the river "makes a close and handsome curve around it." Scenery is still an ornament. She regrets the loss of the "highly valued" elms because they "gave such an ornament" to Hall's meadow.[1] She is not awed so much as frankly distressed by thunder storms. "We sat upstairs and had thunder and lightning, as usual," she writes, as if they were a dessert; and she thinks herself fortunate that her fears are "shared by the mistress of the house, as that procured blinds and candles."[2] As typical an example as any of her descriptions of scenery is that of the view at Fonwell:

> It was a sweet view — sweet to the eye and mind. English verdure, English culture, English comfort, seen under a sun bright without being oppressive.

Now, these things are set down without the least feeling of regret. She would not have been the Jane Austen of our regard otherwise. The denials of nature, it is true, prevent the fullest development, but they may heighten the excellences which exist. And so far as the mere absence of nature worship is concerned in this lady's work, that is not so important in itself as is its contributive value to the general characteristics we are considering. If it suggests primness, it also hints at a proper restraint and self-knowledge of limitations. If it seems cold, it at least commends itself to our judgment as wholly without artificiality. If it does not show an ardent affection for nature, even so it is a return to that very nature in its lack of ostentation and in its clear-eyed honesty. Moreover, nobody looks for landscape gardening in a miniature, and we should never forget that the chief business of a novelist is to portray character. There is really no room for scenery in Miss Austen's scheme. "It was a beautiful evening, mild and still, and the

---
[1] Austen-Leigh, p. 232.
[2] Brabourne, vol. ii., p. 103.

drive was as pleasant as the serenity of nature could make it." That is enough. The party was returning from Southerton after an unsatisfactory day; and the reader is too much occupied with the comedy to care for the scene in which it is placed.

"Well, Fanny, this has been a fine day for you, upon my word!" said Mrs. Norris, as they drove through the park. "Nothing but pleasure from beginning to end! I am sure you ought to be very much obliged to your aunt Bertram and me for contriving to let you go. A pretty good day's amusement you have had!"

Maria was just discontented enough to say directly, "I think *you* have done pretty well yourself, ma'am. Your lap seems full of good things, and here is a basket of something between us which has been knocking my elbow unmercifully."

"My dear, it is only a beautiful little heath which that nice old gardener would make me take; but if it is in your way I will have it in my lap directly. There, Fanny, you shall carry that parcel for me — take great care of it — do not let it fall; it is a cream cheese, just like the excellent one we had at dinner. Nothing would satisfy that good old Mrs. Whitaker but my taking one of the cheeses. I stood out as long as I could, till the tears almost came into her eyes, and I knew that it was just the sort that my sister would be delighted with. That Mrs. Whitaker is a treasure! She was quite shocked when I asked her whether wine was allowed at the second table, and she has turned away two housemaids for wearing white gowns. Take care of the cheese, Fanny. Now I can manage the other parcel and the basket very well."

"What else have you been sponging?" said Maria, half pleased that Southerton should be so complimented.

"Sponging, my dear! It is nothing but four of those beautiful pheasants' eggs, which Mrs. Whitaker would quite force upon me; she would not take a denial. She said it must be such an amusement to me, as she understood I lived quite alone, to have a few living creatures of that sort; and so to be sure it will. I shall get the dairymaid to set them under the first spare hen, and if they come to good I can have them moved to my own house and borrow a coop; and it will be a great delight to me in my lonely hours to attend to them. And if I have good luck, your mother shall have some."

It was a beautiful evening, mild and still, and the drive was as pleasant as the serenity of nature could make it; but when Mrs. Norris ceased speaking it was altogether a silent drive to those within. Their spirits were in general exhausted; and to determine whether the day had afforded most pleasure or pain might occupy the meditations of almost all.

VII

Taste, however, with Miss Austen, does not halt at the mere conformities of behavior. The faculty of discerning order is with her the power of relishing mental and moral excellence; the elegance is of the spirit. Her chosen field is comedy, — high comedy. Her stories are, I think, the most delicately amusing ever written. There is no storm and stress; we do not go to them for the solution of old problems, or to have our sympathies awakened towards new ones. There is not a death in all her fiction. There is no broad brush work; she never draws a servant. It is the ironies of life she has to deal with, and she faces them with their own mirror; — the ironies, too, of the life she was familiar with, which was the genteel life. With a keen eye she observed the frailties and follies of the world about her. That lay-confessor of ladies' maids, Samuel Richardson, took much pride in his "rules of conduct." Miss Austen turns her laughing eyes that way.

If it be true, as a celebrated author has maintained, that no young lady can be justified in falling in love before the gentleman's love is declared, it must be very improper that a young lady should dream of a gentleman before the gentleman is first known to have dreamt of her.

I trust it will not be considered ungallant to call attention to one of the engaging foibles of the gentler sex, as portrayed by one of its most entertaining representatives:

Mrs. Allen cannot boast similar triumphs when Mrs. Thorpe expatiates on the talents of her sons and the beauty of her daughters, but she consoles herself with the discovery "that the lace on Mrs. Thorpe's pelisse was not half so handsome as that on her own."

She had found some acquaintances; had been so lucky, too, as to find in them the family of a most worthy old friend; and, as the completion of good fortune, had found these friends by no means so expensively dressed as herself.

This is the Mrs. Allen who was

... never satisfied with the day unless she spent the chief of it by the side of Mrs. Thorpe in what they called conversation.

She understood the evanescent quality of girl-friendships:

... overtook the second Miss Thorpe as she was loitering towards Edgar's Buildings between two of the sweetest girls in the world, who had been her dear friends all the morning.

'Northanger Abbey' being a skit at the 'Mysteries of Udolpho,' no opportunity is lost to poke fun at its romanticism. Concerning the room of the late Mrs. Tilney:

"It remains as it was, I suppose?" said she in a tone of feeling.
"Yes, entirely."
"And how long ago may it be that your mother died?"
"She has been dead these nine years." And nine years, Catherine knew, was a trifle of time compared with what generally elapsed after the death of an injured wife, before her room was put to rights.

The Tilneys called for her at the appointed time, and no new difficulty arising, no sudden recollection, no unexpected summons, no impertinent intrusions to disconcert their measures, my heroine was most unnaturally able to fulfil her engagement, though it was made with the hero himself.

This gentle intrusion of common-sense into an artificial sentimentalism, dissolving the mists of unreality into a clear atmosphere, is a new note in fiction, and is only equalled in subsequent success by Thackeray. Miss Austen's heroines, like that master's Charlotte, "went on eating bread and butter," to the disappointment of the devotees of "sensibility," who wanted them to be engaged in more exciting pursuits.

And who that has read this book can ever forget the delightful chapter in which Catherine refers to "something very shocking" which "will soon come out in London," — "more horrible than anything we have met with yet," — "uncommonly dreadful. I shall expect murder and everything of the kind."

And Miss Tilney, misunderstanding her, hopes that the account is exaggerated, and that "if such a design is known beforehand, proper measures will be taken by government to prevent its coming to effect." Then Henry, perceiving the error, has sport at the expense of each. "Miss Morland, do not mind what he says; but have the goodness to satisfy me as to this dreadful riot." "Riot!—what riot?"

"My dear Eleanor, the riot is only in your own brain. The confusion there is scandalous. Miss Morland has been talking of nothing more dreadful than a new publication which is shortly to come out, in three duodecimo volumes, two hundred and seventy-six pages in each, with a frontispiece to the first of two tombstones and a lantern—do you understand? And you, Miss Morland,—my stupid sister has mistaken all your clearest expressions. You talked of expected horrors in London; and instead of instantly conceiving, as any rational creature would have done, that such words could relate only to a circulating library, she immediately pictured to herself a mob of three thousand men assembled in St. George's fields, the Bank attacked, the Tower threatened, the streets of London flowing with blood, a detachment of the Twelfth Light Dragoons (the hopes of the nation) called up from Northampton to quell the insurgents, and the gallant Captain Frederick Tilney, in the moment of charging at the head of his troop, knocked off his horse by a brick-bat from an upper window. Forgive her stupidity. The fears of the sister have added to the weakness of the woman; but she is by no means a simpleton in general."

Miss Tilney then insists that her brother should explain his persiflage to the innocent Catherine. "What am I to do?" "You know what you ought to do. Clear your conduct handsomely before her. Tell her that you think very highly of the understanding of women."

"Miss Morland, I think very highly of the understanding of all the women in the world, especially of those, whoever they may be, with whom I happen to be in company."

"That is not enough. Be more serious."

"Miss Morland, no one can think more highly of the understanding of women than I do. In my opinion, nature has given them so much that they never find it necessary to use more than half."

The romantic folly of over-sensibility is a favorite subject of satire with Miss Austen:

Marianne would have thought herself very inexcusable had she been able to sleep at all the first night after parting from Willoughby. She would have been ashamed to look her family in the face the next morning, had she not risen from her bed in more need of repose than when she lay down in it.

"Well, Marianne," said Elinor, as soon as he had left them, "for one morning I think you have done pretty well. You have already ascertained Mr. Willoughby's opinion in almost every matter of importance. You know what he thinks of Cowper and Scott; you are certain of his estimating their beauties as he ought, and you have received every assurance of his admiring Pope no more than is proper. But how is your acquaintance to be long supported under such extraordinary despatch of every subject for discourse? You will soon have exhausted each favorite topic. Another meeting will suffice to explain his sentiments on picturesque beauty and second marriages, and then you can have nothing farther to ask."

And the sentiments of a girl of seventeen towards a bachelor of thirty-five are thus set forth:

She was perfectly disposed to make every allowance for the colonel's advanced state of life which humanity required.

It is worthy of observation, too, that in all this quiet satire she includes herself whenever she feels her particular likings liable to exaggeration. We know that Miss Austen was fond of Cowper;[1] and she makes her most sentimental heroine rave over that author, as if to hold within check her own enthusiasm. The careful reader of 'Northanger Abbey' sees that Miss Austen is frankly an admirer of Mrs. Radcliffe, notwithstanding her critical perception of her absurdities; — that she shares with others who are not blind to the unrealities a live interest in the excitement of the plots. She is really laughing at herself, as well as at Catherine, all through the book. Like Theophrastus, she can say, "Dear blunderers, I am one of you." And this brings her back to the human touch, which sometimes she seems to avoid with her superior aloofness.

She is equally satirical at the expense of the men, as the immortal Mr. Collins abundantly testifies. Of her baronet in 'Persuasion' she says:

He considered the blessing of beauty as inferior only to the blessing of a baronetcy; and the Sir Walter Elliot who united these gifts was the constant object of his warmest respect and devotion.

She readily finds a reason for Sir John Middleton's

[1] Austen-Leigh, p. 256.

enthusiastic reception of the Dashwoods to his neighborhood:

In settling a family of females only in his cottage, he had all the satisfaction of a sportsman; for a sportsman, though he esteems only those of his sex who are sportsmen likewise, is not often desirous of encouraging their taste by admitting them to a residence within his own manor.

When Wickman transfers his affections to a young lady with the superior attraction of £10,000, Elizabeth Bennet writes to her aunt describing the disappointment of her younger sisters:

"Kitty and Lydia take his defection much more to heart than I do. They are young in the ways of the world, and not yet open to the mortifying conviction that handsome young men must have something to live on, as well as the plain."

In a mere snatch of dialogue, she sums up one of the principal charges against careless literary expression:

"I do not understand you."
"Then we are on very unequal terms, for I understand you perfectly well."
"Me? yes; I cannot speak well enough to be unintelligible."
"Bravo! an excellent satire on modern language."

This Henry Tilney would probably be thought a little patronizing by a latter-day Catherine; but Miss Austen puts into his mouth much of her own satire on the heavy didacticism of her time:

"I am come, young ladies, in a very moralizing strain, to observe that our pleasures in this world are always to be paid for, and that we often purchase them at a great disadvantage, giving ready-monied actual happiness for a draught on the future that may not be honored."

We are constantly surprised by the neat little "asides" she drops as her characters develop themselves; and this without the digressions which sometimes arrest the interest of Thackeray's pages:

Everybody at all addicted to letter-writing, without having much to say, which will include a large portion of the female world at least . . .

She was heartily ashamed of her ignorance — a misplaced shame. Where people wish to attach, they should always be ignorant. To come with a well-informed mind is to come with an inability of administering to the vanity of others, which a sensible person would always wish to avoid. A woman, especially, if she have the misfortune of knowing anything, should conceal it as well as she can.

Their vanity was in such good order that they seemed to be quite free from it, and gave themselves no airs; while the praises attending such behavior. . . served to strengthen them in believing they had no faults.

This brilliant characterization sometimes clarifies into the sharpness of a "saying;" and it is to Miss Austen's great credit that the radical fault of the Maxim — that a great truth can seldom be folded in such narrow limits without sacrificing some parts of it — is avoided by her discriminating care, either by hedging her selections with a humorous perversity, as in —

Selfishness must always be forgiven, you know, because there is no hope of a cure.

When people are determined on a mode of conduct which they know to be wrong, they feel injured by the expectation of anything better from them.

or by limiting the application by some saving verb or adverb, as in —

A sanguine temper, though for ever expecting more good than occurs, does not always pay for its hopes by any proportionate depression.

Goldsmith tells us that, when lovely woman stoops to folly, she has nothing to do but to die; and when she stoops to be disagreeable, it is equally to be recommended as a clearer of ill-fame.

Wickedness is always wickedness, but folly is not always folly.

A mind lively and at ease can do with seeing nothing, and can see nothing that does not answer.

One may be continually abusive without saying anything just; but one cannot be always laughing at a man without now and then stumbling on something witty.

VIII

It is always the humorous view with Miss Austen, whether it be a neat crystallized characterization, or a chance laughing word dropped in passing, or a dry retort to some generality.[1]

---

[1] Her letters are full of this humorous observation. In a letter to her nephew, she says: "We saw a countless number of postchaises full of boys pass by, yesterday morning, full of future heroes, legislators, fools, and villains." (Austen-Leigh, p. 307). There are other ways of reporting such events, but it was the "destiny which stands by

"Younger sons cannot marry where they like."

"Unless where they like women of fortune, which I think they very often do."

Herein is observed her dramatic power. To many critical readers, the interest of her story is not so great as the interest in its narration, — in her way of telling the story. It is remarkable how little comment there is by the author: the characters develop themselves through the dialogue.[1] Hers are not novels of incident, yet they are dramatic, — a singular distinction. Not descriptive, eschewing the theatrical, a quiet student of character, she is nevertheless more highly dramatic than most, in that she develops all her effects through the speech and actions of her characters. She combines the constructive abilities of Fielding — and without his improbability of situation — with Richardson's consistency in piecing the parts into a harmonious whole.

This dramatic use of the dialogue clearly manifests a thorough fundamental knowledge of her characters and a logical power in developing their peculiarities. We know Miss Thorpe sufficiently well towards the close of the novel to appreciate the effectiveness of

---

sarcastic, with our *dramatis personæ* folded in her hands," which appealed to her dramatic sense.

[1] No better entertainment for a cultivated house party could be devised than the acting of certain typical scenes from Miss Austen's novels. This is put within the reach of the ambitious by Mrs. Dowson's little book, 'Duologues and Scenes from the Novels of Jane Austen.' Arranged and adapted for drawing-room performance by Rosina Filippi [Mrs. Dowson]. With illustrations by Miss Fletcher. London: J. M. Dent & Co. 1895. No scenery is necessary for the representations, as our author never depended upon that to heighten her effect; and Miss Fletcher's illustrations give all the necessary hints for costumes.

letting her seal her own fate with us out of her own lips (for out of our own mouths are we condemned). She is confessing her ardent affection for Captain Tilney:

"He is the only man I ever did or could love, and I know you will convince him of it. The spring fashions are partly down, and the hats the most frightful you can imagine."

Miss Bingley is allowed to rattle on, her creator grimly standing by and shrugging her shoulders:

"My ideas flow so rapidly that I have not time to express them — by which means my letters convey no ideas at all to my correspondents."

And however vacillating Mr. Bingley may be, one of the indications that he is not a fool is his reply to his sister's expressed desire to substitute conversation for dancing at a ball:

"I should like balls infinitely better if they were carried on in a different manner. . . . It surely would be much more rational if conversation instead of dancing made the order of the day."

"Much more rational, my dear Caroline, I dare say, but it would not be near so much like a ball."

Mr. Collins, proposing to Elizabeth Bennet, declares that to fortune he is perfectly indifferent, and that he shall make no demand of that nature on her father, "since I am well aware that it would not be complied with." He is not disturbed by Elizabeth's rejection, but when she tells him that Lady Catherine would not approve of her, *that*, he gravely confesses, would be an objection. It is a pity Elizabeth Bennet could not have stepped into Dorothea's place when Casaubon asked her to marry him: it would have prevented much subsequent trouble.

"Her indifferent state of health unhappily prevents her being in town; and by that means, as I told Lady Catherine myself one day, has deprived the British court of its brightest ornament. Her ladyship seemed pleased with the idea; and you may imagine that I am happy on every occasion to offer those little delicate compliments which are always acceptable to ladies. I have more than once observed to Lady Catherine that her charming daughter seemed born to be a duchess, and that the most elevated rank, instead of giving her consequence, would be adorned by her. These are the kind of little things which please her ladyship and it is a sort of attention which I consider myself peculiarly bound to pay."

"You judge very properly," said Mr. Bennet, "and it is happy for you that you possess the talent of flattering with delicacy. May I ask whether these pleasing attentions proceed from the impulse of the moment, or are the result of previous study?"

"They arise chiefly from what is passing at the time, and though I sometimes amuse myself with suggesting and arranging such little elegant compliments as may be adapted to ordinary occasions, I always wish to give them as unstudied an air as possible."

The elegance of Miss Austen's disdain, and its entire freedom from malice; her high ladyhood, with perhaps a touch of superciliousness, softened, however, by humor; the clear look of wondering contempt as she passes, and yet the lingering, amused at herself for her interest over some whimsical conceit; sane-eyed queen of serenity, and never harsh, even in the rare instances where she is indignant; not expecting overmuch from a self-deceiving human nature, yet with a feminine freedom from cynicism, and without the bitterness of a disappointed ideality — where else shall we find a similar charm?

When Mr. Collins could be forgotten, there was really a great air of comfort throughout, and by Charlotte's evident enjoyment of it, Elizabeth supposed he must be often forgotten.

Elizabeth, referring to Bingley's inattention to others in his devotion to Jane, asks: "Is not general incivility the very essence of love?"

IX

We are prepared for the full development of Mrs. Norris's character by the little sarcasms casually dropped in the early part of the story:

. . . consoled herself for the loss of her husband by considering that she could do very well without him; and for her reduction of income by the evident necessity of stricter economy.

. . . and no other attempt made at secrecy than Mrs. Norris's talking of it everywhere as a matter not to be talked of at present.

And there is not a discordant note in the harmony of that lady's conduct throughout the book, all discordant, all out of harmony as that life is. It is a very great gift to be able to draw such a character without repelling the reader. Mrs. Norris is, in fact, a repulsive creature. None of us would willingly live in the same house with her for twenty-four hours. Yet so great is the humor with which her selfishness is portrayed, and so logical is the sequence of her development, that the very repulse becomes an impulse, and we confess ourselves eager for her reappearance whenever she is absent from the stage. We don't feel that way about Mrs. Reed or Mr. Brocklehurst. I was reading 'Mansfield Park' aloud, the other evening, when one of the listeners, impatient at the description of the scenes at Portsmouth, cried out: "Skip all that, and give us some more of Mrs. Norris." Yet that young man would have been among the first to have fled from Mrs. Norris in the flesh. Mighty is humor!

The bores in Miss Austen's novels are all purposely so; which is the precise opposite of most bores in fiction. Miss Burney did not intend to make Sir Clement Willoughby a bore, yet he is a most intolerable specimen of that variety. In the notable article on our author by Archbishop Whately above referred to, Miss Austen is compared with Shakspere in her discriminating skill in drawing fools, —

"a merit which is far from common. To invent, indeed, a conversation full of wisdom, or of wit, requires that the writer should himself possess ability; but the converse does not hold good: it is no fool that can describe fools well, and many who have succeeded pretty well in painting superior characters have failed in giving individuality to those weaker ones which it is necessary to introduce in order to give a faithful representation of real life: they exhibit to us mere folly in the abstract, forgetting that to the eye of a skilful naturalist the insects on a leaf present as wide differences as exist between the elephant and the lion."

To the complaint that her fools are too much like nature, he replies:

"Such critics must find 'The Merry Wives of Windsor' and 'Twelfth Night' very tiresome; and those who look with pleasure at Wilkie's pictures, or those of the Dutch school, must admit that excellence of imitation may confer attraction on that which would be insipid or disagreeable in the reality."

"I love the things which make me gay," said Miss Mitford, "therefore, amongst other things, I love Miss Austen." "Dear books," says Mrs. Ritchie, "dear books, bright, sparkling with wit and animation, in which the homely heroines charm, the dull hours fly, and the very bores are enchanting."

It is partly in this supremely logical charm of Miss Austen that we find the completeness of her art. We are constantly delighted by each new situation, not because it hints at a new trait, but because it develops the trait already manifested, and in accordance with itself. It is not the charm of discovery, not the delightfulness of surprise, which enthralls us, but the recognition of consistency in character-drawing even where there is surprise. Each character is at unity with itself. Mr. Bennet, for example, cannot be shaken from his ironical habit of looking at things by the disgrace which has overtaken his family. He is excessively distressed, of course, and hurries to London to try to discover the wayward daughter. Upon his return, he blames himself for the affair, and when Elizabeth tells him he must not be too severe upon himself, he says:

"You may well warn me against such an evil. Human nature is so prone to fall into it! No, Lizzy, let me once in my life feel how much I have been to blame. I am not afraid of being overpowered by the impression. It will pass away soon enough."

"Do you suppose them to be in London?"

"Yes; where else can they be so well concealed?"

"And Lydia used to want to go to London," added Kitty.

"She is happy, then," said her father, dryly; "and her residence there will probably be of some duration."

Then, after a short silence, he continued, "Lizzy, I bear you no ill-will for being justified in your advice to me last May, which, considering the event, shows some greatness of mind."

They were interrupted by Miss Bennet, who came to fetch her mother's tea.

"This is a parade," he cried, "which does one good; it gives such an elegance to misfortune! Another day I will do the same; I will sit in my library, in my night-cap and powdering gown, and give as much trouble as I can, — or perhaps I may defer it till Kitty runs away."

"I am not going to run away, papa," said Kitty, fretfully; "if *I* should ever go to Brighton, I would behave better than Lydia."

"*You* go to Brighton! I would not trust you so near as East Bourne for fifty pounds! No, Kitty, I have at least learnt to be cautious, and you will feel the effects of it. No officer is ever to enter my house again, nor even to pass through the village. Balls will be absolutely prohibited, unless you stand up with one of your sisters. And you are never to stir out of doors, till you can prove that you have spent ten minutes of every day in a rational manner."

Kitty, who took all these threats in a serious light, began to cry.

"Well, well," said he, "do not make yourself unhappy. If you are a good girl for the next ten years, I will take you to a review at the end of them."

Mr. Collins concludes a delightfully Collinsy letter to Mr. Bennet anent this misfortune in this wise:

"Let me advise you, then, my dear sir, to console yourself as much as possible, to throw off your unworthy child from your affection forever, and leave her to reap the fruits of her own heinous offence."

After Lydia's marriage, there is another letter from this exemplary parson, in which he says:

"I am truly rejoiced that my cousin Lydia's sad business has been so well hushed up, and am only concerned that their living together before the marriage took place should be so generally known. I must not, however, neglect the duties of my station, or refrain from declaring my amazement at hearing that you received the young couple into your house as soon as they were married. It was an encouragement of vice; and had I been the rector of Longbourn, I should very strenuously have opposed it. You ought certainly to forgive them as a Christian, but never to admit them in your sight, or allow their names to be mentioned in your hearing."

And this same letter cautions Mr. Bennet against his acceptance of Mr. Darcy's proposal for the hand of Elizabeth, because of the disapproval of Lady Catherine de Bourgh; which causes Mr. Bennet to declare:

"Much as I abominate writing, I would not give up Mr. Collins's correspondence for any consideration. Nay, when I read a letter of his, I cannot help giving him the preference even over Wickham, much as I value the impudence and hypocrisy of my son-in-law."

Later he writes Mr. Collins:

"I must trouble you once more for congratulations. Elizabeth will soon be the wife of Mr. Darcy. Console Lady Catherine as well as you can. But if I were you, I would stand by the nephew. He has more to give."

Finally, this incorrigible gentleman, having in quick succession seen three of his daughters disposed of, says, in dismissing the third from his library:

"If any young men come for Mary or Kitty, send them in, for I am quite at leisure."

And Mrs. Bennet! It will be remembered that she wished to go to Brighton with all the family, and she now insists that if that plan had been carried out the disaster would not have occurred:

"And now here's Mr. Bennet gone away, and I know he will fight Wickham wherever he meets him, and then he will be killed, and what is to become of us all? The Collinses will turn us out before he is cold in his grave; and if you are not kind to us, brother, I do not know what we shall do."

Mr. Gardiner calming her with the assurance that he will assist in the search for Lydia, she immediately jumps to the conclusion that he will find her, and that the marriage will follow:

"And as for wedding clothes, do not let them wait for that, but tell Lydia she shall have as much money as she chooses to buy them after they are married. . . . And tell my dear Lydia not to give any directions about her clothes till she has seen me, for she does not know which are the best warehouses. Oh, brother, how kind you are! I know you will contrive it all."

Notwithstanding her dread that Mr. Bennet will be killed in the duel which her fears have conjured up, she cries out, on hearing of his return without Lydia:

"What! is he coming home, and without poor Lydia? ... Sure he will not leave London before he has found them. Who is to fight Wickham, and make him marry her, if he comes away?"

The girl having been at last discovered and the letter received announcing that the marriage would probably soon take place, —

Mrs. Bennet could hardly contain herself. As soon as Jane had read Mr. Gardiner's hope of Lydia's being soon married, her joy burst forth, and every following sentence added to its exuberance. She was now in an irritation as violent from delight as she had ever been fidgety from alarm and vexation. To know that her daughter would be married was enough. She was disturbed by no fear for her felicity, nor humbled by any remembrance of her misconduct.

"My dear, dear Lydia!" she cried: "this is delightful indeed! She will be married! I shall see her again! She will be married at sixteen! My good, kind brother! I knew how it would be — I knew he would manage everything. How I long to see her! and to see dear Wickham too! But the clothes, the wedding clothes! I will write to my sister Gardiner about them directly. Lizzy, my dear, run down to your father, and ask him how much he will give her. Stay, stay, I will go myself. Ring the bell, Kitty, for Hill. I will put on my things in a moment. My dear, dear Lydia! How merry we shall be together when we meet!"

Her eldest daughter endeavored to give some relief to the violence of these transports by leading her thoughts to the obligations which Mr. Gardiner's behavior laid them all under.

"For we must attribute this happy conclusion," she added, "in a great measure to his kindness. We are persuaded that he has pledged himself to assist Mr. Wickham with money."

"Well," cried her mother, "it is all very right; who should do it but her own uncle? If he had not had a family of his own, I and my children must have had all his money, you know; and it is the very first time we have ever had anything from him except a few presents. Well! I am so happy. In a short time I shall have a daughter married. Mrs. Wickham! How well it sounds! And she was only sixteen last June. My dear Jane, I am in such a flutter, that I am sure I can't write; so I will dictate and you write for me. We will settle with your father about the money afterwards; but the things should be ordered immediately."

She was then proceeding to all the particulars of calico, muslin, and cambric, and would soon have dictated some very plentiful orders, had not Jane, though with some difficulty, persuaded her to wait till her father was at leisure to be consulted. One day's delay, she observed, would be of small importance; and her mother was too happy to be quite so obstinate as usual. Other schemes, too, came into her head.

"I will go to Meryton," said she, "as soon as I am dressed, and tell the good, good news to my sister Philips. And as I come back I can call on Lady Lucas and Mrs. Long. Kitty, run down and order the carriage. An airing would do me a great deal of good, I am sure. Girls, can I do anything for you in Meryton? Oh! here comes Hill. My dear Hill, have you heard the good news? Miss Lydia is going to be married; and you shall all have a bowl of punch to make merry at her wedding."

It was a fortnight since Mrs. Bennet had been downstairs, but on this happy day she again took her seat at the head of her table, and in spirits oppressively high. No sentiment of shame gave a damp to her triumph. The marriage of a daughter, which had been the first object of her wishes since Jane was sixteen, was now on the point of accomplishment, and her thoughts and her words ran wholly on those attendants of elegant nuptials, fine muslins, new carriages, and servants. She was busily searching through the neighborhood for a proper situation for her daughter; and without knowing or considering what their income might be, rejected many as deficient in size and importance.

"Hyde Park might do," said she, "if the Gouldings would quit it, or the great house at Stoke, if the drawing-room were larger; but Ashworth is too far off. I could not bear to have her ten miles from me; and as for Purvis Lodge, the attics are dreadful."

Her husband allowed her to talk on without interruption while the servants remained. But when they had withdrawn, he said to her, "Mrs. Bennet, before you take any, or all of these houses, for your son and daughter, let us come to a right understanding. Into *one* house in this neighborhood they shall never have admittance. I will not encourage the imprudence of either by receiving them at Longbourn."

A long dispute followed this declaration; but Mr. Bennet was firm: it soon led to another; and Mrs. Bennet found, to her amazement and horror, that her husband would not advance a guinea to buy clothes for his daughter. He protested that she should receive from him no mark of affection whatever on the occasion. Mrs. Bennet could hardly comprehend it. That his anger could be carried to such a point of inconceivable resentment as to refuse his daughter a privilege without which her marriage would scarcely seem valid, exceeded all that she could believe possible. She was more alive to the disgrace which her want of new clothes must reflect on her daughter's nuptials than to any sense of shame at her eloping and living with Wickham a fortnight before they took place.

Mrs. Bennet declares that she hates the very sight of Mr. Darcy, but when Elizabeth makes known her engagement, —

Its effect was most extraordinary; for, on first hearing it Mrs. Bennet sat quite still, and unable to utter a syllable. Nor was it under many, many minutes, that she could comprehend what she heard, though not in general backward to credit what was for the advantage of her family, or that came in the shape of a lover to any of them. She began at length to recover, to fidget about in her chair, get up, sit down again, wonder, and bless herself.

"Good gracious! Lord bless me! only think! dear me! Mr. Darcy! who would have thought it? And is it really true? Oh, my sweetest Lizzy! how rich and how great you will be! What pin-money, what jewels, what carriages you will have! Jane's is nothing to it — nothing at all. I am so pleased — so happy. Such a charming man! so handsome, so tall! Oh, my dear Lizzy! A house in town! Everything that is charming! Three daughters married! Ten thousand a year! Oh, Lord! what will become of me? I shall go distracted."

Mr. Woodhouse is incapable of penetrating the somewhat deceptive character of Frank Churchill, but thinks that young man "is not quite the thing" — why? "He has been opening the doors very often this evening, and keeping them open very inconsiderately. He does not think of the draught. I do not mean to set you against him, but indeed, he is not quite the thing." Every view of Mr. Woodhouse is from the standpoint of the valetudinarian, and all moral judgments are filtered through the mists of his delicate health. When Emma exhibits her portrait of Miss Smith for the approval of the family, her father's only criticism is that the subject of the sketch "seems to be sitting out of doors, with only a little shawl over her shoulders; and it makes one think she must catch cold."

"But, my dear papa, it is supposed to be summer, a warm day in the summer. Look at the trees."
"But it is never safe to sit out of doors, my dear."

When Emma consents to marry Knightley, every reader asks himself how can Mr. Woodhouse's approval be gained? and, as expected, he is "so miserable" when the subject is proposed to him that the couple are "almost hopeless." But with her usual comic gift and logical consistency, Miss Austen turns this same habitual nervousness into the reason for his final acquiescence:

In this state of suspense they were befriended, not by any sudden illumination of Mr. Woodhouse's mind, or any wonderful change of his nervous system, but by the operation of the same system in another way. Mrs. Weston's poultry house was robbed one night of all her turkeys,— evidently by the ingenuity of man. Other poultry yards in the neighborhood also suffered. Pilfering was *house-breaking* to Mr. Woodhouse's fears. He was very uneasy; and but for the sense of his son-in law's protection would have been under wretched alarm every night of his life. The strength, resolution, and presence of mind of the Mr. Knightleys commanded his fullest dependence. While either of them protected him and his, Hartfield was safe. But Mr. John Knightley must be in London again by the end of the first week in November.

The result of this distress was, that with a much more voluntary cheerful consent than his daughter had ever presumed to hope for at the moment, she was able to fix her wedding-day; and Mr. Elton was called on, within a month from the marriage of Mr. and Mrs. Robert Martin, to join the hands of Mr. Knightley and Miss Woodhouse.

It is in castastrophe that character shines. We do not realize the nature of asbestos until the fire attacks it. The temptation of the novelist to bring out some hitherto unsuspected quality in some sharp moment of peril or disaster is not often enough resisted, with the result of a lack of agreement between the climax and what has led up to it. Miss Austen's logic is too sure to permit her ever making that mistake. Each of her characters is true to itself always; and when such truthfulness illustrates inconsequence, and such consequence illumines self-deceit, the end gained is as amusing to behold as it is difficult to accomplish. Satire has to do with foolish people. Now, foolish people are never logical in any broad sense, yet frequently logical in a narrow sense. For example, when Sir John Middleton is made acquainted with Willoughby's baseness, his censure does not find an outlet in moral indignation, but in a mere disappointment that " so bold a rider " could act thus. " It was only the last time they met that he had offered him one of Folly's puppies. And this was the end of it ! " The habitually light cannot be roused by tremendous events from their levity, and great events have the same narrow judgments as small events.

Mrs. Palmer, in her way, was equally angry. She was determined to drop his acquaintance immediately, and she was very thankful that she had never been acquainted with him at all. She wished with all her heart Combe Magna was not so near Cleveland; but it did not signify, for it was a great deal too far off to visit; she hated him so much that she was resolved never to mention his name again, and she should tell everybody she saw how good-for-nothing he was.

"He that is unjust, let him be unjust still; and he which is filthy, let him be filthy still; and he that is righteous let him be righteous still; and he that is holy let him be holy still." And this by a girl not yet in her majority!

X

No one knew better the winding self-deceits of the human heart. Her lack of the broadest sympathies concentrated her gaze all the more keenly at the particular weakness. She was a great diagnostician. She does not hate, although she scorns. She is therefore not distracted by an indignation which distorts the vision into seeing faults which do not exist; and if she magnifies the faults, it is in the same way that the naturalist magnifies the insect under his glass. She never blackens a character, no matter how black the character may be. She knows it is not necessary to make John Dashwood brutal or insolent to his sister and her family. "His manners to them, though calm, were perfectly kind." Yet he forces them, through his cruel selfishness, to the point of destitution, deceiving himself all the while with such specious excuses that he would have thought a grave injustice done him had he been called to account.

Mr. John Dashwood had not the strong feelings of the rest of the family; but he was affected by the recommendation of such a nature at such a time, and he promised to do everything in his power to make them comfortable. His father was rendered easy by such an assurance, and Mr. John Dashwood had then leisure to consider how much there might prudently be in his power to do for them.

He was not an ill-disposed young man, unless to be rather cold-hearted and rather selfish is to be ill-disposed; but he was in general well-respected, for he conducted himself with propriety in the discharge of his ordinary duties. Had he married a more amiable woman, he might have been made still more respectable than he was; he might even have been made amiable himself, for he was very young when he married and very fond of his wife. But Mrs. John Dashwood was a strong caricature of himself; more narrow-minded and selfish.

When he gave his promise to his father, he meditated within himself to increase the fortunes of his sisters by the present of a thousand pounds apiece. He then really thought himself equal to it. The prospect of four thousand a year, in addition to his present income, besides the remaining half of his own mother's fortune, warmed his heart and made him feel capable of generosity. "Yes, he would give them three thousand pounds; it would be liberal and handsome! It would be enough to make them completely easy. Three thousand pounds! he could spare so considerable a sum with little inconvenience." He thought of it all day long and for many days successively, and he did not repent. . . .

Mrs. John Dashwood did not at all approve of what her husband intended to do for his sisters. To take three thousand pounds from the fortune of their dear little boy would be impoverishing him to the most dreadful degree. She begged him to think again on the subject. How could he answer to himself to rob his child, and his only child, too, of so large a sum? And what possible claim could the Miss Dashwoods, who were related to him only by half blood, which she considered as no relationship at all, have on his generosity to so large an amount? It was very well known that no affection was ever supposed to exist between the children of any man by different marriages; and why was he to ruin himself, and their poor little Harry, by giving away all his money to his half-sisters?

"It was my father's last request to me," replied her husband, "that I should assist his widow and daughters."

"He did not know what he was talking of, I daresay; ten to one but he was light-headed at the time. Had he been in his right senses he could not have thought of such a thing as begging you to give away half your fortune from your own child."

"He did not stipulate for any particular sum, my dear Fanny; he only requested me, in general terms, to assist them, and to make their situation more comfortable than it was in his power to do. Perhaps it would have been as well if he had left it wholly to myself. He could hardly suppose I should neglect them. But as he required the promise, I could not do less than give it, — at least, I thought so at the time. The promise therefore was given, and must be performed. Something must be done for them —"

"Well then *let* something be done for them; but *that* something need not be three thousand pounds. Consider," she added, "that when the money is once parted with, it never can return. Your sisters will marry, and it will be gone for ever. If, indeed, it could ever be restored to our poor little boy —"

"Why, to be sure," said her husband, very gravely, "that would make a great difference. "The time may come when Harry will regret that so large a sum was parted with. If he should have a numerous family, for instance, it would be a very convenient addition."

"To be sure it would."

"Perhaps, then, it would be better for all parties if the sum were diminished one-half. Five hundred pounds would be a prodigious increase to their fortunes!"

"Oh! beyond anything great! What brother on earth would do half as much for his sisters, even if *really* his sisters! And as it is — only half-blood! But you have such a generous spirit!"

"I would not wish to do anything mean," he replied. "One had rather, on such occasions, do too much than too little. No one, at least, can think I have not done enough for them: even themselves, they can hardly expect more."

"There is no knowing what *they* may expect," said the lady; "but we are not to think of their expectations: the question is, what you can afford to do."

"Certainly; and I think I may afford to give them five hundred pounds apiece. As it is, without any addition of mine, they will each have three thousand pounds on their mother's death — a very comfortable income for any young woman."

"To be sure it is; and indeed, it strikes me that they can want no addition at all. They will have ten thousand pounds divided amongst them. If they marry, they will be sure of doing well, and if they do not, they may all live very comfortably together on the interest of ten thousand pounds."

"That is very true, and therefore I do not know whether upon the whole it would not be more advisable to do something for their mother while she lives, rather than for them — something of the annuity kind, I mean. My sisters would feel the good effects of it as well as herself. A hundred a year would make them all perfectly comfortable."

His wife hesitated a little, however, in giving her consent to this plan.

"To be sure," said she, "it is better than parting with fifteen hundred pounds at once. But then, if Mrs. Dashwood should live fifteen years, we shall be completely taken in."

"Fifteen years! my dear Fanny, her life cannot be worth half that purchase."

"Certainly not; but if you observe, people always live for ever when there is any annuity to be paid them; and she is very stout and healthy, and hardly forty. An annuity is a very serious business; it comes over and over every year, and there is no getting rid of it. You are not aware of what you are doing. I have known a great deal of the trouble of annuities; for my mother was clogged with the payment of three to old superannuated servants by my father's will, and it is amazing how disagreeable she found it. Twice every year these annuities were to be paid; and then there was the trouble of getting it to them; and then one of them was said to have died, and afterwards it turned out to be no such thing. My mother was quite sick of it. Her income was not her own, she said, with such perpetual claims on it; and it was the more unkind in my father because, otherwise, the money would have been entirely at my mother's disposal without any restriction whatever. It has given me such an abhorrence of annuities, that I am sure I would not pin myself down to the payment of one for all the world."

"It is certainly an unpleasant thing," replied Mr. Dashwood, "to have those kind of yearly drains on one's income. One's fortune, as your mother justly says, is *not* one's own. To be tied down to the regular payment of such a sum, on every rent day, is by no means desirable; it takes away one's independence."

"Undoubtedly; and after all, you have no thanks for it.

They think themselves secure; you do no more than what is expected, and it raises no gratitude at all. If I were you, whatever I did should be done at my own discretion entirely. I would not bind myself to allow them anything yearly. It may be very inconvenient some years to spare a hundred, or even fifty pounds, from our own expenses."

"I believe you are right, my love; it will be better that there should be no annuity in the case: whatever I may give them occasionally will be of far greater assistance than a yearly allowance, because they would only enlarge their style of living if they felt sure of a larger income, and would not be sixpence the richer for it at the end of the year. It will certainly be much the best way. A present of fifty pounds now and then will prevent their ever being distressed for money, and will, I think, be amply discharging my promise to my father."

"To be sure it will. Indeed, to say the truth, I am convinced within myself that your father had no idea of your giving them any money at all. The assistance he thought of, I dare say, was only such as might be reasonably expected of you; for instance, such as looking out for a comfortable small house for them, helping them to move their things, and sending them presents of fish and game, and so forth, whenever they are in season. I'll lay my life that he meant nothing farther; indeed, it would be very strange and unreasonable if he did. Do but consider, my dear Mr. Dashwood, how excessively comfortable your mother-in-law and her daughters may live on the interest of seven thousand pounds, besides the thousand pounds belonging to each of the girls, which brings them in fifty pounds a year apiece, and of course, they will pay their mother for their board out of it. Altogether, they will have five hundred a year amongst them; and what on earth can four women want for more than that? They will live so cheap! Their housekeeping will be nothing at all. They will have no carriage, no horses, and hardly any servant; they will keep no company, and can have no expenses of any kind! Only conceive how comfortable they will be! Five hundred a year! I am sure I cannot imagine how they will spend half of it; and as to your giving them more, it is quite absurd to think of it. They will be much more able to give *you* something."

"Upon my word," said Mr. Dashwood, "I believe you are perfectly right. My father certainly could mean nothing more by his request to me than what you say. I clearly understand it now, and I will strictly fulfil my engagement by such acts of assistance and kindness as you have described. When my mother removes into another house my services shall be readily given to accommodate her as far as I can. Some little present of furniture, too, may be acceptable then."

"Certainly," returned Mrs. John Dashwood. "But, however, *one* thing must be considered. When your father and mother moved to Norland, though the furniture of Shanhill was sold, all the china, plate, and linen was saved, and is now left to your mother. Her house will therefore be almost completely fitted up as soon as she takes it."

"That is a material consideration undoubtedly. A valuable legacy indeed! and yet some of the plate would have been a very pleasant addition to our own stock here."

"Yes; and the set of breakfast-china is twice as handsome as what belongs to this house; a great deal too handsome, in my opinion, for any place *they* can afford to live in. But, however, so it is. Your father thought only of *them*. And I must say this, that you owe no particular gratitude to him, nor attention to his wishes; for we very well know that if he could he would have left almost everything in the world to *them*."

This argument was irresistible. It gave to his intentions whatever of decision was wanting before; and he finally resolved that it would be absolutely unnecessary, if not highly indecorous, to do more for the widow and children of his father than such kind of neighborly acts as his own wife pointed out.

His is pre-eminently the standpoint of the worship of mammon, which discovers the highest virtue in the biggest bank account. "His manners to them, though calm, were perfectly kind . . . and on Colonel Brandon's coming in, soon after himself, he eyed him with a curiosity which seemed to say that he only wanted to know him to be rich, to be equally civil to *him*." Did you not observe this same John Dashwood at the reception last night? The world is full of him.

When her father asks Elizabeth Elliot how they can retrench, she,

in the first ardor of female alarm, set seriously to think what could be done, and had finally proposed these two branches of economy, — to cut off some unnecessary charities, and to refrain from new furnishing the drawing-room; to which expedients she afterwards added the happy thought of their taking no present down to Anne, as had been the usual yearly custom.

There is always this exquisite truth of portrayal. Lady Middleton exclaims, on hearing of Willoughby's villainy, "Very shocking!" yet in the interest of her assemblies thinks herself justified in leaving her card with Mrs. Willoughby, as she would be a woman of elegance and fortune. And her "calm and polite unconcern" is contrasted with the affectionate anxiety of Elinor, who is forced to see, with that cruel insight which experience with the world brings, that —

> every qualification is raised at times by the circumstances of the moment to more than its real value; and she was sometimes worried down by officious condolence to rate good breeding as more indispensable to comfort than good nature.

XI

Enough has been shown to substantiate the claim we have made that Miss Austen occupies the highest rank as a mistress of taste, and that her elegant discernment is more than a mere worldly insight as to social conformities. It is the reflection of inward grace; the elegance is of the mind. And like some subtle acid which can, with unfailing accuracy, discover the purity or the impurity of the metal subjected to its test, Miss Austen's real elegance, coming in contact with the false, reveals the difference between the two. Knowing that one does not have to go out of one's class in one's search for vulgarities, she does not go out of hers to secure her contrasts: even Mrs. Elton is connected with it. I fancy this keen-eyed girl saw her Mrs. Elton many times in her walk through life. In one of her letters she records calling on a Miss A. at Lyme, " who sat darning a pair of stockings the whole of my visit."[1] One of Mrs. Elton's charming little familiarities is her habit of addressing Mr. Knightley by his surname.

"And who do you think came in while we were there?"
Emma was quite at a loss. The tone implied some old acquaintance, and how could she possibly guess?

[1] Austen-Leigh, p. 242.

"Knightley!" continued Mrs. Elton; — "Knightley himself! Was it not lucky? For, not being within when he called the other day, I had never seen him before; and, of course, as so particular a friend of Mr. E.'s, I had a great curiosity. 'My friend Knightley' had been so often mentioned that I was really impatient to see him; and I must do my *caro sposo* the justice to say that he need not be ashamed of his friend. Knightley is quite the gentleman; I like him very much. Decidedly, I think, a very gentlemanlike man."

This instance of unrefinement was perhaps not so uncommon in Miss Austen's day as may be supposed. Mr. Russell tells of Lady Holland, "whose curiosity was restrained by no considerations of courtesy," questioning the famous Henry Luttrell about his age: "Now, Luttrell, we are all dying to know how old you are. Just tell me." "If I live till next year," said Luttrell, in reply, "I shall be — devilish old."[1] "The Miss Burneys," says this delightful raconteur, "who had been the correspondents of Horace Walpole, and who carried down to the fifties the most refined traditions of the social life of the last century, habitually 'damned' the teakettle if it burned their fingers, and called their male friends by their surnames. 'Come, Milnes, will you have a cup of tea?' 'Now, Macaulay, we have had enough of that subject.'"[2]

Her Mrs. Eltons may still be found in every parish. This cannot be said of the characters of most fiction one hundred years old, and it is one of the chief "notes" of her genius. I doubt if you could catch

---

[1] 'Collections and Recollections,' p. 176.
[2] *Ib.*, p. 76.

her napping on any of the small points of etiquette mentioned in her novels. She has been criticised for allowing Mr. Bingley to send out *verbal* invitations to balls; which is as valuable as most criticisms of the sort, because " Mrs. Bennet . . . was particularly flattered by receiving an invitation from Mr. Bingley himself, instead of a ceremonious card." The special fact recorded, the particular character emphasized, in Miss Austen's work are always true in themselves, true to the circumstance and type of the moment, but — and here lies the line of demarkation — also true to the broad general type governing all ages and above all changes of time and custom. The reader cannot construct for himself any broad picture of the times out of ' Clarissa Harlowe.' The concern is entirely local; and, on the other hand, the book has no living human interest to-day, because of its disconnection with the interests which abide through all ages. Richardson is not an observer of general life, and we therefore get from him characters, but not types. This is true also, in a less degree, of Miss Edgeworth, for we are not so certain what her young women would do in other circumstances than those in which she had placed them; whereas Elinor Dashwood and Anne Elliot might be introduced into any situation without any fear as to their ease of behavior there. The romanticists suffer from the opposite fault, for with them the characters become mere chess-pieces. How many *names* can even the interested reader of Walpole and Mrs. Radcliffe recall to memory? It is a great distinction to be known as the creator of a character which remains a character while not ceasing to be a type, and remains a type without becoming a puppet.

'Northanger Abbey,' 'Pride and Prejudice,' and 'Sense and Sensibility' are contemporaneous with 'Camilla;' yet 'Camilla' is as extinct as the pterodactyl, while Catherine Morland, Elizabeth Bennet, and Elinor Dashwood still interest us as deeply as the heroine of any novel written in the past ten years. They are as real to us as Mary Queen of Scots, and visitors to the scenes they once graced with their imagined presence are chiefly interested in the localities for that reason. Apropos, there is a good story told of Tennyson at Lyme-Regis. When some one wanted to show him the precise spot where the Duke of Monmouth landed, he broke out: "Don't talk to me of the Duke of Monmouth. Show me the precise spot where Louise Musgrove fell." Miss Austen did not conform to the favorite standards of her day as closely as did Miss Burney and Miss Ferrier; yet by reason of her attitude towards the abiding realities of every day she is alive to this day with a perpetual youth, while they are read only as "curiosities of literature." She conformed to the inner sense appropriate to all time.

If, as Aristotle maintains, epic and tragic poetry is more philosophical than history, because the latter, dealing with the individual, may fail to illustrate the general, whereas the former gives a comprehensive general view from which the particular may be deduced, — if this is true, it is equally true of the novel, which would doubtless have been included in Aristotle's comparison had it existed in his day. What we ask for in the novel is the general, with the individual in agreement with it, not an exception to it. This is what makes nearly every one of Miss Austen's characters a success. The curates in 'Shirley' are a comic failure because the indignation, the personal resentment, of their creator interfered with the objective truth; and a comparison with the elder lady's Mr. Collins, Mr. Elton, and Dr. Grant will illustrate the point. Instead of a passionate scorn, there is an intellectual contempt. The humor softens the observation, and the interest is *in* the characters, not *away* from them, as with Miss Brontë. Because of this, notwithstanding the smallness of Miss Austen's scale, — notwithstanding the "three or four families in a country village" which she deemed enough to work on, her scheme is not provincial. She is parochial, but not provincial, for it is not the limited scene which makes for provincialism in literature, but the spirit which controls the painter of the scene. 'Middlemarch' is a study of a provincial community, not a provincial study. Lydgate and Dorothea, typifying the universal caught in the network of the provincial, constitute the world-wide interest of the story. So in Miss Austen we get a perfect picture of the country life of the early century; her microcosm corresponds with the macrocosm, and the universal is there in the individual.[1] She is old-fashioned, and yet modern, — a proof of which uniquely distinguished position is that it is impos-

---

[1] It is characteristic of the important distinction between these two things that while we see certain situations in Miss Austen's fiction prompted by similar situations in her family, we cannot place the scenes as we can with Charlotte Brontë. The son of Mr. Weston becomes a Churchill as the son of Mr. Austen becomes a Knight. William Price was presumably suggested by one of her sailor brothers. There is the same relationship between Chawton Cottage and Chawton House that there is between the Great House and Upper Cross Cottage in 'Persuasion.' But her art makes the similarity purely accidental; and whenever she wishes to hide a locality, she does so.

sible to burlesque her. Of none of the works of her female contemporaries could scenes be collected for theatrical representation to-day, unless with the avowed intention of caricature.

XII

In its last analysis genius is common-sense. How can it be when it is so uncommon? But common-sense, too, is uncommon; and the one is no more uncommon than the other. The Aristotelian view is that this sense is the faculty which has the power to reduce the other conflicting senses into unity, — that it is the schoolmaster of the senses. That implies power not given to all: it is common in a complimentary sense, only, — applicable to the mind as it should be, and as it would be if unhampered by error and vice. A man with a squint cannot see straight; and those possessed of mental squints are far more numerous than the physically deformed.

The appreciation of the totality of impressions requires gifts denied the herd, or which the herd decline to use. One perceives sight; another, touch; a third, smell; but the master only perceives the general sense of life — which is a second definition of common-sense. If we adopt the Scotch philosophy, the point is still maintainable, for it also implies a faculty, — a power to test truth by " the complement of those cognitions or convictions which we receive from nature." But how few are really receptive! And how few of those few make use of their receptivity! Intellectual training is not essential. The genius may be a backwoodsman, and the professor of mental science may not be a genius. The power may be of the soul; insight may take the place of pains-taking system; and insight is but the flash-light manifestation of this same faculty.

The metaphysical definitions of common-sense meet only that constitution of the human mind which is beneficently full-powered. It is the normal mind intended by the Great Framer, not the average mind of our acquaintance. Genius is uncommon; and it is that general sense which is called " common," but which becomes special (through the general incapacity to use it), and therefore uncommon.

Miss Austen's near approach to this universal standard is what lifts her above the passing standards of any particular time. Common-sense, and humor, which is its minister, the dramatic gift, and the constant remembrance of the purpose of the novel, are what make her as distinguished to-day as when she wrote her immortal fictions.

Her view is "worldly," let us admit. She is not moved by any deep spirituality, for reasons that we have seen. Her books generally open with an inventory of the earthly possessions of her characters. Her remarks are sometimes tinged by a vague "tired," or perhaps one had better say impatient, note, as though the highest trust had been dampened by experience beyond much hope of a return to childish optimism. There is not the slightest bitterness, but the touch is delicately unexpectant of enthusiasm. Her letters are witty, bantering, sprightly, rather than blithe. After describing a new hat to her sister, she writes: "I flatter myself, however, that you can understand very little of it from this description. Heaven forbid that I should ever offer such encouragement to explanations as to give a clear one on any occasion myself."[1] She can speak coolly of 'Don Giovanni': "They revelled last night in 'Don Juan,' whom we left in hell at half-past eleven. We had scaramouch and a ghost and were delighted. I speak of *them;* my delight was very tranquil."[2] And she confesses Miss O'Neill in 'Isabella' not equal to her expectation: "I fancy I want something more than can be. I took two pocket-handkerchiefs, but had very little occasion for either. She is an elegant creature, however, and hugs Mr. Young delightfully."[3]

One would call Miss Austen a thorough woman of the world but for the danger of misconstruing the term into something more than it stands for in her case. She certainly took a real delight in its obvious pleasures; but her sense of humor appreciated its absurdities too keenly to permit her wishing to become a devotee of fashion. She is distinctly not a snob, for she makes Mrs. Gardiner, a City woman, as real a lady as any of her characters, — nay, much more of a *gentle*woman than Lady de Bourgh; and Darcy has to blush for his aunt as much as for his mother-in-law. The "impatient" note is inseparable from a "worldly" view; and her elegant femininity transmuted what would have been cynicism in an equally endowed male into its softened counterpart.

---

[1] Brabourne, vol. i., p. 187. Here see the modern note of impatience. Miss Repplier might have written it yesterday.

[2] *Ib.*, ii., p. 149. There was good reason for the tired note on this occasion, for they got a great deal for their money in those days at the opera. On this particular night, 'Don Giovanni' was the last of "three musical things." And after the 'Merchant of Venice,' on another occasion, Elliston appeared in a three-act comedy. [Brabourne, ii., p. 323.] The "continuous performance" is evidently not a modern invention.

[3] Brabourne, ii., p. 321.

She is all the moralist that a novel writer need be. Too true an artist, too keen a humorist, to obtrude the moral, it is nevertheless there. Granting things which exist in Miss Austen's case, a "worldly" writer can best criticise worldliness,—witness Thackeray. The confessed "worldliness" of him and of Miss Austen passes into the satire of the thing they are in their separate degrees; which is what makes them lovable, though they would be more lovable were they less "worldly" without at the same time being less human, which is generally the fault of the less worldly.

But all serious novels are, after all, novels of purpose. If we do not find any deep emotion in Miss Austen's ethics, we must recall once more the times in which she wrote. It was, in the first place, a great accomplishment to make a novel at once interesting and clean; for cleanliness is not only next to godliness, it is next before it. There was, besides the clean hands of Miss Austen, the pure heart; and her distinguished delicacy was but the reflection of a sound inward undefilement. The common-sense of which we have spoken throws the situation into a clear light, in which morality can work out its destiny. "What have wealth and grandeur to do with happiness?" cries the sentimental Marianne. "Grandeur has but little," says Elinor, "but wealth has much to do with it." The purpose of this novel is thus to contrast the "sense" of Elinor with the "sensibility" of Marianne, and to show that the real sensibility lay in Elinor. "Sensibility" in that day — and not exclusively in that day either — was really a gross sentimentality, all the more harmfully fatal in that it was cultivated as ideally true. It is not the frauds that do the most harm in the world; it is the honestly mistaken people. And the conclusion is that —

Marianne Dashwood was born to an extraordinary fate. She was born to discover the falsehood of her own opinions, and to counteract by her conduct her most favorite maxims. She was born to overcome an affection formed so late in life as at seventeen and, with no sentiment superior to strong esteem and lively friendship, voluntarily to give her hand to another! and *that* other, a man who had suffered no less than herself under the event of a former attachment, whom, two years before she had considered too old to be married, — and who still sought the constitutional safeguard of a flannel waistcoat!

That is not the only moral, however, of 'Sense and Sensibility.' Selfishness is there, as elsewhere, the chief object of Miss Austen's satire; and Elinor's just course is contrasted not only with her sister's absorbing sentimentality, but with the equally insistent selfishness of Lucy Steele.

The whole of Lucy's behavior in the affair, and the prosperity which crowned it, therefore, may be held forth as a most encouraging instance of what an earnest, an unceasing attention to self-interest, however its progress may be apparently obstructed, will do in securing every advantage of fortune, with no other sacrifice than that of time and conscience.

There are not many stronger pictures in fiction of a busy-bodied selfishness than the scenes in which Mrs. Norris and Mrs. John Dashwood disport themselves. She does not say, like Miss Edgeworth," This is taken from real life;" she has her laugh at the didacticists who conclude with a sermon; she allows her delighted readers to apply the moral, and finishes 'Northanger Abbey' with shocking levity:

... and professing myself ... convinced that the General's unjust interference, so far from being really injurious to their felicity, was perhaps rather conducive to it, by improving their knowledge of each other, and adding strength to their attachment, I leave it to be settled by whomsoever it may concern whether the tendency of this work be altogether to recommend paternal tyranny or reward filial disobedience.

But the moral is nowhere more evident than in Miss Austen, and the Nemesis never more sure. Her dramatic sense always prompts the comic situation, as well as the comic dialogue. How delicious the humor with which the appreciation of Miss Bates is conveyed for the good time she had had at the party the previous evening! The good lady calls from her window to Mr. Knightley passing on horseback below —

"Oh, Mr. Knightley, what a delightful party last night! how extremely pleasant! Did you ever see such dancing? Was not it delightful? Miss Woodhouse and Mr. Frank Churchill; I never saw anything equal to it" —

those two young persons being in the adjoining room, and, of course, hearing it all. Mr. Knightley replies:

"Oh, very delightful indeed! I can say nothing less, for I suppose Miss Woodhouse and Mr. Frank Churchill are hearing everything that passes. And (raising his voice still more) I do not see why Miss Fairfax should not be mentioned, too. I think Miss Fairfax dances very well; and Mrs. Weston is the very best country-dance player, without exception, in England. Now, if your friends have any gratitude, they will say something pretty loud about you and me in return."

This dramatic power in a purely comic scene prompts one to expect a mastery of irony extended to the *moral* situations; and the expectation is fulfilled. Lady de Bourgh's visit to Elizabeth brings about the very thing she wishes to prevent. Mrs. Norris is compelled to live with the disgraced niece she has chiefly helped to spoil; and Mrs. Ferrars disinherits Edward in behalf of Robert, who straightway marries the girl his brother was disinherited for not giving up. Of the evil effects of riotous match-making, Emma, Mrs. Norris, and Mrs. Jennings are standing warnings; and for Emma there is a special Nemesis for each of her offences, — the first making the man she despises propose to her, and the second making the girl she despises fall in love with the man she wishes to propose to her! It is no less — it is all the more — a Nemesis because it wears a comic mask.

Not that she is frivolous in treating of the graver issues of life. She does not flirt with tragedy; she avoids it. "Let other pens dwell on guilt and misery," she says. "I quit such odious subjects as soon as I can, impatient to restore everybody not greatly in fault themselves to tolerable comfort, and to have done with all the rest." Her logical comedy leads up to the tragic episode in 'Mansfield Park;' but because her field *is* comedy, the circumstance *is* episodical. The treatment is severe enough while it lasts. "In all the important preparations of the mind she was complete; being prepared for matrimony by a hatred of home restraint and tranquillity, by the misery of disappointed affection, and contempt for the man she was to marry. The rest might wait."

Too late he became aware how unfavorable to the character of any young people must be the totally opposite treatment which Maria and Julia had always been experiencing at home, where the excessive indulgence and flattery of their aunt had been continually contrasted with his own severity. He saw how ill he had judged, in expecting to counteract what was wrong in Mrs. Norris by its reverse in himself, clearly saw that he had but increased the evil, by teaching them to repress their spirits in his presence, so as to make their real disposition unknown to him, and sending them all for their indulgences to a person who had been able to attach them only by the blindness of her affection and the excess of her praise. Here had been grievous mismanagement; but, bad as it was, he gradually grew to feel that it had not been the most direful mistake in his plan of education. Something must have been wanting *within*, or time would have worn away much of its ill effect. He feared that principle, active principle, had been wanting; that they had never been properly taught to govern their inclinations and tempers by that sense of duty which can alone suffice. They had been instructed theoretically in their religion, but never required to bring it into daily practice. To be distinguished for elegance and accomplishments — the authorized object of their youth — could have had no useful influence that way, no moral effect on the mind. He had meant them to be good, but his cares had been directed to the understanding and manners, not the disposition; and of the necessity of self-denial and humility he feared they had never heard from any lips that could profit them.

Bitterly did he deplore a deficiency which now he could scarcely comprehend to have been possible. Wretchedly did he feel that, with all the cost and care of an anxious and expensive education, he had brought up his daughters without their understanding their first duties, or his being acquainted with their character and temper.[1]

This proves that when the opportunity called for it, she could be sufficiently serious. Generally, it is enough to present the subject with careless ease.

She had only two daughters, both of whom she had lived to see respectably married, and she had now, therefore, nothing to do but to marry all the rest of the world.

We respect Edmund Bertram for awakening to the real unworthiness of Mary Crawford through the disclosure of her frivolous view of his sister's fall. This is the unanswerable argument for all time to the charge of undue levity on the part of Miss Austen. "This is what the world does," she makes him say of Mary, and the " world " includes parents and relatives.

XIII

This brings us to the amusing picture of the clergy of her day, as represented in these novels. It is safer to be guided by the poetry and fiction and general literature of a day, in attempting to define its religious side, than by its avowed the-

---

[1] The reason for her strong disapproval of the Mansfield Park theatricals is not only because of the absence of Sir Thomas from home, but largely also because of the nature of the play selected, that piece being not unlike the 'Love for Love' which put Miss Mirvan and Evelina "perpetually out of countenance" at Drury Lane. Had something like the 'Duologues,' from Miss Austen's own books, been available then, the plot would have taken another course in her hands.

ology, this latter being too frequently an intolerant revolt from what the day really stood for. The Methodist movement had not spent itself in Miss Austen's time, and the Evangelical revival was at its height. The roughness of the age may be seen in the polemics which we now read — if we read them at all — with amazement; but it should be remembered that not that chiefly, but rather the prevailing laxity of faith and the deadness of enthusiasm against which this bluff heartiness of conviction and hatred of opposing views to what was considered a saving belief finally threw itself, were the leading characteristics of the times. Toplady, the choice saint of the English Calvinists, and the author of the 'Rock of Ages,' attacked Wesley in pamphlets entitled 'An Old Fox Tarred and Feathered,' and wrote, "I much question whether a man that dies an Arminian can go to heaven." "A low and puny tadpole in divinity" is his suming up of the founder of Methodism.[1] "A pair of horrible liars," he calls him and his co-worker, Sellon;[2] and Rowland Hill cries out on him as a "gray-headed enemy of all righteousness."[3]

But this is merely the result of an earnest religious escaping in angry protest from the crass carelessness

---

[1] 'Works of Augustus M. Toplady,' six vols. London, printed for Wm. Baynes & Son, 1825, vol. v., p. 442.

[2] *Ib.*, vol. ii., p. 344.

[3] 'Imposure Detected and the Dead vindicated; in a Letter to a Friend: containing some gentle Strictures on the false and libelous Harangue lately delivered by Mr. John Wesley, upon his laying the first corner-stone of his new Dissenting Meeting-house, near the City Road.' This "Evangelical" preacher, however, repented, in his old age, of the harshness of his controversial style ; and in justice to the Calvinists it must be said that the Arminians — including their English leader — were themselves not altogether guiltless of epithets.

and worse of the church of that and the preceding epoch. "The public have long remarked with indignation," says Knox, "that some of the most distinguished coxcombs, drunkards, debauchees, and gamesters who figure at the watering places and at all public places of resort, are young men of the sacerdotal order."[1] And Arthur Young records hearing of this advertisement: "Wanted, a curacy in a good sporting country, where the duty is light and the neighborhood convivial."[2] The truthfulness of Crabbe's picture of the average young parson has not been disputed:

> A jovial youth who thinks his Sunday task
> As much as God or man can fairly ask.
> . . . .
> Fiddling and fishing were his arts; at times
> He altered sermons and he aim'd at rhymes,
> And his fair friends, not yet intent on cards,
> Oft he amused with riddles and charades.

There can be no doubt that the unfortunate schisms in the English Church at this time were in large part the result of the worldly indifference of the bishops. A little of the "sweet reasonableness" of their professed leader would have urged them to appropriate to that which was already "established" whatever was convincing in this revival, checking the exuberance

---

[1] Essay No. 18, in 'Essays Moral and Literary,' by Vicesimus Knox, M.A.: a new edition complete in one volume. London: Jones & Co., 1827. This has particular weight coming from one of the most liberal and urbane clergymen of the period. See his Essay No. 10, on 'The Respectableness of the Clergy,' in which he argues for the dignified ease of the bishops and deans, which has so frequently been the object of attack from less conservative writers.

[2] 'Travels in France during the Years 1788-8-9.' By Arthur Young. London: Geo. Bell & Sons, 1890, p. 327.

while welcoming the enthusiasm. They were too comfortable, however, in their political security to allow any disturbance of their complacent orthodoxy. That wise observer Crabbe, once more, summed up the typical clergyman in his Vicar:

> Mild were his doctrines and not one discourse
> But gained in softness what it lost in force.
> If ever fretful thought disturbed his breast,
> If aught of gloom that cheerful mind oppressed,
> It sprang from innovation; it was then
> He spake of mischief made by restless men.
> Habit with him was all the test of truth:
> It must be right; I've done it from my youth.

The extravagances of Methodism were regarded as a "spiritual influenza," and a conservative writer like Goldsmith finds an excuse for an opposing coldness in that "men of real sense and understanding prefer a prudent mediocrity to a precarious popularity, and fearing to outdo their duty, leave it half done."[1] And yet Goldsmith was the friend of the "orthodox" Dr. Warner who, describing a dinner with some boon companions, writes: "We . . . have just parted in a tolerable state of insensibility to the ills of human life."[2] And he might have had a more realizing sense of how this awakened conscience was endeavoring to reform such habits among Christians. Yet it is always easy to fall back on a lazy piety — only, we don't call it "lazy," but "quiet" — as an excusing substitute for the noise of a "popular" religion. We presume that the American Christian Endeavorers singing revival

---
[1] Essay IV.: 'On the English Clergy and Popular Preachers.'
[2] 'George Selwyn and His Contemporaries,' with Memoirs and Notes by John Heneage Jesse. London: Richard Bentley, 1844, vol. iv., p. 137.

hymns in Westminster Abbey last summer had a somewhat similar effect upon the dean and chapter of that ancient fane to that produced by the enthusiasm of the early Methodists upon the excellent Goldsmith.

That was the age of formalism, not this, as some vainly imagine. And Miss Austen's clergymen are, as are all her characters, true types of that age: only, in accordance with her determination not to draw vice, she purposely chooses inoffensive types. It was not in her to be moved, like George Eliot, to embody the ideal of a real sanctity in any of her clergymen. There were Tryans in her day, but she did not come in contact with them, and would not have understood them if she had. At a time when fashionable society held assemblies on Good Friday evening,[1] it would require more religious zeal than Miss Austen possessed to picture other than the ecclesiastical attitude she was familiar with; which was orderly, decent, unharassed by doubt and convictions, full of an Erastian content, classical, cold. Religion, as she knew it, was near to her, but it took the form of a well-governing morality rather than livelier aspects. It was near to her, and therefore she did not talk much about it. She was of the age of Goldsmith and Johnson in point of religion, and would doubtless have laughed sympathetically over the doctor's reply to Miss Monkton's declaration that she was affected by the pathos of Sterne, " Why, that is because, dearest, you are a dunce."

See how nearly Miss Austen reflects the times. Arthur Young's " advertisement " is recalled when we read of Charles Hayter's living, in ' Persuasion.'

[1] 'Collections and Recollections,' p. 87.

"And a very good living it was, only five and twenty miles from Uppercross, and in a very fine country — fine part of Dorsetshire, in the centre of some of the best preserves in the kingdom, surrounded by three great proprietors, each more careful and jealous than the other; and to two of the three, at least, Charles Hayter might get a special recommendation. Not that he will value it as he ought; Charles is too cool about sporting. That's the worst of him."

A Church *living* — mark the word. It is thought of chiefly for its value, as a means of material happiness, and for offering a parson the opportunity to do what he most wants to do — marry. It is natural that we think of these charade-writing priests as men rather than as clergymen, and so Miss Austen regards them; these Tilneys, who spend most of their time at Bath and at their father's manors making themselves agreeable to the ladies, and interrupting such pleasant pastimes with an enforced Sunday now and then at their rectories; and these Eltons, who are in error only when they fall in love with the wrong girl, and not when they pass their mornings reading poetry and making conundrums with the right one. Mr. Collins avows his determination to "demean himself with grateful respect towards" his patroness, and "be ever ready to perform those rites and ceremonies which are instituted by the Church of England." For "even the clergyman," says Mrs. Clay, "even the clergyman, you know, is obliged to go into infected rooms, and expose his health and looks to all the injury of a poisonous atmosphere."

Miss Austen belonged to a clerical family, and in her brother Henry found an example of those who took up the Church as a profession rather than as a calling. He became a clergyman late in life, after failure in other things.[1] The sister was, of course, appreciative of the humor of the situation. "Uncle Henry," she tells a nephew, "writes very superior sermons. You and I must try to get hold of one or two, and put them in our novels: it would be a fine help to a volume; and we could make our heroines read it aloud on Sunday evening, just as well as Isabella Wardour in the 'Antiquary' is made to read the 'History of the Hartz Demon' in the ruins of St. Ruth, though I believe, on recollection, Lovell is the reader."[2] And later, referring to Henry's first appearance in a clerical capacity: "It will be a nervous hour for our pew."[3]

It was a day when a clergyman thought it wrong to read novels, but had no scruples about playing at cards for money, or dancing at public balls; a day when the patron of a living, like Sir Thomas Bertram, could sell its presentation to any Dr. Grant who could pay the price necessary to cancel his debts, although by such an action he is not only bringing into his neighborhood an unworthy priest, but is doing an injustice to his son, who is destined for that living. One can see from these novels what has helped to retard the progress of the Anglican communion. With this Dr. Grant before her — this Dr. Grant who would doubtless have some day become a bishop had he not died of apoplexy brought on "by three great institutional dinners in one week" — we have some sympathy with Miss Crawford in her attempt to draw

---

[1] Austen-Leigh, p. 184. Brabourne, vol. i., pp. 94 *seq*.
[2] Austen-Leigh, p. 309.
[3] *Ib.*, p. 314.

Edmund Bertram away from a lazy profession. The "worldliness" was not all on her side; an ambitious woman naturally desires her husband to have some ambitions likewise.

"It will, indeed, be the forerunner of other interesting events; your sister's marriage, and your taking orders."

"Yes."

"Don't be affronted," said she, laughing; "but it does put me in mind of some of the old heathen heroes, who, after performing great exploits in a foreign land, offered sacrifices to the gods on their safe return."

And not one of these clergymen is caricatured,— not even Mr. Collins. If we think this worthy is drawn too broadly, we have only to remember Mr. Clarke with his "august house of Coburg." I suppose Edmund Bertram is her best clergyman from the priestly standpoint, though, as I have said, we can think of none of them as clergymen, but only as men. Personally, I like Tilney the best because of his defiance of his father in coming to Catherine: he may have been a poor priest, but he was a man and a gentleman. And saving Collins, none of them were hypocrites; they were all too frankly secular for that.

XIV

This elegance never allows her to parade her feelings. In all probability, she never suffered from a love affair. A mysterious stranger whom she is said to have met in South Devon figures in some of the romances written about her, but her nephew denies any real knowledge of the episode.[1] If she loved

---

[1] Austen-Leigh, p. 199.

she hid it under a smiling mask, and there is no evidence whatever of such an attachment in her letters. She was herself an "elegant female," loving the niceties of a polite life, and it would have been a transcending love which could have induced her to welcome poverty for its sake. Apart from her matchmaking proclivities, she was more like her own Emma than any one else; and no Knightley crossed her path.

"I do so wonder, Miss Woodhouse, t[hat you] should not be married, or going to be married — so charming as you are."

Emma laughed and replied, —

"My being charming, Harriet, is not quite enough to induce me to marry; I must find other people charming — one other person, at least. And I am not only not going to be married at present, but have very little intention of ever marrying at all."

"Ah, so you say; but I cannot believe it."

"I must see somebody very superior to any one I have seen yet, to be tempted: Mr. Elton, you know (recollecting herself), is out of the question; and I do *not* wish to see any such person. I would rather not be tempted. If I were to marry, I must expect to repent it."

"Dear me! — it is so odd to hear a woman talk so!"

"I have none of the usual inducements of women to marry. Were I to fall in love, indeed, it would be a different thing; but I never have been in love; it is not my way or my nature; and I do not think I ever shall. And without love, I am sure I should be a fool to change such a situation as mine. Fortune I do not want; employment I do not want; consequence I do not want; I believe few married women are half as much mistress of their husband's house as I am of Hartfield; and never, never could I expect to be so truly beloved and important, so always first and always right in any man's eyes as I am in my father's."

"Never mind, Harriet, I shall not be a poor old maid; and it is poverty only which makes celibacy contemptible to a generous public! A single woman with a very narrow income must be a ridiculous disagreeable old maid! the proper sport of boys and girls; but a single woman of good fortune is always respectable, and may be as sensible and pleasant as anybody else! And the distinction is not quite so much against the candor and common-sense of the world as appears at first, for a very narrow income has a tendency to contract the mind, and sour the temper. Those who can barely live, and who live perforce in a very small, and generally, very inferior society, may well be illiberal and cross. . . . If I know myself, Harriet, mine is an active, busy mind, with a great many independent resources; and I do not perceive why I should be more in want of employment at forty or fifty than at one-and-twenty. Woman's usual occupations of eye, and hand, and mind will be as open to me then as they are now, or with no important variation. If I draw less, I shall read more; if I give up music, I shall take to carpetwork. And as for objects of interest, objects for the affections, which is, in truth, the great point of inferiority, the want of which is really the great evil to be avoided in *not* marrying, I shall be very well off, with all the children of a sister I love so much to care about. There will be enough of them, in all probability, to supply every sort of sensation that declining life can need. There will be enough for every hope and every fear; and though my attachment to none can equal that of a parent, it suits my ideas of comfort better than what is warmer and blinder. My nephews and nieces, — I shall often have a niece with me."

She kept her own counsel about the things nearest her heart, if anything was nearer to it than the affection of her sister. And while one might not be led to expect much valuable advice on the subject of matrimony from one who refers to the fact of the mistress of Lord Craven living with him at Ashdown Park as "the only *unpleasant* circumstance about him," — not sufficiently unpleasant, however, to prevent her sister-in-law from meeting him and finding "his manners very pleasing indeed,"[1] — still, the letter she writes her niece on such a subject is all that the most anxious mother could desire, notwithstanding its amusing admixture of the "worldly" view. She refers to the rarity of such a combination of virtues as reside in the young man in question:

"There are such beings in the world, perhaps one in a thousand, as the creature you and I should think perfection, whose grace and spirit are united to worth, where the manners are equal to the heart and understanding; but such a person may not come in your way, or, if he does, he may not be the eldest son of a man of fortune, the near relation of your particular friend, and belonging to your own country."[2]

Prudent Jane! But then she concludes by urging the niece not to marry unless there is real affection. Good Jane!

It was reserved for the great glory of Charlotte Brontë to paint the full picture of the *passion* of love from the woman's standpoint. Jane Austen presents the *sentiment* merely. It was still a day when a

---

[1] Brabourne, vol. i., p. 257. Compare this with a similar situation in 'Mansfield Park.'

[2] *Ib.*, vol. ii., p. 281.

woman's love was regarded as the natural return of gratitude for the man's. One would not say that it was impossible to portray the later view in Miss Austen's day, and yet the age was against it. Except in 'Persuasion,' we are charmed, not moved, by her love scenes. Still, she rose superior to the romantic ideals of her day. Henry Tilney's love had its source in a pity for Catherine's love for him. "It is a new circumstance in romance, I acknowledge, dreadfully derogatory to a heroine's dignity; but if it be as new in common life, the credit of a wild imagination will at least be all my own." Jane Austen is right here, as always. Catherine did not fling herself at Henry, as Miss Bingley did at Darcy, for she would not have been Miss Austen's heroine thus: it is the difference between sweet frankness and vulgar ambition. Love must spring from something; why not from that which is confessedly akin to it?

Her heroes and her heroines always marry, and there is a general rightness in all the sentiment. When the first love is worthy, it is rewarded, and when not, not. When she sets out to draw a fulllength portrait of a lover, she makes a success of it. What could be more hopeless than Darcy's unpardonable rudeness to Elizabeth at the dance? But we are forced to acknowledge, step by step, with his repentance, that pride of race must make liberal demands on Love before it can swallow Mrs. Bennet as a mother-in-law; and in the completeness of this wonderful woman's art, this love finally becomes supreme, — the "pride" of a Darcy checked and humbled by the worth of a Bennet, and the "prejudice" of a girl transformed into affection for a character which the "pride" merely cloaked and could not hide. The "pride" was not a bar, it was a gate, to love, and opened to it. And true love is the humor of it all.

She does not dwell on the unhappiness of ill-mated marriages, although opportunities offer. Mr. and Mrs. Bennet, Sir Thomas and Lady Bertram, are certainly in this class. The conservative, pleasant view is taken that these things did not matter much, so long as the material comfort of a home was provided. This is evidently true of Mr. and Mrs. Collins. But in each of these cases Miss Austen makes it very plain that the wife is not capable of happiness, and is therefore an object of intellectual contempt rather than a subject for sympathetic pity. Such marriages are part of the comic scheme. She would probably have said, if questioned closely, that one's happiness does not depend entirely on any one person, notwithstanding the romantic notion to the contrary. The idea of the "predestination of love" was not predominant then, though we see it hinted at. She looks out on the waves and sees them troubled, but believes they will break peacefully upon the shore at last; and it is not their *breaking* on the shore which affects her. Her cheerful view takes the happiness of her well-mated couples as a matter-of-course not demanding any analysis. Mr. and Mrs. John Knightley, Mr. and Mrs. Gardiner, Admiral and Mrs. Croft, Mr. and Mrs. Weston are perfectly happy, and even Mr. John Dashwood has a wife eminently suited to his standards of bliss.

But in 'Persuasion' we strike a deeper note. It is the loveliest of her stories. She felt the approach of death as she wrote it, and she was moved to throw aside her reticence. There, if nowhere else, she utters the true woman's appeal:

We certainly do not forget you so soon as you forget us. It is perhaps our fate rather than our merit. We cannot help ourselves. We live at home, quiet, confined, and our feelings prey upon us. You are forced on exertion. You have always a profession, pursuits, business of some sort or other, to take you back into the world immediately, and continual occupation and change soon weaken impressions.

The male auditor arguing that this does not apply to the case in point, Anne says that if the change be not from outward circumstances, it must be from within; "it must be nature, man's nature, which has done the business for Captain Benwick." Captain Harville will not allow this either, believing the reverse, and discovers a true analogy between the bodily and mental frame: "As our bodies are the strongest, so are our feelings." Anne grants that they may be, "but by the same spirit of analogy. . . ours are the most tender," and shows that while man is more robust than woman he is not longer lived, which explains her point of view of the nature of their attachments. If woman's feelings were to be added to the difficulties, privations, and dangers of a man's life, "it would be too hard, indeed." Harville then quotes the songs and proverbs against her, which leads Miss Elliot to retort that the men have the advantage over her sex in being permitted to tell their own story. "I believe you capable," she concludes,

of everything great and good in your married lives. I believe you equal to every important exertion, and to every domestic forbearance so long as — if I may be allowed the expression — so long as you have an object. I mean while the woman you love lives and lives for you. All the privilege I claim for my own sex (it is not a very enviable one, — you need not covet it) is that of loving longest when existence or when hope is gone.

Yet Miss Austen is a just woman, for she makes Frederick, who has been overhearing this, immediately write to Anne, even as she is speaking, declaring to her that his own long years of waiting prove one exception to her rule, and the one exception in all the world she is most anxious to acknowledge.

Originally, it will be remembered, this scene was differently arranged, and the chapter containing this most beautiful defence of woman's love is a substitute for the first draught. This is more than an indication of the great care she gave to all her compositions; it was an inspiration at the gate of the tomb.

XV

Her heroines are joys forever. Each has her distinctive excellence, each makes her individual appeal. One cannot separate them into groups, although there are teasing points of similarity, — another indication of her equal mastery of particular and general.

The girl Jane Austen reveals in her letters possibilities of romantic inclination which her critical faculties held in reserve. Her Emma corrects her Catherine. Her earlier heroine is the personification of simple-mindedness. She is simple, but not silly. A more complex nature would have resented the superior wit of Tilney at the expense of her ignorance, and would have retorted in kind. But Catherine is clear-sighted enough to see that there is nothing ill-tempered in his persiflage, and is humble enough to know that she is ignorant; so she accepts the first in the spirit in which it is offered, and sets about to remedy the second. With all her romanticism, she is the reverse of a fool. She sees through the designs of Isabelle Thorpe and refuses to be taken in by them. Thackeray's women are not so wise.

Like Catherine, Fanny Price, notwithstanding her gentle, yielding nature, can be firm on occasion. She is faithful at once to the dictates of heart and head, which is not such a common virtue. Sir Thomas recognizes this strength and fears it, and Miss Austen cunningly aims a shaft at " perfidious man " in noting the fact:

> He could not help fearing that if such very long allowances of time and habit were necessary for her, she might not have persuaded herself into receiving his addresses properly, before the young man's inclinations for paying them were over.

She represents the clinging-vine ideal perhaps more than the other heroines, but it clings in the way every true-hearted man would desire. She is sweet, yet strong; as delicate as a flower under the snow, but as steady as truth itself. She should have been named Violet.

And Anne Elliot is Viola! There we have the true " sensibility," as we also have it in Elinor Dashwood,—the sensibility suffering in silence, governed by the " sense " which is too proud and too gentle to give it voice. "She pined in thought," even while "smiling at grief;" and every reader exclaims, "Was not this love, indeed?" With Emma the ladyhood is at times predominant over the womanhood: the pensive burden of Anne Elliot's thought is a note of sad womanhood, into which is steeped the brilliant lady quality Miss Austen gives to all her heroines. Elizabeth Bennet's voice laughs silvery down the ages. Anne Elliot's rings a mellow golden cadence. She is inwardly pensive, not outwardly melancholy. Her love lays a care upon her, but it makes her hide it that she may care for others the more. And with what deft art is co҈҈҈҈d her real melancholy with the sentimentality҈҈҈҈shrinking " sense " with the unshrinking " sensibility," of Captain Benwick!

For though shy, he did not seem reserved; it had rather the appearance of feelings glad to burst their usual restraints; and having talked of poetry, the richness of the present age, and gone through a brief comparison of opinions as to the first-rate poets, trying to ascertain whether 'Marmion' or 'The Lady of the Lake' were to be preferred, and how ranked the 'Giaour' and 'The Bride of Abydos,' and moreover, how the 'Giaour' was to be pronounced, he showed himself so intimately acquainted with all the tenderest songs of the one poet, and the impassioned descriptions of hopeless agony of the other; he repeated with such tremulous feeling the various lines which imaged a broken heart or a mind destroyed by wretchedness, and looked so entirely as if he meant to be understood, that she ventured to hope he did not always read only poetry; and to say that she thought it was the misfortune of poetry to be seldom safely enjoyed by those who enjoyed it completely; and that the strong feelings which alone could estimate it truly were the very feelings which ought to taste it but sparingly.

The woman who does not love Anne Elliot is not a good woman.[1]

We see that the gentleness of a girl like this does not stand in the way of her wisdom. The heroines of Jane Austen are clear-sighted like herself; they not only choose the best ends, but also the best means for accomplishing them. They are witty, but refined; satirical rather than sarcastic; never biting; not keen in the pursuit of prey; not cultivating a high pitch, but manifesting a high cultivation in a natural pitch. There is about none of her women the sharp strain we detect in the characterizations of certain "lady novelists" whom we could name; nothing — unless we happen to be fools ourselves — to cause us uneasiness in their society. Emma is the only occasional exception, and that interesting young woman is made to suffer for the excess.[2]

---

[1] In the famous article of Archbishop Whately already referred to more than once, the assertion is made that the situation in 'Persuasion' is so true that it must have been the result of a personal experience. But since the Archbishop's day, more particularly than before it, has the artist been allowed to stand apart from the man; and if Miss Moira O'Neill, who perhaps may be called the chief of living Irish singers, can, in 'Denny's Daughter,' feel instinctively a man's pain at a woman's refusal, cannot Miss Austen be permitted this artist's freedom, much more easily imagined in her case because applied to her own sex?

[2] The only error we can charge against Miss Austen's art in this field lies in this character. It has always struck me as a queer mistake to have allowed Emma to devise an attachment between Harriet Smith and a young man of such aristocratic connections as Frank Churchill. The marriage with Elton would have been well enough; but fancy the dismay at Enscombe over the announcement of an engagement between those two! There ought to have been another man in the story to have given Emma's second mistake freer scope. Miss Austen might have retorted, if charged with the "slip," that a zeal for matchmaking makes even the wisest fools, and that this very absurdity was purposely selected to emphasize the fact. Still, a

We have said that Emma is more like her creator than the other characters: she reflects the "worldliness" more than the rest. Yet there is the redeeming human quality in both. "Poor Mrs. Stent!" writes Miss Austen to her sister. "It has been her lot to be always in the way; but we must be merciful, for perhaps in time we may come to be Mrs. Stents ourselves, unequal to anything, and unwelcome to everybody."[1] Here we see Miss Bates *in posse*, and the "impatient note" of a bright spirit bored at dulness; but with all Emma's mimicry, Miss Austen subdues it to a kind level, punishing her heroine in the one instance where it offends the poor lady by visiting it with Mr. Knightley's rebuke. Our author was notably independent, considering her age, in the expression of her views, and she is never restrained by any false standard of "female modesty." Referring to a certain music master, she writes: "I have not Fanny's fondness for masters, and Mr. M. does not give me any longing after them. The truth is, I think that they are all, at least music-masters, made of too much consequence, and allowed to take too many liberties with their scholars' time."[2] Yet nothing could have been more shocking to Miss Austen than the kind of independence advocated for women in these latter days. She had the old-fashioned belief, which is still shared by the majority of her sisters, that no matter how superior the woman is to the man in many things, the fit relationship of the sexes lies in the recognition of man's general superiority in

---

young woman of Emma's elegant perceptions, one would say, would hardly be led astray in this fashion.

[1] Austen-Leigh, p. 245.
[2] Brabourne, vol. ii., p. 259.

judgment and strength, which makes him the *master*, although, of course, in the spirit of Christian courtesy and forbearance. So her wittiest and most independent heroine is made "inferior" to the hero, and Emma sweetly and cheerfully acknowledges the justice of Knightley's rebukes. She is not a snob, because she is too intrinsically genteel to ape gentility; but her faults lie towards superciliousness, which is corrected in the most natural way by her real good-nature and by the love with which she reads her mentor's mind. She is the most distinguished of Miss Austen's young ladies. While in point of years she is not much older than Elizabeth Bennet, she reflects her creator's more mature thought. And in the last analysis there is something very human about her.

Half-way between Anne Elliot and Emma stands Elinor Dashwood, and this position indicates the variety which Miss Austen gives to her characters. Macaulay delighted to point out the differences between her clergymen, notwithstanding their points of similarity; this is much more noticeable in her heroines. Elinor, like Anne, suffers from an unhappily retarded success in love. She carries herself with the same dignity, and hides her grief with an equal unselfishness. But there is a more sharply defined *aplomb* about her. The circumstances of her case make it necessary for her to show her hand more frequently, and she does it with the fine flavor of wit; at times we forget the pathos of the situation in the gallantry with which it is maintained.

But what shall we say of Elizabeth Bennet? She is, all in all, one of the most satisfactory heroines in fiction,—one of the first half-dozen we would pick out above all the rest as the most charming. We admire Emma in spite of her faults; we love Elizabeth without thinking of faults at all. We could see, if we wanted to, the lurking possibilities of faults in her character, but they do not come to the surface; and to so fashion a personality is very rare art. She is not perhaps without actual imperfections, but the imperfections are not actionable, and she is not "faultless" like Thackeray's women. We admire Emma too much to love her; our admiration for Eliz 's lost in our love. The "sweet careless mus Walter Scott gives no strain like the melody which the bare mention of Elizabeth Bennet's name awakens in the memory. It was characteristic of that master's fine chivalry to make even Di Vernon, his queen of women, a little too perfect for our limited minds to grasp. We apprehend that sort of a heroine; we comprehend Elizabeth Bennet. She was Miss Austen's own favorite, by which token she should be ours also. With characteristic playful fondness, she pretended to search for her characters in real life. She mentions in one of her letters seeing a portrait of Mrs. Bingley at the exhibition in Spring Gardens, " but there was no Mrs. Darcy. [There was no chance of that in any collection of Sir Joshuas.] Mrs. Bingley is exactly herself, — size, shaped face, features, and sweetness. She is dressed in a white gown, with green ornaments, which convinces me of what I had always supposed, that green was a favorite color with her. I dare say Mrs. Darcy will be in yellow."[1] After a visit to other galleries, she confesses her disappointment at not finding anything like Mrs. Darcy there. "I can only imagine that Mr. Darcy prizes any picture of her too

---

[1] Brabourne, vol. ii., pp. 139, 140.

much to like to see it exposed to the public eye. I can imagine he would have that sort of feeling, that mixture of love and pride and delicacy."[1]

Even that belittler of woman's art, Mr. Saintsbury, says in his Preface to 'Pride and Prejudice':

> In the novels of the last one hundred years, there are vast numbers of young ladies with whom it might be a pleasure to fall in love; there are at least five with whom, as it seems to me, no man of taste and spirit can help doing so. Their names are, in chronological order, Elizabeth Bennet, Diana Vernon, Argemone Lavington, Beatrix Esmond, and Barbara Grant.

And while confessing that he should have been most in love with Beatrix and Argemone, none of the others, he maintains, could come into competition with Elizabeth as a wife for daily companionship. As for me, when I first read these novels, I wanted to marry each of the heroines as she was presented, — except Emma, of whom I am still a little afraid; I should feel nervous about asking my bachelor friends home to dinner, for fear that she would want to marry them off to Harriet Smith.

Even the subordinate women of her stories are distinguished. It is a mistake to rank Marianne Dashwood with the hopelessly silly group consisting of Isabelle Thorpe and the Steeles. Her type is different from all the others. She is not selfishly vain, and is not spoiled by the world. She has no trace of the vulgarity of the worst of her class, and she is so truthful that she cannot even fib in " society," or appear to be other than she is. Eleanor Tilney is what the playwrights would call the second leading lady of the

[1] Brabourne, vol. ii., p. 143.

book; yet of her the Earl of Iddesleigh can write: "Surely the whole House of Lords envied the unnamed viscount who became her husband."[1]

XVI

It is difficult to speak with critical nicety as to the comparative merits of such novels as these; for as with persons, so with fiction, one may have a personal favorite, although aware of the superiority of another. In the matter of plot there is not much choice. Whatever surprises she has in store for us are kept well in hand. No one can foresee how Edward Ferrars is to be released from Lucy Steele. Half-way through 'Persuasion' we are uncertain whether Elliot, Benwick, or Wentworth is to marry Anne, and we are well on in 'Emma' before we can decide as to whether Mrs. Weston's surmise is correct that Knightley is in love with Jane Fairfax, or whether Churchill is not himself, or again, whether Knightley is in love with Emma. Yet the plots are not sensationally developed. The earlier pages naturally lead up to the swiftness of interest in the concluding chapters; and as with all true realists, the character-drawing and the charm of narration occupy us more than the mere story. I would say that 'Pride and Prejudice' is the most brilliant of the fictions, 'Emma' the most elegant, 'Mansfield Park' the most carefully detailed, 'Persuasion' the most beautiful. But it is foolish to dwell on a comparison where all are brilliant, all elegant, all worked out most carefully, and all beautiful. We notice, indeed,

[1] *Nineteenth Century*, May, 1900.

a maturity in the later novels which gives them a more chiselled grace; Lady Bertram is done with less exuberance than Mrs. Bennet; and although Miss Austen let herself go on Miss Bates —

"How would he bear to have Miss Bates belonging to him? To have her haunting the Abbey, and thanking him all day long for his great kindness in marrying Jane? 'So very kind and obliging! But he always had been such a very kind neighbor!' And then fly off, through half a sentence, to her mother's old petticoat. 'Not that it was such a very old petticoat either, — for still it would last a great while, — and indeed, she must thankfully say that their petticoats were all very strong'" —

yet she suffers herself to be rebuked for her wit when it becomes unkind. "The hand which drew Miss Bates," says Mr. Goldwin Smith, "though it could not have drawn Lady Macbeth, could have drawn Dame Quickly and the Nurse in 'Romeo and Juliet.'"[1]

But restraint was always evident in Miss Austen's work, and good taste always controlled it. We see it in her avoidance of the highfalutin' names of the popular heroines of her day. Instead of Honoria we have Elinor; instead of Indiana, Fanny; instead of Eugenia, Catherine; instead of Camilla, Elizabeth; instead of Evelina, Anne. We see it in the faithful realism which did not permit her to extend her fancy beyond the limits of her experience. It has been pointed out that she has drawn no scene in which men alone are the actors; she could not have imagined the Rainbow Tavern chapter in 'Silas Marner,'

[1] 'Life of Jane Austen,' by Goldwin Smith. London: Walter Scott, 1890, p. 139.

— an evidence that she is *not* Shaksperean in the sense that George Eliot is. Her men are not done with so sure a hand as her women. An indication of Richardson's effeminacy is that Clarissa is truer to life than Lovelace: the same superiority with Miss Austen simply proves her femininity. Just what view she would have taken of the present standards of the higher education of women, it is impossible to say; her conservative instincts led her to cover any ambitions of her time in that direction with ridicule:

> Mrs. Goddard was the mistress of a school, — not of a seminary, or an establishment, or anything which professed, in long sentences of refined nonsense, to combine liberal acquirements with elegant morality, upon new principles and new systems, — and where young ladies for enormous pay might be screwed out of health and into vanity, — but a real, honest, old-fashioned boarding-school, where a reasonable quantity of accomplishments were sold at a reasonable price, and where girls might be sent to be out of the way, and scramble themselves into a little education without any danger of coming back prodigies.

She did her best, by the use of a genuine drama, to remove theatricality from English fiction. She substituted art for artifice. She pleads not guilty to the favorite fatuity of creating an improbability and then taking refuge in piety by calling the escape "providential;" reminding one of the Sunday-school teacher's answer to the question why the people mentioned in the Bible as walking on the roofs of houses did not fall off, — "Because all things are possible with God." She was not a learned woman, and, as we have seen, humorously confessed her profound ignorance of philosophy. She was well acquainted with many forms of "polite literature," however. It was an age when, as Gibbon complained, there were no public libraries suitable for a scholar's use, although the circulating library was flourishing like the green bay tree. She amusingly criticises Egerton's 'Fitz-Albini,' and refers to Boswell's 'Tour to the Hebrides' and his 'Johnson;' "and, as some money will yet remain in Burdon's hands, it is to be laid out in the purchase of Cowper's works. This would please Mr. Clarke, could he know it."[1] She is quite determined not to be pleased with Mrs. West's 'Alicia DeLacy,' and thinks she can be stout against anything written by that lady.[2] Of Miss S. S. Burney's 'Alphonsine,' she says: "'Alphonsine' will not do. We were disgusted in twenty pages, as, independent of a bad translation, it has indelicacies which disgrace a pen hitherto so pure; and we changed it for the 'Female Quixote,' which now makes our evening amusement; to me a very high one, as I find the work quite equal to what I remembered it."[3] She is not much pleased with 'Marmion,' which she reads aloud, evenings.[4] Espriella's 'Letters' are "horribly anti-English."[5] In regard to Mrs. Hawkins she comments, "As to love, her heroines have very comical feelings."[6] Miss Owenson's 'Ida of Athens' she acknowledges must be very clever, "because it was written, as the

---

[1] Brabourne, vol. i., pp. 169, 170.
[2] *Ib.*, vol. ii., p. 318.
[3] *Ib.*, vol. i., p. 316. She approves of Mrs. Lenox probably because of points of similarity between the 'Quixote' and the attitude of herself in 'Northanger Abbey.'
[4] *Ib.*, vol. i., p. 356.
[5] *Ib.*, vol. ii., p. 8.
[6] Austen-Leigh, p. 286.

authoress says, in three months . . . If the warmth of her language could affect the body it might be worth reading in this weather."¹ She is "very fond of Sherlock's sermons," preferring them "to almost any."² She speaks of Goldsmith, Hume, and Robertson as her old guides in history, and to Miss Lloyd she writes: "I am reading 'Henry's History of England,' which I will repeat to you in any manner you may prefer, — either in a loose, desultory, unconnected stream, or dividing my recital as the historian divides it himself, into seven parts . . . so that for every evening in the week there will be a different subject."³ There are references to most of the living poets in either the letters or the novels; and occasionally we are surprised by her quoting some more recondite author, as Mary Crawford's citation of Isaak Hawkins Browne.

She knew enough to be a good critic, her exquisite taste and her never-failing humor always standing her in good stead. How cheerful her laugh at her niece's manuscript!

"His having been in love with the aunt gives Cecilia an additional interest in him. I like the idea — a very proper compliment to an aunt! I rather imagine, indeed, that nieces are seldom chosen but out of compliment to some aunt or another. I daresay Ben was in love with me once, and would never have thought of you if he had not supposed me dead of scarlet fever."⁴

"Devereux Forester's being ruined by his vanity," she writes this same young relative, concerning an-

[1] Brabourne, vol. ii., p. 62.　　[2] *Ib.*
[3] Austen-Leigh, p. 235.
[4] Brabourne, vol. ii., p. 323.

other of her characters, "is extremely good, but I wish you would not let him plunge into a 'vortex of dissipation.' I do not object to the thing, but I cannot bear the expression; it is such thorough novel slang, and so old that I dare say Adam met with it in the first novel he opened."[1] She guessed that 'Waverley' was written by Scott before the secret was out: "Walter Scott has no business to write novels, especially good ones. It is not fair. He has fame and profit enough as a poet, and ought not to be taking the bread out of other people's mouths."[2] So when a woman like Jane Austen deliberately cancels a 'Lady Susan,' and relegates a family of 'Watsons' to obscurity, we confess to feeling more curiosity about it than interest in it; for we have enough faith in the critical faculty of one who can, in the crucial pain of her last hours, cancel a chapter for the purpose of substituting a better one, to abide by that faculty in leaving cancelled, in the time of her health, two entire novels.

But this elegance of restraint is finest when it smilingly rebukes an unnecessary desire for details which she considered indelicate to enumerate. When Knightley proposes, "What did she say?" asks Miss Austen of Emma, knowing that that is just what her sentimental audience wishes to learn. "Just what she ought, of course. A lady always does." She knows that the genuine lovers of Elizabeth

---

[1] Brabourne, vol. ii., p. 317.
[2] Austen-Leigh, p. 257. This letter is quoted more fully by Lord Brabourne, who gives the date of it, Sept. 28, 1814, about two months after the publication of the novel. This may, of course, merely indicate, that the authorship was more generally known than has been supposed.

Bennet are absolute on the unalloyed sincerity of that young lady's regard for Darcy, — that this regard is not in the slightest degree increased by the prospective delights of Pemberley. She also knows, however, that many readers will suspect such an explanation for the esteem; so, in answer to her sister's inquiries as to how long she had loved Mr. Darcy, Elizabeth is made to reply: "I believe I must date it from my first seeing his beautiful grounds at Pemberley." Perhaps very young readers do not much admire Miss Austen.

XVII

The appreciation of Miss Austen has come to be one of the marks of literary taste. She is appreciated even where the preference is for other styles of workmanship. More and more is our age less easily amused, requiring greater intricacy and subtler tangles than before, just as a latter-day audience demands more and more hazardous performances on the trapeze to gratify its pampered taste for daring skill, which would not put up with the simpler exploits which amazed our fathers. Notwithstanding this, the simplicity of Miss Austen's art satisfies the jaded sense, — satisfies it, indeed, because it is jaded with these new wines with which it has been experimenting, and glad to taste again the grateful product of a sounder vintage. "I find myself every now and then," says fine old Walter Scott, "with one of her novels in my hands." For the Homeric quality of laughter inextinguishable is hers: we can never think of her without thinking of Mr. Collins, who had the kind intention of christening, marrying, and burying his parishioners whenever it did not conflict with his duties to Lady Catherine de Bourgh; and of Mr. Woodhouse loving to see the cloth laid, but convinced that everything on it was unwholesome; and of Mrs. Norris going home "with all the supernumerary jellies."

It is almost impossible to overestimate her importance. Her star rose at the close of a dull night in a gray morning presaging a clear day. The haunting delicacy of her idea is of the virginal beauty of dawn. Out of its sloth and degradation, fiction, at her bidding, put on new life, —

> . . . youth irrepressibly fair
> wakes like a wondering rose.

Her skill was all-complete, the bright elegance of her charm all-perfect. She is the Meissonier of literary art, and the fair mistress of its subtlest intricacies. And her life, moving along the high level tracks of serene good sense, and glittering with the distinction of wit, was in finest accord with the best creations of her fancy. "I can indeed bear witness," says her nephew, "that there was scarcely a charm in her most delightful characters that was not a true reflection of her own sweet temper and loving heart."

She was buried in the grand minster under whose gracious shade she came to rest in the sweet eventide which fell so swiftly on her noon. She lies almost opposite the tomb of William of Wykeham, and round about her is the crumbling dust of mighty saints and great witnesses for truth. And not unworthily sleeps she there among the sculptured dead.

www.ingramcontent.com/pod-product-compliance
Lightning Source LLC
Chambersburg PA
CBHW050934300426
44108CB00011BA/736